The Communicator's Commentary

Proverbs

THE COMMUNICATOR'S COMMENTARY SERIES
OLD TESTAMENT

Library of Congress Cataloging in Publication Data
Main entry under title:

The Communicator's Commentary.
  Bibliography: p.
  Contents: OT15A. Proverbs/by David A. Hubbard
  1. Bible. O.T.—Commentaries. I. Ogilvie, Lloyd
John. II. Hubbard, David A., 1928–
BS1151.2.C66 1986 221.7′7 86–11138
ISBN 0–8499–0421–8 (v. OT15A)

Printed in the United States of America

5 6 7 8 9 9 AGF 9 8 7 6

Lloyd J. Ogilvie

———— General Editor ————

The Communicator's Commentary

Proverbs

David A. Hubbard

WORD BOOKS, PUBLISHER • DALLAS, TEXAS

To
Mary and Dean,
David and Jeffrey,
the generations following

Contents

WORDS OF THE WISE: PROVERBS 22:17–24:34

PROVERBS OF SOLOMON THROUGH HEZEKIAH'S SCRIBES:
PROVERBS 25:1–29:27

WORDS OF AGUR: PROVERBS 30:1–33

WORDS OF LEMUEL: PROVERBS 31:1–31

Editor's Preface

God has called all of His people to be communicators. Everyone who is in Christ is called into ministry. As ministers of "the manifold grace of God," all of us—clergy and laity—are commissioned with the challenge to communicate our faith to individuals and groups, classes and congregations.

The Bible, God's Word, is the objective basis of the truth of His love and power that we seek to communicate. In response to the urgent, expressed needs of pastors, teachers, Bible study leaders, church school teachers, small group enablers, and individual Christians, the Communicator's Commentary is offered as a penetrating search of the Scriptures of the Old and New Testament to enable vital personal and practical communication of the abundant life.

Many current commentaries and Bible study guides provide only some aspects of a communicator's needs. Some offer in-depth scholarship but no application to daily life. Others are so popular in approach that biblical roots are left unexplained. Few offer impelling illustrations that open windows for the reader to see the exciting application for today's struggles. And most of all, seldom have the expositors given the valuable outlines of passages so needed to help the preacher or teacher in his or her busy life to prepare for communicating the Word to congregations or classes.

This Communicator's Commentary series brings all of these elements together. The authors are scholar-preachers and teachers outstanding in their ability to make the Scriptures come alive for individuals and groups. They are noted for bringing together excellence in biblical scholarship, knowledge of the original Hebrew and Greek, sensitivity to people's needs, vivid illustrative material from biblical, classical, and contemporary sources, and lucid communication by the use of clear outlines of thought. Each has been selected to contribute to this series because of his Spirit-empowered ability to help people live in the skins of biblical characters and provide a "you-are-there" intensity to the drama of events of the Bible which have so much to say about our relationships and responsibilities today.

The design for the Communicator's Commentary gives the reader
an overall outline of each book of the Bible. Following the introduction, which reveals the author's approach and salient background on
the book, each chapter of the commentary provides the Scripture to
be exposited. The New King James Bible has been chosen for the
Communicator's Commentary because it combines with integrity the
beauty of language, underlying Hebrew and Greek textual basis, and
thought-flow of the 1611 King James Version, while replacing obsolete verb forms and other archaisms with their everyday contemporary counterparts for greater readability. Reverence for God is
preserved in the capitalization of all pronouns referring to the
Father, Son, or Holy Spirit. Readers who are more comfortable with
another translation can readily find the parallel passage by means of
the chapter and verse reference at the end of each passage being exposited. The paragraphs of exposition combine fresh insights to the
Scripture, application, rich illustrative material, and innovative ways
of utilizing the vibrant truth for his or her own life and for the challenge of communicating it with vigor and vitality.

It has been gratifying to me as editor of this series to receive enthusiastic progress reports from each contributor. As they worked, all
were gripped with new truths from the Scripture—God-given insights into passages, previously not written in the literature of biblical
explanation. A prime objective of this series is for each user to find
the same awareness: that God speaks with newness through the
Scriptures when we approach them with a ready mind and a willingness to communicate what He has given; that God delights to give
communicators of His Word "I-never-saw-that-in-that-verse-before"
intellectual insights so that our listeners and readers can have "I-
never-realized-all-that-was-in-that-verse" spiritual experiences.

The thrust of the commentary series unequivocally affirms that
God speaks through the Scriptures today to engender faith, enable
adventuresome living of the abundant life, and establish the basis of
obedient discipleship. The Bible, the unique Word of God, is unlim-
ited as a resource for Christians in communicating our hope to others. It is our weapon in the battle for truth, the guide for ministry,
and the irresistible force for introducing others to God.

A biblically rooted communication of the Gospel holds in unity
and oneness what divergent movements have wrought asunder. This
commentary series courageously presents personal faith, caring for
individuals, and social responsibility as essential, inseparable dimensions of biblical Christianity. It seeks to present the quadrilateral
Gospel in its fullness which calls us to unreserved commitment to

Christ, unrestricted self-esteem in His grace, unqualified love for others in personal evangelism, and undying efforts to work for justice and righteousness in a sick and suffering world.

A growing renaissance in the church today is being led by clergy and laity who are biblically rooted, Christ-centered, and Holy Spirit-empowered. They have dared to listen to people's most urgent questions and deepest needs and then to God as He speaks through the Bible. Biblical preaching is the secret of growing churches. Bible study classes and small groups are equipping the laity for ministry in the world. Dynamic Christians are finding that daily study of God's Word allows the Spirit to do in them what He wishes to communicate through them to others. These days are the most exciting time since Pentecost. The Communicator's Commentary is offered to be a primary resource of new life for this renaissance.

It has been very encouraging to receive the enthusiastic responses of pastors and teachers to the twelve New Testament volumes of the Communicator's Commentary series. The letters from communicators on the firing line in pulpits, classes, study groups, and Bible fellowship clusters across the nation, as well as the reviews of scholars and publication analysts, have indicated that we have been on target in meeting a need for a distinctly different kind of commentary on the Scriptures, a commentary that is primarily aimed at helping interpreters of the Bible to equip the laity for ministry.

This positive response has led the publisher to press on with an additional twenty-one volumes covering the books of the Old Testament. These new volumes rest upon the same goals and guidelines that undergird the New Testament volumes. Scholar-preachers with facility in Hebrew as well as vivid contemporary exposition have been selected as authors. The purpose throughout is to aid the preacher and teacher in the challenge and adventure of Old Testament exposition in communication. In each volume you will meet Yahweh, the "I AM" Lord who is Creator, Sustainer, and Redeemer in the unfolding drama of His call and care of Israel. He is the Lord who acts, intervenes, judges, and presses His people into the immense challenges and privileges of being a chosen people, a holy nation. And in the descriptive exposition of each passage, the implications of the ultimate revelation of Yahweh in Jesus Christ, His Son, our Lord, are carefully spelled out to maintain unity and oneness in the preaching and teaching of the Gospel.

It is my pleasure to introduce the author of this commentary, Dr. David A. Hubbard. Most readers will already have been impacted by his ministry of scholarship and leadership. Dr. Hubbard is in constant demand as a speaker whose engagements have taken him to every continent on the globe. A prolific author, he has written more than thirty books, not to mention dozens of articles. For twenty-five years he has been Professor of Old Testament and President of Fuller Theological Seminary in Pasadena, California. During these tumultuous times he has piloted Fuller into a position of national and international Christian leadership.

Dr. Hubbard applies his expertise as an Old Testament scholar to this Communicator's Commentary volume on Proverbs. Every page exemplifies his encyclopedic knowledge of the Scriptures, the Hebrew language, the history of Israel, and the culture of the ancient Near East. But Dr. Hubbard writes not just for his academic peers but for every contemporary communicator of Scripture. Two outstanding features of this commentary are specifically designed to assist today's teacher or preacher. In his introduction Dr. Hubbard proposes six guidelines for interpretation that enable us to appreciate the unique genre of Proverbs, a book which is "a collection of collections of materials." This genre also commands an unusual structuring of the commentary itself. Rather than treating 10:1–22:16 in a verse-by-verse fashion, Dr. Hubbard approaches the text thematically, collecting proverbs of similar content, enabling the communicator to utilize passages of Proverbs which are otherwise difficult to teach or to preach.

According to David Hubbard, Proverbs was designed initially as a training manual for Israel's potential leaders. God's standards for leadership remain, even though the cultural setting changes. Therefore, as Hubbard explains, "The contents of Proverbs speak volumes to our modern age as they have to every generation. Modulating power with wisdom and compassion is the basic message of Proverbs. Can such a lesson ever be irrelevant, ever obsolete, ever misdirected?" Certainly not! Those of us called to contemporary Christian leadership need more than ever to follow God's ways as presented in Proverbs.

Dr. Hubbard reminds us to understand Proverbs in the context of God's covenant with Israel. When we apply the text to our own lives, we do so in awareness of God's new covenant in Jesus Christ, who is the wisdom of God incarnate. When taken this way, the proverbs become not stepping stones to legalism, but signposts to grace. As Dr. Hubbard notes, "they are designed to enable us to live out the full meaning of the life that springs daily from the hand of the Creator and Savior."

Proverbs presents us with the wisdom of God for daily living. Dr. Hubbard provides access to that wisdom through the commentary, which reflects God's gifts of wisdom to a man of profound intellect, broad experience, and solid integrity. I am grateful to David Hubbard for his outstanding contribution to this commentary series, and I commend it to you with confidence and enthusiasm.

LLOYD OGILVIE

Abbreviations

AB	Anchor Bible
AV	Authorized (King James) Version
Heb.	Hebrew
JB	Jerusalem Bible
LXX	Septuagint Greek Version
MT	Masoretic Text of Hebrew Bible
NASB	New American Standard Bible
NEB	New English Bible
NIV	New International Version
NKJV	New King James Version
RSV	Revised Standard Version
TEV	Today's English Version

Author's Preface

I have welcomed Lloyd Ogilvie's invitation to comment on Proverbs. For more than half my life I have taught, preached, and written on this book. Tackling this commentary has afforded me the luxury of examining every word in this important, though oft neglected, portion of Scripture. In the process I have had the opportunity of asking again what the proverbs meant to their original users in Israel's community of faith, why they have consistently ministered to believers and unbelievers in the past twenty centuries and more, and what they can mean to Christ's people at the end of the twentieth century.

Their initial use and meaning have been my primary concern. Though bridging between the *then* and the *now* is part of the purpose of the Communicator's Commentary, its most important role is to try to unlock the message of the text and thus to head the teacher, preacher, and other Bible students in the direction of contemporary application. If my expositions have been a bit more technical and less anecdotal than some in this series, I apologize. While I preach with some regularity, scholarly study is my vocation and daily métier. My entire ministry has been spent in the academic side of Christian endeavor.

The contents of Proverbs speak volumes to our modern age as they have to every generation. Modulating power with wisdom and compassion is the basic message of Proverbs. Can such a lesson ever be irrelevant, ever obsolete, ever misdirected? Not so long as the sons and daughters of Eve and Adam seek to make sense of human life in a world where folly is in large supply, arrogance knows no shortage, and fickleness is a way of life.

A study like this is beholden to the works of many others. The important commentaries of the past decades have been my daily companions. Those in English are listed in the Bibliography. Where I have been consciously and specifically dependent on any of them, I have tried to note that. But their indelible yet intangible impact on my work is far more present than I can directly acknowledge.

Help in processing the manuscript has come from my assistant Vera Wils, our secretary Shirley Coe, David Sielaff of the Word Processing crew at Fuller, and especially from my colleague in things *Hebraica*, Dr. John McKenna, who has read the entire text and offered innumerable suggestions for its condensation, clarification, correction, and illustration. My heartfelt thanks to the whole team!

Ruth, my bride and companion over the past forty years, has made her own unique contribution to this book. Her wisdom, love, and persistent faith in the face of adversity have been enduring illustrations of what wisdom literature teaches. She has put up with my preoccupation with a task that left other tasks untended and with my listening to a biblical text when she needed my ear. My debt to her in this venture, as in all others, is immeasurable.

The dedication to our daughter Mary, our son-in-law Dean Given, and our grandsons David and Jeffrey is a modest token of appreciation for the love, joy, peace, and hope that God's Spirit brings daily into our lives through theirs.

Introduction

When did you last hear or preach a sermon on a text from Proverbs? I have leafed through the card catalog of my memory and come up wanting, except for a dozen or so sermons I once broadcast on *The Joyful Sound* radio ministry some fifteen years ago. Proverbs, my hunch is, gets much more use as a source of devotional or inspirational reading than as material for public presentation, whether in preaching or teaching.

Why? Worshipers in synagogues and churches have rarely questioned the book's right to be in the sacred canon. Its material is quoted directly as Scripture in the New Testament (3:11–12 in Heb. 12:5–6; 3:34 in James 4:6 and 1 Pet. 5:5; 11:31 in 1 Pet. 4:18; 25:21–22 in Rom. 12:20; 26:11 in 2 Pet. 2:22). Its descriptions of wisdom (8:22–36), moreover, form the background both of Jesus' claims to be divine wisdom (Matt. 12:42; 23:34) and the apostolic descriptions of Christ's uniqueness and preexistence (John 1:1–4; Col. 1:15–20; Heb. 1:1–3). Besides, the practical nature of the proverbs and the sage advice they tender in so many aspects of personal, social, economic, and political life make them a handy guide for instruction to young and old alike. Their topics are current, and their language is still compelling.

Why, then, are they not used more in the worship and teaching of God's people? A significant reason may be their supposedly moralistic tone. They seem to stress how we ought to behave more than what God has done for us. A further reason for their neglect may be the detached nature of the sayings, especially those in 10:1–22:16 where verse-by-verse exposition is difficult and discovery of the context of a given proverb even more so.

At bottom, the problem seems to be one of understanding the materials in Proverbs from within their own setting and background. How do we read them in the ancient context? How do we hear them alongside their first hearers? Then how do we apply them with biblical integrity and practical fruitfulness to our modern circumstances? Some guidelines for interpretation and proclamation may be suggested in this introduction in order to prepare us for their use in the Commentary.[1]

GUIDELINE 1: *See the book as a collection of collections of wisdom materials.* The Outline of Proverbs that follows this introduction is based on a sevenfold division of the book derived from the separate headings that introduce its major sections at 1:1; 10:1; 22:17; 24:23; 25:1; 30:1; 31:1. It is likely that each section comprises a distinct collection, marked by differences in literary form and instructional content. Grasping these differences, which are pointed out in the appropriate chapters of the Commentary, will help us look for the clues to dealing with them that the authors or collectors have placed within each cluster of teachings.

GUIDELINE 2: *Recognize the various forms of literature of which Proverbs is composed.* Two major forms dominate the first collection (1:1–9:18), after the brief title (1:1), declaration of purpose (1:2–6), and statement of theme (1:7):

- INSTRUCTIONS are extended admonitions (commands or warnings) usually directed to "my son" or "sons." They either (1) extol the prized qualities of wisdom and urge the young to seek them (2:1–22; 3:1–20; 4:1–9, 20–27; 9:7–12) or (2) sound an alarm of the ways in which folly tempts and traps the unwary (friendship with criminal types, 1:8–19; 4:10–19; strife with neighbors, 3:28–35; deceptive or malicious speech, 4:20–27; sexual promiscuity, 5:1–23; 6:20–35; 7:1–27; rash guarantees of loans, 6:1–5; slothfulness, 6:6–11; duplicity, 6:12–15; clan discord, 6:16–19).

- WISDOM SPEECHES are poems, each of several verses, that picture wisdom as a "person" uttering, to whoever will hear, her call to follow her and become her disciples (1:20–33; 8:1–36; 9:1–6). Folly, wisdom's archenemy, is also depicted in personal imagery trying to lure pupils to her with bribes of "stolen water" and "bread eaten in secret" (9:13–18).

If these two types of speech are the architecture of this collection, a number of other literary forms and devices contribute to its interior design. Spotlighting them will prepare for much of what appears in the other collections of Proverbs.

TYPES OF POETIC PARALLELISM. Hebrew poetry, like that of other semitic literatures, is characterized by the use of structurally balanced lines, usually two but often from three to five, that may be combined in one of three main ways.

Synonymous parallelism has the second line restate the first line, usually with synonyms, so as to reinforce its meaning. One basic point is made, yet with more grace, clarity, and nuance than if only one line had been used (see also 18:6 and many other examples in chaps. 18–19):

> My son, hear the instruction of your father,
> And do not forsake the law of your mother
> *Prov. 1:8*

Antithetic parallelism has the second line state the opposite viewpoint of the first. This form stresses the importance of choosing correctly in order to avoid the fate of those who don't. It contributes greatly to the teaching of "the two ways" which makes clear the differences between wise/righteous and foolish/wicked behavior and the consequences of each (chaps. 10–15 bristle with this antithetic form):

> The curse of the LORD *is* on the house of the
>   wicked,
> But He blesses the home of the just.
> *Prov. 3:33*

Often in chapters 1–9, we find *antithetic summaries* in which two back-to-back verses or lines state the positive and negative outcomes of heeding or spurning wisdom (1:32–33; 2:21–22; 3:33–35; 4:18–19; 8:35–56; 9:12).

Synthetic parallelism uses the second (or third) line to advance and complete the sense of the first. The verse, thus, contains one basic thought, enhanced or elaborated by the additional line or lines (see also 16:3, 6–7, 10, 12, etc.; chaps. 16–22 contain a large number of sayings with synthetic parallelism):

> For whom the LORD loves He corrects,
> Just as a father the son *in whom* he delights.
> *Prov. 3:12*

FORMS OF PROVERBS. The two main kinds of proverbs in the book are *sayings* and *admonitions*. Sayings come in several different styles, each with its own way of making its point. Both types of proverbs can use all three kinds of parallelism, together with other literary techniques to be listed below. This variety of expressions lifts wisdom literature above the dangers of becoming mechanical and, therefore, boring.

Sayings can be identified by their grammar: their mood is indicative not imperative. They give descriptions of how wisdom or folly work, as that work is observable in human experience. Their power centers not so much in the teachers' authority, as respected as that may be (1:8), but in the truth of experience which it captures and condenses (the bulk of the collection in 10:1–22:16 is comprised of sayings, virtually all are two lines in length).

> The wise shall inherit glory,
> But shame shall be the legacy of fools.
> *Prov. 3:35*

Two main subcategories of sayings are of interest: *Comparisons* may be made (1) by laying similar ideas back to back so that one line (sometimes two) illustrates the main point (see also 25:12, 14, 25, 28):

> A whip for the horse,
> A bridle for the donkey,
> And a rod for the fool's back.
> *Prov. 26:3*

(2) by using simile words—*like* or *as*—to express the link between the illustration and the main point (see also 10:1, 11, 18; 27:8, 19):

> Like one who binds a stone in a sling
> *Is* he who gives honor to a fool.
> *Prov. 26:8*

Such similes usually feature the absurdity of the illustration in order to highlight the folly of a fool's conduct. And (3) by beginning with the word "better" to demonstrate how wise behavior, even in humble circumstances, outweighs power or affluence when folly is their price (see also 12:9; 15:16; 16:8, 19; 17:1; 19:1; 27:5, 10b):

> Better *is* a dinner of herbs where love is,
> Than a fatted calf with hatred.
> *Prov. 15:17*

Love is not merely preferable to hatred; it is so much superior that it reverses the value of what goes with it—the common vegetables and the choice veal roast.

Numerical sayings were probably derived from games or riddles. They usually follow an *x, x + 1* pattern where the second number is one digit higher than the first and determines the length of the list (see also 30:15b–16, 21–23, 24–28, 29–31):

> There are three *things which* are too wonderful for
>   me,
> Yes, four *which* I do not understand . . .
> > *Prov. 30:18*

The final item in the sequence is often the point of the proverb— 30:18–19 is about the wonders of human affection, not eagles, serpents, or ships. So 6:16–19, the seven deadly sins, climaxes in the denunciation of "The one who sows discord."

Admonitions feature the imperative (or jussive, a third-person command in Heb. [Let him (or it) obey, hear, etc.]) mood. They give positive *commands*, often followed by the reasons, introduced by "for" (see also 21:1–2, 26–28):

> But let your heart keep my commands;
> For length of days and long life
> And peace they will add to you.
> > *Prov. 3:1b–2*

They also frame negative *prohibitions*, whose reason may be introduced by "for" or "lest" (see also 23:22–23; 23:6–8; note that the two collections of Sayings of the Wise [22:17–24:22 and 24:23–34] feature admonitions as do chaps. 1–9):

> My son, do not walk in the way with them,
> Keep your foot from their path;
> For their feet run to evil,
> And they make haste to shed blood.
> > *Prov. 1:15–16*

For a prohibition with "lest," see 22:24–25. Admonitions illustrate the reasonableness of the wise teachers. They did not merely pull rank and cram their commands down the throats of their pupils. More often than not they gave solid reasons, cogent motivations, in support of their instructions. Again the role of experience as the foundation of the call to right behavior is crucial.

OTHER LITERARY FORMS. Six additional forms help fill out the inventory of the teaching techniques of Israel's sages:

Rhetorical questions were used to clinch an argument by forcing the pupil to come up with the right answer. The very form of the question insisted on it (see also 6:28; 30:4):

> Can a man take fire to his bosom,
> And his clothes not be burned?
> *Prov. 6:27*

No! is the only feasible answer. So the question makes the case against adultery crystal clear.

Calls to attention dot the pages of Proverbs and serve to pinpoint the importance of the issue, identify the hearer, underscore the authority, and guarantee the attention warranted by the subject (see also 1:8–9; 4:1–2; 6:20–22; 7:1–5, 24–27; 8:1–9, 32–33; 22:17–21; 23:19, 22–25, 26; note that the bulk of these cluster in the collections of chaps. 1–9 and of 22:17–24:34):

> My son, pay attention to my wisdom;
> Lend your ear to my understanding, . . .
> *Prov. 5:1*

Reflections on experiences are a technique used by at least one teacher to cite his own parents' instruction and its use to him in later life as a motivation for his own children (4:3–9).

Account of personal observations is a another form of argument from experience (7:6–23). It lends credibility to the teacher's admonitions against fornication to have him describe what he has observed first hand in watching from his window the suave and crafty come-ons of a harlot. Personal observation played a central role in the Preacher's acquisition of wisdom (Eccles. 1:13, 14, 16; 2:1; 3:16; 4:1, 7; 9:11).

Beatitudes are promises or exclamations of happiness; at times reinforced by an explanation (see also 8:32, 34; 16:20; 20:7; 28:14; 29:18; see Matt. 5:1–12 for Jesus' use of this wisdom form):

> Happy *is* the man *who* finds wisdom,
> And the man *who* gains understanding;
> For her proceeds *are* better than the profits of silver,
> And her gain than fine gold.
> *Prov. 3:13–14*

The opposite of "happy" was apparently "woe," meaning "trouble" (23:29), as Luke's form of the beatitudes reminds us (Luke 6:20–26).

Allegory or *extended metaphor* is an instance of the sages' subtlety (5:15–23). It begins with imagery—*water, cistern, running water, well, fountains, streams of water*—and gradually becomes literal, as it interprets itself—*wife of your youth, breasts, love*. Nowhere in the Bible, outside of the Song of Songs, do we find so attractive a poem on sexual fidelity and the mutuality and exclusiveness of the marriage covenant.

GUIDELINE 3: *Watch for other literary clues*. The list is long. We can suggest only a few.

• REPETITION is a standard device in Hebrew for making connections between sections and verses or bringing special emphasis to an idea. Chapter 30 furnishes some illustrations. The questions beginning "who" or "what" (v. 4)—four of one, two of the other—are an example of hammering home the majesty and mystery of the Holy God (see v. 3) by the insistent repetition of the interrogative form. Likewise, "generation" (vv. 11–14) becomes the catchword both to connect the four verses—in Hebrew it stands first each time—and to make abundantly plain the widespread character of the sins that are being condemned: not just a handful of culprits but an entrenched mob. Note also how the repetition of "way" (vv. 18–19) puts emphasis not on an occasional act but on an ingrained pattern of life. Moreover, "way" in the numerical saying serves as a linking word (catchword) with the "way" of the adulteress (v. 20) who has her own endemic habits. The editor has deliberately set up both the connection and the contrast—"virgin" and "adulterous woman"—with the repetition of "way."

• CATCHWORDS are a specific instance of repetition. They often account for the linking or pairing of individual sayings. Again in chapter 30, the mention of king in verse 28 may explain the position of the numerical saying on stateliness that follows it and climaxes in the picture of the king with his troops (vv. 29–31). Chapter 11 contains examples of sayings grouped because of thematic or verbal links (11:3–8, 9–14, 18–20, 30–31; see also 15:13–17).

• INCLUSIONS (or ENVELOPES) are another case of repetition that sends us clues as to meaning and structure. Take the declaration of purpose and theme, for instance. It begins "to know *wisdom and instruction*" (1:2); it ends "*wisdom and instruction* fools despise" (1:7). The statement is obviously wrapped or included in this phrase, which sets the tone for the whole book by affirming what is important to know and by noting plainly at the outset that a mark of fools is their scorn of what this book treasures. Chapter 7 begins and ends with calls to attention that serve as symmetrical bookends (7:1–5, 24–27) to the description of the harlot's ploys that is the center-piece of the chapter (vv. 6–23). The calls to attention signal the main emphasis of the chapter—not the harlot's enticement but our need for alertness. The packaging of a passage with similar opening and closing words, phrases, or sentences helps us to know how to divide the text into sections.

• SYNONYMS are sometimes piled up in Proverbs to convey the power and splendor of wisdom. The declaration of purpose (1:2–7) deliberately overwhelms us by citing most of the key terms for wisdom in order to tempt us to succumb to her charms. Chapter 2 re-inforces this (vv. 1–11) by repeating virtually all of the lexicon of wisdom as part of the inducement to choose the ways of the wise (see also Wisdom's own call in 8:12–14). This stacking of synonyms reminds us that our interpretative task is not so much to stress the individual meaning of each word as to catch the accumulative im-pact of the combination of terms that trumpet the glories and worth of wisdom.

• ACROSTIC (or ALPHABETICAL) POETRY appears in splendid form to close the book (31:10–31). Its beauty, its aid to memory, and its comprehensive (A to Z, *aleph* to *tau*) affect are discussed in the commentary.

GUIDELINE 4: *Interpret the book on its own terms.* There is much profit in noting the relationship between Proverbs and other parts of the Bible: (1) comparisons between the instructions of the wise and the laws of Moses can be fruitful; (2) lining up the prophets' concerns for justice and righteousness with those of the sages can shed light on both the differences and similarities between the two groups of leaders; (3) setting wisdom psalms and other parts of the psalter alongside the proverbs reveals both common ground and divergent emphases; (4) tracing the contribution of Proverbs to major inter-testamental works like Ecclesiasticus (Ben Sirach) or the Wisdom of Solomon is highly informative; (5) following the tracks of verses, themes, and literary forms from Proverbs into the New Testament provides a way, not always explored, to understand the Bible's unity. But none of these steps can be taken profitably until we understand the book from within itself.

Proverbs is wisdom literature and as such has its own way of looking at life. It sees *experience as a means of revelation.* In Israel's view of the giving of the law, the reception of prophetic oracles, or the apocalyptic visions, revelation from the Lord breaks into human life from beyond. It opens to us knowledge that we could not otherwise have garnered. Proverbs, in contrast, brings us insight gained from personal and social experience, often at considerable pain. Think how many embarrassing situations lie behind "a stitch in time saves nine."

Proverbs also sees *creation as the basis of order.* This is the chief reason that experience can teach us truths about the will of God for human living. The abundant references to Yahweh's acts of creation in chapter 8 set the tone for the whole book, whose primary purpose is to display the order that holds together all of life. The *analogies* and *comparisons* between animal life and human experience (see chap. 30) make sense because behind both stands the hand of the one Creator. It is that hand which underlies the *cause-and-effect* pattern of proverbs, where good conduct carries its own reward and bad behavior brings its own woe. It is that hand also that dictates the *right time* for the application of a given wise saying or action.

Not that we can learn everything we need to know from creation. Proverbs have *limits.* Their very literary form means that they overstate or oversimplify. They carry no fine print, no footnotes, no lists of exceptions. That is why we need so many of them. We need both "Haste makes waste" and "He who hesitates is lost." Each is precisely true in certain situations; neither is true in every circumstance. Knowing when and where to use them is part of wisdom.

Another limit of proverbs is even more important: *the mystery of Yahweh's sovereignty.* Creation tells us much about God, but not everything. What creation ought to tell us is that we are creatures, often blind to God's ways and heedless of God's thoughts. Our fear of the Lord ought to place major restrictions on our self-confidence. We cannot use proverbs like subway tokens, guaranteed to open the turnstile every time. They are guidelines, not mechanical formulas. They are procedures that we follow, not promises that we claim. We heed them as best we can, try to gain the wisdom that experience can teach, and then leave large amounts of room for God to surprise us with outcomes different from what our plans prescribe (16:1–4, 9, 33; 19:21; 21:30–31).

As wisdom literature, Proverbs not only has its own way of looking at life, it also has its own way of using words. Our handiest tool in any kind of Bible study is a concordance. I hold a Hebrew concordance on my lap through the long months of writing any commentary. I do this not just to discover where else in the Bible a given word occurs but especially to see how it is used in the book under study. In a sense all biblical books are self-contained documents.

Virtually all of them were written to be used for some instructive or devotional purpose before they were included in the Scripture. Their composition, then, calls for them to be understood first on their own terms and then in relation to the whole Bible.

Words like "way," "walk," "stumble," "fall" have their own connotations in wisdom literature as pictures of patterns of life, deeply ingrained habits, and of our failures to follow God's way. "Know," "understand," "fear" call for precise definitions dictated by the contexts in Proverbs. So do "fool," "simple," and "scoffer," common terms in wisdom vocabulary. "Law" usually means the authoritative instruction of teacher or parent, not the statutes of Moses. Illustrations could be multiplied, but I think the point is clear. And in the comments on the various proverbs I have sought to cite where possible the occurrences in other Proverbs passages which contain the word under discussion so as to give the reader further opportunity to grasp its meaning.

GUIDELINE 5: *Remember the initial purpose of the book.* Piecing together the evidence as best we can, we come to the conclusion that Proverbs is a collection of collections of materials designed initially for use by the young men of Israel's society who were being groomed for positions of leadership. The centralization of the government of Israel's twelve tribes under David and Solomon changed permanently the way of life of God's covenant people. Building projects, international diplomacy and trade, census taking, military mobilization, tax collection, judicial procedures—these and many more governmental functions called for a whole cadre of administrators to be recruited and trained for positions of responsibility within the government.

How this training took place we are not told. Egypt, Assyria, and Babylonia have left ample documentation of schools and training centers in both court and temple. In Jewish life the first mention of "school," dated about 180 B.C., is found in Ecclus. (Sir.) 51:23, eight hundred years after the monarchy's beginning. We are almost obligated to assume, although we cannot prove, that Israel's court had set up some kind of schooling system to meet the intense and widespread need for formal learning, beginning probably in Solomon's day, given the close association of his name with the collections in Proverbs (1:1; 10:1; 25:1).

The use of many of the individual sayings, of course, goes back trackless centuries into the early life of Israel and the cultures of their ancestors. The clan would undoubtedly have been the source of many sayings, seasoned and ripened by generations of use in training the young in the mores, skills, and practices of family and tribe. The emphasis on respect for parental teaching (1:8; 7:20; 31:26) and on the children's obligation to hear (2:1–2; 3:1–2; 4:1–9) may be reflections of this clan background as are many of the individual sayings (see esp. chaps. 25–27, which teach the young to read wisdom's lessons in all that surrounds them).

The court (see chaps. 28–29 for instructions to rulers) would be the logical place for these sayings to have been polished, edited, collected, and taught. The nature of this task is described in Eccles. 12:9–11. If schools did exist, patterned after the Egyptian (remember Solomon's personal and commercial ties to Egypt [10:28–11:1]) centers of instruction for bureaucrats and scribes, the teachers for them may also have been trained in the court. Proverbs may well have been part of their curriculum.

These suggestions about the initial use of the book are grounded in a number of observations from its contents. First, Proverbs, in common with Job and Ecclesiastes, reflects the life of the landowning upper classes. It abounds with pictures of luxury: the home of the temptress (7:16–20); the precious stones or jewelry with which wisdom is compared (3:15; 8:11; 20:15; 31:10); the lavish menus featuring meat and wine (17:1; 23:1–2, 20–21, 29–35; 30:8–10); the affluence in the enterprises of the excellent woman (31:15–16, 18, 22). It speaks with concern *about* the poor but not *to* them. The poor (with the slaves) are to be cared for (22:22), but the station they represent is one to be avoided, not to be escaped from. It commends economic prosperity as a good to be retained, not squandered or jeopardized by laziness or rash pledges (11:15).

Second, the frequent references to royalty point to a courtly context for much if not all of the book. Beyond the references to Solomon (1:1; 10:1; 25:1) are the mentions of Hezekiah (25:1), Agur, and Lemuel; the latter two are designated "king" in 30:1 and 31:1. It is enough here to note the commentary discussions of royal responsibility (chaps. 16 and 31) and the proper courtly responses to it (chaps. 16, 23, and 25).

Third, the masculine orientation of Proverbs is best accounted for if the specific initial purpose of the book was to support the training of leaders for political and mercantile responsibility. Those positions evidently were not open to women in that age and society. "Sons" are the ones addressed and their duties featured. Women are mentioned as wives, mothers, and temptresses—the basic roles they played in the lives of the men. Their part in society could be negative (the harlot or the quarrelsome spouse), but it also could be beautifully positive (see "Feminine Dignity" in chap. 27, the remarkable instruction of King Lemuel's mother in chap. 31, including the magnificent acrostic poem to the excellent woman in vv. 10–31).

The teachings of the Bible, to be shown as pertinent to our day and situation, must always be interpreted cross-culturally. We do not live in a monarchy whose basic enterprise is agriculture. Nor do we live in a society that stems from common ethnic, religious, and cultural roots. Our politics, our economics, our technology, and our pluralism all separate us from the world of Israel's sages. We must make careful adjustments to apply God's infallible Word to our lives.

One such adjustment is in our understanding of the role of women in leadership. This is an adjustment made necessary by the further revelation of God in the New Testament. Jesus' treatment of women, the genderless character of spiritual gifts, the realization that in Christ there is neither male nor female, the fulfillment at Pentecost of Joel's prophecy that daughters will prophesy along with sons, that maidservants would be blessed by the Spirit along with manservants, the examples of women who bear key responsibilities in the Pauline churches—these factors all combine to point to a new day in God's program for his people. Part of that new day sees women assuming offices and duties in churchly and public life that earlier generations reserved for men. As that happens, the pages of Proverbs with its important moral, social, financial, political, and spiritual lessons need to be opened by and to women. The last page of Proverbs has always belonged to them. So now must the rest of the book. It is God's inspired word, full of power and profit not only to its first audience but to all the generations following, especially ours.

How and when the entire collection of Proverbs was compiled are hard to say. Solomon's name probably points more to the start (about 950 B.C.) than to the completion of the task. Hezekiah's name tells us that the process was not yet finished by 700 B.C. The differences in outlook between Proverbs and Ecclesiasticus (180 B.C) suggest a date before the Exile (586–539 B.C.) for the bulk of the work. It may be that the sections assigned to Agur (chap. 30) and Lemuel (chap. 31) were added during or after the Exile. The book's present form is based more on content and style than on the date of its parts. What is quite sure is that it is unsafe to date the work on the basis of theories of development. Longer sayings (chaps. 1–9) are not necessarily later than shorter ones. And sayings that express openly the teachers' unique commitment to Yahweh are not necessarily younger than so-called secular ones.

GUIDELINE 6: *Acknowledge the covenantal setting of the biblical proverbs.* Israel's sages did not have a religion different from that of the prophets and psalmists. Everything that we know about them suggests that they worshiped Yahweh in the temple, prayed to God regularly, held the law in devout esteem, and sought to practice justice and righteousness in the community. Yet they had tasks distinct from those of the other religious leaders. They left it to others to interpret law, recite Israel's history and receive oracles that shed light on national crises. Their role was to call the best of Israel's youth and the more seasoned statesmen and administrators to apply their covenant faith in all its ramifications to everyday life. They focused the lamp of creation on the day-by-day decisions and transactions and thus reinforced and complemented the ethical commands of law and prophecy. So doing, they put heart, feet, hands, and tongue to the conviction that Yahweh, the Creator-Redeemer-Lawgiver-King, was indeed Lord of everyone and everything.

The wise coopted the phrase "Fear of the Lord" as their most precise and encompassing expression of the chief duty of their disciples. It embraced religious loyalty as well as neighbor love. It brought covenant and creation together and gave a vertical dimension to social responsibility. Fidelity to all obligations and charity in all relationships were more than clever ways to retain peace in a community. They were reflections of the character of the one, true, living God.

Their confidence in Yahweh's gracious sovereignty over the whole creation gave the sages boldness to reach beyond Israel's borders for insight and understanding. All truth belonged to and ultimately derived from their Lord no matter who experienced and expressed it. Agur (chap. 30) and Lemuel (chap. 31) both seem to be leaders of non-Israelite groups (see on 30:1). Yet their words are part of wisdom's and our canon. And we would not want to be without them.

The same situation seems to be the case with the collection of the Sayings of the Wise (22:17–24:22). The beginning of this section (22:17–23:16) resembles Egyptian instructions from the hand of Amenemope. His thirty chapters (about 1000 B.C. or earlier) contained admonitions against (1) robbing the poor (Prov. 22:22–23; Amen. II); (2) removing boundary markers (Prov. 23:10; Amen. VI); (3) eating with a king (Prov. 23:1–3; Amen. XXIII); (4) banking on wealth (Prov. 23:5b; Amen. VIII). Other similarities are noted in the "call to hear" (Prov. 22:17–18; Amen. I) and the use of "thirty" to enumerate the sections (see on 22:20). Not slavish copying but remarkable innovation in artistic and theological elaboration was the style of Israel's teachers, who used only a fraction of the Egyptian material. Most importantly, they recast what they did borrow to reflect their covenant faith; for example, the injunction against plundering the poor is given in Proverbs a reason that flows from the heart of the wise men's faith: "For the Lord (Yahweh) will plead their cause" (22:23a).

This covenant setting is what keeps the proverbs from shriveling into legalism. Their ground rules for life are not a prescription for salvation. God's elective grace to Abraham, to the tribes in Egypt, and to the succeeding generations in Canaan had provided for that. The proverbs are not bite-size tablets of the law but neither are they sparkling tokens of grace. Like the law of Moses, they represent obligation, to be sure, but obligation grounded in deep gratitude. They are designed to enable us to live out the full meaning of the life that springs fresh daily from the hand of the Creator and Savior. We can preach and teach them as Good News, especially since our Lord Jesus Christ has given them clearer meaning and given us stronger power to keep them through his life, death, and resurrection.

Worshipers in the Eastern Orthodox churches lift their gold-clad Bibles in worship, as their priests chant the single word: "Wisdom!"[2] It would be hard to comb through the dictionary for a better description of Scripture than that, especially in the light of the pivotal role that Proverbs must play in the nurture of God's people.

The eighth-century Irish prayer that we know as "Be Thou My Vision" contains these graceful lines:

> Be Thou my wisdom, and thou my true Word,
> I ever with thee, and thou with me, Lord.
> (translated by Mary Byrne)

NOTES

1. Some material in this introduction is adapted from my articles on "Proverb" and "Proverbs, Book of" in *The International Standard Biblical Encyclopedia*, rev. ed. (Grand Rapids, Mich.: William B. Eerdmans, 1986), 3:1012-20.

2. A. Ugolnik, *The Illuminating Icon* (Grand Rapids, Mich.: William B. Eerdmans, 1989), 50.

An Outline of Proverbs

I. Instructions to Seek Wisdom: 1:1–9:18
   A. Bad Company and Good Counsel: 1:1–33
      1. Title: 1:1
      2. Purpose: 1:2–6
      3. Theme: 1:7
      4. Call to Attention: 1:8–9
      5. Warning against Bad Company: 1:10–18
      6. Summary Appraisal: 1:19
      7. Wisdom's Denunciation of Fools: 1:20–31
      8. Antithetic Summary: 1:32–33
   B. Perverted Speech and Loose Sexuality: 2:1–22
      1. Argument: 2:1–9
      2. Illustrations: 2:10–15
      3. The Illustration of the Immoral Woman: 2:16–20
      4. Antithetical Summary: 2:21–22
   C. Admonitions to Piety and Arguments for Sagacity: 3:1–35
      1. Admonitions to Piety—A: 3:1–12
      2. A Practical Argument for Sagacity: 3:13–18
      3. A Theological Argument for Sagacity: 3:19–20
      4. Admonitions to Piety—B: 3:21–26
      5. Admonitions to Generosity: 3:27–32
      6. Antithetic Summary 3:33–35
   D. Personal Illustration and Practical Advice: 4:1–27
      1. Call to Attention: 4:1–2
      2. Personal Illustration: 4:3–9
      3. Practical Exhortations: 4:10–17
      4. Antithetic Summary: 4:18–19
      5. More Practical Exhortations: 4:20–27
   E. Bitter Honey and Sweet Water: 5:1–23
      1. Beware the Wanton's Wily Words: 5:1–6
      2. Beware the Dire Results of Adultery: 5:7–14
      3. Practice Fidelity with Joy: 5:15–20
      4. Negative Concluding Summary: 5:21–23

F. Social Responsibility and Family Unity: 6:1–35
    1. Disengage Yourselves from Rash Pledges: 6:1–5
    2. Learn Diligence from the Ant: 6:6–11
    3. Perverse People Are Dangerous: 6:12–15
    4. Divisive People Are Deadly: 6:16–19
    5. Call to Attention: 6:20–22
    6. Shun Adultery: 6:23–35
G. Smooth Coaxings and Deadly Results: 7:1–27
    1. Introductory Call to Attention—Positive: 7:1–5
    2. Illustration from Personal Observation: 7:6–23
    3. Concluding Call to Attention—Negative: 7:24–27
H. Ancient Credentials and Contemporary Calling: 8:1–36
    1. Introductory Call to Attention—Extended: 8:1–9
    2. Self-Description of Assets: 8:10–21
    3. Self-Description of Presence at Creation: 8:22–31
    4. Concluding Call to Attention: 8:32–33
    5. Beatitude as Summary: 8:34
    6. Antithetic Summary: 8:35–36
I. Two Calls and Two Responses: 9:1–18
    1. Description of Wisdom's Wholesome Invitation:
        9:1–6
    2. Admonitions on Differences between Scoffers and
        Wise: 9:7–9
    3. Theme Repeated from 1:7: Inclusion: 9:10–11
    4. Antithetic Summary: 9:12
    5. Description of Folly's Fatal Invitation: 9:13–18
II. Proverbs of Solomon: 10:1–22:16 (Note: *The detached nature of
the proverbs in this section makes detailed analysis impossible. In-
stead, this outline pinpoints the topics discussed in each chapter of
the commentary.*)
A. Wisdom and Work: 10:1–32
    1. Rewards for Conduct
    2. Diligence in Work
B. Generosity and Rashness: 11:1–31
    1. Generosity in Giving
    2. Risks of Rash Pledges
C. Honesty and Kindness: 12:1–28
    1. Honest Speaking
    2. Kindness to Animals
D. Violence and Hope: 13:1–25
    1. The Dangers of Violence
    2. The Significance of Hope

E. Fear of the Lord and Control of the Self: 14:1–35
  1. Reverent Obedience
  2. Personal Discipline
F. Prudent Speech and Fervent Prayer: 15:1–33
  1. Effective Conversation
  2. Devout Worship
G. The Lord's Eyes and the King's Face: 16:1–33
  1. Dependence on God
  2. Respect for the King
H. Family Ties and Friendly Bonds: 17:1–28
  1. Honor to Parents
  2. Love of Friends
I. Peace in Society and Purity in Speech: 18:1–24
  1. Peace in Society
  2. Integrity in Conversation
J. Open Ears and Full Hands: 19:1–29
  1. Heeding Instruction
  2. Handling Wealth
K. Firm Hands and Fair Scales: 20:1–30
  1. Discipline of Children
  2. Honesty in Business
L. Rewards of Conduct and Problems of Pride: 21:1–31
  1. Risks of Folly
  2. Gains of Humility
M. Cautious Conduct and Passionate Justice: 22:1–16
  1. Disciplining Ourselves
  2. Defending Others
III. Words of the Wise: 22:17–24:34
  A. First Collection: 22:17–24:22
    1. Saying 1. Call to Attention to Value of Wisdom: 22:17–21
    2. Saying 2. Admonition on Care for the Poor: 22:22–23
    3. Saying 3. Admonition on Association with the Angry: 22:24–25
    4. Saying 4. Admonition on Rash Pledges: 22:26–27
    5. Saying 5. Admonition on Moving Boundaries: 22:28
    6. Saying 6. Question on the Importance of Talent: 22:29
    7. Saying 7. Admonitions on Etiquette with Royalty: 23:1–3
    8. Saying 8. Admonition on Financial Ambition: 23:4–5

An Index of Proverbs

Text	Chapter	Page	Text	Chapter	Page	Text	Chapter	Page
19:15	10	157	20:17	20	311	21:18	21	331
19:16	19	290	20:18	19	287	21:19	27	427
19:17	11/19	167/297	20:19	18	274	21:20	14	206
19:18	20	305	20:20	17	258	21:21	21	331
19:19	14	210	20:21	20	312	21:22	21	325
19:20	19	286	20:22	20	302	21:23	18	277
19:21	16	238	20:23	20	309	21:24	21	337
19:22	12	178/184	20:24	16	236	21:25	10	155
19:23	14	201	20:25	15	230	21:26	11	168
19:24	10	155	20:26	16	247	21:27	15	228
19:25	19	282	20:27	16	240	21:28	12	180/184
19:26	17	258	20:28	16	249	21:29	22	342
19:27	19	284	20:29	20	306	21:30	16	238
19:28	12	180	20:30	14	212	21:31	16	238
19:29	21	325						
			21:1	16	250	22:1	22	340
20:1	14	205	21:2	16	242	22:2	16	240
20:2	16	248	21:3	16	244	22:3	22	343
20:3	14	211	21:4	21	337	22:4	14	203
20:4	10	156	21:5	22	344	22:5	22	343
20:5	14	212	21:6	20	311	22:6	20	304
20:6	26	411	21:7	13	195	22:7	19	296
20:7	20	303	21:8	21	320	22:8	22	347
20:8	16	247	21:9	27	427	22:9	11	165
20:9	20	301	21:10	17	262	22:10	18	270
20:10	20	307/308	21:11	19	283	22:11	18	277
20:11	20	306	21:12	21	326	22:12	16	240
20:12	16	239	21:13	11	165	22:13	10	156
20:13	10	158	21:14	22	344	22:14	27	429
20:14	20	310	21:15	21	330	22:15	20	304
20:15	18	276	21:16	21	330	22:16	22	348
20:16	11	172	21:17	14	206			

II. Solomon's Proverbs Copied by Hezekiah's Scribes: 25:1–29:27

Text	Chapter	Page	Text	Chapter	Page	Text	Chapter	Page
25:1	25	387	25:14	25	398	25:27	26	414
25:2	25	389	25:15	25	394	25:28	29	447
25:3	25	389	25:16	29	446			
25:4	25	390	25:17	26	413	26:1	28	436
25:5	25	390	25:18	26	405	26:2	26	406
25:6	25	394	25:19	26	405	26:3	28	438
25:7	25/26	394/412	25:20	26	413	26:4	25	398
25:8	26	412	25:21	25	402	26:5	25	398
25:9	26	412	25:22	25	402	26:6	26	414
25:10	26	412	25:23	26	406	26:7	25	399
25:11	25	396	25:24	27	427	26:8	28	436
25:12	25	397	25:25	15	226	26:9	25	399
25:13	25	397	25:26	28	435	26:10	28	437

Text	Chapter	Page	Text	Chapter	Page	Text	Chapter	Page
26:11	19	282	27:17	19	289	28:24	26	410
26:12	21	335	27:18	19	417	28:25	29	449
26:13	27	419	27:19	14	213	28:26	28	436
26:14	27	420	27:20	16/29	235/449	28:27	25	402
26:15	27	420	27:21	25	401	28:28	28	441
26:16	27	420	27:22	28	438			
26:17	26	407	27:23	27	418	29:1	19	290
26:18	26	407	27:24	27	418	29:2	25	392
26:19	26	407	27:25	27	418	29:3	17	259
26:20	26	408	27:26	27	418	29:4	25	392
26:21	26	408	27:27	27	418	29:5	28	437
26:22	18/26	273/408				29:6	28	443
26:23	26	409	28:1	28	439	29:7	25	402
26:24	26	409	28:2	28	440	29:8	29	451
26:25	26	409	28:3	13	193	29:9	29	450
26:26	26	409	28:4	15/28	230/440	29:10	13	194
26:27	26	409	28:5	28	441	29:11	29	451
26:28	26	410	28:6	18/28	272/432	29:12	25	393
			28:7	17	259	29:13	16	241
27:1	21	336	28:8	28	433	29:14	25	393
27:2	21	336	28:9	19	290	29:15	29	453
27:3	25	399	28:10	28	435	29:16	28	443
27:4	27	421	28:11	28	432	29:17	29	453
27:5	27	422	28:12	28	441	29:18	15	230
27:6	27	423	28:13	28	442	29:19	29	453
27:7	29	447	28:14	14	200	29:20	25	400
27:8	29	448	28:15	25	391	29:21	29	454
27:9	29	448	28:16	25	391	29:22	29	450
27:10	27	423	28:17	13	193	29:23	21	333
27:11	17	256	28:18	28	442	29:24	26	411
27:12	28	439	28:19	27	419	29:25	14	202
27:13	11	172	28:20	28	433	29:26	25	395
27:14	25	400	28:21	28	433	29:27	28	439
27:15	27	430	28:22	28	434			
27:16	27	430	28:23	26	410			

Instructions to Seek Wisdom

Proverbs 1:1–9:18

CHAPTER ONE

Bad Company and Good Counsel

Proverbs 1:1–33

Israel's teachers were persistently passionate in their concern to lead their students in the right path. They argued, badgered, reasoned, illustrated, pleaded, warned, and commanded in order to make their points. In short, they cared. And they voiced that care with every technique in a repertoire that had been in the making among the wise of the ancient world for two thousand years before Solomon mounted Israel's throne.

The bulk of Proverbs divides into two major kinds of literature: instructive speeches, chapters 1–9; wisdom sayings, chapters 10–31. The speeches had as their main purpose to state every possible reason why wisdom should be valued and folly despised. The larger canvas of the speeches gave them more room to make their claims than did the small sketch pad of the individual sayings, and they took advantage of every square centimeter of space. Wisdom for them was a matter of nothing less than life or death. It was the way in which children of the covenant with Yahweh were to live. And it was the only course in life that made both present and ultimate sense.

Incentives to wise living and illustrations of what that entails— these two themes are the point and counterpoint of the first nine chapters, where bright encouragement and dark warning find artful interplay. The warnings anticipate and amplify some of the key topics covered by the clusters of sayings in chapters 10–31: perverted speech (chap. 2), loose sexuality (chaps. 2, 5, 6, 7), ungodly self-reliance (chap. 3), greed (chap. 3), rashness in guaranteeing the financial obligations of others (chap. 6), laziness (chap. 6), lying (chap. 6), disruptive social behavior (chap. 6). This typical combination of general exhortation to wisdom and specific application of it shapes the form of chapter 1, once the title (1:1), purpose (1:2–6), and theme (1:7) of Proverbs have been stated.

TITLE

1:1 The proverbs of Solomon the son of David, king
of Israel:

Prov. 1:1

The title intends to cover the whole book, even though sections
that do not derive from Solomon are noted later (30:1; 31:1). Proverbial sayings played a role in Israel's clan life from the beginning—
conserving, organizing, packaging, and transmitting the lessons
learned from apt observation and painful experience. But not until
Solomon came along, with his divinely gifted skills at wisdom and
his need to transmit it to those who managed his burgeoning administration, was there a means to collect, edit, and disseminate the
varied sayings that had been used to train Israel's young. Solomon's
hand in all of this was noted in Israel's historical summaries (1
Kings 4:29–34; 10:1) as well as in the annotations of Prov. 10:1 and
25:1. Hezekiah seems to have been one royal successor who
grasped the importance of serving the people by supplying them
with wisdom (Prov. 25:1).

Solomon's traditional role as sponsor and patron of wisdom may
help to explain the titles of two other Old Testament books. We
should note, however, that the Song and Ecclesiastes allude to
Solomon in different ways from the title in Prov. 1:1. Ecclesiastes
does not mention Solomon by name but hints at his participation
cryptically, "the son of David, king in Jerusalem," and this only in
the first two chapters. The Song, while naming Solomon in 1:1; 3:8–
9, 11; 8:11–12, frequently describes the lover as a rustic shepherd
whose love and loyalty are likened to royal conduct. All this is to
suggest that the titles of the three books are not meant to be read
alike and that the role of the historic Solomon in the collection and
composition of Proverbs is probably more prominent than any part
assigned to him in the other two works.

"*Proverbs*" states the genre of the book as do "song" (Song of Sol.
1:1), "vision" (Isa. 1:1), "burden" (Nah. 1:1), "history" (Gen. 2:4), and
"gospel" (Mark 1:1). Knowledge of the genre is essential to the interpretation. A valentine is not a recipe—a literal reading of one will
dull the edge of love; a figurative reading of the other will blunt
the edge of appetite. Taking care to understand how to read the Bible
is as important as trusting in its power and authority. Our author has
done us a favor by stating at the outset the kind of literature with
which we deal. However, we must understand proverbs (Heb. *māshāl*

in singular) to cover a much wider range of forms than does our English word. "Lesson" or "artistic instruction," often based on comparisons as the Hebrew root suggests, may be closer English equivalents to *māshāl*. The rich inventory of speeches and sayings in the book will give us the best clues as to the meaning of proverbs (see verse 6 for a sampling).

Purpose

1:2 To know wisdom and instruction,
   To perceive the words of understanding,
3 To receive the instruction of wisdom,
   Justice, judgment, and equity;
4 To give prudence to the simple,
   To the young man knowledge and discretion—
5 A wise *man* will hear and increase learning,
   And a man of understanding will attain wise
      counsel,
6 To understand a proverb and an enigma,
   The words of the wise and their riddles.

Prov. 1:2–6

Chock full of meaty morsels about wisdom, this paragraph is designed to whet the appetite of even the most casual reader. Its synonyms, piled one on another, are calculated to show wisdom's well-stocked larder. They are an instance of the use of repetition by Hebrew authors to expand, reinforce, and enrich the meaning of a concept. It is their accumulative force that conveys the teacher's intention, more than the precise nuance of each term, though each word adds something to our understanding of wisdom.

The regnant word is "wisdom"—Hebrew *hokmāh* (vv. 2, 7) the broadest, most inclusive term available to depict the combination of observation, obedience, careful planning, prudent conduct, and sensitivity to God's will that Israel's wise treasured and taught; it is the only term used when wisdom is treated as a person whose calls, claims, and promises are quoted directly (e.g., 1:20–33; 8:1–36; 9:1–6, 10–11).

"*Instruction*" (vv. 2–3) includes correction and discipline in its orbit of meaning; the Hebrew *mûsār* is a favorite in Proverbs (1:7; 5:12, 23; 6:23; 8:33; etc.; more than thirty occurrences all told), expressing as it does the painful process of garnering wisdom.

"*Understanding*" (vv. 2, 5, 6) is the ability to look to the heart of an issue and to discern the differences at stake in the choices being weighed; Hebrew root *bîn* as a verb and in a whole clutch of nouns turns up more than sixty times in Proverbs.

"Wisdom" (v. 3) is better read as "well-used skill"; Hebrew *śākal* (about sixteen times in Proverbs) connotes both the ability to apply wisdom and the success or prosperity that come with that application.

"Prudence" may not quite catch the sharp edge of Hebrew *ʿormāh*, which conveys ideas like "shrewdness," "cunning," "cleverness," even to the point of deceit (Exod. 21:14; Josh. 9:4; a related form describes the serpent in Gen. 3:1), although that is precluded here by the stellar virtues in verse 3.

"Knowledge" (vv. 2, 4) is a pivotal term for Proverbs as well as for Hosea (see 2:20; 4:1, 6; 6:3, 6), Jeremiah (see 10:14; 22:16), and John (see 17:3; 1 John 2:3–4); Hebrew *yādaʿ* and its related nouns appear over seventy times; beyond numerical count, the centrality and scope of knowledge is signaled in its use as a term parallel to the "fear of the Lord" (1:7; 9:10); implied in such use is knowing and doing what God requires, as fervently and consistently as possible.

"Discretion" (v. 4), used here positively, is the same term that is denounced later as "evil devices" (12:2); Hebrew *mᵉzimmāh* focuses on "prudent planning," a key component of wisdom.

"Learning" (v. 5) springs from the root *lāqaḥ*, "take" or "grasp"; it embraces "comprehension of truth well enough to teach it" (Deut. 32:2) and the "ability to teach" or persuade others (Prov. 7:21; note again the negative as well as positive use).

"Wise counsel" (v. 5) has to do with "accurate guidance," literally "sound steering of the right course" (Heb. *taḥbulôth* see 11:14; 12:5; 20:18; 24:6).

The vastness of the teacher's subject, documented in these nine terms, is matched by the range of the audience addressed: *"the simple"* (v. 4), that is, naive, easily influenced, readily seduced (the same root, Heb. *ptʾ*, shows up negatively in 1:10; see also 1:22; 7:7; 8:5; 9:4, 6, 16; 14:15, 18, etc.); *"the young man"* (v. 4), used in parallel with *"simple,"* to denote the tenderfeet, the apprentices in the curriculum of wisdom; at the other end of the scale are the persons of accomplishment, *"wise"* and *"understanding"* veterans of wisdom's long march, yet with much to learn given wisdom's unconquerable and overwhelming topography. As the Tetons offer some climbing sites safe for beginners and others boggling for experts, so wisdom has terrain profitable to the neophytes and inexhaustible to the masters.

Another aspect of wisdom's wealth is her dazzling array of forms.

She comes at us with the versatility of a great actress, capable of adapting herself to any part assigned her. *"Proverb"* (v. 6) is the master category, bracketing the other expressions and focusing on the powerful lessons to be conveyed in artful teaching (see on 1:1). *"Enigma"* is an allusive saying, hard to puzzle out because it may be deliberately ambiguous and may also project a biting sarcasm (see Hab. 2:6). *"Words of the wise"* are sayings like those found in 22:17–24:34, which bear this very heading. Their aim is practical instruction through a combination of exhortations supported by good reasons and of recitations of personal experience (see 24:30–34). *"Riddles"* are teasing questions that are clear enough to give clues to their solution and cryptic enough to throw the careless off track, like the side-paths which Agatha Christie invites us to take in most of her mystery stories. Their playful use at Samson's wedding feast (Judg. 14:12–19) is balanced by their political use in the visit to Solomon of Sheba's queen (1 Kings 10:1). Proverbs that begin with clusters of questions may be classified as riddles or their offspring (see 23:29–30; 30:4), as may be some of the numerical sayings in chapters 6 and 30. Proverbs may use playful language but its aim is deadly serious. The teachers were not training candidates for quiz shows or even Phi Beta Kappa keys. They were recruiting and shaping generations of leaders whose obligation was to practice the fundamental virtues of Israel as laid down by law and ratified by experience. That is why *"justice"* (or "righteousness"), *"judgment"* (or "justice"), and *"equity"* (or "uprightness") are concerned with conduct that is fair and bolstered by trustworthiness and integrity. Amos pairs the first two terms in his famous call to renewal (5:24), while Job embodies the last one in the total rightness of how he behaved (Job 1–2).

Theme

> 1:7 The fear of the LORD *is* the beginning of
>   knowledge,
> *But* fools despise wisdom and instruction.
>   *Prov. 1:7*

These familiar words stand out in isolation from the long purpose sentence of 1:2–6 and the call to attention that begins the two wisdom speeches (1:10–19, 20–33) that comprise the bulk of the chapter. Their form—a saying in the indicative, not an admonition in the imperative (see vv. 8, 10)—their new thought, *"fear,"* their mention of the Lord's name for the first time and their antithetic style all combine to spotlight this text as the theme of the entire book. Its periodic echoes will be heard and analyzed in chapter 14, so brief comments will suffice here. "Fear" is best understood as "reverent obedience." Although it includes worship, it does not end there. It radiates out from our adoration and devotion to our everyday conduct that sees each moment as the Lord's time, each relationship as the Lord's opportunity, each duty as the Lord's command, and each blessing as the Lord's gift. It is a new way of looking at life and seeing what it is meant to be when viewed from God's perspective.

"Beginning" means more than commencement, although it does mean that. There can surely be nothing that the Bible classifies as true "knowledge" (see on 1:2–6) that does not commence with awe that leads to action. But "beginning" is also culmination. The Hebrew root, an offshoot of the word for "head" (see its use in 8:22–26), suggests that which is first in importance as well as in time. The point is not that we begin our quest for knowledge by fearing God and then venture forward to be made perfect by the flesh (Gal. 3:3). The point is that obeying God is the ceiling as well as the foundation of life. It should lead to knowledge, and, in turn, all knowledge should enhance it.

"Fools" (Heb. ᵉwîl), one of the two basic descriptors (see also kāsîl at 1:22–23) of those who choose against God's way, disrupt society, shame their families, and bear the dreadful consequences, do not even begin this cycle. "Wisdom and instruction" (see on 1:2–6) are not only ignored, they are totally devalued (despised) by them. The antithetical structure shows that the fear of the Lord comes last, not first ("beginning") with them. That is why they are fools. Their basic lack is not intelligence quotient, educational opportunity, or positive examples. They are not so much stupid as wicked (see chap. 10).

CALL TO ATTENTION

> 1:8 My son, hear the instruction of your father,
> And do not forsake the law of your mother;
> 9 For they *will be* a graceful ornament on your
> head,
> And chains about your neck.
>
> Prov. 1:8–9

What the fools despise (v. 7) is a source of elegance, delight, and beauty. No yoke pictured here. No back-to-the-wall, nose-to-thegrindstone kind of clenched-jaw obedience. The teacher knows better than that, as did the psalmist (Ps. 1:2). To fear God and to act on that fear as it was compressed into the fiber of parental instruction is to be graced with eye-catching beauty like the chains or necklace that adorned the beloved in the Song (4:9). *"Ornament"* is probably a wreath or garland of greenery or flowers (see 4:9). Obedience makes a person delightfully outstanding to others and gives one something to cherish and value for oneself. That is the promise to the one open to *"hear"* the words and the meaning of the parents' teachings. *"Law"* (Heb. *tôrāh*) is here not primarily the Mosaic commandments, though they may have been included, but all necessary instructions for wise and godly life, even though accompanied by pain (for *"instruction,"* see 1:2–6).

That both parents are mentioned is a tribute to the prominent role of Israel's mothers. We find no similar reference to mother as teacher in Babylonian or Egyptian wisdom literature. This call to attention (see 4:1, 10, 20; 5:1, 7; 7:24; 8:32–33) is a form well known to psalmists (see Psalms 49 and 78) and prophets (see Amos 3:1; 4:1; 5:1; Hos. 5:1) as well as the wise. Here it may form a bridge between what the pupils had learned at home, which they were not to *"forsake"* or abandon (for other uses of the verb *nātash,* see 17:14; Deut. 32:15; Neh. 10:22) and what they were about to learn more formally from the teachers who were preparing them for their roles as leaders in the land.

WARNING AGAINST BAD COMPANY

1:10 My son, if sinners entice you,
    Do not consent.
 11 If they say, "Come with us,
    Let us lie in wait to *shed* blood;
    Let us lurk secretly for the innocent without
      cause;
 12 Let us swallow them alive like Sheol,
    And whole, like those who go down to the Pit;
 13 We shall find all *kinds* of precious possessions,
    We shall fill our houses with spoil;
 14 Cast in your lot among us,
    Let us all have one purse"—
 15 My son, do not walk in the way with them,
    Keep your foot from their path;
 16 For their feet run to evil,
    And they make haste to shed blood.

17 Surely, in vain the net is spread
   In the sight of any bird;
18 But they lie in wait for their *own* blood,
   They lurk secretly for their *own* lives.

Prov. 1:10–18

The teachers knew that life was lived in groups. Their society was still deeply affected by the instincts of Israel's tribal and clannish beginnings. As strong as were the parental ties saluted in verses 8–9, the voices of mother, father, or teacher were not the only calls vying for attention. People with malice on their minds, *"sinners"* (v. 10) openly committed to create mayhem or murder (*"shed blood"*) in the name of greed (v. 11) were also uttering their seductive (*"entice,"* v. 10) invitations. The fact that this alarm of the dangers of bad company is the first specific warning sounded in Proverbs suggests that folly is not just an individual matter but a social one as well. We travel in groups—whether they are our social friends, our service club, our prayer partners, our tennis set, our business colleagues, or our street gang. What we become is determined in some significant measure by the company we keep.

Introduction
  The social setting
  The modern scene
Unsound friendships may be empty   (24:1–2)
  Perversion of mind
  Corruption of speech
Unsound friendships may prove harmful   (22:24–25)
  Edgy anger
  Tempting wrath
Unsound friendships may lead to disaster   (1:10–19)
  Greed's false promises
  Evil's inevitable outcome
Conclusion
  Be concerned
  Be careful
  Be realistic
  Be thankful

The proverbs seem to have towns and cities as their *social setting*. They reflect a time of increased urbanization (hear wisdom calling in the *city* streets [vv. 20–21]) and pluralization. Younger persons had left their homes to find jobs or hold offices in Jerusalem. This move severed their clan roots and put them in touch with Canaanites and other non-Israelites, as well as with renegade Hebrews, who had overthrown their covenantal obligations and were living as sheer pagans (sinners, v. 10) who deliberately defied the law by looting the possessions of others even to the point of murder (vv. 11, 16). These were purely wanton acts motivated by greed (v. 13) and committed against persons who had done them no harm whatsoever. Note *"innocent"* and *"without cause"* (v. 11). The fact that the teachers began with this note and amplified it through ten verses is good evidence that the temptation to hang out with these criminals was real. They probably could have expanded their comments with horror stories of what had happened to some of their pupils who had scorned their counsel.

In our modern scene every teenager knows the questions: "Where are you going?" "How will you get there?" "What time will you be home?" And increasingly an even more important question is added: "Who else will be there?" To the answer to this last query, wise parents give closest attention. Unfamiliar names prompt further inquiry. Well they know the telling influence that friends assert. Family, teachers, bosses all make their contribution. But in our society the peer group, the tight circle of intimates, may determine whether a young person dabbles with drugs, experiments with sex, or toys with crime.

Unsound friendships may be empty. The teachers were both reasonable and realistic in making such assertions. Their realism taught them that the young are often enticed by the ways of wicked people. Their reasonableness pushed them to help their pupils scratch beneath the surface and eye the deeper consequences of their behavior.

> Do not be envious of evil men,
> Nor desire to be with them;
> For their heart devises violence,
> And their lips talk of troublemaking.
> *Prov. 24:1–2*

This verse summarizes the teaching of 1:10–19 by exposing the perversion of mind (*"heart"*) that leads to wrong choices and wrong deeds. The warning is apt: who of us can say that he or she has felt no tug of attraction, no glint of envy (the Heb. root can mean to be *"jealous of"*), upon hearing stories of wealthy criminals, flamboyant desperadoes, or fast-living gangsters? Which of us has not silently cheered for the robbers in some police stories we have read or seen? There is enough rebellion in all of us to lure us to look sympathetically at a life of waywardness, particularly if we can keep from getting caught. A heart that meditates about destruction— what a misuse of our human ability to think and choose! Our hearts or minds (Heb. includes both English concepts) were made to frame prayers, memorize Scripture, write poems, plan acts of love, compose symphonies, design buildings, discover medicines. Yet the evil people in Proverbs used that God-given capacity for plots of violence. Whose cattle could they rustle? Whose house could they loot? Whose caravan could they hijack? Whose reputation could they ruin? Whose blood could they spill? An exercise in emptiness it was to make common cause with such perverted minds.

That internal perversion vented itself in corruption of speech. We hear it in verses 11–14 of our primary text, where the teacher actually quotes both the blandishment and the cruelty of the criminals' words. What a misuse of lips that were equipped by God for other purposes: to croon lullabies, whisper comfort, share hope, give advice, sing hymns, confess faith, bless God. Empty is the life lived in the presence of those whose hearts mull over the disaster of others and whose lips have mayhem for their main theme.

Unsound friendships may prove harmful. This is the case especially when the would-be friend has an uncontrollable temper.

> Make no friendship with an angry man,
> And with a furious man do not go,
> Lest you learn his ways
> And set a snare for your soul.
> *Prov. 22:24–25*

Low boiling points may speed up cooking. They do not, however, cement friendships. Edgy anger chafes and cuts the persons exposed to it. I remember an unpleasant bus ride to an airport of one of our great cities. What made me uncomfortable was the unkind, even hostile way the driver treated a passenger who had asked an innocent question. I was glad to escape from the bus and to let other sounds drown out the voice of that boorish driver. It is wounding to be in the presence of anger, even when it is not directed at me. Part of anger's edginess is the fear it engenders that I will be its next victim.

What the wise feared most was that their students would succumb to such tempting wrath. Brash personalities use their tempers like bullwhips to keep everyone under control. Their churlishness can be contagious. We watch them throw their weight around, muscle more timid persons into submission, challenge the manners of our society—and something within us wants to do that, too. That is the snare within which, like dumb birds, we trap ourselves, unless we take deliberate steps to behave correctly in the face of the dangers present in the ways of the angry.

Unsound friendships may lead to disaster. That is the chief point of 1:10–19. It exposes greed's false promises: precious goods, spoil, one purse (vv. 13–14). But such advertisements do not tell the whole story. No mention is made of pained consciences, lives that stew in regret, heartache for friends and family, fear of being caught by authorities or betrayed by comrades who want the one purse for themselves, as did Judas in the apostolic company.

Evil's inevitable outcome is a lesson not to be missed. Like 22:25, the picture is of bird trapping (vv. 17–18). This time the criminals are more stupid than the bird that will shun a snare set while it is watching. But the lying-in-wait and the secret lurking which they described so vividly in verse 11 are the height of stupidity, since the sinners themselves are their own prey, the ultimate victims of their crimes. Like drunken cats they have stalked their own tails; like tipsy hunters they fired into the moving bushes only to shoot their own feet; the very feet that run in the eagerness to work their evil crimes, violently hurrying to shed blood (v. 16) are maimed by their avid greed. We should not miss the fact that Paul includes 1:16 in his list of sinful traits that describe the whole human family and make us subject to divine wrath (Rom. 3:15). In God's sight we are all bad company, capable of any crime mentionable or unmentionable including murder.

Summary Appraisal

> 1:19 So *are* the ways of everyone who is greedy for
>   gain;
>   It takes away the life of its owners.
>
> *Prov. 1:19*

Verse 19 is a general conclusion to the subject of bad company as verse 10 is a general introduction. As Hebrew poets frequently do, it takes the figurative pictures of loot, purse, and snare and restates them in simple, literal, unambiguous terms. In good proverbial form, the moral of the teaching is generalized and applied not just to specific instances known to the author but to *"everyone"* who is grasped in the clenched fist of greed. Nothing is said directly about who does the punishing because that is not the point here. The point is that God, though not mentioned, has so directed life by control as Creator that evil deeds carry evil consequences. Not to know that is the depth of folly.

In conclusion, we may note that Proverbs seems to consider such sinners as beyond help. We, this side of Christ's cross, need to protect ourselves from evil influences but we need to do more. Here are four suggestions. *Be concerned.* Beneath the shells of the rude and hostile, of the greedy and wayward, are persons made and loved by God. *Be careful* how you show your concern. Such persons are hot to handle. We have to monitor our progress to see whether God is using us to open them to divine love and life. Above all, we need to evaluate ourselves for any negative impact they may have on us. *Be realistic.* Some persons are better equipped in spiritual gifts and emotional stability to work with the rough and tough. We are not the Savior. Jesus is. We must reckon on our limitations and at the same time rejoice in God's goodness and grace. *Be thankful* that people who seem as hard to handle as cuddling a porcupine are not beyond God's embraces. For our own good we may have to limit our contacts and shun their company completely. But God is in the business of changing lives, and we do what we can to contribute to that change.

WISDOM'S DENUNCIATION OF FOOLS

1:20 Wisdom calls aloud outside;
  She raises her voice in the open squares.
 21 She cries out in the chief concourses,
  At the openings of the gates in the city
  She speaks her words:
 22 "How long, you simple ones, will you love
   simplicity?
  For scorners delight in their scorning.
  And fools hate knowledge.
 23 Turn at my rebuke;
  Surely I will pour out my spirit on you;
  I will make my words known to you.
 24 Because I have called and you refused,
  I have stretched out my hand and no one
   regarded,
 25 Because you disdained all my counsel,
  And would have none of my rebuke,

> 26 I also will laugh at your calamity;
>   I will mock when your terror comes,
> 27 When your terror comes like a storm,
>   And your destruction comes like a whirlwind,
>   When distress and anguish come upon you.
> 28 "Then they will call on me, but I will not
>   answer;
>   They will seek me diligently, but they will not
>   find me.
> 29 Because they hated knowledge
>   And did not choose the fear of the LORD,
> 30 They would have none of my counsel
>   *And* despised my every rebuke,
> 31 Therefore they shall eat the fruit of their own
>   way,
>   And be filled to the full with their own fancies."
>
> *Prov. 1:20–31*

The siren song of the wicked (1:11–14), as enticing as it may be to the young and venturesome, is more than matched by the stern voice of wisdom recorded here in a terrifying denunciation of fools, which has a fire and fury akin to the judgment speeches of the prophets. Its largely negative tone reinforces and amplifies the picture of the dire consequences that await the practitioners of ruthless greed just described by applying it to all expressions of folly. This section should be read as the negative half of an antithesis whose positive statement is found in chapter 8. The harmony of the two passages is seen not only in their treatment of wisdom as a person able to call, command, promise, and make claims for herself but in the prominence given to the fear of the Lord (1:29; 8:13), which as we have already observed (at 1:7) is a major theme of the entire book.

Wisdom's setting is the city (vv. 20–21), the very place that offered such opportunity and such temptation to Israel's future leaders. Like a town crier or even a sentinel announcing danger, shouting in full voice (*"calls aloud"*; see also 8:3), she strides from the *"open squares"* (plazas used as markets) to the boulevards rumbling with the noise of traffic (*"chief concourses"*) to the several *"gates"* where open spaces allowed people to assemble for trade or official business. No behind-the-hand seductive whispering here (see v. 10); wisdom is a public figure, making her claims in the open and calling her disciples boldly to follow her. The Hebrew word for wisdom (see on 1:2–6) is plural (v. 20) and consequently may point to her majestic manysidedness already made clear in the cluster of synonyms with which the purpose of Proverbs is stated. She is formidable, compelling, and inescapable.

Wisdom's invitation is both bitter and brief (vv. 22–23). *"How long"* sounds like a psalm of complaint (Ps. 6:3), but is a device used in Proverbs as well to register strong dissatisfaction (see 6:9; 23:35). It is not a true question but an implied statement: you have had long enough; you should have answered my call by now. It is addressed to the *"simple ones,"* the young and naive (see on 1:4) who have yet to make full commitment to either wisdom or folly. To wait longer, to prolong the naiveté, is to edge closer to the scorners who deride God's will and ways (see 9:7, 8, 12; 14:6; 15:12; 19:25; 20:1, etc.; Ps. 1:1) and to the fools (Heb. *kāsîl* along with *ʾewîl*, see on 1:7, the key word in Proverbs to denote unbridled disdain of right conduct; see 3:35; 8:5 and very frequently in chaps. 10–22, 25–29) who *"hate,"* utterly reject, the true *"knowledge"* (see on 1:2–6, 7) of what God requires of His people.

The invitation centers in the verb *"turn"* (or return) as is so often the case in the prophets (see Hos. 3:6; 14:1–2). Deliberate choice is called for. Wisdom has done the confronting (*"reproof,"* the decision as to what is right and wrong; see 10:17; 12:1; 13:18; 15:5, 10, 31–32, etc.). How will the simple respond? If positively, they will receive wisdom's own *"spirit"* poured out on them (the language is similar to Joel 2:28) and thus be empowered to carry out the implications of the turning and to know more fully what wisdom wants to teach them. Note the close connection between *"spirit"* and *"words"*—a connection sound theology has always made in refusing to choose one above the other or to play them against each other.

Wisdom's rejection (vv. 24–31) is treated much more extensively than her invitation. Her rejection of them is in answer to their rejection of her: *"you refused"* my call (the verbs are plural; the simple acted as a group with no one courageous enough to dissent from the others), *"no one regarded"* my helping *"hand"* (v. 24, listened carefully, paid full attention; see 4:1, 20; 5:1; 7:24 where the verb *qāshad* is used in calls to attention); *"you disdained"* (ignored, neglected; see 4:15; 13:18; 15:32; 29:18) *"my counsel"* (Heb. *ʿēṣāh*, first time here in Proverbs; see 8:14; 12:15; 19:20, 21; 20:5, 18; 21:30; for the key role of counsel as plan of appropriate and wise action, see Jer. 18:18; Isa. 30:1); you did not choose or respond to (v. 25, *"would have none of"*; see v. 30) my reproof (see vv. 24, 30).

That rejection is so strong and thorough that wisdom, beginning at verse 29, speaks *about* the simple, not *to* them—a technique akin to Hosea's (see 8:14 for *about*; 9:1 for *to*). But her picture of their rejection remains the same. *"Hated knowledge"* (v. 29) confirms the fact that the simple have joined the camp of the fools (see on v. 22). *"Did not choose the fear of the Lord"* (v. 29) means that they decided against wisdom's beginning point and top priority (see on 1:7). Failure to respond to counsel and reproof (see on vv. 22, 23) is evidence that they have not turned. Indeed they have turned the wrong way (v. 32, the word may be translated *"apostasy,"* *"backsliding"*; see Hos. 11:7; 14:4; Jeremiah 3). Disdain (v. 30) is a very strong word—*"despise"* (see Deut. 5:12; 15:5; 32:19), summing up the total and intentional commitment to folly which the simple have made.

If the *reason* for wisdom's rejection of the foolish is described in the clauses that depict their rejection of her, the *results* of that rejection are reflected in two ways: wisdom's personal reaction and the natural consequences of wicked/stupid behavior. Wisdom's reaction is sarcasm—laughing, mocking (v. 26) as would enemies over the disasters of their foes (see 17:5; 30:17; Ps. 2:4)—and silence— refusal to answer or to allow them to find her (v. 28). The ask-receive, seek-find pattern has time limits built into it in both Testaments (Isa. 55:6; Matt. 7:7). The natural consequences are depicted as (1) a *"storm"* from without, a *"whirlwind,"* carrying with it unbearable distress and anguish as they lose all control of their circumstances (v. 27); (2) a food that does not nourish or satisfy because they feed on their own empty hollow resources—the *"fruit"* of their own way of life, ill-chosen and ill-destined (v. 31), and the fruit of their own presumptuous plans (*"fancies"*; the Hebrew word is almost always negative and describes conduct denounced by the prophets and psalmists; Jer. 7:24; Hos. 11:6; Mic. 6:16; Pss. 5:10; 81:12; the only positive use is Prov. 22:20); (3) a slaying (v. 32), perhaps suicide is implied, since the destructive agents—*"turning away"* (see above) and *"complacency"* (careless ease toward God; see 17:1; Jer. 22:21; Ezek. 16:49)—are wielded by their victims. Again nobody is named as the inflicter of this punishment. The order coded by God into the creation imposes it.

ANTITHETIC SUMMARY

> 1:32 *"For the turning away of the simple will slay them,
> And the complacency of fools will destroy them;

33 But whoever listens to me will dwell safely,
And will be secure, without fear of evil."
Prov. 1:32–33

The final two verses encapsulate the outcomes of heeding wisdom's cries (vv. 20–21) or giving them a deaf ear. This antithetic pattern builds on 1:7 and introduces the dominant emphasis on choice and its consequences that pervades the book (see 2:21–22; 3:33–35; 4:18–19; 8:35–36 for other antithetical summaries in chaps. 1–9). Destruction versus security is the contrast in results, while *"turning away"/"complacency"* and *"listens to me"* describe the poles of decision. *"Whoever"* returns the grammar to the singular and focuses again on the individual's responsibility for sound choices however the group may behave. *"Safely"* is used elsewhere in Proverbs for the positive results of good conduct, which, given the divine order, should not lead to harm or danger (3:23, 29; 10:9). In the prophets it pictures the security of the new age, after judgment has done its work (Hos. 2:18; Ezek. 28:26). *"Be secure"* is used positively in verse 33, meaning "untroubled," "undisturbed" in parallel to safely (see Isa. 32:18; note the negative use, "at ease, complacent," in Isa. 32:9). *"Evil"* is deliberately ambiguous in Hebrew, defining both wicked conduct and the harmful results of that conduct. Here it is the latter that wisdom alludes to as she concludes her first, and most threatening, speech.

CHAPTER TWO

Perverted Speech and Loose Sexuality

Proverbs 2:1–22

Wisdom is nothing less than the key to survival. Israel's teachers looked out on a world fraught with menace and proclaimed wisdom as the savior. To deliver or rescue is its chief mission (vv. 12, 16). The means given by God to achieve this salvation are described in military nouns and verbs: "shield" (v. 7), "guards" (v. 8) or "keeps" (v. 11; the two Hebrew words are the same), and "preserves" (vv. 8, 11). Wisdom's value is noted in passing as part of the encouragement to seek it (v. 4), but it is its effective protectiveness that dominates the chapter.

This wisdom speech is complete and self-contained, though it has strong verbal and thematic ties to the one that preceded it and to those that follow. "*My son,*" marks a new beginning and resumes a pattern set in 1:8, 10, 15. The address is singular in contrast to wisdom's speech in 1:22–33 which points to the simple, the mockers, the fools. And wisdom is described in third not first person language (v. 2). Even more striking is the visibility given to God in chapter 2: not only are fear and knowledge of God mentioned (v. 5) but Yahweh, the Lord, is celebrated as the Giver of wisdom (v. 6) and serves as the subject of verses 6–8; moreover, the "covenant of her God" is the description of a wedding ceremony in verse 17. This means that the major theme of the fear of Yahweh, placarded in 1:7 and spotlighted in 1:29, is here floodlighted into even greater prominence. What is implicit in all of Proverbs, chapter 2 makes brightly explicit: wisdom comes from God and no one can enjoy it who does not choose God's paths.

No chapter in Proverbs is more tightly knit than this. Read in Hebrew, it is virtually one continuous sentence. Since the number of its lines (and verses) is twenty-two it may be designed to mirror the completeness of the Hebrew alphabet, whose twenty-two letters form the framework of the acrostic (alphabetic) song in 31:10–31. The structure of this speech is further testimony to its compactness and unity. It is also a window to the ways in which the teachers combined *argument* and *illustration* to bundle and cinch their lessons.

Argument	2:1–9
condition	2:1–4
result	2:5
reason	2:6–9
Illustrations	2:10–20
men of perverse speech	2:10–15
women of loose sexuality	2:16–20
Antithetic conclusion	2:21–22
positive	2:21
negative	2:22

Since it is the illustrations that lend clarity to the argument, our chapter heading features them. If wisdom is shield and guard, the enemies that threaten are the two kinds of persons whose foolish activities are pictured in the illustrations.

ARGUMENT

2:1 My son, if you receive my words,
And treasure my commands within you,
2 So that you incline your ear to wisdom,
And apply your heart to understanding;
3 Yes, if you cry out for discernment,
And lift up your voice for understanding,
4 If you seek her as silver,
And search for her as *for* hidden treasures;
5 Then you will understand the fear of the LORD,
And find the knowledge of God.
6 For the LORD gives wisdom;
From His mouth *come* knowledge and
understanding;
7 He stores up sound wisdom for the upright;
He is a shield to those who walk uprightly;
8 He guards the paths of justice,
And preserves the way of His saints.
9 Then you will understand righteousness and
justice,
Equity *and* every good path.
Prov. 2:1–9

"Take my teaching seriously" is what every dedicated teacher asks of a student. No talking, no sleeping, no gazing out of the window, no snapping the notebook shut before the bell rings. The entire flow of the argument in 2:1–9 is designed to evoke that sense of seriousness. *"My son"* (v. 1) recalls again the teacher's role of authority over and intimacy with the pupil. *"Receive . . . treasure . . . incline . . . apply . . . cry out . . . lift up your voice . . . seek . . . search"* —verb is heaped on verb to build a monument to wisdom's importance. Like *"silver,"* once so rare in Palestine that it outranked gold in value, like hidden treasures (the Hebrew word depicts the money that Joseph slipped surreptitiously into the grain bags of his brothers, Gen. 43:23), wisdom is to be garnered and then put to work (v. 4). The wealth of wisdom is again showcased in the rich array of synonyms (see on 1:2–6, for both the cumulative impact and the meanings of the individual words). The only new term inserted here is *"sound wisdom"* (v. 7; Heb. *tushîyyāh*), a term that stresses the successful results of wisdom's activities: "ability" (NEB), "help," (JB), "victory," (NIV).

The condition (vv. 1–4), the if-then form of argument, conveys a couple of emphases: (1) it pinpoints the importance of choice; there is nothing automatic about going wisdom's way; one does not drift into it lazily; it takes a deliberate decision to begin and constant attention later to follow wisdom; (2) it pictures the actuality of results; wisdom is not a will-o'-the-wisp, playfully or spitefully illusive; her calls come in the open; she is a public figure (1:20–21; 8:1–3); those who respond she helps. Meet the *"if"*—the condition (vv. 1–4)—and you may plan on the *"then"*—the result (v. 5). The condition is both intense and specific, as the verbs in verses 1–4 indicate. They imply focused passion, single-hearted devotion to discovering and doing what is right. *"Cry out . . . lift up your voice"* (v. 3) are the very acts that wisdom performs in her passion to make disciples (1:20–21; 8:1). To be wisdom's apt pupil one must match that intensity and answer her, cry for cry, call for call.

The result (v. 5), simply stated, is that wisdom's true suitor will know what to do to please God and how to do it. *"Fear"* and *"knowledge"* are words of attitude and action (see on 1:7, 29), as well as information. They are code terms for the total response in life—worship, obedience, service, love—which God enables those to make who fully commit their ways to Him (see Prov. 3:5–6). They describe an exclusive relation that transforms all other relationships: to ourselves, our neighbors, our things, our work, our world.

The reason (v. 6), introduced by *"for,"* underscores the importance of the if-then argument and shows why it works: it puts us in direct touch with the grace and power of God, who both *"gives"* (v. 6) and *"guards"* (v. 8), equipping us with the wisdom of his very words (*"from His mouth"*) and serving as a shield to those who pursue life (*"walk"*) in terms of his integrity (*"upright," "uprightly"*; see chapter 10 for these and other synonyms for righteous conduct). The threat against which God protects the wise seems to be injustice (v. 8): *"He guards the paths of justice,"* that is, his wisdom works in us to fend off our tendencies toward injustice, unfair treatment of our neighbors and fellow citizens, and to ward off and correct the injustices with which they may afflict us. The outcome of such protection (v. 9) is a life characterized (*"you will understand"* [experience and appreciate]) by the three social virtues cataloged in the statement of purpose with which Proverbs began (see 1:2–6): *"righteousness . . . justice . . . equity."* And in case that trio is not comprehensive enough, *"every good path"* (lit. "cow track" or "wagon rut," see vv. 15, 18, for this synonym to the standard words for way and path as metaphors for conduct, behavior, and course of life) is added to cover a whole range of blessings and virtues received and practiced because God is Giver to the wise and Guardian of them. In the outline of this chapter, I have followed the paragraphing and translation of NKJV which makes a major break between verses 9 and 10 and begins verse 10 with "when" as the lead word of the paragraph that ends in verse 15. The alternate approach which may capture more closely the nuances of the Hebrew would make verse 10 the concluding sentence of the argument paragraph, translating the initial word as "for." The consequences of this would be to revise the structural outline found above as follows:

condition (vv. 1–4)   key word—*if*
result A (v. 5)   key word—*then*
reason A (vv. 6–8)   key word—*for*
result B (v. 9)   key word—*then*
reason B (v. 10)   key word—*for*

This structure is reflected in NEB, NASB, NIV. The balance of style and thought in verses 5–10 becomes more clear on this reading:

Then you will understand . . . (v. 5)
For the Lord gives wisdom . . . (v. 6)
Then you will understand . . . (v. 9)
[For] wisdom enters . . . (v. 10)

An added insight of this approach is that "fear" and "knowledge" (v. 5) are amplified and made practical by their parallels in verse 9: "righteousness," "justice," "equity." The structural balance casts light on the thematic connections.

ILLUSTRATIONS

2:10 When wisdom enters your heart,
    And knowledge is pleasant to your soul,
11 Discretion will preserve you;
    Understanding will keep you,
12 To deliver you from the way of evil,
    From the man who speaks perverse things,
13 From those who leave the paths of uprightness
    To walk in the ways of darkness;
14 Who rejoice in doing evil,
    And delight in the perversity of the wicked;
15 Whose ways *are* crooked,
    And *who are* devious in their paths;

Prov. 2:10–15

Structurally, the two illustrations (vv. 11–15 and vv. 16–20) are amplifications of the reason why the if-then argument is both reliable and practical. "Shield" and "guard" (vv. 7–8) are here applied to two specific threats from which the wise need preservation—men of perverted speech and women of loose sexuality. Verse 10 is better heard as the closing lines of the argument, summing up the gift of wisdom and knowledge promised in verses 5–6 (see discussion above). *"Pleasant"* is a very attractive Hebrew word, used to sum up the woman's beauty in Song of Sol. 7:6 and to name little girls as did Naomi's parents (Ruth 1:19–20); examples of the noun and verb in Proverbs are found in 3:17; 9:17; 15:26; 16:24; 24:25. Wisdom is wonderfully winsome as well as prudently useful.

The illustration picturing men of perverted speech has two centers. First, what wisdom (*"discretion," "understanding,"* see on 1:2–6) can do, described in military-guard language (vv. 11–12): *"preserve," "keep"* (see v. 8), *"deliver."* Second, why wisdom is needed, documented in the bundle of terms for persons whose values have become so distorted as to be plainly dangerous. How these wicked persons lived is seen as crooked and misleading from every angle. Three words for way, path, and tracks are used to document this (vv. 11, 15). *"Evil"* appears twice (vv. 12, 14). *"Perverse"* and *"perversity"*

(vv. 12, 14) are the controlling words, picturing a value system turned upside down: truth becomes error and error becomes truth; right is branded wrong and wrong is praised as right (see 6:14; 8:13; 10:31–32; 16:28, 30; 23:33). The depth of the perversity finds evidence in the preferences for *"darkness"* over *"uprightness"* (v. 13) and for the *"crooked"* and *"devious"* (see 3:31–32; 14:2) over the straight (v. 15). Jesus knew such persons and also denounced them (John 3:19). What should have shamed and saddened sparked them to *"rejoice"* and *"delight"* (v. 14); and perhaps worst of all, they spoke brashly about all of these topsy-turvy forms of thought and behavior (v. 12). They boasted in the evil and argued grandly that others should join them. They pitted their call to perversity against wisdom's cry to discipleship. To the naive and uninitiated the choice was not easy. That was why the teacher argued so cogently and illustrated so graphically the risk-gain results of wrong or right choice.

THE ILLUSTRATION OF THE IMMORAL WOMAN

> 2:16 To deliver you from the immoral woman,
>   From the seductress *who* flatters with her
>   words,
> 17 Who forsakes the companion of her youth,
>   And forgets the covenant of her God.
> 18 For her house leads down to death,
>   And her paths to the dead;
> 19 None who go to her return,
>   Nor do they regain the paths of life—
> 20 So you may walk in the way of goodness,
>   And keep *to* the paths of righteousness.
> *Prov. 2:16–20*

The illustration depicting women of loose sexuality builds immediately on what preceded it. Verse 11 introduced it as well as verses 12–15. The structure runs like this:

> Discretion will preserve you;
> Understanding will keep you (v. 11)
>   To deliver you . . . from the man who . . . (v. 12)
>   To deliver you . . . from the immoral woman . . . (v. 16)
> So you may walk in the way of goodness . . . (v. 20).

This is further evidence that chapter 2 is a seamless garment and that our attempts to divide it are arbitrary decisions made for the convenience of commenting section by section. Communicators will do well to recognize the indivisible character of passages like this and to teach or preach them as a whole or, at the very least, to set any chosen portion in the context of the whole passage, and, indeed, of the entire book. What we have, then, in verses 16–20 is not an isolated warning about fornication or adultery but a further description of wisdom's ability to serve as shield and guard (vv. 7–8)—"to deliver" (v. 16)—in life's temptation. Wisdom's power is the chief subject, not the wanton's wiles. And wisdom's chief aim in empowering and protecting is that we "walk [live all of life] in the way of goodness" (lit., "good people"), as the concluding lines of the illustration sections indicate (v. 20).

"Immoral woman" and "seductress" (v. 16) are appropriate translations of terms that suggest "foreignness." Their point is not so much that the woman comes from a strange land and resides in Israel as an ethnic alien. Rather, she is a spiritual and social outsider because she has deliberately chosen to violate the covenant mores of her people. She violates the law as she "forsakes" and abandons her husband ("companion of her youth"), and even worse she "forgets," that is, deliberately fails to obey (see Hos. 2:13, for a similar use of "forget") her marriage vows made before God and in His name as a "covenant" (the only instance of the term in Proverbs) to which God is party (see Mal. 2:14, for a kindred expression). The ugliness of her actions stands in sharp contrast to the attractiveness of her seductive techniques: she "flatters [lit., "says smooth and pleasing things"] with her words."

So susceptible is the male ego to such "sweet nothings" that the teacher has to unmask both the unthinkable obscenity of her adulterous ways (v. 17) and to predict the deadly effects on anyone who consorts with her (vv. 18–19).

The immoral woman seems to describe both a literal and a figurative presence in Israel's society. Her dominant role in these wisdom speeches (note 5:3–6, 20; 6:23–35; 7:1–27; 9:13–18) is clear evidence that the literal physical chastity of their students was a constant concern of the teachers, and apparently with good reason, given the power and prevalence of the temptations that surrounded them. If the emphasis seems one-sided, slanted toward the seductiveness of women and the gullibility of men, the reasons are understandable: (1) Proverbs by its very purpose centers in the needs of the men who were to play strategic roles in public life; (2) in that society women would have been much more protected than men by their families from whose watchful care they would have little opportunity to stray.

Behind this literal picture of sexual seduction stands a figurative idea of religious compromise. As wisdom is personified in terms of a wise mother calling her young or an older sister guiding a younger brother (7:4–5), so "folly," rebellion and waywardness against the paths of God, may be portrayed as an immoral woman using every blandishment to tease the simple into her embraces (see especially 7:4–5; 9:13–18). Folly is nothing less than pagan living, foreign to God's people and fraught with the threat of physical and spiritual *death* (v. 18). The mention of death and *the dead* (v. 18) may suggest some connection between dame folly and the mythology of the Canaanites, for whom death was a deity that had to be conquered every spring to ensure the fertility of crop and flock and the dead (Heb. *r'phā'îm*, "weak," "feeble," "lifeless"; 9:18; 21:16) were shades or spirits that hobnobbed with death. In other words, folly may have been not merely the absence of Israel's covenant ideals but also the blatant presence of Canaan's pagan practices. Hosea, Jeremiah, and Ezekiel each tarred Israel's drift into Canaanite religious practices as expressions of spiritual adultery; in their parlance Israel was the woman and Baal or other foreign deities the seductive man. Whether literally or figuratively, dallying with the loose woman meant a descent to an underworld in which *death* not *life* was ruler (v. 19) and from which *return* was impossible. Israel may have learned from its Babylonian neighbors to call death "the land-of-no-return," since God had not yet revealed to His people any full-blown view of afterlife or resurrection.

Verse 20 snatches our attention from the realm of the dead to the ultimate aims of wisdom. *"So"* (or "in order that") makes a grammatical and logical connection to verse 11 and the key verbs of purpose—"to deliver" (vv. 12, 16). Discretion preserves us (v. 11) by rescuing from men of topsy-turvy speech (v. 12) and women of pagan sexual values (v. 16) to the end that ("so") we may live ("walk") the way good and righteous (see on 1:2–6) people should. The two negative illustrations show how positive wisdom's purpose is. The envelope of wisdom's impressive power (v. 11) and benevolent purpose (v. 20) makes this clear.

ANTITHETIC SUMMARY

2:21 For the upright will dwell in the land,
  And the blameless will remain in it;

> 22 But the wicked will be cut off from the earth,
> And the unfaithful will be uprooted from it.
> *Prov. 2:21–22*

Like 1:32–33, these verses distill the intent of the speech by a summary of the contrasting outcomes. The "if" clauses at the beginning (vv. 1–4) spelled out the need for choice. The antithesis at the end, which serves as a final motivation to the entire speech, makes clear the consequences: life or death. Though *"the land"* (v. 21) may refer to Palestine and *"dwell"* and *"remain"* to continuous possession of it, guaranteed where obedience prevails and denied (*"cut off,"* *"uprooted"* or *"torn from"*; v. 22) where it does not (see Deut. 30:15–18), it is more likely that physical existence or at least physical welfare are in view rather than national security. Death not exile is the threat. The address ("my son," v. 1) and the key verb ("you may walk," v. 20) suggest that individual pupils, not the entire people, are the subjects of instruction. Failure to heed wisdom's call leads either to premature death or to a life so void of happiness as to be a living death in which none of the God-given blessings of the *"earth"* (v. 22) or *"land,"* (v. 21; the Hebrew word is the same both places) is available to lend any joy or meaning to life.

CHAPTER THREE

Admonitions to Piety and Arguments for Sagacity

Proverbs 3:1–35

The teachers showed no letup in their eagerness to pound home wisdom's merits. Commands, arguments, illustrations, summaries—they have used all of these tools in the first two speeches, and they keep them at the ready in chapter 3, but with a change in target. What they had pinpointed earlier were the threats from contexts in which their pupils lived, threats like greedy and murderous thieves (1:10–19), persons of perverted values and teachings (2:11–15), and easy, adulterous women (2:16–19). In the third speech, however, the temptations that are exposed lie within the hearts of the students (see vv. 1, 3, 5 for "heart"). Inner life more than outer is the focus. What counts, say the teachers, is the fear of the Lord (vv. 1–26) and the care for one's neighbor (vv. 27–32). The combination of these two themes recalls the two tables of the ten commandments. Note that the obedient life is lived in the sight of both God and man (v. 4).

The structure and movement of chapter 3 can be charted like this:

Admonitions to Piety—A	3:1–12
Keep the commandments	3:1–4
Trust the Lord's guidance	3:5–8
Honor the Lord's provision	3:9–10
Accept the Lord's correction	3:11–12
Arguments for sagacity	3:13–20
Practical: a beatitude	3:13–18
Theological: an affirmation	3:19–20
Admonitions to piety—B	3:21–26
Guard wisdom	3:21–24
Don't fear disaster	3:25–26
Admonitions to generosity	3:27–32
General	3:27
Specific	3:28–32

ADMONITIONS TO PIETY—A

3:1 My son, do not forget my law,
    But let your heart keep my commands;
 2 For length of days and long life
    And peace they will add to you.

 3 Let not mercy and truth forsake you;
    Bind them around your neck,
    Write them on the tablet of your heart
 4 *And* so find favor and high esteem
    In the sight of God and man.
 5 Trust in the LORD with all your heart,
    And lean not on your own understanding;
 6 In all your ways acknowledge Him,
    And He shall direct your paths.

 7 Do not be wise in your own eyes;
    Fear the LORD and depart from evil.
 8 It will be health to your flesh,
    And strength to your bones.

 9 Honor the LORD with your possessions,
    And with the firstfruits of all your increase;
10 So your barns will be filled with plenty,
    And your vats will overflow with new wine.

11 My son, do not despise the chastening of the
      LORD,
    Nor detest His correction;
12 For whom the LORD loves He corrects,
    Just as a father the son *in whom* he delights.

Prov. 3:1–12

In the flow of these admonitions—commands followed by reasons for them (note vv. 2, 4, 8, 10, 12)—the more general words of urging to obedience, *"do not forget," "bind them around your neck,"* etc., are followed by very specific imperatives like *"trust"* (v. 5), *"honor"* (v. 9), *"do not despise"* (v. 11). Proverbs and other poetry books of the Old Testament do this frequently, beginning with an umbrella statement followed by a series of more detailed instances of the general principle and then sometimes returning to an overall summation (see vv. 33–35).

In the first admonition, *"keep my commands,"* *"law"* and *"command"* (v. 1) remind us that the words of the wise were more than opinions or suggestions. They had a binding quality to them because they were based on the teachers' God-fearing observations of how life under divine control really worked. They were close cousins to the statutes of Moses which the prophets applied regularly to Israel's covenant relations. That is why *"mercy"* (Heb. *ḥesed*), the primary term for Yahweh's commitment to His people and their reciprocal love and loyalty to Him and to each other (Ps. 136; Hos. 6:6), and *"truth"* (Heb. *ᵉmet*), a key word for God's utter reliability in word and deed and the people's pledge of integrity in turn (Hos. 4:1), are used (v. 3) to show the meaning and impact of law and command. This obedience is not lip service or outward show but is to become an integral part of the disciple, written on the heart (see Jer. 31:33), bound around the neck (see 1:9), and thus influencing every choice and movement. The reasons given for motivation are these: *"long life"* (v. 2, lit., "years of life"), *"favor"* (v. 4, "grace" or "mercy"), and *"high esteem"* (i.e., "success" based on wise choices). Verse 4 may have influenced the wording of Luke's summary of Jesus' growth to maturity: "And Jesus increased in wisdom and stature, and in favor with God and men" (2:52).

"Command" used in tandem with "reason" recalls the style of the Decalogue where long life in the land is the promised result of honoring one's parents (Exod. 21:12). *"Tablet"* (v. 3) is a further tie to the Mosaic law. The teachers expected their instruction to play a part in the lives of the young akin to that of Moses' decalogue.

In the second admonition, "trust the Lord's guidance" (vv. 5–8), we come upon the words most frequently quoted from the Book of Proverbs by Christian believers. These phrases are to Christ's disciples what the wedding ceremony is to newlyweds. They spell out what is and is not to be done within that relationship. They set the terms of what it means to live with God at the outset of our commitment to Him and through every step of our pilgrimage. They are the "to have and to hold from this day forward" of our marriage-covenant with God. We need to reflect on them regularly as wedding anniversaries encourage us to do on our wedding vows. Forty years later, now, my wife Ruth and I remember that our vows signaled the beginning of what we determined would be a lifelong loyalty. But to make sure this loyalty remains strong we affirm it again and again. The marriage ceremony is like our conversion—the initial pledge of troth. But that trust must continue, must grow. And we cannot assume that the growth will be automatic. The wise called discipleship not a pole vault or a long jump but a *walk*. Reaffirming, reexperiencing those first steps and then taking fresh ones day by day, year upon year, is what trust is about. How long does it take to build a good marriage? A lifetime of walking arm in arm is the only accurate answer. Trusting God is like that.

It begins with commitment. Nothing less than *"with all your heart"* (v. 5) is sufficient. Choices, decisions, motives, intentions must all be directed to what God wants and what God can do. *"Trust"* steps onto the bridge of God's loving power and leaves the shoreline of our own abilities and ambitions behind. Such belief means literally to "bet your life" on God's truth and wisdom.

Our trust in God continues with renunciation: (1) of our *"own understanding"* (v. 5), not tempered and not molded by God's will and guidance; (2) of our own wisdom in which it is so easy and so foolish to take pride (v. 7) and, so doing, cancel its effectiveness and expose it not as wisdom but stupidity; (3) of *"evil"* in its many-headed manifestations, but especially, in this context, in its most dangerous form—arrogant self-reliance from which all fear of God is drained (v. 7).

Our trust of God issues in relationship, as the verbs *"acknowledge"* (v. 6; lit., "know," "recognize"; see comments on "knowledge of God" at 1:7, 29 and 2:5) and *"fear"* (see the same passages) signal. These are terms of personal bonding which result in changes of behavior. They combine the senses of awe, intimacy, and obligation which mark sound relationships. They suggest that God's people want to know Him so well that they do His bidding virtually without having to be reminded. The path we walk is marked out (directed, v. 6) by Him, and the power to walk is His gift.

Such trust in God leads to well-being in the very depths of our persons (v. 8). *"Bones"* and *"flesh"* are descriptors not just of the structure and tissue of our bodies but of our whole selves, body-spirit, tangible-intangible. This reward outstrips the promises of wealth and abundance (v. 10), as valued as those material blessings are. Health is a wholistic not just a physical word; it connotes thriving and radiant wellness (see the use of a related noun in 4:22; 6:15; 12:18; 13:17; 14:30; 15:4; 16:24; 29:1). The frequency of the concept is a key to the fact that, for Proverbs, "health" or "healing" is a code word for the total personal prosperity that is God's gift to those who walk in wisdom's way. It is rightly called refreshment, like a cool drink to a thirsty traveler.

These ingredients of trust do sound like an outline of a wedding ceremony. *Commitment* is symbolized in the giving and receiving of rings and the endowing of the partner "with all my worldly goods." *Renunciation* is clearly voiced in "forsaking all others, will you keep you only unto her so long as you both shall live?" *Relationship* is chimed not only in "to have and to hold from this day forward" but especially in "to love and to cherish." *Well-being* is promised in the benediction where the Lord is invoked to "make His face to shine upon you, be gracious unto you, and give you peace" (*shālôm*, total welfare). Do we need special anniversary celebrations to renew our trust in God as we do our troth to our partners?

The third admonition, *"honor the Lord with your possessions"* (v. 9, lit., "wealth"), takes us closer to the realm of temple regulations than Proverbs usually does. *"Firstfruits"* echoes Deut. 26:2, 10 and is a reminder that the practitioners of wisdom were also children of the covenant and at times took covenant stipulations and restated them in wisdom's parlance. The interplay between Proverbs and Deuteronomy is often remarked upon. In our passage it shows up not only in the offering to God of the first and best products of the harvest but in the promise of *"barns . . . filled with plenty"* and *"vats [overflowing] with new wine"* (v. 10, or grape juice of which wine will come in the fermentation process) which seems to be an answer to the prayer for blessing with which the ceremony of first-fruits ends (Deut 26:15). Moreover, the admonition to generosity in Prov. 3:27 parallels Moses' command to share crops with Levite, sojourner, fatherless, and widow, "that they may eat within your gates and be filled" (Deut. 26:12). Prosperity, gratitude, and charity are an indivisible triad of experiences in biblical thought, and notably in Proverbs (see chaps. 11 and 25).

The fourth admonition (vv. 11–12) *"accept the Lord's correction"* (lit., "discipline" or *"chastening"*; see on 1:2–6) witnesses to the perceptive realism of the teachers. Cherish as they did their commandments, chide as they did their pupils, they knew that perfect obedience was an impossibility. The temptations were too pressing and attractive; individuals were too gullible and willful. No matter how clearly God marked out the paths of righteousness, some would miss them by carelessness and others would leave them by stubbornness. And when they did, because their basic trust was in God and their deep-seated desire was to please Him, He would meet them as a disciplining Father determined to point out their mistakes and return them to the right road. *"Correction"* (or *"reproof"*; see wisdom's use of this in 1:23, 25, 30) is the appropriate term for this and *"love"* is its motivation. So well did this picture of divine parenting, both stern and loving, capture the nature of God and our need to understand our Creator that the author of the Book of Hebrews centuries later found no better text than this with which to bring divine comfort to a people in pain (Heb. 12:5–6).

A PRACTICAL ARGUMENT FOR SAGACITY

3:13 Happy *is* the man *who* finds wisdom
      And the man *who* gains understanding;
  14 For her proceeds *are* better than the profits
      of silver,
      And her gain than fine gold.
  15 She *is* more precious than rubies,
      And all things you may desire cannot compare
      with her.
  16 Length of days *is* in her right hand,
      In her left hand riches and honor.
  17 Her ways *are* ways of pleasantness,
      And all her paths *are* peace.
  18 She *is* a tree of life to those who take hold
      of her,
      And happy *are all* who retain her.
                                        Prov. 3:13–18

This speech interrupts the stream of admonitions to insert a double argument in favor of wisdom's excellence: a practical argument in the form of a beatitude and a theological argument expressed as an affirmation. The literary touch is graceful and changes the pace from the incessant series of commands found in verses 1–12 and resumed in 21–32. So placed, the argument serves to underscore the first set of admonitions and blaze the trail for the second.

The beatitude, with its practical promise of reward, is an expression, almost an exclamation, of the gains to be found in attaining wisdom (v. 13). The opposite of beatitude is woe, as the antithetical style of Jesus informs us (Luke 6:20–26). The use of happy and woe may have originated in attempts to instruct children on the beneficial or harmful results of good and bad conduct: happy are those who do the one; woe (or "trouble," JB) to those who do the other. The typical emphasis of a beatitude, as we see it here and elsewhere (Ps. 1, 32; Matt. 5:3–12), is on the relationship between wise conduct and its happy outcome. Here, as in Psalm 1, more attention is paid to the outcome than to the specifics of the conduct. The latter is expressed simply: *"finds wisdom," "gains understanding"* (v. 13; see 1:2–6 for meaning of terms). The next five verses embellish the outcome in lavish strokes: (1) even fabulous wealth (vv. 14–15)— *"silver,"* mentioned first perhaps because of its rarity in Israel's antiquity; *"fine gold,"* unusually pure and carefully smelted; *"rubies,"* also translated as "red coral," "pearls," or "jewelry," since the exact meaning of this and other Hebrew words for gems cannot always be stated with precision; *"things you may desire,"* probably other precious gems or gold and silver artifacts as the context suggests— *"cannot compare"* ("be equal, likened to") with wisdom which is off the chart not only of commodities but of the most exquisite luxuries and badges of wealth with which the scions of Israel's upper class were either familiar or would like to have been; (2) perhaps, even more to be cherished were the longevity (v. 16 *"length of days"*; see on v. 2) and *"honor"* (or "glory") in the community that accompanied such blessings; the same root (Heb. *kbd*) described the honor due to God through offerings in verse 9; who in wisdom honors God with goods in return receives *"honor"* and *"riches,"* the most general term in Hebrew for wealth or valuable belongings of any kind; (3) beyond that, wisdom offers smooth, straight, peaceful *"paths"* to all who go her way (v. 17); (4) she is like a life-producing *"tree,"* full of nourishing fruit to sustain weary, hungry travelers who eat of her produce and stretch out in her shade (v. 18); (5) *"happy"* in the final line points again to the beginning of the beatitude which is wrapped top and bottom with the theme of happiness and blessedness. We have already seen the ties between Proverbs 3 and the law of Moses. The similarity of this beatitude to that of Psalm 1 reinforces that tie: (1) here wisdom is sought; there the law is to be treasured (note Prov. 3:1 where wisdom teaching is *"my law"*); (2) here wisdom is likened to a "life-giving tree"; there the one who is nourished by the law is like a tree; (3) here wisdom's *"ways"* are *"pleasantness"* (for Heb. word see on 2:10); there the *"way"* of the righteous is known by God. Hence, in language both elegant and familiar, the teachers have displayed the superlative claims of wisdom with the firm hope that it will prove irresistible to their disciples.

A Theological Argument for Sagacity

3:19 The LORD by wisdom founded the earth;
By understanding He established the heavens;
20 By His knowledge the depths were broken up,
And clouds drop down the dew.

Prov. 3:19–20

This affirmation, fraught with theological significance, lauds and commends wisdom to the young by linking it to God's creative work at the beginning. Wisdom's antiquity, usefulness, and intimate connection with Yahweh are what the argument points to. For the synonyms *"understanding"* and *"knowledge,"* see on 1:2–6. Here as there we are not to distinguish among them but see them as facets of wisdom which when used together lend splendor to that magnificent virtue. Wisdom is pictured here not so much as companion to Yahweh (see on 8:22–31) as a tool used by Him to do what only He could do. The argument is clear: if Yahweh with wisdom as His tool could accomplish the wonders of the various phases of creation—settling the *"earth"* on its foundations, setting the *"heavens"* in their appointed place (v. 19), breaking up the *"depths"* to irrigate the dry land through wells, springs, and streams, and watering the earth with *"dew"* from the clouds (v. 20; a key source of moisture for truck gardening and other crops in Palestine is dew)—think what wisdom will do, better, what Yahweh will do through wisdom in the lives of those who find it.

Admonitions to Piety—B

3:21 My son, let them not depart from your eyes—
Keep sound wisdom and discretion;
22 So they will be life to your soul
And grace to your neck.
23 Then you will walk safely in your way,
And your foot will not stumble.
24 When you lie down, you will not be afraid;
Yes, you will lie down and your sleep will
be sweet.
25 Do not be afraid of sudden terror,
Nor of trouble from the wicked when it comes;
26 For the LORD will be your confidence,
And will keep your foot from being caught.

Prov. 3:21–26

Wisdom so valuable that it outweighs all wealth (vv. 13–18) and wisdom so powerful that it was employed by Yahweh to frame the creation is surely too precious to turn our *"eyes"* from, even for a moment. "Guard wisdom with your life" is the first admonition in this second series (vv. 21–24). Guard it because it is your life (*"life to your soul,"* v. 22), might be the better way to put it. The mutual relationship of learner to wisdom pivots on the word *"keep"* (or *"guard,"* v. 21): in Prov. 2:8, 11 wisdom guards those who seek it; in Prov. 3:21, those who seek it guard it. A mutual protection society are wisdom and its followers. Beauty like an attractive pendant (*"grace to your neck,"* see on 1:9; 3:3), surefootedness like a goat on a mountain path (v. 23), secure sleep, *"sweet"* like a child's (v. 24)— these are wisdom's treasures bequeathed to those who treasure it. *"Sound wisdom"* (see on 2:7) and *"discretion"* (see on 1:4; 2:11) are again part of the chain of synonyms which stretches back to verses 19–20. Despite the change in literary form from affirmation to admonition, the vocabulary forges a link between the sections.

The second admonition (vv. 25–26) continues and sharpens the picture of safety and security presented in the first: "Don't fear disaster." Here the threat is not natural calamity like stumbling on a stony path (v. 23) but stems from the *"trouble"* (lit., "ruin" or "storm") of *"the wicked"* (v. 25), the only allusions in this speech to danger from outsiders. *"Your confidence"* (v. 26) may also be translated as "at your side." Either way, the important thing is that God's powerful presence—remember His work in creation (vv. 19–20)—*"will keep your foot from being caught"* in the vicious snares or traps set by the wicked (v. 26). To go the way of true wisdom is to have the Lord's protection close at hand.

ADMONITIONS TO GENEROSITY

3:27 Do not withhold good from those to whom it is
     due,
    When it is in the power of your hand to do *so.*
28 Do not say to your neighbor,
    "Go, and come back,
    And tomorrow I will give *it,"*
    When *you have* it with you.
29 Do not devise evil against your neighbor,
    For he dwells by you for safety's sake.
30 Do not strive with a man without cause,
    If he has done you no harm.

> 31 Do not envy the oppressor,
>   And choose none of his ways;
> 32 For the perverse *person is* an abomination to
>   the LORD,
>   But His secret *counsel is* with the upright.
>   *Prov. 3:27–32*

The security and protection offered by the Lord of wisdom put us under obligation to be generous to others. The principle of generosity is stated in general yet striking terms in verse 27 and then elaborated in four more specific admonitions. All five commands are framed in negative terms—a reminder that both wisdom and law help us cope with our human frailty and self-centeredness by telling us what *not* to do. Every parent knows why: "don't" more than "do" salts our vocabulary as we equip young children both to stay alive and to fit the structures of human society. Before we can really know how to do right we must learn to avoid the dangerous and cruel ways to which we are compulsively attracted.

"Good" (v. 27), as frequently in Scripture, is the most comprehensive word for generosity in a whole range of activities ("favour," NEB)—but particularly in the sharing of material goods. *"To whom it is due"* is literally "its owners." One way to construe the meaning makes it address the question of paying debts on time and in full measure. More likely, "its owners" is a graphic way of describing "the needy" (so the LXX) who, under the principle of neighbor love, have a claim on any goods that we can spare to help meet their needs. This is what seems to be intended by *"in the power of your hand."* The specific admonition of verse 28, "don't turn away a needy neighbor," is intended as a commentary on the more general words of verse 27. The command pointedly picks up a persistent human foible by quoting the actual words which ring with the wish to procrastinate. *"Tomorrow,"* whether in Hebrew, Arabic, or Spanish (*mañana*), can be a ploy of infinite postponement.

The final three admonitions (vv. 29–32) define generosity as maintaining peace in the neighborhood. The "Neighborhood Watch" signs on our block remind us that we live side by side *"for safety's sake"* (v. 29) as well as for convenience. Trust is a central ingredient of community. Where it is betrayed by devising (or plotting) evil (harm) against a neighbor, no community is possible. It is now every family for itself, guarding its property, strengthening its fences, protecting its members. When neighbors become threats to each other, we can say with accuracy and regret, "There goes the neighborhood." Quarreling (*"do not strive"*) can be as upsetting as plotting harm (v. 30). Groundless (*"without cause"*) arguments and petty disputes are the height of selfishness. They spring from lack of generosity. The picky, petulant person knows no compromise and refuses to grant the neighbor the benefit of the doubt. Every misgiving or misunderstanding becomes a reason for criticism or conflict. Part of neighborliness is the willingness to be wrong and the ability to bite one's tongue when we think we are right. Few issues in life are worth breaking relationships to prove our correctness.

One step beyond contentiousness stands violence (v. 31). When the person given to physical or emotional attack on others (*"oppressor"*) becomes a hero, we personally and our community generally have hit bottom. Of all people unworthy of envy the oppressor heads the list. To be jealous of his prowess is to play the fool and to suffer the consequences. *"None of his ways,"* personal habits or modes of conduct is worth emulating. No person is as sick, no society in as grave condition as the person or society that lionizes the wicked and sets the violent on pedestals of adulation. In a culture where Canaanite views of the abuse of power in all manner of greed and cruelty were threatening to prevail, Israel's prospective leaders needed this warning. Given the level of violence that prevails in our communities, whether local or international, the admonition has lost none of its cogency.

Verse 32 supplies the motivation for all five negative commands (vv. 27–31). Absence of generosity in all its forms *"is an abomination to the Lord"* (see on 11:20; 12:22; 15:26; 17:15; it may be Hebrew's strongest term of divine abhorrence), who cares about neighborliness and community. Generosity is the way the *"upright,"* the people of rectitude and integrity, live. To withhold it and hence destroy community is to choose the wrong path and get lost, as *"perverse"* literally means. The opposite of this is to be on intimate, insider terms with God so that we know what He wants and are given power to do it. *"Secret counsel"* means to be taken "into His (Yahweh's) confidence" (see NEB, JB, NIV). Can there be any stronger motivation to neighbor-love than this? Certainly, not short of the Cross.

ANTITHETIC SUMMARY

3:33 The curse of the LORD *is* on the house of the
wicked,
But He blesses the home of the just.

34 Surely He scorns the scornful,
   But gives grace to the humble.
35 The wise shall inherit glory,
   But shame shall be the legacy of fools.

Prov. 3:33–35

The lengthy speech draws to its close with this trio of summary-evaluations which capture the consequence of obedience or disobedience of the featured admonitions. Each verse contains two points of comparison which can be charted like this:

	humanly chosen conduct	*divinely assigned result*
v. 33	wicked/just	curse/blessing
v. 34	scornful/humble	scorns/gives grace
v. 35	wise/fools	glory/shame

As we have seen frequently in Proverbs the clusters of synonyms reinforce and augment each other. Their power is in the build-up of intensity effected by their repetition rather than in the meaning of the individual terms. On the nouns and adjectives of "conduct," see chapter 10. The nouns and verbs *of result* deal with status in the community as the outcome of obedience to God. The text seems to say that what we wrongheadedly thought we could gain from a neighbor by greed, deceit, quarrel, or violence—namely, power, wealth, and status—are attainable only as gifts of God and then only on His terms of uprightness and humble dependence. The theme of honor ties the speech together like a thread: in humble gratitude we honor the Lord with our substance (v. 9); this and other acts of obedience put us in touch with wisdom who holds riches and honor in her hand (v. 16); that honor (lit., "glory") God makes available to those who live in loving and peaceful community with their neighbors, who are His creatures and beloved ones as well (v. 35).

CHAPTER FOUR

Personal Illustration and Practical Advice

Proverbs 4:1–27

The most important things about us do not appear on our résumés. Academic degrees, denominational responsibilities, places of ministry, publications, honors—these all happen too late in life to make as much difference as we think they do. My résumé (curriculum vitae, if you prefer) needs to include names like Helen Funnell, my counselor and English teacher at Frick Junior High, Pearl Sindel, my junior department Sunday school teacher at Elim Tabernacle, and Paul Huchthausen who introduced me to Greek in my freshman year at California Concordia College. I cannot think of myself without appreciating the patient and loving contribution that each of them made to my life. And even more important were my parents Helena and John and my siblings—Paul, John, Laura, and Bob. From them in a myriad of different ways I learned the whats, hows, whys, and wherefores of life, especially as it is lived in a Christian setting and with a Christian outlook. In turn, what I have learned from them I am passing on consciously or unconsciously to our daughter, Mary, and her children, David and Jeffrey.

That chain of tradition linking the wisdom of the generations is the basic theme of this fourth wisdom speech. The teacher not only lists his parents on his résumé but (1) credits them for the quality of life that their wisdom provided him (v. 3), (2) recommends that tried and true wisdom to his children (vv. 4–9), (3) specifies the nature of part of that wisdom (vv. 10–27), and (4) tacitly, at least, encourages them to follow that example and teach their own children the devout wisdom of their family tradition. Let the cycle of wisdom roll on, is one thing he is saying. Family cycles are well known to sociologists: abused children often become abusing parents; offspring of alcoholics have a high incidence of alcoholism;

delinquents may rear delinquents. Breaking the bad cycles and continuing the good ones are what wise parenting entails. This chapter shows us a wise parent at work.

CALL TO ATTENTION

4:1 Hear, *my* children, the instruction of a father,
And give attention to know understanding;
2 For I give you good doctrine:
Do not forsake my law.

Prov. 4:1–2

These verses, ringing with authority, almost jar the ears of us moderns. We are part of a generation of whom it has been said, with a substantial dose of truth, "Ours may be the first generation in history that did not know how to raise its own young." We have tended especially in the decades immediately following World War II to doubt our traditional wisdom, to derive our approaches to child training from experts who were much more permissive than our instincts were prompting us to be, or even to delegate much more of our parental responsibility to outsiders in the schools and day-care centers of our land.

"*Hear . . . and give attention*" (see on 1:8) are not the words of a timid parent or insecure teacher. Nor is any loss of nerve signaled in the terms that describe what he wants the "*children*"—the plural form of "son" is used only here (see vv. 10, 20 for singular) and points to a classroom or family setting with a number of pupils present—to hear: "*instruction*" and "*understanding*" (see on 1:2–6), standard synonyms for wisdom and its various aspects, also labeled as "*doctrine*" (or teaching, see on 1:5) and even "*law*" (Heb. *tôrāh*) to show their binding and authoritative character. Note also "my commandments" in verse 5 (Heb. *miṣwāh*), a term frequent in the legal sections of the Old Testament and Jewish law. "*Father*" is the fundamental word in the call. It connotes concern, relationship, intimacy, right, and authority. "Parents know best" is not an affirmation that would have cued laughs from an audience of Israelites. They expected such teaching and were expected to give it heed at the time and to cling to it throughout the years—"*Do not forsake*" (see also the imperatives in vv. 3–9).

PERSONAL ILLUSTRATION

4:3 When I was my father's son,
    Tender and the only one in the sight of my
       mother,
  4 He also taught me, and said to me:
    "Let your heart retain my words;
    Keep my commands, and live.
  5 Get wisdom! Get understanding!
    Do not forget, nor turn away from the words
      of my mouth.
  6 Do not forsake her, and she will preserve you;
    Love her, and she will keep you.
  7 Wisdom *is* the principal thing;
    Therefore get wisdom.
    And in all your getting, get understanding.
  8 Exalt her, and she will promote you;
    She will bring you honor, when you embrace
      her.
  9 She will place on your head an ornament
      of grace;
    A crown of glory she will deliver to you."
                            Prov. 4:3–9

The intent of the illustration, which forms the heart of this speech and its major contribution to chapters 1–9, is not nostalgia. Much more is involved than tender reminiscence. At issue is the right of the parent-teacher to impose instruction in command form, admonition, upon the younger generation. That right is explained and defended, as the teacher cites the setting and content of his own education at the feet of his parents. *"My mother"* (see on 1:8; 6:20) underscores her role in the curriculum. She was particularly solicitous of her son's nurture, since he seems to have been frail or weak (*"tender"*), and as the *"only"* child he carried with him the survival of the family's name and destiny (v. 3).

The quotation of the father's words (vv. 4–9) is a showcase of a number of themes already displayed in chapters 1–3: (1) *"wisdom"* and *"understanding"* are synonyms; the latter term is used in the poetic parallelism so that "wisdom" will not have to be repeated (vv. 5, 7; see 1:2–6; 2:2, 6; 3:13, 19); (2) wisdom, which at times is given a personality that speaks for itself (see 1:20–33), is basically conveyed through the *"words"* of parents or teachers (vv. 4, 6; see 2:1–5), though its ultimate source is Yahweh (2:6), whose name is not mentioned in this speech; (3) wisdom's primacy (*"principal thing,"* v. 7) is featured, though not specifically connected with the fear of the Lord which is what makes wisdom uppermost in the teachers' priority list (see on 1:7, 29; 2:5); (4) wisdom's prowess to *"preserve"* and *"keep"* (guard) is advertised in a context made especially appropriate by the allusion to the teacher's own childhood frailty (vv. 3, 6; see on 2:6–8, 11); (5) wisdom's legacy is *"life,"* the power and ability to survive whatever snares and pitfalls one may encounter (v. 4; see also vv. 10, 22; 3:16, 18, 22); (6) when duly *"loved"* (v. 6), *"exalted,"* *"embraced"* (v. 8), wisdom will repay in kind with status (*"promote,"* v. 8), *"honor"* (v. 9), and public approval as evidenced in the festive *"ornament"* (or garland, see on 1:9; 3:22) and *"crown,"* not here a sign of power but of popular acclamation, like the winning of a contest. The teacher has made his point. He has found his father's words true and his own right to lay similar urgings on his children valid.

PRACTICAL EXHORTATIONS

> 4:10 Hear, my son, and receive my sayings,
>   And the years of your life will be many.
> 11 I have taught you in the way of wisdom;
>   I have led you in right paths.
> 12 When you walk, your steps will not be
>   hindered,
>   And when you run, you will not stumble.
> 13 Take firm hold of instruction, do not let go;
>   Keep her, for she *is* your life.
>
> 14 Do not enter the path of the wicked,
>   And do not walk in the way of evil.
> 15 Avoid it, do not travel on it;
>   Turn away from it and pass on.
> 16 For they do not sleep unless they have done
>   evil;
>   And their sleep is taken away unless they
>   make *someone* fall.
> 17 For they eat the bread of wickedness,
>   And drink the wine of violence.
>
> *Prov. 4:10–17*

The teacher proceeds immediately to exercise the right to instruct, launching into a series of admonitions—two sets of them (vv. 10–17; vv. 20–27) separated and connected by an antithetical summary

(vv. 18–19). The rapid-fire style of these commands is witness to the fact that he has made his case. Beginning at verse 13, they are a closely linked chain of imperatives, embellished only on occasion with explanations to establish the reason for or to describe the outcome of obedience to the command (vv. 13b, 16–17, 22, 26b). Lacing the admonitions together is a consistent use of one of Proverbs' most dominant metaphors, path or way. Its role in this context is strategic. The teacher aims to equip his young for a lifetime as his parents had done for him. His topic was not so much individual, day-by-day issues but the whole course of life—how to survive it with joy and success. Given this purpose, no language was more appropriate than the language of the journey. For a time, the urban setting of much of Proverbs (see on 1:20–21) is laid aside and the rugged topography of Palestine is in view. The scene recalls Psalm 23 with the gang of threats that stalk those who journey over craggy hills, rock-studded cliffs, or the moonscape stretches of the wilderness. It is a land of dark shadows, paths that beckon and lead to nowhere, false turns, dead ends, slippery clefts and yawning gullies, ominous caves and treacherous pits. And with all, the enemies are lurking—whether bestial or human—against whom wisdom and understanding, like the Lord's rod and staff, offer the only adequate defense to the young traveler. Note that the audience which began plural, my children (v. 1), now narrows to a single person, perhaps the eldest among them, *"my son"* (vv. 10, 20).

The language bristles with components of the extended metaphor. First, the nouns "way," "path," and "track" (usually all read as "path" in NKJV) occur eight times all together (vv. 11, 14, 18, 19, 26) in synonymous pairs. Second, the verbs are more numerous—"taught" (v. 11, lit., "guided"), "led" (v. 11), "walk" (v. 12), "run" (v. 12), "stumble" (vv. 12, 19), "enter" (v. 14), "walk" (or "step," v. 14), "avoid" (v. 15), "travel" (v. 15, also translated "pass on"), "turn away" (v. 15), "turn" (v. 27), "remove" (v. 27). Third, expressions of the nature of the right are informative—"straight" ("right," v. 11), smooth, without impediment or cause for stumbling (v. 12), filled with increasing "light" (v. 18), not pitch-black "darkness" (v. 19), demanding "eyes" to be fixed on it (v. 25), and "feet" disciplined from wandering right or left (v. 27).

Within this encompassing theme of "path" as the chief description of habitual, consistent conduct, two specific pitfalls are spotlighted, each in its own cluster of admonitions: (1) avoid violence (vv. 10–17); (2) avoid dishonesty (vv. 20–27).

Avoid violence was the first specific instruction found in Proverbs (see on 1:10–19). Shun the very company of those prone to it was the advice there. That advice is only echoed here (vv. 14–17) with special emphasis on staying clear of any paths they walk, that is, any association with them or their violent life patterns, patterns so stamped by *"wickedness,"* their turbulent drives to challenge the ways of God, and *"violence,"* their unbridled practice of harming others, that the evil actions form their very diet—their *"bread"* and *"wine"* (v. 17). So crooked is their life path, so deviant from the straight, that they can *"sleep"* the sleep of the satisfied (v. 16) only on those nights when they have done harm (*"evil"*) to the innocent and made well-meaning people *"fall"* flat on their faces (*"stumble,"* see vv. 12, 19). The inclusion of sleep and diet in descriptions of the path shows how comprehensive the term is. Any of us with skills of honest recollection can remember shameful things we did as part of a gang or group that we would not have initiated on our own. The caring teacher-parent had learned that at his own childhood table and did not miss the opportunity to expose afresh the diabolically seductive influence of malicious people.

ANTITHETIC SUMMARY

4:18 But the path of the just *is* like the shining sun,
    That shines ever brighter unto the perfect day.
  19 The way of the wicked *is* like darkness;
    They do not know what makes them stumble.
Prov. 4:18–19

This summary concludes and distills the lessons about the dangers of violent people by contrasting the two ways in terms of light and darkness. The figure is of two groups of travelers. One, the *"just"* ("righteous" or "innocent," see chap. 10), begin life's path at daybreak and walk it in sunlight that *"shines ever brighter"* until midday when the light is at its full and the day is totally established (*"perfect"*) in its ability to illumine every obstacle and turning of the path. Threats are almost nonexistent, so well can the daytime travelers see. The other group, *"the wicked,"* set out on their way at dusk, only to find themselves immersed in *"darkness"* so dense that they *"stumble"* without knowing why. Dawn and dusk may each offer the same level of light to the prospective journeyers. But their pilgrimage ends poles apart: one, secure in the ability to scan from horizon to horizon and know precisely how the land lies; the other, ambling aimlessly with every familiar landmark obliterated by the impenetrable pall and every step an exercise in fear and futility.

MORE PRACTICAL EXHORTATIONS

4:20 My son, give attention to my words;
    Incline your ear to my sayings.
21 Do not let them depart from your eyes;
    Keep them in the midst of your heart;
22 For they *are* life to those who find them,
    And health to all their flesh.
23 Keep your heart with all diligence,
    For out of it *spring* the issues of life.
24 Put away from you a deceitful mouth,
    And put perverse lips far from you.
25 Let your eyes look straight ahead,
    And your eyelids look right before you.
26 Ponder the path of your feet,
    And let all your ways be established.
27 Do not turn to the right or the left;
    Remove your foot from evil.
Prov. 4:20–27

Avoid dishonesty, the second admonition (vv. 20–27), sought to ward off temptation from within as avoid violence (vv. 10–17) had guarded the student from without. Both commands are set in contexts where wisdom is viewed as life giving (vv. 13, 22) and where its aim is to induce the young people to follow the right path, the right course of total conduct in life (vv. 11–12, 25–27). The honesty to be sought centers in speech: its enemy is *a deceitful mouth* (given to crookedness; see the ampler description at 6:12) and *perverse lips,* a phrase virtually synonymous with its mate (v. 24). So crucial are words as windows on the inner life, rafters that join person to person in the family and community, and doors of instruction and encouragement to friends and neighbors that when they go crooked all social stability topples in a heap (see on 2:11–15 where *the man who speaks perverse things* is branded an archenemy). The total context of this final admonition should catch our eye. The continuity of sound teaching passed from generation to generation (vv. 1–9) like a sterling silver sugar bowl will lose its effectiveness and beauty anytime the tin of dishonesty is substituted for the original precious metal.

The honesty commended centers in speech (v. 24) but it embraces the whole person. Few passages in Proverbs declare with such force that the path of God laid out in wisdom is both all-demanding and all-rewarding. If it offers its prizes of life, honor, esteem, security, and success (vv. 8–10), it also asks for total surrender to its claims and directions.

The list of nouns in verses 20–27 is a lesson in the anatomy of discipleship. The *"ear"* must receive and retain the words of the wise parent (v. 20). The *"eyes"* must be riveted to them in their written form, a reminder of the literacy of Israel's aristocracy (v. 21) and must at the same time be fixed on the path to spot any obstacle or deviation (v. 25). The *"heart"* serves as a vault within which the treasures of wisdom are to be guarded and from which they are to be withdrawn and skillfully employed (vv. 21, 23; in the latter text "issues" is a noun derived from a Heb. root "go out" and carries a range of meanings from "exits" [Ezek. 48:30] to "limits" [1 Chron. 5:16] or "boundaries" [Josh. 15:4]). The force in Prov. 4:23 may be to see the heart as a wellspring and its "outgoings" as the vivifying waters that refresh wise persons and those around them. Scarcely any treasure in those desert realms was more coveted than fresh spring water; to keep it from turning brackish was a noble goal.

The *"mouth"* and *"lips"* are the conduit from which the water of the heart (wise and sound decisions and observations) flows in either fresh or fetid form (v. 24). The *"eyelids"* are probably better understood as "eye rays," quick, discerning flashes of insight and perception (v. 25). The *"feet"* do the actual walking, following directions of heart and eye; the safety of the journeyer depends on their ability to implement quickly the commands they receive (vv. 26–27). The *"right [hand]"* and the *"left [hand]"* (the literal Hebrew) symbolize the tendency to roam aimlessly to one side or another of wisdom's chosen path; they are seen as figures of the options to stray which seem so gorgeously attractive and which require such assiduous discipline to resist (v. 27).

More important in this wisdom speech than the specific commands is the domineering presence of representatives of three generations: the teacher, his parents, his children. He knew that his résumé would be inaccurate unless appropriate prominence were given to the contribution to his life of those who preceded and those who followed him. He was right. Many of us want to salute our parents in red letters, so prominent were their gifts of wisdom to us. What about our children? Whose names will appear on their résumés?

CHAPTER FIVE

Bitter Honey and Sweet Water

Proverbs 5:1–23

Unworthy company and unreliable words—these are the two major enemies that set snares in the paths of the wise. A hallmark of the prudent pupil is to know why and how to avoid them. As important as truth telling is (see on 2:11–15; 4:20–24; 6:12–15), choosing right companions is an even more dominant theme (see on 1:10–19; 2:11–15, 16–20; 4:10–17; 6:23–35; 7:1–27; 9:13–18). The wisdom speeches begin with a warning against hobnobbing with greedy men (1:10–19) and conclude with an indictment of a lustful woman (9:13–18). Between this beginning and conclusion, the speeches direct pivotal paragraphs (2:16–20; 6:23–35) and entire chapters (5 and 7) to the death-dealing dangers of consorting sexually with a person outside of wedlock.

The intent of these sections can be stated plainly, given our understanding that the chief purpose of the opening speeches in Proverbs is to motivate the hearers to desire wisdom and then behave wisely: nothing in life so clouds our judgment and makes stupid fools out of the wisest of us as succumbing to illicit passion. All our useful energies are drained off to defend or conceal that behavior. The colossal compromise of adultery colors all our other value judgments and causes us to stagger along life's road half-tipsy.

To the teachers it was worth every possible effort to prevent their young people from falling into this bottle-dungeon of perverted sexuality whose walls sloped inward to the top and made escape only a wild fantasy. We shall chart their efforts as we comment on the succeeding chapters. Here it is enough to point to the passage where this theme was first broached (2:16–20). There the warning was simply stated: no matter how flattering are the words of the temptress, she is totally unreliable, having broken her covenant with her husband and her God; the outcome of such treachery for her and her unauthorized companion is death.

Chapter 5 picks up that theme of smooth yet fatal words and restates it, first in the minor key, elucidating its terrors for both
parties—first the woman (vv. 5–6), next the man (vv. 7–14). Then
the mode turns major, articulating the bright opportunities of love
and affection between wife and husband (vv. 15–20). Along with
Gen. 2:24–25 and the Song of Solomon, this paragraph sounds the
note of unembarrassed passion, of open delight, that should fill
the air of every household which interprets marital love as a joyous
expression of God's love for His people. The minor key may be
named "bitter honey" (vv. 3–4)—its first taste brings a, smile; its last,
a grimace. The major key is called "sweet water"—its taste is constant; its affect, refreshing; its impact, life giving.

BEWARE THE WANTON'S WILY WORDS

5:1 My son, pay attention to my wisdom;
Lend your ear to my understanding,
2 That you may preserve discretion,
And your lips may keep knowledge.
3 For the lips of an immoral woman drip honey,
And her mouth *is* smoother than oil;
4 But in the end she is bitter as wormwood,
Sharp as a two-edged sword.
5 Her feet go down to death,
Her steps lay hold of hell.
6 Lest you ponder *her* path of life—
Her ways are unstable;
You do not know *them*.

Prov. 5:1–6

The call to attention (vv. 1–2; see on 1:8–9; 4:1, 10, 20) carries a
note of urgency. It forces the student ("*my son*") to choose between
the teacher's manifold "*wisdom*," whose splendor gleams in the three
additional synonyms (see on 1:2–6), and the saccharine (refined
"*honey*") and lubricious (filtered olive "*oil*") speech of the "*immoral
woman*," whose ways were foreign to teachings of the covenant (see
on 2:16–17), though she may or may not have been a native Israelite.
To hear the teacher is to muffle the call of the temptress and vice
versa. Refusal to answer her or responding with a forthright "no" is
the way that "*lips keep* [or guard] *knowledge*" (v. 2).

The teacher's insistence is supported with strong reasons, introduced by "*for*" (vv. 3–6). First, to listen to her is to be poisoned

by *"wormwood"* (v. 4) always a symbol of bitterness in the Bible (Lam. 3:19; Amos 6:12) and also in Shakespeare, where Juliet's nurse reminded her ward of the weaning process accomplished by dabbing on her breast wormwood, distilled from a shrub *Artemisia absinthium,* to squelch the young girl's desire to suckle. Second, to listen to the immoral woman (v. 3) is to be mutilated as her words take on the sharpness of *"a two-edged sword"* (v. 4; lit., *"two-mouthed"* as though the sword ate alive its victim). Third, to walk with her is to embark on the *"path"* to *"death"* and *"hell"* (v. 5), Sheol, the grave and the abode of the dead in Old Testament parlance. Fourth, to consort with her is to share her disorientation intoxicated as she is by passion, and to wander (as *"unstable"* means) off the path of life, the pattern of conduct that leads to survival and success (see emphasis on path in chap. 4), and to be hopelessly lost with her (v. 6).

BEWARE THE DIRE RESULT OF ADULTERY

5:7 Therefore hear me now, *my* children,
    And do not depart from the words of my
       mouth.
  8 Remove your way far from her,
    And do not go near the door of her house,
  9 Lest you give your honor to others,
    And your years to the cruel *one;*
10 Lest aliens be filled with your wealth,
    And your labors *go* to the house of a foreigner;
11 And you mourn at last,
    When your flesh and your body are consumed,
12 And say:
    "How I have hated instruction,
    And my heart despised correction!
13 I have not obeyed the voice of my teachers,
    Nor inclined my ear to those who instructed
      me!
14 I was on the verge of total ruin,
    In the midst of the assembly and congregation."
                             Prov. 5:7–14

The teacher turns to a wider audience, *"my children"* (v. 7), as though he had focused first on one student in the initial warning and now wants to catch the attention of the whole group with a second call to attention (see v. 1; 4:1 contains a similar plural form of address). The call to attention serves as a timely pause in the argument and then immediately locks in the interest of the class as the admonitions continue. This time they center not on the confusion and disorientation suffered by the woman but the public loss of dignity endured by a man caught in her clutches. The teacher's eyes seem to have swung again from the larger group of his children to the solitary individual, since the verbs that describe the hearer are all singular.

The dire results of adultery are listed first as loss of what every sane person values (vv. 9–10): *"honor"* and respect in the community; *"years"* of building up one's reputation for integrity and reliability, only to have it tarnished by a cruel person who will take vengeful delight in public exposure; *"wealth"* (lit., what gives one *"strength"* to cope with life's needs), which may be lost from the family inheritance and squandered, perhaps by blackmail, into the hands of the harlot and her comrades; *"labors"* of a lifetime and all that they have allowed a person to accumulate, as they fly out the window and settle in a place where they do not belong—the house of a foreigner, which may refer also to the place where the adulteress resides.

The second set of bleak outcomes is the bitter regret that will be banefully acknowledged by the transgressor (vv. 11–14). Bereft of all that sustains life—self-esteem and material goods—he is left with nothing to do but to *"mourn,"* literally "groan" or "growl" like a beast mortally wounded, flesh and body *"consumed."* The teacher's technique here is powerful: he places a litany of gray regrets on his student's lips that were earlier commissioned to guard wisdom (v. 2). Guard it they do, but too late. The words of confession have a chalky taste: "What I should have treasured and preserved, I have hated and despised (or disdained)—instruction even to the point of pain (see on 1:2–6) and reproof, setting wrong things right (see on 1:23, 30). The calls to attention which punctuated the teachers' lessons (see on 1:8–9; 4:1–2; 5:1–2, 7), my ears have resisted with stony obstinance (v. 13). The sorry denouement of my life script was public embarrassment before an assembly of my countrymen (v. 14)." How literally we should read this last verse is hard to say. It may describe with dramatic license the fact that the entire neighborhood and a whole cadre of his peers would find out about his secret dalliance, or more literally, it may suggest that an offended husband had hailed him into court to press charges against him.

The shattering, soul-destroying affect of adultery is the point. It can rarely be kept secret, and its perpetrators are damned if it is and damned if it is not. Kept hidden, it grinds on the spirit and conscience of those who practice it until exposure seems a kind of relief. And many a person has deliberately left traces of a sin for others to discover, as a desperate plea for rescue from enslaving behavior. Made public, adultery brings personal shame, humiliation to loved ones, and loss of respect in the larger community. In recent times, a number of politicians and religious leaders could be summoned to verify the accuracy of the teacher's words.

PRACTICE FIDELITY WITH JOY

5:15 Drink water from your own cistern,
    And running water from your own well.
  16 Should your fountains be dispersed abroad,
    Streams of water in the streets?
  17 Let them be only your own,
    And not for strangers with you.
  18 Let your fountain be blessed,
    And rejoice with the wife of your youth.
  19 *As a* loving deer and a graceful doe,
    Let her breasts satisfy you at all times;
    And always be enraptured with her love.
  20 For why should you, my son, be enraptured by
    an immoral woman,
    And be embraced in the arms of a seductress?
Prov. 5:15–20

The best admonitions, like Cana's wedding wine, were saved to the last. The teacher has brought the melody of bitter honey to its doleful cadence. Now, using his own words, not his pupil's, he moves into his air and variations on the joys of fidelity and sings them lustily and artfully in the major key. The commands to chastity are embroidered with an extended metaphor—a double metaphor, in fact—and comprise as winsome a stanza of poetry as Proverbs contains. If sexual looseness has its dangers, sexual loyalty has its advantages, so sings the teacher-poet in verses 15–20.

Fidelity is the opening theme (v. 15). *"Cistern"* and *"well"* were prized possessions in a climate where rainfall was scarce and a time when the techniques of drilling deep wells were not yet discovered. The cistern collected rain water and could store any overflow of a well fed by a spring (*"running water"*). The two nouns describe the wife, and the *"water,"* fresh from a spring, pictures the refreshment of love making (see also Song of Sol. 4:12, 15). The contrast between the harlot's honey that goes bitter (vv. 3–4) and the wife's water that stays sweet ("running") is the point of the whole chapter.

Fertility is the subject of the rhetorical questions and the two admonitions that follow it (vv. 16–18). *"Fountains"* and *"streams of water"* (v. 16) are pictures of male sexual vigor, perhaps even semen, which should be reserved for the woman he is pledged to and the children she is to bear. Impregnating *"strangers"* (v. 17) is a misuse of masculine potency and a squandering of the help, blessing, and strength that a large number of children can bring to a family whose financial stability, community influence, and long-term survival depend on them. Job's seven sons and three daughters seem to exhibit the ideal size and shape of an ancient Hebrew family. The psalmist put the matter graphically:

> Like arrows in the hand of a warrior are the sons of
>   one's youth.
> Happy is the man who has his quiver full of them.
> *Ps. 127:4–5*

The psalmist's "happy" is what the teacher means by *"blessed"* (v. 18). *"Your fountain"* points to the wife as did "cistern" and "well." The blessing that prompts them to rejoice together is pregnancy and childbirth.

The final admonition and its follow-up question (vv. 19–20) add warmth and tenderness to the whole speech. They portray marital loyalty as an experience of fondness as well as fertility and fidelity. The young man, with the rest of our male species through the centuries, is exhorted not just to a steely willed commitment or to a paternal pride but also to a single-hearted, impassioned affection for his bride. To sketch the note of fondness, the teacher reaches again for the palette of love language with its splendid array of hues. Not fountain this time, as appropriate as was that symbol of fertility, but *"loving deer"* and *"graceful doe,"* expressions of the wife's beauty and gentleness. Besides, who can resist wanting to pet and stroke such an attractive, guileless creature? The attention to *"breasts"* recalls the description of the woman in another love poem:

> Your breasts are like two fawns,
>   twins of a gazelle,
> that feed among the lilies.
> *Song of Sol. 4:5; also 7:3*

The passion is made even more explicit in the last line of verse 19. *"Love"* means "love making" as it does frequently in Solomon's Song, and *"be enraptured"* derives from a verb that suggests intoxication. When this kind of companionship is available at home, is it not sheer stupidity to seek it in the arms of a person whose name, values, and habits of life are foreign to you? So runs the teacher's clinching question (v. 20).

NEGATIVE CONCLUDING SUMMARY

> 5:21 For the ways of man *are* before the eyes of
>   the LORD,
>   And He ponders all his paths.
>   22 His own iniquities entrap the wicked *man,*
>   And he is caught in the cords of his sin.
>   23 He shall die for lack of instruction,
>   And in the greatness of his folly he shall
>   go astray.
> *Prov. 5:21–23*

As cogent as have been the notes of fidelity, fertility, and fondness, the teacher cannot let the anthem end there. One other grave consideration must be stated: Yahweh's interest in how temptation is dealt with and especially what happens when we yield to it. The God before whom we, knowingly or unknowingly, pledged our vows is a partisan observer of our performance. Part of what we have been taught to pray to Him is:

> And do not lead us into temptation,
> But deliver us from the evil one.
> *Matt. 6:13*

Our failure to voice that prayer or our refusal to help answer it lead to disaster. We become entrapped in snares of our own making (v. 22). Our twisted, distorted ways (*"iniquities"*) catch us in their nets; our penchant for straying from God's clearly marked path or missing the target of His righteous requirements (*"sin"*) lassos us with our own lariat.

The final verse (v. 23) echoes three notes from the whole composition: (1) death is the expected result of sexual immorality, since life is robbed of its roots in love and loyalty; physical life may struggle on but the guilt, compromise, and failure of adultery are a walking death (see v. 5); (2) rebellion against *"instruction,"* the disciplined self-control that bears suffering and learns from it, is a mistake from which it is hard to recover (see v. 12); (3) one should be intoxicated with the love of a spouse (v. 19) not the love of an immoral woman (v. 20); where the latter is the case, it is tantamount to being intoxicated (*"go astray"* is the same verb as *"enraptured"* in vv. 19–20) or overdosed with massive folly; the outcome is lethal.

The living waters of covenant loyalty or the fatal chemistry of bitter honey—day by day, year after year, we moderns face that choice with even greater intensity than did the ancients to whom Proverbs was first directed. We have cars; we travel widely; we frequent large cities where anonymity is possible; we have the mechanical or chemical means to avert pregnancy; we live in a society where adultery makes smaller waves than a tiny pebble in a windswept pond. As much as any generation that ever lived, we need to open our hearts to the teacher's counsel. Adultery can still be death dealing—even literally given the spread of AIDS. Our best choices are still our own partners, with whom we need to keep affections alive, courtships strong, passions kindled. Whatever attracted us to each other in the first place can be recalled and experienced afresh. Water is not sweeter elsewhere nor grass greener. Not as long as God is in heaven and our ways *are before the eyes of the Lord.* God has called us to be loyal to each other in order to portray to the whole human family how deathlessly loyal He is to us. Heeding that call or not heeding it has consequences that are nothing less than cosmic.

CHAPTER SIX

Social Responsibility and Family Unity

Proverbs 6:1–35

"So many things to learn; so little time to learn them!" Some such thought must have prompted the teacher to fill this speech with a variety of topics, each deemed indispensable to the nurture and growth of the pupil. We teachers are always tempted to load on our students more material than they can handle and in a shorter time than they need to absorb it.

We can learn from this chapter how to choose crucial topics and how to convey them winsomely. The topics line up like this:

Rash pledges	6:1–5
Laziness	6:6–11
Perverseness	6:12–15
Disruptiveness	6:16–19
Adultery	6:23–35

The artistic variety that expresses them is many-splendored:

metaphors from bird trapping and deer hunting (vv. 2, 5)
object lesson from the habits of ants (vv. 6–8)
complaining questions (v. 9)
metaphors of hobos and beggars (v. 11)
description of the body language of a perverse, destructive
    person (vv. 12–13)
numerical saying to highlight the seventh and final crime
    mentioned (vv. 16–19)
compact list of activities that undermine social stability
    (vv. 16–19)
call to attention to prepare hearer for final and most
    important topic (vv. 20–22)
rhetorical questions that dictate their own answers
    (vv. 27–28, 30)

description of an outraged husband pressing charges
against an adulterer (vv. 33–35).

Admonitions are the backbone of the literary style. But in two
sections of the speech, the form is deliberately varied for the sake of
interest and emphasis: the sayings on perverseness (vv. 12–15) and
the numerical sequence that builds to its climax with the picture of
discord (vv. 16–19); both describe the problems without issuing
specific commands. A word to the wise is sufficient. Moreover, the
sayings stated in the indicative mood retain a double edge: they
alert the hearer to persons in society who are perverted and disruptive; they also warn against engaging in such malicious behavior.
"There are those who do this; watch out for them and don't be like
them" is the force of these sayings. The admonitions, couched in
imperatives, are pointed directly at the hearer and call for personal
response, whether in obedience or rejection.

DISENGAGE YOURSELVES FROM RASH PLEDGES

6:1 My son, if you become surety for your friend,
    If you have shaken hands in pledge for a
        stranger,
  2 You are snared by the words of your mouth;
    You are taken by the words of your mouth.
  3 So do this, my son, and deliver yourself;
    For you have come into the hand of your
        friend:
    Go and humble yourself;
    Plead with your friend.
  4 Give no sleep to your eyes,
    Nor slumber to your eyelids.
  5 Deliver yourself like a gazelle from the hand *of
    the hunter,*
    And like a bird from the hand of the fowler.

Prov. 6:1–5

The three parties to this rash transaction seem to be named in
verse 1: *"my son,"* the pupil who is being warned; *"your friend"* probably the lender, who shows up again in verse 3; and *"a stranger,"* either
a resident alien or a person who lives outside the moral and ethical
boundaries of the community, who originally borrowed the money.
The nature of such commercial transactions is discussed below (see
chap. 11). They may have been more complicated than anything the

pupil had run into in his youth which he probably spent in a more agricultural setting.

The primary theme of the passage surfaces in verse 3. The command there is not "Don't do it," though that is obviously a subliminal point (see on 11:15; 17:18; 22:26, each of which warns against such financial entanglements). Rather the imperatives are *go and humble yourself* (a troublesome verb that may also mean "hurry;" see JB, "go quickly"), and *plead* (or even "pester," NEB). The lesson, then, is, "Swallow hard and eat your humble pie." A quick pledge, sealed with a hasty hand slap (v. 1) and with brash promises—*words of your mouth* is repeated verbatim in verse 2 without any attempt at stylistic variety—can put the naive young person in a trap (*"snared"* and *"taken"* or *"caught"* are hunting terms; see v. 5). The friendly lender into whose hand (i.e., "power," v. 3) the youth may stride is both *"hunter"* and *"fowler"* (v. 5). But the youth is even more stupid than a confused *"gazelle"* or a baffled *"bird,"* since he himself wove his own net (v. 2).

In a society where pride and self-esteem governed public conduct and made apology rare and groveling before a creditor even more rare, this lesson would have cut to the quick. It called for admitting a faux pas, reneging on a promise, and badgering a powerful neighbor for relief from it. Distasteful but necessary. And a wholesome reminder that prudence would have avoided the predicament in the first place. It was not brother or uncle for whom he rashly pledged collateral and cosigned an agreement. It was someone to whom he had no primarily obligation and who, in turn, was not at all accountable to him.

Perhaps my inherent caution is owed to the fact that my dad, warm-spirited and kindhearted preacher that he was, almost always came out short in such financial matters. But I have developed strong convictions about the risks of financial involvement between ministers and their friends or parishioners. Successful deals may engender feelings of obligation; unsuccessful ones may breed hostility. We learn from the teacher to take hat in hand and beg for mercy when we must; we also learn the wisdom of avoiding obligations whose outcome augurs pain.

LEARN DILIGENCE FROM THE ANT

> 6:6 Go to the ant, you sluggard!
>   Consider her ways and be wise,

7 Which, having no captain,
　Overseer or ruler,
8 Provides her supplies in the summer,
　And gathers her food in the harvest.
9 How long will you slumber, O sluggard?
　When will you rise from your sleep?
10 A little sleep, a little slumber,
　A little folding of the hands to sleep—
11 So shall your poverty come on you like
　　a prowler,
　And your need like an armed man.

Prov. 6:6–11

This sarcastic bit of artistry is one of the choice pieces of biblical poetry. Dramatically it addresses the pupil not as who he is but as who he may become—a *"sluggard"* (vv. 6, 9). It imagines his inexhaustible potential for laziness, mocks it by the comparison with the *"ant"* (vv. 6–8), complains about it in the questions that begin *"how long"* and *"when"* (v. 9; the style imitates the complaints against enemies or even God in passages like Pss. 4:2; 6:3; 13:1–2), taunts its practitioner with his own words (v. 10), and then pictures its outcome with metaphors of vagrants and their surprise assaults on the unsuspecting (v. 11).

The bite of sarcasm is felt in the contrast between the diligence of the ant and the indolence of the sluggard. The contrast is humiliating. A person over 5 feet tall and weighing 130 pounds or more is told to let an ant be teacher, an ant less than a quarter of an inch long, weighing a slight fraction of an ounce. A person with gifts of speech, with a brain the size of a whole anthill, is told to bend over, peer down, and learn from the lowly ant. The irony is powerful. The stupid sluggard lags behind the ant in two chief ways. First, she needs no leader; she is not part of a Solomonic bureaucracy (v. 7) with its *"captain, overseer* [or record keeper], *and ruler* [or counselor]." The sluggard may fail despite an organizational structure that ought to promote achievement; the ant succeeds on her own. Second, she plans ahead. She understands the seasons. The cycles of life—harvest season and dormant periods—are coded into her instincts. She works while food is plentiful and stores it against the season of want. The contrast leads to a sarcastic complaint (v. 9). The teacher is frustrated, even angry. Laziness is a breach of love. It refuses to carry its own weight let alone help with the loads of the rest of us who plod along supporting our young, our aged, our infirm. We have no surplus energy to carry those who can walk and will not. "How long" and "when" are the right questions.

The sting of the sarcasm comes through in the caricature of the sluggard. One of the sluggard's traits is cartooned here—the tendency to deny the laziness. Verse 10 may be a quotation of the sluggard's rationalizations: "I'm not lazy at all, I'm only snatching a slight snooze, seizing the pause that refreshes." The teacher uses the caricature to draw the sarcastic consequences (see also 24:33–34): You may call it snoozing. But while your eyes lie shut and your hands folded, *"your poverty"* will panhandle everything you own like a hobo ("tramp" is a more accurate translation than *"prowler,"* v. 11) and your need (or total lack of goods) will take the rest like a cheeky beggar (*"armed,"* in light of Arabic and Ugaritic roots ought to be translated as either "an insolent man" or "a beggar"). Hard work ought to be the normal routine of us who serve a carpenter-Christ, who follow the lead of a tentmaker-Apostle, and who call ourselves children of a Father who is still working (John 5:17).

PERVERSE PEOPLE ARE DANGEROUS

6:12 A worthless person, a wicked man,
     Walks with a perverse mouth;
  13 He winks with his eyes,
     He shuffles his feet,
     He points with his fingers;
  14 Perversity *is* in his heart,
     He devises evil continually,
     He sows discord.
  15 Therefore his calamity shall come suddenly;
     Suddenly he shall be broken without remedy.
                      Prov. 6:12–15

This is not a picture of a good neighbor. To a stable community such a person spells disruption. The young leaders to whom Proverbs is addressed had to be put on guard against him. They would meet his like and needed to recognize him at first glance and deal with him or steer clear of him, as the situation warranted.

His motives are wretched (v. 12): he is out to eat people alive, swallow them whole, in his ambitious corruption (some such force lies beneath the difficult word *"worthless"* [Heb. *bᵉlîyaʿal*]); his life is a zero, emptied of all truth, goodness, righteousness, and justice (so suggests the Hebrew word for wicked used here, *ʾāwen*; see 6:18;

10:29; 11:7; 12:21; 17:4; 19:28; 21:15; 22:8; 30:20; also Hos. 6:8; Amos 5:5; Mic. 2:1); his speech (*"mouth"*) betrays his crookedness.

His manners are malicious (v. 13). The body language probably implies more than shiftiness or subterfuge, though both are involved. The signs made by *"eyes," "feet,"* and *"fingers"* may suggest magic or witchcraft. Hexes, spells, evil eyes, harmful omens—these are all part of his bag of tricks. They are also evidences of the insidious yet explosive danger of such devices. Biblical faith is dead-set against these practices not only because they give evil persons the power of fear and anxiety over their fellow citizens but especially because they seize the helm of life from Yahweh's hands and seek to replace him as Lord of history (Deut. 18:9–14).

The methods used by the wicked are expressions of the *"perversity"* (the topsy-turviness; see on 2:12, 14 for the use of this word found nine times in Proverbs and elsewhere only in Deut. 32:20) of the wicked and especially of the evil plots that boil in them *"continually"* (v. 14). All their choices (*"heart"*) are malicious, because discord among the people, disruption of community consensus and family unity, are their aim. Such discord may even carry them into court to try to give legal expression to their contentiousness (ten times the Hebrew word for discord, *midyān,* is found in Proverbs and nowhere else in the Old Testament; its root suggests public dispute or judicial strife).

What ultimately crushes (*"be broken"*) such a wretch is not described (v. 15). It may be a righteous uprising of the community; it may be a negative decision by the town's elders in the litigation that takes place in the city gate. In any case, the defeat is so devastating that all temptation to copy the perverse person is quelled. These words are not wasted on our modern society where both wicked manipulation by magic and mean contention in court are daily realities. The first is an insult to divine power; the second, an outrage to divine love. Perverse people are dangerous, then and now.

DIVISIVE PEOPLE ARE DEADLY

6:16 These six *things* the LORD hates,
    Yes, seven *are* an abomination to Him:
    17 A proud look,
        A lying tongue,
        Hands that shed innocent blood,
    18 A heart that devises wicked plans,
        Feet that are swift in running to evil,

19 A false witness *who* speaks lies,
And one who sows discord among brethren.
                                    Prov. 6:16–19

This familiar list of "seven deadly sins" may well be a commentary on the previous paragraph since the climactic line of each is *"sows discord"* (vv. 14, 19). Certainly, that catch phrase accounts for the back-to-back positioning of the passages in this wisdom speech. In the prior text, the emphasis was on the dangers of perversity and the disastrous fate of its perpetrator. Here the evil conduct is evaluated from God's viewpoint, as *"hates"* and *"abomination"* (a favorite word in Proverbs and Deuteronomy to describe what is utterly outrageous to God in its insolence or evil; see on Prov. 3:32) declare.

The numerical pattern—*"six . . . seven"*—plays several roles: (1) it aids memory by numbering the items in a list; (2) it encourages recitation or repetition of the items by making a game, almost a riddle, of the text; (3) it thrusts into bold relief the final item, here the seventh, as the climax and center of the list (see comments on other numerical proverbs at 30:7–9, 15–16, 18–19, 21–23, 24–28, 29–31; for a prophet's use of the pattern, see Amos 1–2).

If we are right in seeing *"discord"* (v. 19) as the heart of the passage and in finding frivolous or malicious litigation as a chief expression of that discord, then we may see a contentious note in each of the first six rungs in the ladder by which we ascend to the climax of the final clause (v. 19b). *"A proud look"* (v. 17; lit., "raised eyes") may be a general reference to the haughtiness that God detests as an intrusion on his sovereignty (see Isa. 2:11–19); it may also refer specifically to the claim to being one up that the perverse person wants to sustain in court. *"A lying tongue"* (v. 17) may be a general penchant to play loose with the truth; it may also point to falsehood in setting up or testifying in a legal encounter. *"Hands that shed innocent blood"* (v. 17) may describe violence of many kinds (its opposite is "clean hands"; Pss. 24:4; 73:13), including the unjustified violence that a verdict against an innocent person produces. *"A heart that devises* [lit., "plows" to prepare the soil] *wicked plans"* (v. 18; see the identical idea in v. 14) may well speak of scheming against the guiltless in a rigged trial. *"Feet that are swift in running to evil"* (v. 18) catches the note of urgency involved in the crime—no step spared, no second wasted, no base left uncovered in the execution of the plot. *"A false witness who speaks lies"* (v. 19) helps to clinch the point that illicit legal action is in view (see at chap. 12 for a sustained discussion of the importance of truth telling in court). The discord, then, sown on soil plowed ("devised") in wicked plans (v. 19; see vv. 14, 18) is not unspecified divisiveness. It is an attempt to drive wedges into the solidarity of the community or clan (note *brethren*) by spurious legal claims.

Three observations need making in light of this passage (vv. 16–19) and the one that introduced it. First, the focus on parts of the body demonstrates the total involvement of the wicked people in their scheme—"eyes" (vv. 13, 17), "mouth" or "tongue" (vv. 12, 17), "feet" (vv. 13, 18), "finger" or "hand" (vv. 13, 17), "heart" (vv. 14, 18). They epitomize, with this consuming engagement of their whole selves in plotting harm to others, the kind of life against which the teacher sharply warned in 4:20–27, which also abounds with body talk.

Second, the seriousness of the legal system is being stressed in these verses. They witness to the importance of due process to the social welfare of Israel's society. Persons who tampered with it threatened to distort life beyond recognition, to turn upside down the props that support decent human relations.

Finally, our modern society in which court dockets are crammed with acrimonious and greedy lawsuits needs to look at itself in light of this list of behaviors that God hates. One of my attorney friends, a law school professor, has embarked on a crusade to try to make arbitration or mediation, not litigation, the normal way of settling disputes in our land. With tears in his eyes, he has lamented to me that the system in which someone has to win big and another lose lavishly whenever claims are made cannot be right. "Jesus does not want us to live that way" is the simple, irrefutable conclusion to which his Christian commitment has led him. The Sermon on the Mount (6:21–26, 38–42) and its application by Paul (1 Cor. 6:1–8) brand that conclusion as right.

CALL TO ATTENTION

6:20 My son, keep your father's command,
       And do not forsake the law of your mother.
   21 Bind them continually upon your heart;
       Tie them around your neck.
   22 When you roam, they will lead you;
       When you sleep, they will keep you;
       And *when* you awake, they will speak
          with you.

Prov. 6:20–22

This admonition to obedience combines three familiar ingredients and adds a new one. Familiar are (1) the equation of wisdom teaching with *command* and *law* (v. 20; see 3:1) to show that obedience is not a matter of option or choice but of responsibility or rebellion, (2) the mention of both parents as sources of authoritative instruction (v. 20; see on 1:8; 4:3), a reminder that school was seen as an extension of the home in its obligation to nurture the young, (3) the metaphors of tying or binding (v. 21; see 1:9; 3:3, 22) to depict the tenacity with which wisdom is to be grasped and the central part it plays in every aspect of life. New are the trio of clauses that picture wisdom's constant role during the key activities of each day (v. 22): a guide during the goings and comings (*"roam"* suggests *"going astray"* which is not the point here) that work and leisure demand; a guard during the helpless hours of sleep; a concerned companion (*"speak"* understates the attention wisdom pays to its wards), present in the early waking hours before dawn and family break the silence. The threefold time frame parallels closely the words of the *Shema*: "You shall teach them diligently to your children, and shall talk of them when you sit in your house, and when you walk by the way, and when you lie down and when you rise up" (Deut. 6:7).

SHUN ADULTERY

6:23 For the commandment *is* a lamp,
    And the law a light;
    Reproofs of instruction *are* the way of life,

24 To keep you from the evil woman,
    From the flattering tongue of a seductress.

25 Do not lust after her beauty in your heart,
    Nor let her allure you with her eyelids.

26 For by means of a harlot
    A man is reduced to a crust of bread;
    And an adulteress will prey upon his precious
        life.

27 Can a man take fire to his bosom,
    And his clothes not be burned?

28 Can one walk on hot coals,
    And his feet not be seared?

29 So *is* he who goes in to his neighbor's wife;
    Whoever touches her shall not be innocent.

30 *People* do not despise a thief
    If he steals to satisfy himself when he is
        starving.

31 Yet *when* he is found, he must restore
   sevenfold;
   He may have to give up all the substance of
   his house.
32 Whoever commits adultery with a woman
   lacks understanding;
   He *who* does so destroys his own soul.
33 Wounds and dishonor he will get,
   And his reproach will not be wiped away.
34 For jealousy *is* a husband's fury;
   Therefore he will not spare in the day of
   vengeance.
35 He will accept no recompense,
   Nor will he be appeased though you give
   many gifts.

Prov. 6:23–35

It is clear from the outset of this passage that law and command featured in the call to attention (vv. 20–22) do not have in mind the whole range of human conduct but serve to summon the hearers to the seventh command, the prohibition of adultery (see Exod. 20:14; Deut. 5:18). One difference between Mosaic law and Solomonic wisdom becomes clear in this prolonged speech. Nothing is said here about Exodus or Covenant, with which the Ten Commandments are prefaced. Nor does the command stand alone, starkly stated without introduction or explanation. Of the thirteen verses only verse 25 contains commands. The rest of the speech (1) describes the role of wisdom as guard under the analogies of *"lamp," "light,"* and safe road (*"way,"* vv. 23–24); light almost uniformly in Scripture speaks of secure guidance, thanks to illumination that brightens the journey and exposes any threats or enemies; (2) features the seductive blandishments of the adulteress (v. 24); and (3) enumerates the manifold perils that await the adulterer (vv. 26–35).

The role of wisdom as guard (*"keep,"* v. 24) echoes the note in verse 22 and reprises a familiar theme (see on 2:8, 11; 4:6). *"Reproofs of instruction"* (or "discipline," v. 23) combines two favorite wisdom words that try to set wanderers straight and especially to head off any wandering even though the correction may be painful and embarrassing (see on 1:2–6, 23, 25, 30). The *"flattering tongue"* ("smooth speech," "sweet talk," v. 24) is a constant characteristic of the teachers' temptress (2:16; 5:3; 7:21). *"Eyelids"* (v. 25) here embellish the picture of charm—hence "eyelashes" in RSV—but elsewhere in Proverbs suggest a gaze fixed forward so as not to miss the path (v. 4) or a haughty look akin to that forbidden in verse 17 (30:13).

The command itself is simple and direct (v. 25). It warns not only against the act but against the coveting (*"lust"*) that leads to the act. Again we are close to the Decalogue—commandment ten: "you shall not covet your neighbor's wife" (Exod. 20:17). It realistically guards against the wiles of *"beauty"* of face and form and especially the ability of the eyes or eyelids, perhaps glistening with makeup or lustrous material, to *"allure,"* that is, "take in," "capture" as an army would take prisoners. Nothing feeds adultery like fantasy. Imagination, savoring in the soul the delights of an unlawful partner, is the fuel by which immorality is fired.

The range of new arguments mustered to reinforce the command is impressive (vv. 26–35; note *"for"* as the transition from admonition to motivation). First, a contrast is made between consorting casually with a *"harlot"* whose quick services can be purchased for a loaf of bread and entering an entangling alliance with an *"adulteress"* who will stalk *"his precious life"* as would a lioness a prized deer (v. 26). The Hebrew text is so brief that NKJV has added *"a man is reduced to"* (so NASB and NIV) and thus made the two lines of the verse synonymous and identified the harlot and the adulteress (lit., "wife of a man") as the same woman. (See RSV, NEB, JB for my interpretation.) The aim of this verse is not to condone harlotry (see 7:10; 23:27; 29:3) but to show how utterly destructive a semi-permanent sub rosa relationship can be.

Second, two rhetorical questions call attention to the third-degree burns suffered by those who expose themselves intimately to the fires of physical lust (vv. 27–29). *"Bosom"* (or "lap") and *"feet"* (at times a euphemism in the Old Testament for male genitals; Isa. 7:20; Gen. 49:10; 2 Sam. 11:8) speak of sexual activity. Engage them in the blazing ovens of illicit intercourse and your masculinity will be seared for life. There can be nothing *"innocent"* about such an act or those who indulge in it; they are guilty as sin. They know it, and so will the whole community once it is exposed (v. 29).

Third, a comparison is struck between an apprehended adulterer and a thief who *"steals"* to sate his hunger (vv. 30–31). Verse 30 should be heard as a question (see RSV; NEB treats v. 31 as a question also). Though the Hebrew text does not contain the usual indicators for interrogatives, the context suggests a rhetorical query which strengthens the contrast between thief and adulterer. Anyone who steals draws the spite of the community even though his personal need may be pressing. The punishment for such an offense is grievous: *"sevenfold"* restitution, a demand that seems to exceed what the law required (Exod. 22:1–8), even though it may take all his substance or material wealth to pay the fine. How much more expensive is the penalty for adultery, so runs the argument. The act stamps the adulterer as stupid (*"lacks understanding"* or "heart") and ultimately destroys his life, as *"soul"* here should be understood (v. 32).

Fourth, the *"fury"* of the husband's jealousy is unleashed on the adulterer (vv. 33–35). This assault seems to be carried on in public. Shame and reproach are the direct opposites of the honor and exaltation that wisdom proffers (4:8–9). Adulterers are losers not winners no matter how sweet their stolen hours may have seemed at the time. *"A day of vengeance,"* probably in court, is scheduled against them and neither an expensive bribe (so *"recompense"* may suggest) nor a multitude of *"gifts"* will save their skins. Whether or not the law of capital punishment (Lev. 20:10) was regularly enforced in such cases, we cannot know. But even if it were not, the inner guilt and social ostracism are a form of walking death.

This speech needs no specific illustration. Your mind like mine has conjured up a dozen memories of talented, dedicated, charming persons who committed emotional suicide and revoked their own credentials as Christian leaders by seeking gratification with persons off-limits to them. If Henry Kissinger's maxim is correct—"power is the ultimate aphrodisiac"—then leaders face a special responsibility to curb their lusts. If this was true of Israel's budding bureaucrats in Proverbs whose opportunities to be alone with married women were carefully delimited by the social mores, how much more does it apply to spiritual leaders today, much of whose ministry is one on one with persons who hang on their every word. Were Proverbs being written for our times it would alert us to the dangers of transference and countertransference where authority figure and eager follower, say counselor and counselee, entertain legitimate feelings for and expectations of each other. What starts as an arm's length face-to-face relationship tragically ends, all too often, as an intimate embrace more destructive to both parties than any outraged mother bear could inflict on a dog that tampered with her cub.

CHAPTER SEVEN

Smooth Coaxings and Deadly Results

Proverbs 7:1–27

You will see them on the streets of almost every large city. From sunset till well after midnight you can see them, standing on the corners, clustered at the entrances to bars, slipping into doorways of cheap hotels. Their dress is usually gaudy and tasteless; their cosmetics seem to have been applied with a palette knife.

Prostitutes they are, earning a living for themselves and their "managers" by selling their charms to anyone who will meet their price. There is nothing new about their practice. Harlots have plied their trade for thousands of years. The earliest written records of life in the Middle East mention prostitution as a part of the culture. They feed on the loneliness, boredom, lust, and insecurity of their customers. They live off the fragility and uncertainty of the male ego. The demand for their services does not seem to be waning.

All this is not to pick on them. Without gullible males they would be out of business. They are to be pitied as well as censured. I describe them and their work because they are a visible symbol of the agelong problem of chastity. The need for sexual discipline, the need to say "no" to offers of physical intimacy outside of marriage, is the dominant theme in the wisdom speeches of Proverbs 1–9. In chapter 7, it occupies the entire speech and centers in the peculiar temptations offered to the leaders in commerce and government which the young men of Proverbs were being trained to become.

If we can reconstruct the setting of the scene described here (vv. 6–23), it appears that a husband and wife of foreign citizenship are residing in Jerusalem. They are obviously people of means, perhaps diplomats or merchants. The husband has departed the country for a month, and the wife is left alone filled with desire and furnished with opportunity to engage in sexual activities with an upper-class Israelite man. To arrange the liaison she attires herself as a harlot in order to gain access to and attract the attention of someone for whom she craves. Her maneuvers are watched by the teacher who undergirds his warnings to the young by his personal experience.

The structure of the speech reflects the teacher's urgency. It begins and ends with calls to attention—the first positive, pointing to the benefits of a close attachment to wisdom and the sexual continence which that attachment will bring (vv. 1–5); the second negative, listing the deadly results awaiting those who buy the slick coaxings of the aristocratic harlot (vv. 24–27). Between the two calls is an extended description of the occasion of the seduction (vv. 6–9), the tactics of the temptress (vv. 10–20), and the response of the man who is the target of her wiles (vv. 21–23). "Chastity always makes sense" is the teacher's premise, and he makes the seduction especially attractive to pound home his point. An outline of the speech for teaching or preaching might look like this:

Introduction
    Rely on wisdom in times of temptation   7:1–5
Immorality is deceptive   7:6–9
    It is more apparent to others than to us
    It blocks the flow of our common sense
Immorality is hurtful to others   7:10–20
    The woman is degraded by her conduct
    The husband is betrayed by her infidelity
Immorality is death dealing in its outcome   7:21–23
    The overture is bright with promise
    The epilogue is dark with defeat
Conclusion
    Reject the seductive opportunity; it is a dance of death   7:24–27

INTRODUCTORY CALL TO ATTENTION—POSITIVE

7:1 My son, keep my words,
    And treasure my commands within you.
2 Keep my commands and live,
    And my law as the apple of your eye.
3 Bind them on your fingers;
    Write them on the tablet of your heart.
4 Say to wisdom, "You *are* my sister,"
    And call understanding *your* nearest kin.
5 That they may keep you from the immoral
    woman,

> From the seductress *who* flatters with her
> words.
>
> *Prov. 7:1–5*

The teacher uses a whole cluster of techniques to rivet the student's attention on the subject. First, the quartet of nouns in verses 1–2 emphasize the inescapable character of the admonitions— *"words," "commands"* (twice), and *"law"* (see at 6:20, 23) are not options or casual suggestions. Second, the vital nature of the theme is spotlighted in its life-giving (*"keep . . . and live"*; see Amos's *"seek me and live"* in 5:4) and light-bringing (*"the apple* [or pupil] *of the eye"* governs the amount of the light and the focus of our vision) qualities (v. 2). Third, *"bind"* and *"write"* (v. 3) mark it as a permanent and indelible truth to be carried with us and stamped within us, like Moses' command to love the Lord (Deut. 6:6, 8). Fourth, treasuring the teacher's law is tantamount to treating wisdom (and *"understanding"*) as *"sister"* and *"nearest kin"* (see Ruth 2:1; 3:2 for the same Hebrew root) and so making her not an abstract idea but a person whose love and care will protect (*"keep"* or guard) us from the flattery of the seductress (vv. 4–5), as Miriam guarded the young Moses, cradled in the reed basket and floating in the shallows of the Nile (Exod. 2:1–10). Fifth, the artistic use of word order in Hebrew thrusts the imperative verbs into urgent prominence by placing them first and last in their clauses: *"keep* my words and my commands *treasure"* (v. 1); *"say* to wisdom . . . and understanding *call"* (v. 4); the technique is called chiasm from the Greek letter *chi*, shaped like an *x*.

> Keep my words
> my commands treasure.

Draw a line connecting the verbs and another connecting the nouns and an *x* is formed. Sixth, the flattering (or smooth) words of the harlot (v. 5; see also 2:16; 5:3; 6:24) stand in bold contrast to the lawgiving, life-preserving words of the teacher (v. 1).

ILLUSTRATION FROM PERSONAL OBSERVATION

> 7:6 For at the window of my house
>   I looked through my lattice,
>   7 And saw among the simple,

I perceived among the youths,
A young man devoid of understanding,

8 Passing along the street near her corner;
And he took the path to her house

9 In the twilight, in the evening,
In the black and dark night.

10 And there a woman met him,
With the attire of a harlot, and a crafty heart.

11 She *was* loud and rebellious,
Her feet would not stay at home.

12 At times *she was* outside, at times in the open
square,
Lurking at every corner.

13 So she caught him and kissed him;
With an impudent face she said to him:

14 "*I have* peace offerings with me;
Today I have paid my vows.

15 So I came out to meet you,
Diligently to seek your face,
And I have found you.

16 I have spread my bed with tapestry,
Colored coverings of Egyptian linen.

17 I have perfumed my bed
With myrrh, aloes, and cinnamon.

18 Come, let us take our fill of love until morning;
Let us delight ourselves with love.

19 For my husband *is* not at home;
He has gone on a long journey;

20 He has taken a bag of money with him,
And will come home on the appointed day."

21 With her enticing speech she caused him
to yield,
With her flattering lips she seduced him.

22 Immediately he went after her, as an ox goes
to the slaughter,
Or as a fool to the correction of the stocks,

23 Till an arrow struck his liver.
As a bird hastens to the snare,
He did not know it *would cost* his life.

Prov. 7:6–23

Like any good teacher the wise one draws on personal experience to clinch the point. He apparently made it a practice to observe the habits of the young, as they gathered in the evening in the streets and

squares near his home (vv. 6–9). The *"window,"* designed to circulate
air and vent cooking smoke and other fumes, was conveniently
screened for shade and privacy. He could linger there *"in the twilight,"*
take in the scene, and never be discovered by the youth below.
"Simple" he called them, not in this case wicked but naive. One *"young
man"* was branded *"devoid of understanding"* (Heb. "heart") on the
basis of the bad choice he later made. That choice was not, apparently, the decision to walk near the harlot's *"house,"* although that did
ultimately have dire consequences. The bad choice began with the
impulse to leave the group and venture out alone into an evening so
"black" and *"dark"* that it seemed to offer anonymity and obscurity.
The thirst for illicit adventures, untried experiences, is part of the de-
ceptiveness of immorality. It was as though the teacher could have
predicted what the youth had only subliminal hankerings for. Naiveté
with a taste for the lurid had blocked the flow of the young man's
common sense.

The plot thickens with the appearances of the *"woman,"* whose encounter with the man is heralded in the Hebrew text with "behold"
(v. 10), marking the transition to the next scene. Her equipment is
twofold: *"the attire of a harlot,"* a cloak or veil perhaps combined
with erotic or outlandish jewelry (see Tamar's garb in Gen. 38:12–19
or Gomer/Israel's in Hos. 2:2, 13); *"a crafty heart,"* which concealed
an evil plan. Both the teacher and the youth discerned the clothing
in the fading light; only the teacher could penetrate the outer garments and read the woman's evil intent. He had dealt with the likes
of her before.

. He spotted her wantonness in her mannerisms—the *"loud"* and
unconventional (*"rebellious"* or stubborn) speech, blanched of all
grace and refinement (v. 11), the rapid, shifty movements that pro-
pelled her from her own property to the streets, plazas (*"square[s]"*),
and corners where she kept lurking, as though in ambush for her
prey (vv. 11–12). One can sense the teacher's outrage as he describes her degraded comportment. The hurtfulness of immorality
knows no bounds. Brazen lust has an aristocratic woman in its
clutches and it reduces her to the status of a sex-starved clown. Her
face was empty of all shame (*"impudent"*) as she smothered the
young man in her embraces and showered him with kisses (v. 13). Is
it possible that she knew him through the professional circles that
she and her husband frequented? The answer turns on whether the
"you" of verse 15 is specific—"you and no one else"—or general
"you," that is, "anyone" and "you happened to be he."

The text features her lust but not only her lust. Religious rituals seemed to have played a part in her frenzied search for the partner, (vv. 14–15). The *"peace offerings"* were to have been eaten in communion with others, and she needed a companion to dine with her in her empty home. The *"vows"* she paid may have included a vow to enjoy sexual intercourse as a ritual act of obedience to the priests before whom she took her vows. Hosea makes clear how much pagan practice of religious immorality had permeated Israel's life and culture. Whether these religious explanations were rationalizations for raw passion or whether they were part of her inner motivation we cannot say. The text surely indicates an eagerness that outruns any sense of mere duty. While the embroidered (*"colored"*) couch *"coverings"* and fragrant spices may have had a ceremonial meaning (vv. 16–17), the bottom line of the invitation is to passionate and prolonged lovemaking, as both Hebrew words for "love" make clear. The Song of Solomon uses them both and with great regularity to portray the delights of marital love. The clincher in this depiction of illicit, though perhaps religious passion, is the woman's explanation that her *"husband"* is away on *"a long journey,"* probably out of the country, and is not slated to return until the "full moon," as *"appointed day"* is better translated (vv. 19–20). The entire absence may be a month, since the description of darkness (v. 9) and the time of sacrifice (v. 14) may suggest that the whole episode began at the new moon. Her invitation may be first to one night (*"until morning,"* v. 18) and then to many more.

A double standard, where males were granted sexual liberties denied to women, was not uncommon in the ancient world; nor is it today. The fact that she pinpoints the absence of her man as the occasion for the rendezvous strongly suggests that she took no such freedom when he was around. Add then to immorality's list of its walking wounded the name of the husband betrayed and deceived yet able to do nothing about it. His reputation was bound to be battered, his ego assaulted at its most fragile point. Was the wise teacher the only observer of the shameful scene? Not likely.

The proposition, so slickly put, so piously argued, so winsomely supported, gained the response she had in mind (vv. 21–22). *"He immediately went after her,"* without pausing to reflect, investigate, or seek outside counsel. At that moment the foreign woman became his authority, replacing the law of Moses and the commands of his teacher. The outcome was not what she had advertised—not the final outcome at least. Ecstasy there may have been, the stupefying satisfaction of embraces and orgasms spiced by a whole cupboard of erotic techniques and enjoyed in a setting of exotic sights and smells.

But, as the teacher brilliantly perceived, immorality's destructive powers are massive. The bedroom was a slaughterhouse and the lad a dumb *"ox"* who walked blandly into the butcher's knife (v. 22) or a stag who pranced gleefully to the hunter's noose only to feel the bite of an *"arrow"* in his *"liver"* (read this kind of emendation of the Hebrew with NEB, JB, and NIV), or a *"bird"* flitting into the *"snare"* that spells its doom. The first thing said about him in this detailed account of the setting and springing of the trap was that he was "devoid of understanding" (v. 7). The last thing showed how devoid he was: *"he did not know"* that the chance encounter would cost him his life (v. 23). Evidently there is something about sexual immorality that anesthetizes our judgment. Part of it, I suppose, is the sheer passion involved. More than one sorry culprit has said to me, "I never thought it could happen. Before I really knew what was going on I had committed the adulterous act." Adrenalin shoots through our systems, hormones race about in our bodies, our nerves are all a-tingling. The chemistry and neurology that God placed within us to urge us to populate the earth and to bind us to our life partners is set to boiling in the wrong laboratory and with the wrong coworker. Nothing less than sheer mayhem is the result.

CONCLUDING CALL TO ATTENTION—NEGATIVE

7:24 Now therefore, listen to me, *my* children;
    Pay attention to the words of my mouth:
  25 Do not let your heart turn aside to her ways,
    Do not stray into her paths;
  26 For she has cast down many wounded,
    And all who were slain by her were strong *men*.
  27 Her house *is* the way to hell,
    Descending to the chambers of death.
                       Prov. 7:24–27

The audience is expanded to include the whole classroom—*"my children"* (v. 24)—despite the fact that the lesson began with an address to an individual—my son (v. 1). The temptation to sexual immorality is universal, though it touches some with greater intensity than others. The naive young man began his downfall by taking the wrong path (v. 8). His fellows are warned once more against that choice (v. 25). The roads of life are strewn with the bones of those who followed the siren songs of temptresses like this one. Even the *"strong"* turn weak when they pause to ponder her melody (v. 26). The roads to Sheol (*"hell,"* the grave or the dim, gray, joyless abode of the dead) pass through her house, and from there keep descending to the realm of *"death"* (v. 27).

There were pagan overtones in the harlot's account of sacrifices and vows (v. 14). If she was a non-Israelite, resident in the holy land, as we have assumed, she would have been a devotee of pagan gods, either of Egypt (see v. 16) or Canaan. If the latter is the case, there may be another echo of pagan mythology in the mention of "Sheol" and "death" in verse 27. Death (Mot) was a Canaanite deity to whom was credited the long winter drought which Baal had to conquer if the vernal fertility was to be enjoyed in the land. The ritual act of intercourse to which the woman invited the young man was designed to encourage Baal to have intercourse with the goddess Anat and thus fertilize the land. In a subtle yet telling bit of irony, this wisdom speech, as its last word, may be saying that Mot not Baal, death not sexual prosperity, is the ultimate conqueror when the divine command is paid no heed.

CHAPTER EIGHT

Ancient Credentials and Contemporary Calling

Proverbs 8:1–36

The aim of the speeches in Proverbs 1–9 has been to accent wisdom's worth and thus attract the young students who will be Israel's future leaders to pursue it with might and mane. This chapter is the core course in the teacher's curriculum. It weaves together a number of key themes: (1) it features the attractiveness of wisdom by bringing to full bloom the buds of personification that sprouted in 1:20–33 and 7:4, as wisdom, in human guise, calls for attention and describes her credentials in most impressive terms; (2) it fills in the details of the picture of wisdom's presence at creation sketched in 3:19–20; (3) it connects wisdom with the fear of the Lord by naming wisdom as the chief God-fearer (v. 13; see on 1:7); (4) it links wisdom to practical deeds of righteousness and justice (v. 20; see on 2:9–15); (5) it contrasts wisdom's positive and profitable call with the seductive beckonings of the temptress whose face has appeared on virtually every page of these speeches (2:16–19; 5:1–23; 6:23–35; 7:1–27); (6) it illuminates the path of righteousness, the only viable route in life (v. 32; see on 4:18–27); (7) it underlines the importance of choice by showing that issues which lead to life, on the one hand, or death, on the other (vv. 35–36), call for the strongest personal response—love (vv. 17, 36), absence of which is tantamount to hate.

The breakdown of the chapter follows its literary structure, which in turn gives us clues as to the intention and purpose of each section.

The call to attention (vv. 1–9) is the longest in the book, a fact which in itself shows how passionately the teacher wanted the pupils to face the claims of wisdom. There follow two self-descriptions which argue for the validity of wisdom (vv. 10–21) and the authority of wisdom (vv. 22–31). The speech closes with a three-part conclusion—a brief call to attention (vv. 32–33) that echoes the opening, a beatitude that promises happiness to wisdom's devotees (v. 34), and an antithetic summary (vv. 35–36) that reminds us of life's basic choice and its infinite consequences.

In loftiness and grandeur this speech rises from the pages of Proverbs like the Jungfrau over Interlaken or Rainier above Puget Sound. It is the summit of Old Testament discipleship, inviting all who see it to mount the slopes of righteousness and justice, goodness and mercy, and from there to see life as God intended in those days when He called creation into being and shaped humankind in His own image. Wisdom laughed for joy when He did, and all who truly seek her by fearing God are promised a share in that pristine happiness.

INTRODUCTORY CALL TO ATTENTION—EXTENDED

8:1 Does not wisdom cry out,
    And understanding lift up her voice?
2 She takes her stand on the top of the high hill,
    Beside the way, where the paths meet.
3 She cries out by the gates, at the entry of
    the city,
    At the entrance of the doors:
4 "To you, O men, I call,
    And my voice *is* to the sons of men.
5 O you simple ones, understand prudence,
    And you fools, be of an understanding heart.
6 Listen, for I will speak of excellent things,
    And from the opening of my lips *will come*
    right things;
7 For my mouth will speak truth;
    Wickedness *is* an abomination to my lips.
8 All the words of my mouth *are* with
    righteousness;
    Nothing crooked or perverse *is* in them.
9 They *are* all plain to him who understands,
    And right to those who find knowledge."
Prov. 8:1–9

This is wisdom's call to attention, not just the command of the teacher. As such its components ask for special attention. The extended form (cf. 1:8–9; 4:1–2, 10; 5:1, 7; 7:24) is a clue to the unique importance of this particular call. Its grammatical structure centers in the three imperatives of verses 5–6: *"understand," "be of an understanding heart,"* and *"listen,"* but its meaning centers in the lessons it conveys about wisdom. Those lessons frame the outline of our study.

Wisdom's call is certain (v. 1). The rhetorical question, clearly marked in Hebrew by the question indicator attached to the word *"not,"* tolerates no other answer but "yes." Of course, wisdom does call. She shouts, in fact. She cares too much to keep silent. Her message is too important to be whispered. She has no intention of letting her righteous cause be drowned in the sea of wicked propositions that threaten to engulf the young—propositions from greedy savages (1:10–19), from men of lying speech (2:12–15), from women of smooth words (2:16–19), from the perverters of righteousness (4:14–17), from wretches who sow discord (6:12–15). The battle is joined, and a shaky trumpet will not summon the troops. Wisdom leaves no doubt about the importance and meaning of her call.

Wisdom's call is public (vv. 2–3). Hers is not a private word of inner piety alone. It sounds from the hilltop like a watchman's warning; it rings from the junctions of the main roads where merchants, travelers, pilgrims, farmers, and soldiers salute each other; it echoes in the gates of the city where deals are struck, political decisions made, and judicial verdicts rendered. It is wisdom in the public domain, shaping the entire life of the community. It calls for obedience in politics, commerce, community relations, as well as religious activities. We do well to hear this public call. It tells us that, though church and state may be separated by the First Amendment, our faith must inform and govern our behavior in all areas of life. There can be no true discipleship which is only private. The places from which wisdom lifts her persistent voice are the very places where our witness is needed.

Wisdom's call is personal (vv. 4–5). It is addressed to the human family, called here *"men,"* *"sons of men"* (or "children of Adam"), *"simple ones"* (see on 1:4), and *"fools"* (see on 1:32). In the context, the last two terms may be understood in the light of the first two. Every human being has great capacity for simpleminded foolishness. The address is not specifically to a group of naive or wicked persons but to all of us who carry the constant potential of foolish conduct. We can almost see her gesturing, pointing, beckoning; we can almost hear her shouting, "You, yes, I mean you, wise up." Learn how to be successful by doing the right thing (*"prudence,"* or *"cunning"*; see on 1:4); *"understand"* what common sense (*"heart"*) means and how to apply it in your daily choices.

Wisdom's call is reliable (vv. 6–9). In a society that bristled with perverse speech—crooked, foolish teachings, unreliable opinions and advice (2:12; 6:12–15)—words that you could bank on were worth their weight in platinum. The cluster of terms describing wisdom's teaching is a who's who of commendable expressions: *"excellent"* (or *"outstanding,"* v. 6) suggests a loftiness and nobility of subject matter; *"right things"* (v. 6) and *"right"* (v. 9) ring with integrity and uprightness; *"truth"* (v. 7) connotes accuracy and dependability; *"righteousness"* (v. 8) points to straight talk that has a helpful, healing intent; *"plain"* (v. 9) also means straightforward, on target in terms of truthfulness and moral rectitude. Part of wisdom's reliability is her rejection (*"abomination,"* v. 7) of everything that is the opposite of truth: *"wickedness"* (v. 7) is the inner turbulence of those who choose against God's ways and consequently disrupt the stability of their communities; *"crooked"* and *"perverse"* (v. 8) both depict twistedness, contortedness of speech that bends the truth either by deliberate misstatement or by conscious omission of relevant facts.

Wisdom's call is purposeful. *"Understanding"* (note the verb in v. 9) and *"knowledge"* (v. 9) are its goal. As frequently in Proverbs, knowledge is more than possessing general information, as we would call it—"being knowledgeable," "well read," "thoroughly informed." It almost always is carefully aimed, precise knowledge that the sages commend: the knowledge of God in His gifts of grace and His demands of obedience (see on 1:7). Such knowledge leads not to Phi Beta Kappa keys or large winnings on game shows or even Nobel prizes. It leads to discipleship—no less, no more.

The Apostle Paul sounds like one of wisdom's disciples in his own call to wisdom:

> Whatever things are true, whatever things are noble,
> whatever things are just, whatever things are lovely,
> whatever things are of good report, . . . meditate
> on these things.
>
> *Phil. 4:8*

What wisdom offered in Prov. 8:6–9 is precisely what Paul commends to the Philippian believers and to the rest of us.

SELF-DESCRIPTION OF ASSETS

8:10 "Receive my instruction, and not silver,
    And knowledge rather than choice gold;
11 For wisdom *is* better than rubies,
    And all the things one may desire cannot be
    compared with her.

12 "I, wisdom, dwell with prudence,
   And find out knowledge *and* discretion.
13 The fear of the LORD *is* to hate evil;
   Pride and arrogance and the evil way
   And the perverse mouth I hate.
14 Counsel *is* mine, and sound wisdom;
   I *am* understanding, I have strength.
15 By me kings reign,
   And rulers decree justice.
16 By me princes rule, and nobles,
   All the judges of the earth.
17 I love those who love me,
   And those who seek me diligently will
      find me.
18 Riches and honor *are* with me.
   Enduring riches and righteousness.
19 My fruit *is* better than gold, yes, than fine gold,
   And my revenue than choice silver.
20 I traverse the way of righteousness,
   In the midst of the paths of justice,
21 That I may cause those who love me to inherit
      wealth,
   That I may fill their treasuries."

Prov. 8:10–21

The command *"receive"* marks the beginning of a new section
and reminds us of the imperative mood that begins (vv. 5–6) and
concludes (vv. 32–33) the speech. The admonitions are essential to
help us catch the sense of the passage—wisdom is commanding—
but what the commands actually do is provide a framework within
which wisdom establishes the right to issue her call and the results
in the lives of those who respond. In a typical admonition (e.g.,
24:1) the command is stated in two parallel lines and the motivation to obey it in two more parallel lines. In this section of wisdom's speech, however, the command follows that pattern, but the
motivation, introduced by *"for,"* consumes the next twenty-three
lines. Structure, then, highlights the command but bulk tells us
what wisdom really has in mind. Therefore, the term "self-description"—note the I's, me's, my's—is the appropriate rubric under
which to grasp the meaning of this section and the one that follows
(vv. 22–31).

Wisdom's worth is displayed in terms of the most valuable things
imaginable (vv. 11–12): *"silver,"* in Israel's early history the
most precious metal thanks to its scarcity; *"choice gold,"* thoroughly

refined, purged of dross, and polished to high luster; *"rubies"* or perhaps *"red corals,"* rare and lustrous stones; *"the things one may desire"* may be the blanket term for all manner of wealth, beautiful artifacts and so forth, or it may describe "jewelry" (see NEB) which in antiquity was the most portable, guardable, displayable form of riches. Material success was undoubtedly a high ambition of the "Yuppies" of antiquity. Wisdom claims, with a cogency that our materialistic generation needs to hear, to be of infinitely more value than any material goods.

Wisdom's worth is implied in the variety of terms used to describe her. The thesaurus of synonyms which was showcased in 1:2–6 (see for definitions) is opened once more before us. Wisdom includes understanding or "insight" as the parallelism of verse 1 (see also 7:4) indicates. She has *"prudence"* for a roommate (*"dwell with,"* v. 12), and she possesses the ability to keep discovering (*"find out,"* the tense is imperfect) *"knowledge and discretion"* or knowledge *of* discretion, as the Hebrew may be read. Verses 12–14 comment on the comparison between wisdom and wealth (vv. 10–11) by hinting that wisdom can lead to successful plans that will produce wealth and many other signs of achievement, since both prudence and discretion are terms that to the Israelite ears would convey the picture of practical, tangible success granted to the shrewd or clever.

Wisdom's piety is portrayed in verse 13. The placement of this pronouncement, which seems to separate verse 12 from verse 14, as an abrupt intrusion, reminds us that shrewdness and cleverness can lead to all kinds of trouble when they are not controlled by *"the fear of the Lord,"* which by definition prompts us to *"hate evil,"* especially the evil of *"pride and arrogance"* to which shrewd and clever persons are especially prone. Such pride turns all values upside down, as *"perverse"* literally means (see on 2:14). Bragging of achievements as though we accomplished them without divine grace is theologically as perverse as speech can get. Wisdom's deepest goal is to get us to trust God. Self-trust especially when it is arrogantly broadcast is the constant target of her hatred, because it is the exact opposite of fearing God (see 1:7).

Wisdom's competence can be celebrated because it flows from that very fear (vv. 14–16). It includes precisely what the young leaders needed to serve well their nation and their countrymen. *"Counsel"* is the ability to make decisions and shape plans that will have beneficial outcomes for all involved. *"Sound wisdom"* is strategy that really works and enjoys lasting success (see on 3:21). *"Understanding"* here is not compassion or sympathy, as sometimes it is in our speech but penetrating insight, the skill of dissecting an issue into its component parts and seeing right to the heart of the matter (see on 1:2; 4:1; 7:4). All of these tools allow such significant accomplishment, such effective disposal of problems, such powerful development of courses of action in politics or economics or justice that they can be accompanied by the word *"strength"* or *"might."*

Wisdom is due the credit wherever right decisions (called *"justice"* in v. 15) are taken by the responsible and esteemed leaders of a nation: *"kings"*; dignitaries (*"nobles"* translates an ancient term for *"potentates,"* persons who carry weight in their society, Judg. 5:3); *"princes"* means high government officials and may include military responsibility (*"commanders"*); *"nobles"* (v. 16) reflects a Hebrew title suggesting princely persons who not only hold high rank but are generous in spirit as they wield their authority; *"judges"* may be either a noun or a participle *"judging,"* whose object is probably *"earth"* as NKJV has it, a reading that follows the Greek text and is adopted by most modern versions (NASB is the exception reading with MT, *"rightly"*). Wisdom provides the perspective and the power to see issues clearly and pursue them courageously. What a sorely needed word this is in a world where politicians boast of their exploits and bury their failures in their frenzied efforts to grasp or maintain positions of power! How much more honest would we all be if God's wisdom got the credit for our success and we forthrightly shouldered the blame for our folly!

Wisdom's rewards are listed as the climax of this section (8:17–21). Part of what makes wisdom different is her care (*"love"*) of those who value her (v. 17). Her call conceals no plan to exploit, no desire to use and then abandon. She is not only bright, she is good; she makes herself available to all who single-mindedly pursue her. Their welfare is her aim. And that welfare is detailed in spectacular terms: *"riches,"* *"honor"* (or *"glory"*), *"enduring"* material wealth (the second Hebrew word for *"riches"* is a synonym of the first), and *"right-eousness,"* which here means *"victorious success"* based on maintaining right relations with God and His people (v. 18). She is like a productive orchard or vineyard whose *"fruit"* and *"revenue"* (or *"crop"*) are priceless. Righteousness and justice (see at 2:8–9) may well be the fruit she refers to (v. 20). They describe how she comports herself (*"traverse"* or *"walk"*) and what accordingly she has to teach others (for righteousness and justice as fruit, see Isa. 5:7). *"Wealth"* and *"treasuries"* may also be understood as more than materials. To would-be leaders charged with the implementation of righteousness and justice (see Ps. 72:1–2), what would be a greater boon than to have a vault stocked with those precious necessities?

SELF-DESCRIPTION OF PRESENCE AT CREATION

8:22 "The LORD possessed me at the beginning of
    His way,
    Before His works of old.
  23 I have been established from everlasting,
    From the beginning, before there was ever
    an earth.
  24 When *there were* no depths I was brought
    forth,
    When *there were* no fountains abounding with
    water.
  25 Before the mountains were settled,
    Before the hills, I was brought forth;
  26 While as yet He had not made the earth or
    the fields,
    Or the primal dust of the world.
  27 When He prepared the heavens, I *was* there,
    When He drew a circle on the face of the deep,
  28 When He established the clouds above,
    When He strengthened the fountains of the
    deep,
  29 When He assigned to the sea its limit,
    So that the waters would not transgress His
    command,
    When He marked out the foundations of the
    earth,
  30 Then I was beside Him *as* a master craftsman;
    And I was daily *His* delight,
    Rejoicing always before Him,
  31 Rejoicing in His inhabited world,
    And my delight *was* with the sons of men."

Prov. 8:22–31

Wisdom warms to her task of making clear why she, not Dame Folly, should be heeded and followed. Her self-description turns from her present assets to her past experience, as a witness to and celebrant in God's creation. As Job had learned, an understanding of the mysteries of creation was one major distinction between God and him. God had been there, knew all about it, and was responsible for it. Job had not, did not, and was not (Job 38:1–42:6). What the sages craved more than anything else was insight into the way creation worked. To understand its patterns and processes was to clutch the key to life. Wisdom gives herself the ultimate commendation when she says, "I was there when it happened." Folly can only stand in the corner and cringe with her hand over her mouth in the face of that claim.

Wisdom was present at the creation (vv. 22–29). She recounts her presence and the priority it gives her over all other virtues in some of the loftiest language the Bible contains. First, her antiquity is featured in verses 22–23 where the dominant words are *"beginning,"* *"of old,"* *"from everlasting,"* and *"before."* Second, her priority is stressed in verses 24–26 as she recalls a time when there was not even a drop of water—*"no depths"* or oceans, *"no fountains"* or rivers. Since the Genesis account mentions the deep and waters in its second verse, wisdom's claim is a vaunted one. See also the division of the waters above from the waters below on day two (Gen. 1:6–8). *"Before"* (v. 25) and *"while as yet"* (v. 26) introduce her claim to outrank the *"mountains,"* *"hills,"* *"earth,"* and *"fields,"* all part of the dry land that appeared on the third day (Gen. 1:9–13). Third, throughout this text, wisdom's humility should be noted. Her claims are unique but not overweening: she plainly recognizes the difference between her and the Creator—a crucial recognition. Twice she speaks of her own origin: *"I was brought forth"* (vv. 24–25), the terminology of childbirth. This clear term helps us interpret her claim in verse 22: *"The Lord possessed me"* translates an ambiguous word that can also mean "created me" (see NEB, JB, RSV). The context supports the latter meaning, as does the Greek translation. Vital as is wisdom to the divine plan, she is part of the creation not a cocreator.

Fourth, wisdom's witness to the creation is spelled out in verses 27–29. The clause that governs the meaning and should be repeated with each clause in this section is *"I was there"* (v. 27). The setting in Genesis is again days two and three with the formation of the *"heavens,"* the marking off of the horizon of the sea (v. 27), the division of the waters above (*"clouds"*) from the waters below (*"fountains of the deep,"* v. 28), the setting of the boundaries of the *"sea,"* and the lining out of the earth's *"foundations"* (v. 29). All that divine surveying and construction wisdom watched. She was privy to the how's and what's and Who of those mysterious beginnings—prime credentials for any teacher.

But wisdom was not only present at creation, she was also a participant in creation (vv. 30–31). If we catch her meaning, she was a cheerleader as the repetitions of *"delight"* and *"rejoicing"* ("sporting" or "laughing") imply. *"Master craftsman"* is the conventional rendering of the pivotal word to describe wisdom's role and relationship to the Creator (see RSV, JB, NASB, NIV). A slight change in the Hebrew vowels produces a sense of "young, dependent child" or "ward" (NEB "darling"), a meaning which accords better with all the playfulness inherent in the text. Like a gleeful little kid, wisdom is so excited by the majesty and power of the creation that she jokes and laughs about it *"daily"* with the Creator, who takes exquisite *"delight"* in her jollity. Her joy reaches its apex in the creation of the human family (*"sons of men"*) on the sixth day. Remember that she had cried out to the sons of men in verse 4. No wonder she cared about them; she had watched their mother and father come fresh from the hand of God.

A startling view of creation this is. Not a struggle among the gods for mastery of the cosmos, as the Babylonians saw it, not an ageless, gray, grim quest for survival by adaptation as atheistic evolution views it, but high comedy applauded and enhanced by wisdom herself. We may venture to say that this picture of sporting laughter is more than wisdom's reminiscence. It may be another subtle argument for her infinite superiority to folly. Is she saying, "Follow me, and life will never be drab?" Is she nudging her hearers away from their innate prejudice against discipline by teaching them that creation's order and pattern were formed in a context of humor and should still be *"enjoyed"* while they are being discerned and obeyed?

In the providence of God, this chapter, notably verses 22–29 (and 35–36), has contributed as much to expressions of Christian faith as any text in the whole Old Testament. Three of the strongest affirmations of the deity and preexistence of Jesus Christ are grounded in its thought and language: John 1:1–14; Col. 1:15–20; Heb. 1:1–4. In each case the theme is the unique superiority of Christ over all claimants to equality or intimacy with God. The early church knew from His claims, His miracles, His teaching, and His presence that Jesus was not just a man with incredible spiritual power and perception. They knew, those first Christians, that in dealing with Jesus they were dealing with the eternal God.

But the transcendent monotheism of the Hebrew Scriptures gave them no language with which to express plurality in the Godhead. The unity of God was the relentless note sounded in the Law and the Prophets and the Psalms. How could that now be expanded to include room for the Lord Christ, both preexistent and incarnate? "What language shall I borrow to praise Thee, Savior, Friend?" was the way the hymn writer phrased their question. Proverbs 8 provided the answer. Wisdom's preexistence, participation in the creation, life-giving power, and call to exclusive allegiance furnished the Christian vocabulary for the ultimate exaltation and adoration of Christ.

The links between wisdom and the Messiah are dramatically highlighted in Henry Sloan Coffin's translation of the Old Latin hymn which applies equally to Christ's two comings:

> O come, Thou Wisdom from on high
> And order all things, far and nigh.
> To us the path of knowledge show,
> And cause us in her ways to go.
> Rejoice! Emmanuel shall come to thee, O Israel.

CONCLUDING CALL TO ATTENTION

> 8:32 "Now therefore, listen to me, *my* children,
>   For blessed *are those who* keep my ways.
>   33 Hear instruction and be wise,
>   And do not disdain *it.*"
>   *Prov. 8:32–33*

Wisdom has made her case. Her assets are sterling, her credentials impeccable. She has more than earned the right to be heard. She need say little more about herself, so she returns to her first concern: the welfare of the disciples whom she is recruiting. To them she throws a beatitude as if it were a bouquet. Her *"ways,"* her *"instruction"* or discipline (see on 1:2–6) are the road to happiness (*"blessed,"* see on 3:13). Wisdom has made her case; they now must make their choices. Her self-descriptions are not just erudite lectures, learned discourses on the sequence of creation. They are motivations, impassioned arguments designed to evoke an obedient response. Discipleship is not just studying; it is deciding. *"Hear"* or *"disdain"*—those are the options, whether it is wisdom calling "Listen to me" or Jesus, the greater Wisdom, calling "Follow me."

BEATITUDE AS SUMMARY

> 8:34 "Blessed is the man who listens to me,
>   Watching daily at my gates,
>   Waiting at the posts of my doors."
>   *Prov. 8:34*

Wisdom, who had pictured her own happiness at the prospect of creation and the utter delight which the Lord took in her joy, now throws another bouquet of beatitude to her audience. Joy-bringing-success is what she promises. *"Blessed"* or *"happy"* is one of Hebrew's most comprehensive words for human well-being (see on 3:13–14). It captures the goal of human life as well as any word we have. Its price is total dedication to the claims, aims, and arts of wisdom, dedication symbolized in the vigilant *"watching"* and *"waiting"* (or *"standing guard"*) in front of wisdom's house (see on 9:1).

ANTITHETIC SUMMARY

8:35 "For whoever finds me finds life,
And obtains favor from the LORD;
36 But he who sins against me wrongs his
own soul;
All those who hate me love death."
Prov. 8:35–36

The tug of war between wisdom and folly for the loyalty of the heart is perpetual in Proverbs. It will dominate the argument of chapter 9. Here it is featured as a stark and simple summary of how wisdom sees the issues. They are white and black. The form is antithetic in that the first verse states the positive results of choosing wisdom, and the second the negative. Beyond that it is chiastic. The first line opposes the fourth, and the second line counters the third: *"life"* in line one is the alternative to *"death"* in line four; *"favor from the Lord"* in line two contrasts with *"wrongs [or "does violence to"] his own soul [or "self," "person"]"* in line three. The envelope pattern thrusts the outer lines into prominence—the ultimate contest between life and death. The inner lines define what the outer mean: finding favor from the Lord is an explanation of life; wronging oneself is a description of death.

Thus does wisdom conclude her call. She yields nothing to Joshua (chap. 24) in riveting the attention of her hearers on the ultimacy of their decision. Both say "Choose this day whom you will serve." Both make clear the consequences of that choice.

CHAPTER NINE

Two Calls and Two Responses

Proverbs 9:1–18

Like the last movement of a sonata or symphony, this final chapter of the wisdom speeches recapitulates the major motifs of chapters 1–8. It pits Lady Wisdom (vv. 1–6) and Dame Folly (vv. 13–18) against each other in language that is unmistakably parallel (cf. vv. 4 and 16). The issues of choice that have dotted every page and virtually every paragraph are here made starkly clear. They are nothing less than life (v. 6) or death (v. 18) matters, just as they have been all along. And the choices are put to the same audience that has been in view throughout Proverbs thus far—the simple (or naive), the one who lacks understanding (lit., "heart"; see 7:7). As the two calls of wisdom and folly are compressed in a handful of verses each, so the two possible responses are condensed in a remarkably brief and powerful section (vv. 7–12) which both separates and connects the words of the two archenemies. The possibility of a negative response to wisdom's overture had already been faced in 1:22–32. The benefit of a positive response was the theme of 1:33 and 8:32–36. The two calls, then, and the two possible answers capture much of the mood of the wisdom speeches in a highly digested format.

An analysis of the structure pictures for us the ways in which these closing words sum up both the intent and the content of Proverbs 1–8 and provide a fitting conclusion to this introductory section of the book.

Wisdom's call	9:1–6
Description of feast	9:1–2
Dispatch of maidens as heralds	9:3
Words of invitation	9:4–6
Wisdom's reception	9:7–12
Rejection by wicked scoffers	9:7
Admonitions to teachers	9:8–9
Restatement of theme	9:10–11; see 1:7

Chapter 9 is an envelope: it begins and ends with calls to eat, one issued by wisdom, the other by folly. In the heart of the envelope (vv. 7–12) are the descriptions and commands about dealing with the scoffer and the wise, who mark the two ways in which the calls can be answered. Chapter 9 is an envelope within an envelope, since at the heart of it stand the theme words "the fear of the Lord is the beginning of wisdom" (v. 10) which aims to distill the message of chapters 1–9 just as "the fear of the Lord is the beginning of knowledge" served to anticipate it in 1:7.

What this final speech tells us, then, are these things: (1) wisdom and folly vie for our human allegiance; (2) that ultimate choice lies with us and which call we answer, with whom we choose to eat; (3) scoffers can be so hardened in their choice that they do harm to the teacher who challenges them; the wise are so open to wisdom's call that even her rebuke will spark their affection; (4) behind wisdom's invitation stands Yahweh; to say yes to wisdom is to respond in reverent obedience to Him; (5) to heed folly's call is to forsake the land of the living and to join the company of the dead. All these themes we have met before but never so adroitly packaged, never so compellingly stated. Their bold succinctness and vivid personification give them an irrefutable power.

DESCRIPTION OF WISDOM'S WHOLESOME INVITATION

> 9:1 Wisdom has built her house,
>   She has hewn out her seven pillars;
>   2 She has slaughtered her meat,
>   She has mixed her wine,
>   She has also furnished her table.
>   3 She has sent out her maidens,
>   She cries out from the highest places of
>   the city,
>   4 "Whoever *is* simple, let him turn in here!"
>   *As for* him who lacks understanding, she says
>   to him,

5 "Come, eat of my bread
   And drink of the wine I have mixed.
6 Forsake foolishness and live,
   And go in the way of understanding."

Prov. 9:1–6

What kind of scene is this? Is it a picture of genteel hospitality like a barbecue at an antebellum mansion in Georgia or of a religious festival in Jerusalem's temple? Is conviviality the point or participation in spiritual sacrifice and cleansing? The answer seems almost to be a tossup. Almost, but not quite. The picture of the *"house"* and its *"seven pillars"* (v. 1) seems to fit the architecture of a shrine rather than a family dwelling. The *"furnished* [or "prepared"] *table"* echoes language of Ps. 23:5, which the old Scots paraphrased so memorably:

A table thou hast furnishe'd
in presence of my foes.

The reference is to God's hospitality in the temple as the psalm's closing verse indicates. Perhaps most important the picture of wisdom is designed to counterbalance the sketch of folly inviting the young to commit adultery—both literally and spiritually—in her precincts (v. 17). The contrast, then, takes on the deepest possible significance. The choice is not good conduct versus bad, though that choice is life-shaking; it is at bottom the choice between true worship and false, between Yahweh whose sovereignty and order make wisdom what she is and the fatal attractions of immorality and idolatry for whom folly is the pitchwoman.

If this interpretation is valid and wisdom's invitation is to worship as well as learn, then verse 6 needs to be heard as a description of a turning point in the faith of wisdom's disciples—the plural audience is indicated in the plural form of all three imperatives. *"Forsake foolishness"* means "abandon your foolish tendencies to heed folly's call to fornication and pagan worship"; note that folly is called "simple" (v. 13), a term from the same root as "foolishness" in verse 6. *"Live"* means "accept the gift of life," even "the verdict of life" from the Lord, the righteous Judge; note the identification of the hearer as "just" (v. 9) and the verdict rendered by Yahweh in Ezek. 18:9, when He pronounces the devoutly obedient person as just and then adds the judicial pronouncement: "He shall surely live!" *"Understanding"* (or "insight") may also take on a deeper meaning—"the ability to discern the difference between true worship and false."

ADMONITIONS ON DIFFERENCES BETWEEN SCOFFERS AND WISE

> 9:7 "He who corrects a scoffer gets shame for
>   himself,
>   And he who rebukes a wicked *man only* harms
>   himself.
> 8 Do not correct a scoffer, lest he hate you;
>   Rebuke a wise *man,* and he will love you.
> 9 Give *instruction* to a wise *man,* and he will be
>   still wiser;
>   Teach a just *man,* and he will increase in
>   learning."
>
> *Prov. 9:7–9*

Is wisdom still speaking in this section? "By me" in verse 11 suggests that she is. If so, both the subject and the audience of her call have changed. Her audience now must not be the youth but a wisdom teacher whom she advises on the differing responses to be expected from instructing wise persons or scoffers. The banquet scene of 9:1–6 is out of view. An alternative approach is to read "by me" in verse 11 as "by it," that is, "by the fear of God" or "by the knowledge of the Holy One your days will be multiplied." The Greek text supports such an interpretation at the beginning of verse 11: "For in this manner" replaces "by me" and obviously refers to verse 10. The speaker in that case would be not wisdom but the teacher whose aim is to account for the contrasting responses of the wicked and the righteous hearers so that the students would be thoroughly alert to the strength of the negative reactions which wisdom's call may receive. "Do not underestimate the power of perverseness" is the sage advice of the wise. So perverse is it that attempts to *"correct"* or *"rebuke"* it end in *"shame"* and *"harm"* to the teacher (v. 7). The arrows of instruction seem to bounce off their target and ricochet to strike the one who launched them. *"Shame"* and *"blemish"* describe the insult, the embarrassment, and the sense of rejection that come from reaching out to help a victim of entrenched foolishness (*"a scoffer"*) and getting your hand slashed in the effort. "Beware of the teacher's risks" is the gist of the saying.

"Choose your pupil wisely" is the point of verse 8. Trying to coax one who mocks truth, morality, and wisdom to change his ways will only intensify his ire and turn him completely against you (*"hate"*). Your efforts will only add insult to injury. Spite will be the tuition paid you for your services. Better by far to spend your energies on the teachable; even if you show them where they are wrong they will shower you with appreciation and esteem (*"love"*). So open are they—the *"wise"* person and the *"just"* one (the one who wants to do right and who is fair-minded in evaluating the words of the teacher)—that they take in *"instruction"* like nutrition and become stronger and stronger by it (v. 9).

The very structure of verses 7–9 highlights the two responses to the two calls which begin and close chapter 9. Verse 7 describes the hard-nosed rejection of the scoffer (see on 1:22) in synonymous parallelism, each line reinforcing the other. The first line of verse 8 continues the warning about the scoffer and the dangers of his response. The second line of verse 8 switches suddenly and antithetically to the wise person and the love he accords the teacher. And both lines of verse 9 (it is synonymous like v. 7) amplify that note of positive reception, confirming the notion that time and effort be spent where they result in the nurture and growth of the wise. Jesus' words about good soil in the parable of the seeds (Mark 4:1–20) and about shaking dust from the feet when the message of the kingdom was not received (Mark 6:11) are further comments on the practical truth of this passage for Christian leaders.

THEME REPEATED FROM 1:7: INCLUSION

> 9:10 "The fear of the LORD *is* the beginning of
> wisdom,
> And the knowledge of the Holy One *is*
> understanding.
> 11 For by me your days will be multiplied,
> And years of life will be added to you."
> *Prov. 9:10–11*

These verses accomplish three things in the heart of this speech. First, they reaffirm the central theme which was placarded like a dominant slogan at the beginning of the book. *"The fear of the Lord"* is the first and the last thing said about wisdom in these chapters which so feature her goodness, glory, and gifts. Worship and obedience of Yahweh are the keys to happiness, service, and reputation. No young leader who deigned to amount to anything dared start on the search for success without that fear. It is the *aleph* and *tau*, the *alpha* and *omega* of effective living.

Second, these verses rebuke once for all the scoffer who has been the chief subject of verses 7–9. Scoffing at truth, duty, and goodness are the antithesis of fearing the Lord. The scoffer who chortles over his worldly wisdom and snorts at the person who makes justice an aim has not even started to learn the alphabet of fruitful behavior. His spite will actually shorten his life. Having turned his back on God and knowing Him, he has confined himself to a prison cell of rebellion where crumbs from the table of the wise will be his only diet.

Third, the promise of days multiplied and years added sets up a transition to folly's call at verse 13 and particularly the gloom of death and hell that shrouds the final verse. Fear of God has long life as its destiny. Infatuation with folly is a shortcut to the mortuary.

ANTITHETIC SUMMARY

9:12 "If you are wise, you are wise for yourself,
      And *if* you scoff, you alone will bear *it* alone."
                                            Prov. 9:12

Again the wise person and the scoffer are placed poles apart. In verses 7–9 the focus was on the teacher and the blessings and danger of teaching wise or foolish pupils. Here the words are addressed again to the pupils and the responsibility each bears for his response and the consequences of it. *"Wise for yourself"* means "you personally reap the benefits." *"You alone will bear it alone"* means that "the harmful damages will fall squarely on your shoulders." The context, sandwiched as the verse is between the two calls of the two Ladies, suggests that the mark of the wise is to heed wisdom's call, and the sign of the scoffer is to scorn it and pay court to folly. Verse 12 prevents either party from acting in haste or ignorance. Its contrasting lines spell out the choices and the results more blatantly than the red and green lights that govern our decisions at the crossroads of our towns.

DESCRIPTION OF FOLLY'S FATAL INVITATION

9:13 A foolish woman is clamorous;
       She is simple, and knows nothing.
  14 For she sits at the door of her house,
       On a seat *by* the highest places of the city,

15 To call to those who pass by,
   Who go straight on their way:
16 "Whoever *is* simple, let him turn in here";
   And *as for* him who lacks understanding, she
      says to him,
17 "Stolen water is sweet,
   And bread *eaten* in secret is pleasant."
18 But he does not know that the dead *are* there.
   That her guests *are* in the depths of hell.
                                        Prov. 9:13–18

Folly is portrayed as a woman who overcompensates for her ignorance by raucous talk and wanton conduct (v. 13; see 7:11 where the
adulteress is called loud, the same Hebrew word as *"clamorous"*).
One gets the feeling that she has already been in her cups to fortify
herself to holler her brazen invitation. Her indecorous behavior
seems to be set in a temple (*"her house,"* v. 14), a shrine erected on a
hill high above the city where pagan shrines or "high places" were
often situated. Her target audiences are not those who have intentionally headed for her place but those traveling by on the way to
somewhere else (v. 15), just as the young man in chapter 7 was
snared when he happened to pass the corner where the crafty
woman waited for her prey (7:8–10).

Her call to the passers-by repeats the exact words of wisdom's
cry (v. 16; see v. 4). She too appeals to the naive young men who
play the game of life without a full deck of common sense. The
beginnings of the two calls are the same, but the two consequent
elaborations of the invitation are very different. True, both are invitations to a meal—probably a ritual banquet (v. 17; v. 5). But wisdom's menu is straightforward and above board: bread and wine
mixed with spices. Folly's offerings, on the other hand, have a
shady, suspicious, seductive appeal to them: *"stolen water,"* probably an echo of the allegory in 5:15–23 where water and fountain
describe love making between husband and wife; *"bread eaten in
secret,"* a picture of a forbidden meal which would lead to rebuke
and perhaps banishment from the covenant community if participation in it were made public. The combination conjures a scene of
fornication and idolatry which can result only in spiritual and perhaps physical death.

The teacher's final comment is telling (v. 18). You can find folly's
guest list by reading the daily obituaries. *"Dead"* means "shades,"
gray spirits, bleak shadows of what were once vital but unknowing

young people. What appears to be a portal to pleasure—*"the door of her house"* (v. 14)—is the corridor to *"hell"* (Sheol, the grave or the grim abode of the dead where the full life of God never reaches). Bluntly but truly put, her past *"guests"* are now ghosts.

On that strong word the wisdom speeches of chapter 1–9 abruptly close. Their point on the wonder and worth of wisdom has been well made. Any hearers who make the wrong choice or answer the wrong call have only themselves to blame. The teachers' hands are clean.

Proverbs of Solomon

Proverbs 10:1–22:16

CHAPTER TEN

Wisdom and Work

Proverbs 10:1–32

"Choose wisdom and avoid folly." That was the heart-cry of the first nine chapters. They sounded it by extolling wisdom's beauty, worth, and virtue and by exposing folly's dark ploys and deceptive blandishments. The arguments extended over many verses, sometimes whole chapters, so intent were the teachers (or parents) on capturing the interest and the consent of their pupils. Where specific cases of wicked conduct were mentioned, the goal was illustration— the effort to make clear the concrete choices with which life faces us, together with their consequences.

At 10:1, however, the Book of Proverbs takes a different tack. No more extended arguments, no more lengthy poems in praise of wisdom, no more embellished examples of the wiles of folly. Instead, the menu served from 10:1–22:16 is 375 sayings, usually two lines long. The mode of service is not table d'hôte but á la carte, brief, detached snacks of wisdom, like a vast buffet of hors d'oeuvres.

Attempts to organize them into fifteen groups of twenty-five sayings each, whose total (375) contains the code of Solomon's name when each Hebrew letter is given a numerical value, have not proven helpful to our understanding of how the sayings are organized. Each chapter surveys a wide range of topics, even though the precise form of the proverbs may change from section to section (see *Introduction*).

Since there is no discernible significance to the sequence of the verses, except the loose connectives of occasional catchwords, *our approach to them in this section of the book is topical.*

This method has the advantage of suggesting to preachers and teachers how they may collect and arrange similar sayings in a way that makes for a more coherent form of communication than is possible when each tidbit is offered individually. It is not an exaggeration to say that there are only two ways in which we can deliver the truths embedded in this collection of terse sayings from 10:1–22:16: one at a time or in groups organized by topic.

The task of organizing them is a judgment call; many would fit more than one of the thirty or so subject categories which I have identified. Both the table of topics (see *Introduction*) and the cross references in the commentary will give help in finding how and where each proverb is treated. The basic approach is to deal with two or three topics in each chapter using its relevant verses and also applicable sayings from other chapters.

The two themes expounded on the basis of Proverbs 10 are *Rewards for Conduct* (vv. 13, 6–9, 23–25, 28–30; see also chaps. 21 and 28) and *Diligence in Work* (vv. 4–5, 26; see also chap. 27).

> 10:1 The proverbs of Solomon:
> *Prov. 10:1*

The title [10:1 *"The proverbs of Solomon"*] serves to mark off this collection of proverbs (on the types of proverbs, see *Introduction*) from the longer wisdom speeches that precede it. It also restates the traditional link that binds this material to Solomon, who was honored as the sage par excellence and the patron of Israel's wisdom movement (see *Introduction*). No other title is found until 22:17 when the beginning of a new section is earmarked. The antithetic parallelism—the second line of the couplet restates the proposition in terms opposite to those of the first: wise/foolish; glad/grief, father/mother—dominates the literary tone of chapters 10–15. Its purpose is to illuminate the doctrine of the two ways by demonstrating both the blessings of sound conduct and the dangers of personal instability. *"Father"* and *"mother"* recall 1:8–9 and mark verse 1 not only as an independent proverb but as the implied introduction to the other 374 in this collection. One of the truly compelling arguments for choosing wisdom's ways against those of folly is the impact of our conduct on our parents whom both law (Exod. 20:12; Deut. 5:16) and wisdom command us to honor.

REWARDS FOR CONDUCT

Introduction
    Major theme
    Largest category
    Cause and effect
Importance of choice
    Freedom to decide   10:8; 11:20; 12:8, 20, 26

Our conduct, whether wise or foolish, has ultimate consequences. That is the major theme of Proverbs, and notably of 10:1–22:16. The largest single category in this section—about 75 of the 375 sayings—is comprised of sayings which deal with the weal of wisdom and the woe of folly without giving specific counsel on the types of actions that separate the wise from the foolish. These proverbs assume an inevitable cause-and-effect relationship between human behavior and its outcome. The Lord (Heb. *Yahweh*) has rigged the universe for righteousness. To go His way prompts reward. To go against it leads to failure. An analysis of the proverbs in this category in chapters 10–13 (other studies of them may be found in chaps. 21 and 28) points to two major headings: (1) importance of choice; (2) inventory of outcomes.

The importance of choice is highlighted first in the freedom to make sound decisions which Israel's wise always assumed. Neither wisdom nor folly was a predetermined, inevitable choice for them. No one was predestined to either. Each human being had the opportunity and obligation to make that choice personally. The frequent use of "heart," for instance:

> The wise in heart will receive commands,
> But a prating fool will fall.
>
> *Prov. 10:8*

underscores this. *"Heart"* is the seat of choice, the part of the person that says, "I will" or "I won't." If wise (10:8), it is open to the commands of the knowledgeable and experienced; if foolish, it encourages *"prating"* back talk which resists authority and causes a person to *"fall,"* or, even worse, come to total ruin (see Hos. 4:14).

> Those who are of a perverse heart *are* an
>   abomination to the Lord,
> But *the* blameless in their ways *are* His delight.
> > *Prov. 11:20*

> A man will be commended according to his
>   wisdom,
> But he who is of a perverse heart will be despised.
> > *Prov. 12:8*

The verbal display of folly flows from kinky or muddled thinking as though the *"heart,"* where such thinking gets done in the Hebrew language, were twisted out of shape and could not function with perception and accuracy. *"Perverse"* translates two different Hebrew words with about the same meaning: "twisted."

> Deceit is in the heart of those who devise evil,
> But counselors of peace have joy.
> > *Prov. 12:20*

Foolish choosing as Proverbs sees it may be more than stupid; it may be downright malicious with harm (*"evil"*) not welfare (*"peace"*) to others as its intent.

> The righteous should choose his friends
>   carefully,
> For the way of the wicked leads them astray.
> > *Prov. 12:26*

Freedom of choice seems to be expressed clearly in 12:26, but the Hebrew text is not as lucid as our version makes it, and the LXX seems to chart its own course, lengthening the verse measurably. Above all, the verb *"choose"* is a doubtful reading, while "minds," with a slight change in spelling, is frequently read as "harm" or "misfortune." The two most common retranslations run something like these: "The righteous one will show the way to a companion, but *the way of the wicked leads them astray"* or "the righteous one turns away from evil (or misfortune), but" etc.

Faithfulness to Israel's Lord is the second way in which the importance of choice is understood. Wisdom and folly are at bottom religious not secular terms in Proverbs. The best way to demonstrate this is in the very frequent use of righteousness and wickedness as synonyms for wisdom and folly. Among the verses selected from chapters 10–13 for consideration under the topic *Rewards for Conduct*, fifteen use "wicked" and "righteous" to describe bad and good behavior, while three use "fool" and "wise" or kindred terms.

Righteous (Heb. *ṣaddîq*) speaks of loyal, reliable conduct based on a commitment to God and the covenant which God made with Israel. It is a term of relationship which describes a desire to live a life pleasing to God and fitting to the members of God's family. It means behaving toward God and his people with the same care, compassion, and integrity that the righteous God has shown them. The words that substitute for "righteous," partly for literary variety, bear out this meaning, while their antonyms state the various forms that rebellion may take:

Prov	Synonyms	Antonyms
10:9	integrity (*tôm*)	perversity "twistedness"
10:29	upright (*tôm*)	workers of iniquity a blanket phrase that covers all sorts of mayhem from magic to idolatry to murder (see Job 31:3; Ps. 5:5; Prov. 21:15; Isa. 31:2; Hos. 6:8)
11:3 11:6	upright Heb. *yāshār*, a synonym of *tôm* (see Job 1:1, 8; 2:3)	unfaithful i.e., deceitful or treacherous (see 13:15)
11:5 11:20	blameless Heb. *tāmîm* a sister word to *tôm*	perverse or wicked
12:2	good Heb. *ṭôb*, a general word for excellent conduct, esp. when marked by consideration and generosity	man of wicked devices suggests a deceitful schemer, pursuing selfish gain by hook or crook

Wicked (Heb. *rāshā'*) is best defined as the opposite of all that "righteous" entails: disloyalty to the Lord, rebellion against the covenant standards, disregard of the welfare of the people. Among its synonyms are the following:

perverse   see chart above

iniquitous   see chart above ("workers of iniquity")

unfaithful	see chart above
evil	(11:19, Heb. *rāʾāh*) an all-purpose word for wrong of many kinds and for the harm or misfortune that comes to those who do evil
unjust	(11:7) may be from the same root as *iniquity* in 10:29, but may also be a mistranslation of a word meaning "wealth"; see Hos. 12:8; if so, the line would read "and the hope of [i.e., placed in] riches perishes"
sinners	(13:21) those who willfully miss the mark of God's standards and deviate from their obligation to follow them

Righteousness and wickedness, then, together with wisdom and folly, their counterparts, are not so much specific acts performed under the pressure of immediate decision as they are patterns of life, permanent boxing of the compass or setting of the sail. Faithfulness is a disposition more than a deed. The vocabulary of wisdom literature makes this clear: (1) *walks*—not runs or leaps—is the descriptor of conduct which has become a habit (10:9); (2) *way* or *ways*, the characteristic nouns of behavior, suggest a fixed course in life not a casual or temporary excursion (10:9, 29; 11:5, 20; 12:26, 28; 13:6, 15); (3) *pursues* underscores the fierce intensity with which we plot our course toward wickedness (11:19) or with which disaster systematically stalks sinners (13:21); (4) *sport* or *child's play* pictures the practice of evil (see "wicked devices," 12:2) as something so habitual that it comes just as naturally, readily, and easily to the fool as does wisdom to the man of understanding (10:23).

Fellowship provides a context for human choices and affirms their importance. Our actions, like pebbles tossed in the pond, send ripples or even waves of influence into the lives of others. The level of gladness or grief of our parents is largely determined by our behavior (10:1). So are the welfare and morale of the city.

> When it goes well with the righteous, the city
>   rejoices;
> And when the wicked perish, *there* is shouting.
>   *Prov. 11:10*

The larger community also benefits or suffers from our comportment, rejoicing when the righteous thrive, whose love and thoughtfulness are appreciated, shouting when the wicked collapse (*"perish"*) in the endeavors which are wrought in selfishness, greed, and malice.

Fellowship also helps us make wise choices:

> Where *there is* no counsel, the people fall;
> But in the multitude of counselors *there is* safety.
>
> *Prov. 11:14*

We stand too close to the canvas to see the whole picture and we bring so much emotional fog to our decisions that what we do see is blurred. This may be particularly true in political matters where prudent *"counsel"* (see on 1:5) provides direction, as would a rudder for a ship that wants to sail in *"safety"* (lit., "salvation"). One test of prudence is the consensus of a group (*"multitude"*) of experienced and mature *"counselors,"* planners, and advisers. It does not at all stretch the text to apply this principle to churchly, business, or personal decisions.

In hundreds of different ways, the proverbs say it: our choices in life are important. We have freedom to make them. Our primary choice is faithfulness, our unqualified declaration of loyalty to God, His will, His word, His ways, His work; from that choice all other choices stem. We make pivotal decisions best in a context of fellowship, where we measure their impact on others and seek the help of seasoned friends to protect ourselves and them from nearsightedness and subjectivity.

The inventory of outcomes spells out the character of the rewards credited to our conduct. Their finality, variety, and certainty are described in utterly sobering terms.

Finality is what, in the long run, makes choices so important. Our texts ring with the language of finality. The contrast between the destinies of the righteous and the wicked is the point pounded home, with particular vehemence in the case of the wicked:

Prov	*Righteous*	*Wicked*
10:3	The Lord will not allow (or "cause") a soul ("person"; Heb. *nephesh* can mean "throat" or "gullet") to famish (starve); see Ps. 37:25; Prov. 13:25.	The Lord casts away (drives out and rejects) desires (appetites, cravings for satisfaction), as He banished the Canaanites from the land (Deut. 6:19; 9:4).
10:6	Blessings, words of praise, appreciation, and well wishing are accorded (placed on the head as were the blessings of Joseph on Ephraim and Manasseh; Gen. 48:13).	Violence, perhaps as a form of punishment, stops (covers) the mouth (or face) so that not even a cry for help can be uttered (see also 10:11): NEB "choked by their own violence."
10:7	One's memory (or "name," as that by which one is remembered) will be blessed (become a source of strength and joy) like Abraham's (Gen. 12:3).	One's name (reputation, permanent influence on others) will crumble (rot) to useless pulp like softwood ravaged by moisture, mold, and vermin (Isa. 40:20).

Prov	Righteous	Wicked
10:25	Stands firm in all circumstances because of the unshakeable, enduring foundation of loyalty to God on which life is built (Matt. 7:24–27).	Swept away like chaff (are no more, cease to exist) by the whirlwind, which God uses to expose the futility of their lives (Job 21:18; 37:9; Jer. 4:13).
10:28	Hope, what they look forward to with high anticipation, will issue in gladness (rejoicing) because their good conduct will be rewarded.	Expectation (another Heb. word for hope intently desired) will die completely (perish), come to nothing like a mirage that offers no water or a desert path that leads nowhere (see 11:7, 10).
10:29	Strength (a "fortress") is the lot of those who obey the Lord by walking in His way.	Destruction ("terror," "ruin," a favorite word; Prov. 10:14, 15; 13:3; 14:28; 18:7; 21:15) is the destiny of those who do the opposite.
10:30	Stable and permanent existence (will never be removed) like Jerusalem's (Ps. 46:5) is their reward.	No future dwelling place awaits them, whether in the land of Israel or even the land of the living.
11:3	Integrity ("sincerity" or "innocence"; see Job 2:3, 9; 27:5; 31:6) will serve as guide as did the Lord's pillars of cloud and fire to Israel (Exod. 13:21).	Perversity ("deceitfulness," "treachery"; see 13:6; 15:4; 19:3; 21:12; 22:12 for uses of both verb and noun) will lead to their massive destruction ("destroy" is the prophets' favorite verb for all-out destruction in judgment; Isa. 21:2; Jer. 15:8; Ezek. 32:12; Hos. 10:2; Mic. 2:4).
11:19	The one "steadfast in righteousness" (RSV) has life, not just in terms of duration but also of delight, as a destiny (8:35; 12:28).	The one who pursues evil (see above for both words) gains death, in all its unhappy expressions—emotional, spiritual, and physical—as the result (8:36).
13:15	Good understanding (sound common sense; lit., sense in behavior and advice) gains favor (lit., "grace" or "acceptance"), presumably with God and one's fellows.	The way (practices, habits of conduct) of the unfaithful (deceitful, treacherous) is so self-destructive that it "does not last long" enough (so "hard" may be translated, since the Heb. word cannot mean "hard") to gain favor of any kind.
13:21	Good is the paymaster not the payee or the payment. It stands not only for a righteous life, which carries rewards, but is virtually a synonym for God, the ultimate source of all retribution.	Evil, that is, total disaster, complete misfortune, is the hunter here, not the hunted as in 11:19. Its ability to catch its prey is unerring (see 12:21).

Variety is a feature of the inventory of outcomes, along with finality. The various metaphors of reward and punishment contribute to our understanding of how Israel's teachers looked at
human behavior and its consequences. Stability versus instability,
survival versus extinction, seem to be the outcomes featured in the
word pictures. Most obvious are those drawn from architecture:
10:25 (see above) features the sound foundation on which the
righteous person builds and which survives the blasting whirl-
winds of life that snatch away the wicked.

> The wicked are overthrown and *are* no more,
> But the house of the righteous will stand.
> *Prov. 12:7*

This verse depicts the wicked as *"overthrown,"* blown flat like the
Midianite tent in Gideon's dream (Judg. 7:13), while the *"house"*
("household" or "dynasty"; Heb. *bēth* speaks of both structure and
personnel) of the righteous *"will stand"* upright and secure.

> *Though they join* forces, the wicked will not go
>   unpunished;
> But the posterity of the righteous will be delivered.
> *Prov. 11:21*

Family continuity is also featured here. The *"posterity"* ("seed") of the
righteous will be cleared of all charges (*"delivered"*), while "it is dead
certain" (NKJV, *"join forces,"* misunderstands "hand to hand," which
in Hebrew describes a gesture—slapping or shaking hands—that
seals a bargain and hence becomes an expression of certainty; "be
sure of this," NIV) that the verdict will go against the wicked, whose
"seed," we assume, will be cut off.

> The light of the righteous rejoices,
> But the lamp of the wicked will be put out.
> *Prov. 13:9*

"Lamp" and *"light"* are images of the survival of name, influences,
and descendants. *"Rejoices"* is the opposite of *"will be put out."* Family continuity was life's highest hope, brightest joy, in a society that,
as yet, had been given no clear sense of eternal life or bodily resurrection. The wise had no greater incentive to encourage godly living
among their students than the promise that their progeny would

survive to carry on their name, while the line of those disloyal to God would be snuffed out like a wick charred to its stump.

Agricultural metaphors reinforce this theme of stability and continuity:

> The wicked *man* does deceptive work,
> But he who sows righteousness *will have* a sure
>   reward.
>
> *Prov. 11:18*

"Righteousness" is like good seed that one *"sows"*; the consequent crop (*"reward,"* "wages") is truly dependable (*"sure"*). Sow well; reap well. The connection between sows and *"seed"* (posterity, 11:21) may hint that one reward of righteousness is children to carry on the name (Ps. 127:3–5). In contrast, as this law of moral harvest puts it, the *"deceptive work"* of the wicked is not only false and cheating in its activity but in its results: it produces no lasting crop whether of children or anything else.

> The fruit of the righteous *is a* tree of life
> And he who wins souls *is* wise.
>
> *Prov. 11:30*

"Fruit" further defines reward in 11:18 and the whole picture is amplified by *"tree of life"* which again speaks of prosperity (cf. Ps. 1:3) and continuity—a tree that continues to exhibit its life by bearing fruit from season to season and providing blessing for the community that depends on it. "Violence" (the Hebrew word resembles "wise") seems to be the opposite of "righteousness" in 11:30. Several versions, following LXX, read the second line as antithesis to the first, since the Hebrew words translated as *"wins souls"* must mean, rather, something like "take away life": "but violence means the taking away of life" (NEB). The verse then says in effect, righteousness is life producing, but violence is death dealing.

> A man is not established by wickedness,
> But the root of the righteous cannot be moved.
>
> *Prov. 12:3*

The permanence enjoyed by a life of righteousness is symbolized in the figure of a *"root"* which *"cannot be moved"* (see 10:30).

> The wicked covet the catch of evil *men*,
> But the root of the righteous yields *fruit*.
>
> *Prov. 12:12*

The same idea seems to be conveyed in this difficult verse, both lines of which contain problems. Scott's reading in his commentary in the Anchor Bible series restores the balanced contrast between the lines without undue tampering with the Hebrew text: "The stronghold of the wicked will be blotted out, / But the roots of the just [righteous] are enduring." *"Covet"* in Hebrew resembles "will be blotted out" or "destroyed"; *"catch"* (or "snare") is similar to "stronghold" (or "fortress"); *"yields fruit"* (with help from Arabic) may read "enduring" or "stands firm" (RSV; see also NEB and JB).

Positive, lasting, satisfying results are what the wise promise their disciples in their gallery of word pictures. We will understand their inventory of outcomes and its remarkable variety of expressions better if we look at the means of reward along with the metaphors. At times, the acts of retribution are seen as judicial sentences pronounced and executed by the Lord, who weighs the evidence and announces the verdict as would a judge in court. Forensic retribution we can call this, because it has the sound and look of a courtroom, with all the appropriate legal processes. We see it clearly in 10:3 when God is subject of the verbs: "The Lord will not allow"; "He casts away." Similarly in 12:2, favor is obtained from the Lord, while the man of wicked schemes "He will condemn" ("declare guilty") like a judge.

The Lord's personal stake in human conduct is made startlingly plain in 11:20–21:

> 11:20 Those who are of a perverse heart *are* an
>   abomination to the Lord,
>   But *the* blameless in their ways *are* His delight.
> 21 *Though they join* forces, the wicked will not go
>   unpunished;
>   But the posterity of the righteous will be
>   delivered.
>
> *Prov. 11:20–21*

The *"perverse"* are an *"abomination"* (3:32; 6:16; 8:7), the word used for rejected sacrifices, hypocritical worship, lewd conduct, and flagrant idolatry, while the *"blameless . . . are His delight"* (give Him great pleasure). Technical terms for "not clearing the wicked of guilt" ("*not go unpunished*") and "declaring the righteous free of all charges" ("*delivered*") suggest a courtroom venue, but we cannot be sure whether in this passage the judge is human or divine.

In Proverbs, dynamistic retribution is a much more common means of reward than forensic. Dynamistic means that a crime inevitably carries the power to effect its own consequences. We live in a world, said the wise, when every cause achieves its appropriate effect. What is true in architecture—how well you build determines how well you live—and agriculture—what you sow is what you reap—is true in the realms of business, politics, social welfare, and personal morality. Like a boomerang, what you hurl at life circles back to hit you, for woe or for weal. The "wicked will fall by his own wickedness" (11:5); no outside intervention is mentioned. "The unfaithful will be taken by their own lust" (11:6); what they crave is so inherently wrong that when they get what they want they become prisoners of it—whether sexual lust, chemical dependence, social ambition, or material greed. The same idea is put graphically in these words:

> The desire of the righteous *is* only good,
> *But* the expectation of the wicked *is* wrath.
> *Prov. 11:23*

"*Desire*" describes the future aspirations of the "*righteous*" which will inevitably arrive at a happy outcome ("*good*"); "*the expectation of the wicked*," however, if viewed realistically can only be "*wrath*," the dire results that spark frustration and consequent loss of temper. So powerful is this dynamistic tide of retribution that the trouble ("distress") which the righteous escape invades (comes to) the lives "*of the wicked*" instead (11:8).

> Righteousness guards *him whose* way is blameless.
> But wickedness overthrows the sinner.
> *Prov. 13:6*

"*Righteousness*" acts as "*guard*" and protector, while "*wickedness*" creates upheaval ("*overthrows*," see 19:3; 21:12; 22:12) in the life of the sinner; the meaning is the same even if the words are reversed: "but sin overthrows the wicked" (RSV; the Hebrew text needs a little smoothing and the syntax is ambiguous).

If the righteous will be recompensed on the earth,
How much more the ungodly and the sinner.
Prov. 11:31

The certainty of these results, intimated in almost every item of
the inventory of outcomes, is summarized here. The focus, as is
characteristic of the antithetical verses, is on the lot of the *"wicked."*
It is that which must be avoided at all costs. The argument for the
certainty of punishment is based on the visible, tangible rewards
gained by the *"righteous"* in the land, on *"earth,"* in Israel, before the
eyes of all prudent observers.

The fear of the wicked will come upon him.
And the desire of the righteous will be granted.
Prov. 10:24

He who earnestly seeks good finds favor,
But trouble will come to him who seeks *evil.*
Prov. 11:27

The righteous eats to the satisfying of his soul,
But the stomach of the wicked shall be in want.
Prov. 13:25

"To each his own" is the gist of these sayings. They brook no
doubt about the certainty of reward and deprivation, depending on
which way the sojourner ventures in life, which path he chooses.
The wicked seem to have nagging doubt about their ultimate outcome as well as their interim success. And with good reason. What
they dread most (*"the fear"*) is destined to come their way (10:24).
They have no claim on the Lord to rescue them from the horror
(Heb. *m*gôrāh,* Isa. 66:4, is one of the strongest Old Testament words
for dread) that stalks them; they cannot share the experience to
which the righteous psalmist testified:

I sought the LORD, and He heard me,
And delivered me from all my fears.
Ps. 34:4

While fear is the subject of the first clause in 10:24, Yahweh is the
implied subject of the second. *"Will be granted"* is better read in Hebrew, "He will grant." The righteous aspirations (*"desire"*) of God's

people the Lord Himself can bring to fruition because it is His will
that they seek.

Part of that will is the well-being (*"good"*) of the community
(11:27). The person who gives that top priority (*"diligently seeks"*) is
on a proper quest (*"seeks"*) for the approval (*"favor"*) of his fellow
citizens. He craves their welfare and benefits from their esteem.
They trust his motives and honor him accordingly. Correspondingly,
the lot of the one who searches for ways to do them harm will become the victim of his own plot. *"Trouble"* and *"evil"* translate one
Hebrew word which is both subject and object in the sentence; the
grammar helps make certain the connection between intentions and
their outcome: "But the one who searches for evil, it (the evil) will
come to him" is a literal reading of the three-word clause.

The certainty of reward and punishment is illustrated in daily
matters as mundane as our human appetites (13:25). *"Soul"* is parallel to *"stomach"* and means here *"gullet"* or *"appetite."* Divine justice
would see to it, so the teachers viewed life, that the righteous person would have enough while the wicked suffered *"in want."* The
Lord was not their Shepherd, and they could not claim His promise
of provision (Ps. 23:1).

Such obvious rewards are marks of divine justice and order,
whether carried out in a formal court setting or built into the structures of reality. A fearful thing, indeed, it is to ignore this truth:
righteousness has regularly and consistently been rewarded. To
overlook truth is to make the greatest of all errors: to assume that
our sins will not find us out.

The weighty pull of these proverbs with their black-and-white po-
larizations of wisdom and folly/sin and righteousness is hard on a
generation used to the ethical weightlessness and the vague grayness
of our moonscape morality. True, overstatement, generalization, and
simplification are part of the literary mood of Proverbs. Other biblical writings like Job, Ecclesiastes, Psalms 49 and 73 recognize this.
They play a welcome role in the Bible by telling us that God understands how complex life seems when he chooses not to follow the
formulae of Proverbs. But most of us need to learn to reckon with the
rules before we ponder the exceptions. There is an ultimate and absolute difference between following God and not following Him, between accepting and rejecting His lordship, between pledging our
loyalty to Him in faith and going our own way in rebellion. The results—whether in the impact of our own lives on others, the experience of joy in the midst of our toils, or the final outcome of eternal
life with God or exclusion from His presence—are utterly, finally,

and certainly different. More than any other single lesson, Israel's
wise teachers wanted their hearers—and us—to know that.

DILIGENCE IN WORK

Introduction
    Previous comments   6:6–11
    Impact on   10:1–22:16
Motivations
    Positive: survival   12:9; 16:26
    Negative
        Apathy   19:24; 21:25
        Anxiety   22:13; 20:4
Results
    General
        Negative: destruction   18:9
        Positive: profit   14:23
    Specific
        Bread   12:11; 13:4; 19:15; 20:13
        Prestige   10:5; 20:4
        Well-being   10:26; 15:19
        Power   12:24
        Wealth   10:4; 12:27
Conclusion
    The style of Proverbs
    The world-view of wisdom
    The implications for modern life

Work is one of the chief marks of wisdom. Israel's teachers never
let their students forget that. Their doctrine of creation took seriously the human role in God's care of the earth. They knew that
they were no longer in Eden; they knew also that tilling and tending
were more necessary, if more arduous tasks, than they had been at
the beginning.

Our *previous comments* on 6:6–11 set the tone for what we find in
this section of Proverbs. The ant reminds us that the drive for survival, no matter how much effort is entailed, was built into the very
framework of the creation. To violate that drive is to fly in the teeth
of what God has ordered. He has set timely seasons of sowing and
harvest in the pages of our calendar, and we ignore them only to our
hurt. Sun and moon, night and day are signals that govern our activities. To sleep when work is in order is like ignoring the crossing

barriers at the train track and getting trapped between them with
the engine hurtling toward us. For the wise, poverty was that engine
ready to run us down if we violated the divine signals that told us
when to work and when to rest.

The *impact of this theme* on 10:1–22:16 is seen in the fact that chapter 10 is scarcely started when sayings on work pop up (vv. 4, 5), and
they continue to dot the pages with the persistent regularity of a
mother pushing her children off to school morning by morning. The
implications of diligence and laziness form the subject of some eighteen proverbs, almost one of every twenty in the collection that runs
from 10:1–22:16. They do not cluster. Four are the most to be found
in any chapter, but they insist on being heard, so central is their message to all that Proverbs stands for.

The *motivations* which those sayings employ are practical,
straightforward, and basic. The positive note of persuasion is survival. Work is not an additive to life with which we amuse ourselves
and ward off boredom like spinning a yo-yo or playing solitaire. It is
an utter essential to our humanity. Without it life as we know it
would cease, for us and for all who depend on us.

> The person who labors, labors for himself,
> For his *hungry* mouth drives him *on*.
> *Prov. 16:26*

The bluntest expression of this drive for survival is 16:26. The
focus is on the laborer's "appetite" which "*labors* [the word suggests
harsh toil and is a favorite of Ecclesiastes] *for*" him. "Appetite" is
obviously parallel to "*mouth*" and suggests that it is the correct
translation of Hebrew *nephesh* which, besides meaning "soul" or
"*person*" can mean "neck," "throat," or "belly." Paul echoed this link
between eating and working: "If anyone will not work, neither shall
he eat" (2 Thess. 3:10). The thought in Proverbs is not so much what
the community should force a person to do, but what one's own
physical need "*drives*" (the verb occurs only here and seems to mean
"presses him hard") one to do.

> Better *is the one* who is slighted but has a servant,
> Than he who honors himself but lacks bread.
> *Prov. 12:9*

A similar notion is put forth in 12:9 in the "better" form of comparative proverb. Food outweighs assumed honor by a vast amount,

as the form would indicate with its tendency to extreme comparisons (see *Introduction*). The contrast is between the one who pretends to be reputable and self-sufficient yet is starving and the person who is ignored and treated lightly as though carrying no weight in the community and yet works for himself; *"has a servant"* with a slight change in spelling reads "earn one's own living," NEB, which makes much more sense in the context and strengthens the comparison. Reputation, especially when it is self-assumed, is not fodder for survival.

The negative obstacles to an adequate food supply were not a malevolent creation which was out to destroy humankind. No true Israelite, nurtured on Genesis, Psalms, Job, and Isaiah, could have believed that. Demons were not the enemies, nor hostile spirits that have kept animists cowed through the centuries. Even the stony soil and low annual rainfall of Palestine were not the subject of attention. Human resolve was. One could choose to work hard or not. Turning that choice positive was an aim of the teachers. To do that they had to overcome the apathy of their pupils.

> The desire of the lazy *man* kills him,
> For his hands refuse to labor.
> > *Prov. 21:25*

Strong language is one of their tools (21:25). The choice of the *"slothful"* (a common word in Proverbs, often translated "sluggard"; see 20:4) not *"to labor"* (the word here means simply to get done what needs to be done and holds no hint of sweat or pain) is a choice ultimately fatal (*"kills him"*). The poetic form is synthetic to make clear the reason for the suicidal results of languor.

Humor was used to needle the lazy out of their apathy:

> A lazy *man* buries his hand in the bowl,
> And will not so much as bring it to his mouth
> > again.
> > > *Prov. 19:24*

The epitome of sloth is the person who cannot muster the energy to pull his *"hand"* out of the *"bowl"* that contains the vegetables and sauces which he usually scoops into his mouth with pieces of barley loaf that probably looked something like our pita bread (19:24). The first line of 12:27 (see below) seems to mock a person so lazy that he will not expend the energy even to build a fire to roast the catch he took in hunting.

> The lazy *man* says, *"There is* a lion outside!
> I shall be slain in the streets!"
>
> *Prov. 22:13*

Equally ridiculous was the anxiety of a *"slothful man"* who used the threat of a lion outside (22:13; see 26:13; lions were not unknown in Palestine during Old Testament days, Amos 5:19, but would not have stalked the town streets) to rationalize his indulgence. Some sluggards did not need lions; the inclement weather of winter was enough to keep them from the plow:

> The lazy *man* will not plow because of winter;
> He will beg during harvest and have nothing.
>
> *Prov. 20:4*

The biting humor put across the chief point: laziness was stupid. Beyond that, its *results* could be wicked destruction:

> He who is slothful in his work
> Is a brother to him who is a great destroyer.
>
> *Prov. 18:9*

The one who is *"slothful"* is one who is slack and overrelaxed (see 24:10) *"in his work"* (business or commercial activity; see 22:29; 24:27). Far from being a harmless nuisance, he is *"a brother to* [close kin to, almost like] *him who is a great* [master, lord; Heb. ba‘al] *destroyer"* (see 28:24 for a similar accusation against those who cheat their parents and deny it). Laziness, then, however cool and laid-back it may seem, is big-league mayhem. It saps a society of its will to achieve, undermines the values of the young, makes it dependent on outside resources, and abdicates the divinely assigned role of coregency in the stewardship of creation.

The positive counterpart of this destruction (18:9) is the profit mentioned in this saying:

> In all labor there is profit,
> But idle chatter *leads* only to poverty.
>
> *Prov. 14:23*

Work (*"labor"*) that is willing to sweat and bleed, if necessary, produces *"profit"* (see 21:5); something will be left over for a rainy day, for additional investment, or for acts of charity or generosity. In contrast, talk alone (*"idle chatter,"* words that drop lightly from the lips) produces nothing and consumes time that ought to be used to ward off want (*"poverty"*).

The specific results mentioned in Proverbs amplify both the profitable and the destructive effects of our attitudes toward work. Heading the list of benefits is bread.

> He who tills his land will be satisfied with bread,
> But he who follows frivolity is devoid of
>   understanding.
>
> *Prov. 12:11*

Tilling the land produces concrete results, like a full stomach (*"be satisfied with bread,"* usually baked from barley and the staple diet of the average Israelite); in contrast, scheming to get rich or waiting for a ship to come in is to *"pursue"* (*"follow"*) *"frivolity"* (empty-headed fantasies that produce nothing dependable; see 28:19) and to demonstrate a vast incapacity for making good choices (*"devoid of understanding,"* lit., "lacking of heart"). The lazy wait for the good idea; the wise grasp the plow.

Wishing ("desires") is no substitute for diligence:

> The soul of a lazy *man* desires, and *has* nothing;
> But the soul of the diligent shall be made rich.
>
> *Prov. 13:4*

The one leaves the sluggard's "belly" (lit., "soul"; see above at 16:26) empty; the other fills the stomach (*"soul"*) of the *"diligent"* (who cuts sharply into his work without hesitation) with the satisfying fatness (*"made rich"*) that virtually all cultures save our own have treasured as a sign of blessing and prosperity.

> Laziness casts *one* into a deep sleep,
> And an idle person will suffer hunger.
>
> *Prov. 19:15*

"Deep sleep" is the wrong posture for bread winning (19:15). It renders us as lifeless as Adam's anesthetic (Gen. 2:21) or Abraham's trance (Gen. 15:12). Its only product may be deceitful dreams and realistic *"hunger."*

Do not love sleep, lest you come to poverty;
Open your eyes, *and* you will be satisfied with
　　bread.

Prov. 20:13

The difference between compulsive attachment (*"love"*) for *"sleep"* (here the ordinary word, not the special term of 19:15) and a resolve to keep *"open your eyes"* during the hours of work is the difference between *"poverty"* (lit., *"being dispossessed"*; see 23:21; 30:9) and having your fill of *"bread."*

Prestige is a result of diligence:

He who gathers in summer *is* a wise son,
He who sleeps in harvest *is* a son who causes
　　shame.

Prov. 10:5

It is gained through the *"wise"* practice of toiling as hard as necessary during the summer harvest, which began with barley and wheat in May and June, and ended with the summer fruits and the last of the grapes in September. The *"shame"* brought to the family of the lazy (*"he who sleeps"*) was bitter. They lost face, a painful experience for all of us, and especially for Orientals, because their son was viewed as not knowing, not caring, not contributing. Family welfare was not among his priorities. Sleep during the vital plowing of autumn and winter proved him unsuitable to be called a *"son."* It divorced him from his place among those who toiled because they cared for the clan. The ultimate outcome of such behavior would be to reduce the members of the family to begging (20:4).

Well-being is threatened by laziness:

As vinegar to the teeth and smoke to the eyes,
So *is* the lazy *man* to those who send him.

Prov. 10:26

The sting of that threat is pictured as *"vinegar to the teeth and smoke to the eyes,"* when someone sent to carry an urgent message or perform a vital task proves indolent. Our dependence on others in societies where division of labor is a way of life proves most frustrating when those we count on for an important assignment—plumbers, electricians, administrative assistants, or stockbrokers—fail to do their work on schedule.

The way of the lazy *man is* like a hedge of thorns,
But the way of the upright *is* a highway.
Prov. 15:19

The *"lazy"* person lives as though trapped in a thicket of thorn
hedge. Confined by his laziness he cannot strike out to accomplish
worthwhile tasks; should he sally forth tentatively he recoils from
the prickly pain. The *"upright"* (the LXX suggests that the original
word was "diligent"), on the other hand, faces life like a broad, level
"highway" that offers maximum opportunity for progress.

Power may be a by-product of hard work.

The hand of the diligent will rule,
But the lazy *man* will be put to forced labor.
Prov. 12:24

The gap between the lot of the *"diligent"* (a frequent word in
Proverbs, describing intelligent, focused, and persistent effort that
cuts through the problem and gets the work done; see 10:4;
12:24, 27; 13:4; 21:15) and that of the *"lazy"* (or "slack" like the
string of a useless bow, Hos. 7:16; see also 10:4: 12:24, 27; 19:15) is
monumental: one *"will rule"* (exercise authority over others with
the support of the king); the other *"will be put to forced labor,"* like
the men conscripted by Solomon to break their backs on his massive construction projects (1 Kings 4:6; 5:27–28; 9:15). Indolence so
gnaws at the vitals of a society that it may have to draft persons for
labor if they are fit and yet unwilling to work.

He who has a slack hand becomes poor,
But the hand of the diligent makes rich.
Prov. 10:4

Wealth in contrast to poverty may not mean exorbitant riches, but
only enough on which to be self-sufficient and to be able to help
others. Those of us raised in Depression-era families know that feeling. Just having enough provides incredible exhilaration. The term
"makes rich" is commonly used in Proverbs to describe this sense of
material and social well-being (10:22; 13:7; 21:17; 23:4; 28:20).

The lazy *man* does not roast what he took in
    hunting,
But diligence *is* man's precious possession.
Prov. 12:27

If we read this rightly, *"diligence"* itself is more to be valued than wealth, presumably because it gives the ability to recover wealth lost and to use well wealth retained. Laziness, in contrast, is so crippling that it hampers a person from using even what he has, like game bagged *"in hunting"* (see above on 19:24).

In *conclusion,* we need be reminded that the style of the proverbs leaves no room for contingencies. The generalizations bypass matters of physical fitness, adequate opportunity, effective training, and any number of issues that affect one's competence to work. In a clan society the able family members cared for those who were not able. Spite for the lazy did not squeeze out compassion for the poor and handicapped. Biblical neighborliness was expected to be shown to them. They were part of the community that took its definition of human worth from God's own merciful faithfulness to all His people. But that same Lord, who labored on the six days of creation and everyday but one since then, had the right to expect productive labors from all who were capable of them. To them these proverbs are addressed. And the varieties of literary form—from antithesis (10:4, 5; 12:11, 24, 27; 13:4; 14:23; 15:19) to synthesis (16:26; 18:9; 19:15, 24; 20:4; 21:25; 22:13) and from simple sayings to comparisons (10:26; 12:9) and admonitions (20:13)—are an index of the attention which the wise gave to this keystone issue in personal and societal health.

The world-view of wisdom is seen in the all-encompassing mandate of work. No fit person, whatever his or her station or class, was exempt from it. Our creatureliness as vice-regents of God in charge of the environment with which He gifted us, our membership in an interdependent society from whose beneficence we draw and to whose obligations we contribute, our very physical natures that require exercise for mobility and food for sustenance, and our urges to subdue, innovate, build, sustain, and refine—all of these make work essential to our personal welfare and the achievement of the purposes of our existence.

The implications for modern life are noteworthy. The move from farm to city is a worldwide phenomenon. It is taxing the resources of human ingenuity to find meaningful work for those who are caught in this migratory upheaval. Factories are closing and service industries are burgeoning. Fewer people than ever make our goods and grow our food. Jobs that brought dignity to generations of family members are suddenly obsolete. The economic fallout is frightening. But even more terrifying is the thought of rearing crop after crop of young people who know not the delights of work, who are robbed of the satisfaction of mastering a craft, who are barred from the joy of contributing to the support of their household, and who are paralyzed at the thought of assuming responsibility for their own families.

Along with the social engineering, family planning, governmental stratagems, and industrial efforts being brought to the solution of these problems, there ought to come the prudence of the wise. The theology of work that underlies their thinking sparks an urgency while it also offers a perspective. God the master Worker has built the need and joy of work into the very stuff of His universe and His people. Knowing this is the first step in understanding what He wants us to do about those who can and will not labor and especially about those who will and cannot labor.

CHAPTER ELEVEN

Generosity and Rashness

Proverbs 11:1–31

Money is the common thread that binds together these two prominent and interrelated themes: *Generosity in Giving* (11:24–26) and the
Risks of Rash Pledges (11:15). Both topics are essential for our understanding of the checks and balances intended to keep Israel's social
order on an even keel and prepare their leaders for responsible and
fruitful ministries.

Their access to wealth and consequent accountability made them a
ripe audience for these subjects. The relevance to our affluent times
will be obvious at every turn. The sayings are almost uniformly antithetic, with the word "but" being the characteristic hinge between
the lines. Verses 7 (synonymous), 22 (comparison), and 25 (synonymous) seem to be the exceptions.

GENEROSITY IN GIVING

Introduction
    Admonitions to generosity   3:27–35
    Ingredients in generosity
        goods
        attitudes
Recipients of generosity
    Neighbor   14:21
    Poor   21:13; 22:9; 11:26
Surprises of Generosity   11:24
    Give and get
    Hold and lose
Rewards of generosity
    Enrichment   11:25; 22:9
    Friendship   19:6
    Repayment   19:17
Serendipity of generosity   21:26

Reason for generosity   14:31
Conclusion
   Proverbial style
   Divine order

So embedded in Israel's thinking was the idea of generosity, that admonitions to it were planted in the beginning chapters of Proverbs (see 3:27–35) along with the other major themes that were introduced. People who believed that the whole earth and everything that filled it belonged to their Lord (Ps. 24:1) were not hard put to recognize that the giftedness of their own lives, which, no matter how hard they toiled and how judiciously they spent, was utterly dependent on God's grace. And that grace was given not to be hoarded like Silas Marner's gold coins buried in his workshop cavern and covered with a rug under his loom. It was to be shared like the inexhaustible supply of oil lavished on the widow in Elisha's day (2 Kings 4:1–7). Neighborliness was reason enough, since people lived close to each other for mutual provision and protection (Prov. 3:29). But even more important was the blessing of God promised to those who walked humbly and loyally before God and each other.

> The curse of the LORD *is* on the house of the
>   wicked,
> But He blesses the home of the just.
> *Prov. 3:33*

The commands (admonitions) of 3:27–35 are embellished in the eleven proverbs that carry on this note in 10:1–22:16. The generosity they describe expresses itself in a ready distribution of "goods," especially such goods as a neighbor truly needs and asks for (3:29). Most basic is the supply of food staples in times of want, unemployment, or famine. This is not construed as rewarding bad behavior by caring for the slothful, whose ways are constantly denounced (see chap. 10). It is seen, rather, as a normal duty in a society where all members were in covenant with each other, were related to each other through their tribal ancestors, and were essentially all of one class. Some had been more blessed than others and that blessing called for mercy, not arrogance, for generosity, not miserliness.

The giver's attitude was as important as the goods. Stubbornness in withholding largess (3:27), delay in meeting a pressing need (3:28), scheming how not to give (3:29), arguing over the terms of the transaction, imitating oppressive persons who gave to gain control over the recipient (3:31), showing scorn or spite while helping these needy—all these responses were outlawed. They turned what might have been generosity into something bitter, disdainful, shameful, ungodly.

The individual sayings sprinkled through our section of Solomonic proverbs show us the right ways to meet the needs of others.

> He who despises his neighbor sins;
> But he who has mercy on the poor, happy *is* he.
> > *Prov. 14:21*

The recipients of generosity are named as neighbors, the persons who live near enough to have special claim on us and special commitment to us. In most cases in Israel, they would reside in the same village as their benefactors and be in day-by-day touch with them. Their needs, therefore, would be well known. They were not the drifters, panhandlers, and street people who knock at the door of city churches and tell us tragic and often false stories of urgent need. Nothing in this list of proverbs suggests that con men are in view.

The needy are neighbors and they are *"poor,"* destitute of the basics of life—especially food and raiment (remember Jesus' summary of basic needs in Matt. 6:25). The most common Hebrew words for them in Proverbs are (1) *dal* which speaks of their low estate, their physical and social weakness (10:15; 14:31; 19:4, 17; 21:13; 22:9, 16, 22; 28:3, 8, 11, 15; 29:7, 14) and (2) *rāsh* (also spelled *rā'sh*) which pictures their want and especially their hunger, the single surest sign of poverty (Prov. 10:4; 13:7, 8, 23; 14:20; 17:5; 18:23; 19:1, 7, 22; 22:2, 7; 28:3, 27; 29:13; the noun "poverty," *rē'sh*, from the same root, is found in 6:11; 10:15; 13:18; 24:34; 28:19; 30:8; 31:7); twice occurs the word *'ᵃnāyîm* (14:21; 16:19), a familiar term for lowliness and humility, most common in the Psalms (9:12, 18; 10:12, 17; 25:9; 34:2; 37:11) where it connotes direct dependence on God in the absence of all material props.

So far as we can tell, these *"poor,"* whatever Hebrew word defines them, were not members of a social class but individuals within the society that experienced regular or periodic adversity, at times because oppression not generosity became the response to their plight. That oppression may well have threatened to turn them into a despised and persecuted caste as Amos's passionate concern for their lot may indicate. The advice to Israel's educated, affluent, and influential future leaders was aimed to head that off. How successful the proverbs were is hard to judge, though we can assume that without their salt and light the situation would have become even more dark and tasteless. In fact, the argument is worth noting that the wisdom tradition may have been part of what God used to sharpen Amos's conscience and add bite to his message.

"Poor" and *"neighbor"* are virtual synonyms in 14:21. *"Despises"* and *"has mercy"* (see 14:31) are the poles present in human attitudes when need is prevalent. We can doubt the need, blame the need on the indigence or folly of the needy, or ignore the need in the light of our own financial priorities. The Bible rightly brands these attitudes despiteful (*"sins"*). We can, in contrast, help to meet the need just because it is there, because it is better to err on the side of *"mercy"* than suspicion, and because God has been merciful to us. The promise *"happy is he"* makes a beatitude of this verse and casts light on our Lord's later word, "Blessed ["happy"] are the merciful" (Matt. 5:7).

> He who has a generous eye will be blessed,
> For he gives of his bread to the poor.
> *Prov. 22:9*

That same offer to *"be blessed"* is extended to the person of *"generous eye,"* who sees the need of the hungry (*"bread"*) and opens a hand to them. The synthetic parallelism uses the second line to make complete and specific the nature of the generosity depicted in the first line. "Good eye" in baseball is the skill to see the ball, judge whether it is over the plate, and lay the bat on it. "Good eye" in Proverbs is the knack of spotting a neighbor's need and laying *"bread"* on his or her table.

An opposite case is cited here:

> Whoever shuts his ears to the cry of the poor
> Will also cry himself and not be heard.
> *Prov. 21:13*

Instead of a "good eye," we find a shut ear, utterly indifferent to the passionate, distressed, *"cry"* of the needy (see Mordecai's cry of perplexity and frustration in Esther 4:1). The boomerang of neglect will return to smite him: others will turn deaf in his hour of need. We can assume that the citizenry in general had more than a passing acquaintance with these proverbs. They knew the mores of ancient Israel which called for crops to be shared with them (remember the practice of gleaning in the Book of Ruth).

> The people will curse him who withholds grain,
> But blessing *will be* on the head of him who sells *it*.
> *Prov. 11:26*

Their vehement responses then of *"curse"* (24:24) were the logical outcry toward those who held tight to their own inventories of *"grain"* in an attempt to control the market and jack up the price, just as *"blessing"* was their word for those who made grain available in the marketplace at fair value. Food was life or death. No rebuke was too strong for those who hoarded it; no blessing too rich for those who distributed it. Here the question is not so much the poverty of the consumers but the greed of the suppliers. The saying assumes that normal business practices were being suspended for some devious purpose of the seller.

The surprises of generosity demonstrate the principle of reward that God has woven into the fabric of creation. They also show how different His ways may be from ours.

> There is *one* who scatters, yet increases more;
> And there is *one* who withholds more than is right,
> But it *leads* to poverty.
> *Prov. 11:24*

The one who gives gains; the one who holds loses. A penny saved may be a penny squandered. The Lord did not learn mathematics from *Poor Richard's Almanac. Scatters* is a strong verb used of the dispersal of Jews by their enemies (Joel 3:2; Esther 3:8), the diffusion of the bones of Israel's foes (Ps. 53:6), and the broadcasting of snow and hail by the divine Creator (Ps. 147:16). None of these instances suggests tidiness, care, or caution. "Scatters" here means distributing widely, generously, perhaps brashly, and paying little attention to where the beneficence goes. Yet the wealth of the generous *"increases"* more than the amount given away. The selfish person has the opposite experience. He hangs on to (*"withholds,"* maintains very tight control) his goods more tenaciously than he ought to, given his responsibilities and his neighbors' needs. When he opens his clenched fist, they have disappeared. What he deemed prudence *"leads to poverty."* He who wanted to make sure he had more than he needed ended in complete lack, as "poverty" means literally in Hebrew (see 14:23; 21:5; 22:16). The root word is translated "want" in Ps. 23:1. The selfish person sought to shepherd only himself and gained the pitiful results: he wanted for everything.

The rewards of generosity begin with enrichment:

> The generous soul will be made rich,
> And he who waters will also be watered himself.
> *Prov. 11:25*

"Rich" means literally "fat" and therefore thoroughly prosperous and healthy (see 13:4; 15:30). Such a state comes as the result of blessing others by sharing blessing with them. *"Generous soul"* is literally "soul (or "person") of blessing." The metaphor that describes the resultant prosperity is perhaps an artesian well, pumping an endless supply of water into the gardens of others while continually having more than enough for its own. Jesus gives us a spiritual illustration of this in His sermon at Tabernacles (John 7:37–39). The picture of water in more than abundant supply is especially striking when we remember that it was Palestine's most valued agricultural commodity.

Friendship is another reward, though it may be a mixed blessing.

> Many entreat the favor of the nobility,
> And every man *is* a friend to one who gives gifts.
> *Prov. 19:6*

The noble, influential, even "princely" person (see 17:7, 26) has a special obligation to generosity both because of divine blessing in his life and because he receives income from the people through taxation. Yet he is subject to special blandishments (*"entreat the favor"* means "stroke the face" or "butter up") that are themselves a nuisance; even more he may not know who his true *"friend"* is, so courted is he by fair-weather friends who long for his *"gifts."* None of this lessens his obligation to be generous, but it should remind those of us who may be on the receiving end that no need of ours absolves us from the integrity and sincerity we owe others, especially others whose favor we may court. Gift getting and gift giving were and are constant practices in oriental protocol. We Westerners are tempted often to emulate the manipulative or ambitious aspects of this practice without understanding the graciousness and affirmation that are also elements in it.

Repayment is the most striking reward of generosity.

> He who has pity on the poor lends to the LORD,
> And He will pay back what he has given.
> *Prov. 19:17*

Here a wholly different slant is placed on the transaction. It has the earmarks of a loan. The person who shows mercy (*"has pity"*) to the poor *"lends to the Lord,"* who, in turn will *"pay back"* his fair and accurate recompense (*"what he has given"*; see 3:30; 11:17; 12:14; 31:12 for the language of recompense). Jesus made this thought unforgettable: "Assuredly, I say to you, inasmuch as you did it to one of the least of these My brethren, you did it to Me" (Matt. 25:40). Light on the Lord's commitment to repay comes from Prov. 22:7: "And the borrower is servant to the lender."

> He covets greedily all day long,
> But the righteous gives and does not spare.
> *Prov. 21:26*

A serendipity of generosity is spotlighted in these lines. This verse complements 21:25 which pictures sloth as suicide (see chap. 10): the sluggard dies by his own hand, refusing to lift it to do any work! Instead of engaging in productive labor *"all day long,"* *"he covets greedily"* (the Hebrew structure deliberately magnifies the covetousness) and, thereby, breaks the law (Exod. 20:17; Deut. 5:21), despises his hardworking neighbor, and rots his own soul with bitterness. The *"righteous"* person, in contrast, escapes the sin of covetousness—that is the serendipity—by not grieving over what he does not have but by rejoicing in what he *"gives"* and gives unsparingly. One great gain of generosity is that it protects us from the soul-destructive preoccupation with greed.

The climax, spiritually and theologically, of the sages' teaching on unselfishness comes when the reason for generosity is stated.

> He who oppresses the poor reproaches his Maker,
> But he who honors Him has mercy on the needy.
> *Prov. 14:31*

The Lord is the principal participant in cruel or kind human transactions. Life is triangular in shape, as the Bible sees it. Our person-to-person relationships are like the horizontal base. But the apex to which both ends of the base are attached by upthrust lines is the Lord, who made and cares for both parties: the person who *"oppresses* [the word means "crushes"; 22:16; 28:3] *the poor* ["weak," "needy," "disadvantaged"]" scorns, even blasphemes (*"reproaches"*; 17:5) the poor person's (*"his"*) *"Maker"* (creator). So seriously does biblical faith take the doctrine of God's image in man as a gift of divine creation that acts done to a human being are as weighty as though done to God. Scarcely any idea has more power than this to change life radically. The antithetical second line states the positive side of the proposition: treating the *"needy"* (those in want, who have no means to meet their basic needs; 30:14; 31:9, 20) with *"mercy"* (tender, gracious compassion) by helping to meet their needs demonstrates an appreciation for God's worth and glory (*"honors"*). With Amos (5:21–24), the wise of Israel tolerated no distinction between worship of their Lord and the care of His people.

In conclusion we note how the style of proverbs reinforces their message. For the sages, *observation* was a key to unlock divine truth. They watched how life worked—the long-term impact of selfishness and generosity—and drew their apt conclusions from what they saw. One such conclusion is found in 11:24: give and gain; hold and lose. *Balance* is another feature of proverbs. If all we had were the pointed sayings that prod us to work hard and acquire much (see "Diligence in Work," chap. 10), we could rationalize our compulsive greed and endemic drive to self-protection. But just when we begin to savor that temptation, another set of sayings, equally pointed, goads us to use what our work has produced with lavish generosity to the needy. Compassionate, caring, inclusive capitalism is what the Bible calls for and what our affluent society finds so devilishly difficult to practice. Finally, *authority* is an essential characteristic of Proverbs. They are not casual suggestions as to how life can be improved, light options that raise the level of happiness; they are weighty yet winsome statements of obligation. They unpack, item by item, the implications of covenant living, which has the fear—the reverent, fervent obedience—of God as its core.

The expressions of divine order in proverbs dealing with generosity are highly personal. We are not looking at how life works automatically, so much as at how God has called us to behave. Even more, we are reminded, tacitly, of how God has behaved in generosity toward us. The laws of cause and effect, so essential to our understanding of Proverbs, are not suspended—good sowing does mean good reaping; bad sowing, bad reaping. Yet they are not the whole story. A personal God is at work, not only granting just rewards and fair punishments, but using our acts of generosity to bring His justice and His compassion into the lives of others. That some people will have more than others is assumed. That the talented young people being schooled to serve as leaders will have more than others is especially assumed. With that privilege goes the obligation to bring surprises of grace into the lives of the needy with the same light, openhanded touch with which God has blessed them.

The "poor" in these texts are not censured for their poverty. Biblical realism knows that differing talents, opportunities, backgrounds, and circumstances lead to differing economic states. The needy are not blamed for their deprivation; the affluent are blamed when they fail to help. Their very affluence is not only God's gift to them but God's means of helping others through them. A friend of mine bears the name of one of America's most wealthy and influential families. His masters at the New England prep school where he spent his formative years pounded into him the lesson that his family legacy meant obligation not privilege, service not leisure, philanthropy not consumption. Israel's wise would have approved of that understanding of the way the divine order works.

THE RISKS OF RASH PLEDGES

Some of the earliest stories of the Bible speak of pledges. When Jacob bargained with Tamar, whom he mistook for a harlot, he offered her a young goat as payment for her services (Gen. 38:16–20). Since the goat would be cut from the flock and delivered to Tamar sometime after the transaction was completed, she shrewdly asked for a pledge: Jacob's signet, the cord that held it, and the staff which any acquaintance would recognize as his, all sure signs that Jacob would be the father of any child born of the encounter. Jacob's efforts to exchange the pledge for the goat which he had promptly dispatched were thwarted by Tamar's cunning. For our purposes in Proverbs, the story illustrates the customary purpose of the pledge: to protect the rights of someone who had lent money or rendered services and had to wait for full recompense.

In the Genesis account, two parties are involved. Proverbs that warn against pledges usually imply three parties: (1) a person who is forced to borrow, (2) a person who is asked to lend, and (3) a person who is implored to guarantee repayment should the borrower default on the loan. "Cosigner" is the term that modern banking practices ascribe to the pledger. The transactions assume that the borrower has no equity or collateral to post as guarantee. In a culture where land, goods, and livestock were the common property of families or clans, individual assets were hard to come by. Sometimes a cloak (20:16; 27:13) was all a poor person, particularly a "stranger" (11:15) or foreigner could offer. Lenders necessarily felt that a third party whom they knew and trusted should share the risk. The persons of substance and repute to whom the proverbs are directed were visible targets to be singled out to play the pledger role. Their vulnerability and sometimes gullibility called for special counsel on these matters.

The previous warning (6:1–5) was direct, dramatic, and impassioned. It pictured the binding character of the promise and gave specific advice on the drastic means that one should take to be released from it before it led to inescapable entrapment. Four proverbs pick up the subject and look at it from two different angles—the perspective of the would-be pledger being asked to sponsor a loan (11:15; 17:18) and the perspective of the lender being called upon to accept a guarantee from a pledger (20:16; 27:13).

Rash pledging is a sign of foolishness:

> A man devoid of understanding shakes hands in a
>   pledge,
> *And* becomes surety for his friend.
>
> *Prov. 17:18*

Only a person *"devoid of understanding,"* lacking in sound judgment, prone to make quick and unstable decisions (Heb. "heart" points to the willful choice involved) will fall into the trap of shaking or striking *"hands"* in a gesture of *"pledge"* (or promise) and hence *"become surety for his friend"* (acquaintance or neighbor). "Surety" translates a Hebrew word that implies intertwining of lives, even sharing in responsibilities (see 20:19; 24:21, where "associates with" is the meaning). It is carried over into the New Testament and lends itself to Greek in the form of *arrabōn,* the important word for guarantee or down payment (2 Cor. 1:22; 5:5; Eph. 1:14), which describes the role of the Holy Spirit, God's pledge to His people that the whole work of redemption will one day be complete. In His infinite wisdom and sovereignty God can make and keep such a pledge. Those of us without such resources do well to be more cautious in what we promise.

Rash pledging can be a source of suffering:

> He who is surety for a stranger will suffer,
> But one who hates being surety is secure.
> *Prov. 11:15*

It pulls a train of evils or misfortunes, as *"will suffer"* indicates. Loss of goods in paying off a bad debt, strained relationships with the creditor, hostility toward the debtor, abuse of the family or community that participates in the loss of material assets—all these forms of suffering should be avoided and can be if one registers staunch reluctance (*"hates"*) to be put in that position and refuses to be partner in the hand striking that signals the bargain (*"being surety"*). *"Secure"* is the antonym to *"suffer."* It speaks of safety because one has retained the resources in which one is able to trust (the same Hebrew word means "trusting" in 11:28; 28:26).

From the lender's angle pledging carries its risks, and a suggestion for safety is in order:

> Take the garment of one who is surety *for* a
>   stranger,
> And hold it as a pledge *when it* is for a seductress.
> *Prov. 20:16*

> Take the garment of him who is surety for a
>   stranger,
> And hold it in pledge *when* he is surety for a
>   seductress.
> *Prov. 27:13*

The language of the two sayings is virtually verbatim in Hebrew, though NKJV expands its translation of 27:13. The basic counsel, voiced in the imperatives of an admonition, is that the lender should get a tangible guarantee—the pledger's *"garment,"* his outer cloak—not just a handclasp or a promissory note. Such collateral is especially important when the borrower is a *"stranger,"* a foreigner to the community or the country, whose reputation is unknown and whose assets cannot be attached. The second line of the synonymous parallelism says essentially the same thing. *"Hold it in pledge"* refers to the garment of line one and the word rendered *"seductress"* (see on 2:16; 5:20; 6:24) should be retranslated as "foreigners," a Hebrew synonym for stranger. At stake in these warnings was more than the protection of individual wealth or reputation. The stability of the society was a prime consideration. Promises lightly made or pledges rashly offered contribute to economic uncertainty and interpersonal ill will. They enable shysters and con men to flourish and jeopardize the credit of the reliable. The banking crises of the past few years are warning enough that borrowing, pledging, and lending carry substantial risk of pain. Polonius was not far from the mark in his advice to his son and Hamlet's friend, Laertes:

> Neither a borrower nor a lender be,
> For loan oft loses both itself and friend,
> And borrowing dulleth edge of husbandry.

The caveats against rash pledges may be read as footnotes on the advantages of generosity. In dealing with close friends or relatives, my wife Ruth has taught me that outright gifts may make for less strain and better relations than loans. If the person is able and willing to repay, good and well. Then we have a few dollars to give to someone else. If not, by viewing the transaction as a gift, we are spared both the anxiety of wondering if the repayment will come and the edginess of deciding whether to confront the issue when we see the other person. Jesus' word about keeping the left hand and the right hand in ignorance about the transactions in which each is engaged is a vote for quiet, unheralded generosity as a mode of Christian living.

CHAPTER TWELVE

Honesty and Kindness

Proverbs 12:1–28

Five proverbs in chapter 12 (vv. 6, 13, 17, 19, 22), bolstered by about twenty other sayings form the basis of our study of *Honest Speaking* (see also chap. 26), while verse 10 with 14:4 offers opportunity for brief comment on *Kindness to Animals*, a signal illustration of the teachers' concern for the importance of every facet of God's creation. The two topics are linked by more than coincidence. They remind us that we human beings share the state of creatureliness with the animal world. More than that, they recall that one duty of our God-given creatureliness was to name the animals (Gen. 2:19–20). Implied in that naming was the responsibility to distinguish among them, identify their needs, and as one recent commentator has noted to put "them into a place" in our world. The fact that animals, not things, are given names by our first parents shows their close relationship to the human family. Furthermore, this calling out of names for the animals was the first recorded instance of human speech. The naming marked them off from us as unsuitable partners but linked them to us as those who share the Creator's touch and with us inhabit God's earth. Our care of it includes our care of them. Speech makes all this possible.

HONEST SPEAKING

Despite the antiquity of writing, which by Solomon's reign, had seen more than two thousand years of development, the everyday cultures of the Middle East were largely oral—and in many places still are. We have no way of guessing at the literacy rate among the populace but can conclude only that its percentage was low. "Speaking" and "hearing" are far more frequent in the Bible's parlance than "writing" and "reading." This is true even in the proverbs which we have assumed were directed to the brightest and best of the nation's young, men chosen to become the leaders, administrators, and official scribes of the people. "Hear" is the favorite command directed to them (1:8; 4:1; 5:1; 7:24; 8:6, 32, etc.). Undoubtedly they possessed written skills, but their mandate was to listen. And even their reading may have been done aloud: the Hebrew word "meditate" (Ps. 1:2) means literally to "mutter."

Their way with words was their major art form, given the ban on idolatry which tended to discourage their devotion to the graphic arts. Listen to their stories in Genesis and Samuel; catch their fables and riddles in Judges; follow their disputes in Job or Malachi; grasp their similes and metaphors in Hosea and Jeremiah; puzzle at their visions in Ezekiel and Zechariah; tremble at their excoriations of iniquity in Amos and Isaiah; warm to the love lyrics of the Song of Solomon; lift your hands to the cadences of praise and the pathos of complaint in the Psalter; marvel at the canny and winsome wisdom of Proverbs. Art, all of it is art. This art enhances its spiritual value by clutching at our emotions as well as dazzling our intellects.

The Israelites were not only skilled in words, they were also dependent on them. With them they kept alive their tribal histories and customs. With them they played their games and released their tensions. With them they communicated their feelings, needs, and values, conducted their diplomacy, and regulated their commerce. Written contracts and bills of sale have survived for four millennia, thanks to the sharp stylus of the Akkadian scribes and the durable clay of their sunbaked tablets. But such documents were more the exception than the rule. The vast majority of transactions were never recorded only spoken. And then they were sealed by a gesture of commitment—the hand pressing against the loin, or squeezing the neck, or slapped or clutched by the hand of the partner. Not written documents but honest words were the stuff of which a stable society was built. No wonder Proverbs pays them so much attention!

The legal structure as well as the oral culture needs some comment if the cluster of proverbs under discussion is to be understood. The general outlines of judicial procedure can be reconstructed from Old Testament materials, even though there is no single place where its details are spelled out. It took place in the town gate, a central place of assembly for the prominent leaders of the community, some of whom acted as judges (1:21; 8:3; 22:22; 31:23, 31; Amos 5:15). The plaintiff would present the charge against the defendant, and both parties could summon witnesses. The more serious cases, and perhaps most ordinary ones, could be settled only when at least two witnesses supported the plaintiff's claims (Deut. 19:15; Isa. 8:2).

Material evidence would be presented where applicable: the fragments of an animal not stolen by the defendant but mauled by a wild beast (Exod. 22:12; Amos 3:12); the bed sheets of a woman accused of not being a virgin on her wedding night (Deut. 22:13–17). But the key to the whole endeavor was not only the fairness of the elders but the veracity of the witnesses. Their word had to serve as crucial evidence since the scientific technology available to our criminal investigations was unheard of: no fingerprints, fragments of skin under the fingernails, compromising photos of the accused, tape recordings of damning conversations. Due process, so essential to the welfare, stability, decency, and freedom of all peoples, depended more on the integrity of witnesses than on any other factor. Hence, their role in initiating the death penalty by casting the first stone (Deut. 17:7). Hence, the terse command, left unexplained: "You shall not bear false witness against your neighbor" (Exod. 20:16; Deut. 5:20). Hence, the fixation of the wise on the accuracy of legal testimony.

Two arenas of honesty are singled out for attention in Proverbs: the community and the courts. For both to be the centers of fellowship and justice for which they were designed, honest speaking had to become a way of life.

The welfare of a community is dependent first on the sound reputation of its leading citizens. They must be persons of recognized integrity who live above scandal. Tampering with their esteem without cause is both heinous and foolish.

> Whoever hides hatred *has* lying lips,
> And whoever spreads slander *is* a fool.
> *Prov. 10:18*

Though some translations, following the LXX, interpret the first line as the positive half of an antithesis, the synonymous form of the NKJV can be allowed to stand. *"Hatred"* or hostility, stored in the heart (*"hides"*), may prompt a person to *"lying"* slanderously against an innocent party. Such *"slander"* is as wickedly foolish (see 25:9–10) as was the bad-mouthing of the land of Canaan in which the shortsighted spies engaged in Moses' day (Num. 13:32; 14:36–37; "bad report" is the same Hebrew word as "slander"). The potential good that a citizen can do is undercut and the community itself, of which presumably the *"fool"* is a member, suffers loss of dignity and stability.

> The hypocrite with *his* mouth destroys his
>   neighbor,
> But through knowledge the righteous will be
>   delivered.
> *Prov. 11:9*

Such a rumormonger proves himself profane and godless (*"hypocrite"* may be too weak a word) and therefore untrustworthy. He is out for his neighbor's blood (*"destroy"* means *"slaughter"*). The militant attack calls for appropriate weaponry in defense: *"will be delivered"* means *"will arm himself adequately"* (see Num. 31:3). *"Knowledge"* (see on 1:4, 7), a theme word in Proverbs, used more than thirty times, is the proper armament: it can set straight the facts, discern the wicked motivations, and decide the right ways to present the defense—whether the *"righteous"* person is under assault in the community or in the courts. In legal contexts *"righteous"* may mean "innocent" (Amos 2:6).

> He who is devoid of wisdom despises his neighbor,
> But a man of understanding holds his peace.
> *Prov. 11:12*

The very act of slander in which one *"despises* [devalues in public]
his neighbor" is a badge of empty-headedness. *"Devoid of wisdom"* is
literally "lacking of heart," that is, of power to make right decisions.
Chances are that the facts are wrong, that the damages are irreparable, and that the fool is doing himself immeasurable harm by his
open display of savage immaturity. The contrast is clear: the person
who has the *"understanding"* or insight (see on 2:6) keeps his mouth
shut, as *"holds his peace"* more delicately suggests.

Retaining confidentialities is integral to the protection of sound
reputations within communities.

> A talebearer reveals secrets,
> But he who is of a faithful spirit conceals a matter.
> *Prov. 11:13*

"Secrets" (see 20:19; 25:9) are privileged information. Sharing them
turns one into a *"talebearer"* who has betrayed trust. Had he not
originally been trusted he would not have been made privy to the
secret. By broadcasting it he proved himself not to be a person
"faithful," reliable, dependable (see 25:13; 27:6) of *"spirit,"* disposition, or attitude. "Watch whom you tell your secrets, and watch that
you tell not the secrets of others" is the warning of this saying. Its
fitness to our times has prompted Peter Drucker to say on more than
one occasion, "If one other person knows it, it is no longer a secret,"
a biting comment on the way in which even Christian friendships
are riddled with verbal infidelity.

Honest communication is worth a great deal.

> What is desired in a man is kindness,
> And a poor man is better than a liar.
> *Prov. 19:22*

However deplorable it may seem to be devoid of material goods like
a *"poor man,"* his lot is infinitely richer than that of a *"liar."* The poor
can contribute *"kindness"* (covenant loyalty) to his neighbors, and
that ultimately is what *"is desired"* in others and what we desire for
ourselves. In contrast, the liar is cruel, not kind, robbing his neighbors of their good names and undermining the very foundations of
integrity without which a community will collapse.

Accurate information is essential to the sound decisions that the
wise teachers valued. Our judgments can rarely be better than our
grasp of the facts, and then only by accident!

> A wicked messenger falls into trouble,
> But a faithful ambassador *brings* health.
>
>   Prov. 13:17

The transmission of accurate information in the ancient world depended on a *"messenger"* (see 16:14; 17:11 the same word is translated "angel" in many texts) or an "emissary"; *"ambassador"* is too technical a term for the general conveying of news, plans, requests, or instructions intended here. If he carelessly or, worse, deliberately distorted the message, as *"wicked"* connotes, he brought disaster (*"trouble"*) on himself and the one who tragically trusted him. The *"faithful"* (see 11:13) carrier of information renders one of the services most valued in community life—*"health,"* healing, cure (4:22; 6:15; 12:18; 14:30; 15:4; 16:24; 29:1). Maliciously distorted information can make any situation sick—whether in political negotiating, commercial bargaining, discussions of land or water rights, or trustee meetings dealing with church building plans. The prophets understood full well the importance of the faithful transmission of the messages of their Superior and frequently prefaced them with the standard messenger formula of the day: "Thus says the Lord." For a secular example of this formula, see Gen. 32:4, where Jacob sends messengers to Esau.

> He who winks with the eye causes trouble,
> But a prating fool will fall.
>
>   Prov. 10:10

Candid confrontation may be necessary to keep community life sound. So the LXX understood the meaning of 10:10, where the Hebrew text may well have repeated the closing line of 10:8 by scribal error. In the Greek form the two lines are antithetical (see also RSV, NEB, JB):

> He who winks his eyes with deceit gathers griefs
>   for men,
> But he who reproves with boldness makes peace.

"Winks" must mean overlooking a fault, behaving dishonesty by pretending not to see how bad a situation is (6:13 contains a lengthy picture of such a person; see also 16:30). It is the opposite of *"reproves"* or *"rebukes."* The more closely people live together the more necessary it is to keep short emotional accounts by sharing feelings, clearing the air of misunderstandings, and gently letting each other

know how each feels. Any short-term conflict sparked by such caring confrontation can be the prelude to long-term peace making, a disposition that has the Master's own stamp of approval as a hallmark of the children of God (Matt. 5:9).

In the court the chief concern was for reliable witnesses. Life and death hinged on the words of those who testified, as some of the contrasting proverbs point out.

> The words of the wicked *are*, "Lie in wait for blood,"
> But the mouth of the upright will deliver them.
> > *Prov. 12:6*

> He *who* speaks truth declares righteousness,
> But a false witness, deceit.
> > *Prov. 12:17*

> A faithful witness does not lie,
> But a false witness will utter lies.
> > *Prov. 14:5*

> A true witness delivers souls,
> But a deceitful *witness* speaks lies.
> > *Prov. 14:25*

> A false witness shall perish,
> But the man who hears *him* will speak endlessly.
> > *Prov. 21:28*

Three synonymous proverbs focus on the practice and consequences of false witness. By adding a line that corresponds to, rather than contrasts with, the first, they reinforce the idea (second the motion, if you will) of the first line.

> A disreputable witness scorns justice,
> And the mouth of the wicked devours iniquity.
> > *Prov. 19:28*

Nothing less than havoc is what perjury entails. The description of the perjurer is as vicious as Hebrew can make it. *"Disreputable"* translates *beliyya'al,* a word that means worthlessness or wickedness (6:12; 16:27) and was picked up in the intertestamental period and the New Testament as Beliar or Belial (2 Cor. 6:15), a name for the devil. *"Scorns"* speaks of outrageous behavior that spits in the face of law, order, and piety as do the "scornful" in Ps. 1:1, who are named

Prov	Wicked	Righteous
12:6	*"Wicked"* are virtual murderers who advocate lying in wait (ambushing others; Judg. 20:29; Prov. 1:11, 18; 7:12) *"for blood"* (or bloodshed).	*"Upright"* so speak the truth that their mouths *"will deliver* [snatch from defeat, danger, or death; 2:12, 16; 14:25] *them."*
12:17	*"False witness"* (lit., *"witness of lies")* is not one who misreads the facts or forgets the details but who deliberately and meanly employs *"deceit"* (11:1; 12:5, 20; 14:8, 25) thus undercutting the stability of the whole society.	Speaking truth (what is utterly dependable; 12:22; 28:20) is a declaration of righteousness, a contribution to the wholeness, straightness, and soundness of the community, and ultimately an expression of deliverance and salvation.
14:5	*"False witness"* (lit., *"witness of a lie"*; Heb. *shāqēr* occurs in Proverbs about 20 times in singular and plural, as in 12:17) utters (breathes out, expresses; a favorite word in Proverbs; see 6:19; 14:25; 19:5, 9; 29:8) lies, statements designed to deceive (the noun *kāzāb* is a frequent object of the verb *"to utter"*; 6:19; 14:5, 25; 19:5, 9).	*"Faithful* [trustworthy, reliable] *witness"* does not engage in this kind of self-serving and dangerous act of falsifying (verb *kāzab*; 30:6).
14:25	*"Deceitful"* witness (see on 12:17) expresses the crooked intention of deliberate falsification (*"speaks* [or utters] *lies"*; see 14:5)	*"True witness"* (lit., *"witness of truth"*) is a lifeguard in a community, rescuing (*delivers"* see 12:6) persons (*"souls"*) from the murderous motives of those who lie in court.
21:28	*"False witness* [*"witness of lies"*; Heb. here is *kāzāb*, virtually interchangeable with *shāker; see 14:5*] *shall perish,"* whether literally or in the loss of all status and credibility in the community (see 19:9).	*"The man who hears"* (gets the facts right, truly understands the situation under trial) *"will speak"* *"successfully,"* *"correctly"* (better than *"endlessly"*), and thus maintain status and credibility.

in the company of the ungodly and sinners. To scoff at *"justice"* is to treat with mockery and spite the processes by which decent people protect the rights of others, insist that wrongs be punished and affirm the dignity of their own society. In the biblical context where social and personal justice was a reflection of God's own will for society, such disdain was as base a crime as any. It is as though *"the mouth of the wicked"* witnesses actually *"devours"* (*"gulps down,"* NIV) *"iniquity,"* worthless thoughts and deeds from which nothing good can come. Some translations, influenced by 15:28, change slightly the spelling of the Hebrew verb to read *"pours forth"* rather than *"gulps down"* (see NEB *"fosters"* and NASB *"spreads"*). In either reading the obscenity of perjury is clear. No wonder the punishment

is so severe and so certain: no court of elders will let these despisers
of justice's gate go unscathed.

> A false witness will not go unpunished,
> And *he who* speaks lies will not escape.
>   *Prov. 19:5*

> A false witness will not go unpunished,
> And *he who* speaks lies shall perish.
>   *Prov. 19:9*

"Unpunished" is legal language—to be declared clear or innocent
(6:29; 11:21; 16:5; 17:5; 28:20); "escape" has a similar meaning
here—to escape a guilty verdict and its consequences (see on 11:21).
The sense of all this is plain: those who seek to sabotage the mills of
justice will be ground under the very stones they try to dislodge.

The affects of honesty have been scanned in our look at its arenas.
Here it will be enough to summarize them briefly. Its positive influence is patent in a handful of sayings.

> He who winks with the eye causes trouble,
> But a prating fool will fall.
>   *Prov. 10:10*

Peace making rather than trouble bringing (for *"trouble,"* pain, or
grief, see 15:13; Job 9:28) is one gain. (See above for a revised translation of this proverb.) The following verse likens the mouth (the
speaking) of the neighbor to an artesian well that bubbles its life-
giving refreshment upon a thirsty land.

> The mouth of the righteous *is* a well of life,
> But violence covers the mouth of the wicked.
>   *Prov. 10:11*

(For the choking effect of *"violence,"* see on 10:6.) The metaphor can
turn military:

> The hypocrite with *his* mouth destroys his
>   neighbor,
> But through knowledge the righteous will be
>   delivered.
>   *Prov. 11:9*

"Knowledge" (knowing and telling the facts) is the weaponry through which the *"righteous"* triumph over the slander of the ungodly *"neighbor."*

> A wicked messenger falls into trouble,
> But a faithful ambassador *brings* health.
> *Prov. 13:17*

"Health" not *"trouble"* (misfortune, harm) is the end result when crucial messages are promptly and accurately delivered.

> A true witness delivers souls,
> But a deceitful *witness* speaks lies.
> *Prov. 14:25*

Actual life saving (*"delivers souls"*) is the ultimate positive result of truth telling, whether in the courts or the community.

Its dramatic deliverance is another affect of honesty. It equips the righteous person to evade the snares of the wicked.

> The wicked is ensnared by the transgression of *his*
>   lips,
> But the righteous will come through trouble.
> *Prov. 12:13*

The contrast of the two lines is highlighted if we read *"ensnared"* (lit. *"a snare"*) as what the *"wicked"* by their speech (*"lips"*) try to do to the *"righteous"* rather than what happens to the wicked themselves: "In the *transgression* [rebellion] of the *lips* is the *wicked* person's snare," set and cocked to discredit or condemn—we cannot tell whether or not a legal setting is in view—the righteous. The trap will not work; the righteous will go on their way without getting caught in the *"trouble"* (distress) plotted for him.

On the other hand, those who seek to sway the course of justice by their twisted tongues are the ones who will be caught and duly sentenced.

> A false witness will not go unpunished,
> And *he who* speaks lies will not escape.
> *Prov. 19:5*

> A false witness will not go unpunished,
> And *he who* speaks lies shall perish.
> *Prov. 19:9*

A trustworthy reputation is part of honesty's payoff.

> The truthful lip shall be established forever,
> But a lying tongue *is* but for a moment.
> *Prov. 12:19*

"The truthful lip" will turn into a sure foundation for life, *"established forever."* As long as the person lives and beyond, he will be remembered as credible; his word is solid enough to build on. Not so the *"lying tongue."* It is a flash in the pan. Its words have neither stability nor durability; once spoken, they drift, fade, and vanish. *But for a moment"* is literally *"while I would twinkle,"* the brief instant when the light hits the iris just right and the eye flashes. It is a powerful expression of the fleeting and transitory, as the author of Job knew when he used it to describe the short-lived joy of the godless (Job 20:5).

> A false witness shall perish,
> But the man who hears *him* will speak endlessly.
> *Prov. 21:28*

Prerequisite to the truthful lip is the open ear; sound hearing (getting the facts straight; as *"endlessly"* should be translated; see above) will allow a person to testify and gain a successful verdict. *"Him"* is not in the Hebrew text and should be omitted. The strong silent type may be a vanishing breed. But most of us would instinctively trust our reputations to those who have made their mark by listening at least as much as by speaking.

> A righteous *man* hates lying,
> But a wicked *man* is loathsome and comes to shame.
> *Prov. 13:5*

The language used for those who do not seek the truth before they speak it is strong. Such a person is *"loathsome,"* literally stinking or odious, fouling the air of his household and community. His ordained fate is to blush and flinch with *"shame"* (19:26)—and all because he is the opposite of the *"righteous"* person who utterly detests (*"hates"*) telling lies.

Honesty carries with it a covenantal consistency.

> What is desired in a man is kindness,
> And a poor man is better than a liar.
> *Prov. 19:22*

We see this consistency in the contrast between the *"liar"* and the person who desires *"kindness,"* a key biblical word (*ḥesed*) which smacks of "loyalty." The sharp difference between the Hebrew and LXX texts has prompted a variety of translations of which NIV best captures the sense, especially if we follow the footnote:

> What a man desires is unfailing loyalty;
> better to be poor than a liar.

We can view the matter from the personal or the social perspective and find the proverb equally sound. Lying is a violation of covenant kindness or loyalty. It is worse than poverty in its power to destroy both personal integrity and social stability. What we all desire is to be part of a community where we can rely on what people say because they know that covenantal living thrives only where truth is told.

Honesty's ultimate effect is divine approval.

> Lying lips *are* an abomination to the LORD,
> But those who deal truthfully *are* His delight.
> *Prov. 12:22*

"The Lord" Yahweh is the final judge of the outcome of honest speaking. Truth telling at bottom is not just a pragmatic option based on maxims like "cheaters never prosper" or "honesty is the best policy." Biblical people shun lying because liars have to have long memories and their lying tends to compound itself as lie follows lie, each interpreting and reinforcing the next. But even more than that they know that lying is a violation of the divine character and therefore an obnoxious offense (*"abomination"*; 3:32; 6:16; 8:7) to the God of truth. Only those who value truth as God does will be *"His delight,"* those in whom He takes full pleasure.

In conclusion, three matters call for quick looks. The question of exceptions comes first to mind. As a genre, proverbs major in generalizations. They tell us how to behave in the normal circumstances of life. They warn against the personal and communal damage of deliberately distorting or reversing the truth, especially where the reputation, safety, or legal rights of others are concerned. They leave open, to wise and sober judgment, the matter of how we behave under emergency conditions. May Christians be spies for their governments and engage in the subterfuge that goes with that territory? May Christians harbor refugees from a vicious government and plead ignorance of their whereabouts, as did Danes, Norwegians, and Netherlanders during Hitler's Jewish pogroms? May we lie to lunatics, sociopaths, or known criminals to protect family, friends, or property? The Bible seems to leave room for a "yes" answer. Biblical examples like Rahab's concealment of Joshua's spies (Joshua 2) and biblical principles like the call to resist evil even when the government is the perpetrator as in Daniel's acts of defiant prayer (Daniel 6) or John's promise of reward to those who violate Antichrist's mandate of worshipful submission (Revelation 13) suggest that a Christian conscience may allow or even urge breaches of the principle of truth telling when God's higher purposes are at stake. But most of our living goes on in contexts like the more normal social setting of the proverbs. We need to believe that "an honest women is as good as her bond," that "a handshake is as binding as a contract," that "truth will out" and therefore we should "tell the truth, the whole truth, and nothing but the truth" as our basic pattern of life. If we can accomplish that, by God's grace, we shall be given the wisdom to know the extreme conditions in which other patterns may be required.

Without saying so directly, proverbs implies that words—the gift of intelligible, unambiguous, and reciprocal communication—are *expressions of the divine image* within us. We can say "I and you" to God and to each other like no other members of the creation. This means that, with all else that makes for true humanity, our capacity for speech is not a human achievement but a divine legacy. The antithetic style of so many of the proverbs that deal with this subject is itself a symbol of the fact that the divine legacy has been corrupted by sin. Lying is a deliberate, willful misuse of both the God-given power of speech and the God-ordained principle of neighbor love which is the inevitable obligation of those made in God's image. The most important human characteristic is that we are all—whatever our sex, race, age, status, or culture—made like and for God. This monumental reality should bind us together in worship of God and respect for each other. Lying assaults this reality in both its divine and human dimensions. It is one of the most insidious by-products of our fall in Adam (Genesis 3). Honest speech, on the other hand, is an essential part of our commitment to be what the Creator made us to be, reflectors of God's truthfulness and protectors of the life and reputation of his people.

We do not have to be sages to catch our topic's importance to contemporary life. Playing fast and loose with truth seems to be a feature of our era. *Politically,* we have viewed a series of government hearings through the past two decades which have outraged us by their reports of lying among elected and appointed officials. *Economically,* we have seen vast fortunes made and lost by greed which erupted in dishonest statements, especially in crooked claims of injury before courts of law. *Commercially,* we have watched, heard, and read such a spate of false claims made for saleable products that we have been swamped to cry for rescue by a whole new breed of lifeguards—consumer advocates—to fetch us to the shores of truth. *Legally,* we have gazed at reports of witnesses—our experts, so-called—who have perjured themselves to help gain exorbitant settlements from the juries they deceive. *Materially,* the panderers of merchandise have falsely advertised their wares as keys to happiness and left a whole generation frustrated by what it could not acquire and bored with what it could. *Personally,* we have become so used to shading the truth that we barely know when we are doing it. We shape our words to make us look better than we are, to fabricate excuses for what we did wrong, to fake appointments on our calendars to avoid invitations we do not want to accept, to call in sick when beach or stream look attractive, to give phony reasons for lipstick on the collar. All of this has occupied legions of lawyers and sent insurance rates rocketing. Much worse, it puts our very covenant as a people in jeopardy. In the long run, we stand at risk from many things: sexual immorality, unbridled violence, chemical addiction, savage greed, external attack. It may be that none of them poses a greater threat to what we are as a people, called to live in covenant with the Lord God and each other, than our compulsive failure to tell the truth.

KINDNESS TO ANIMALS

Animal pets, especially dogs, were part of human life from the early stages of civilization as excavations from Jericho's New Stone Age levels (7000–4000 B.C.) reveal. Playful sport with them was noted in Prov. 26:17. In Jesus' day they are pictured as enjoying table (or undertable) privileges in some homes (Matt. 15:26–27; Mark 7:27–28). The wise teachers used their behavior to illustrate foolish and unacceptable conduct (Prov. 26:11, 17). Yet no direct injunctions have been preserved to tell us how to treat them.

With animals whose products—milk and wool—were valuable or who helped to process and haul the crops, the matter is different. Ezekiel 34, though basically a political treatise on the behavior of the nobility, is also a valuable instruction sheet on the care of sheep. Two of the proverbs, conscious of Israel's rural setting with its strong dependence on agriculture and its high proportion of labor dedicated to food production, remind us of the importance of farm animals and the obligation to look after them with kindness.

The sayings recall a pretechnical society when animals, not machines, bore the burden of arduous plowing, tilling, cultivating, hauling, threshing, and milling. On their lives depended the supply of materials hard to store, like wool (of which a constant source was needed for barter, sale, or replacement of material for garments, bedding, and tents) or like milk (which our ancestors had no way, except cheese, to preserve and widely distribute). Farm animals are still valued, but technology has made many of their ancient roles dispensable.

In view of prudence, kindness to animals was recommended behavior.

> Where no oxen *are*, the trough *is* clean;
> But much increase *comes* by the strength of an ox.
> *Prov. 14:4*

While a *"clean* [empty] *trough* [crib or stall for fattening animals; Isa. 1:3]" meant that no grain had to be expended to feed the domestic *"oxen"* that helped with the chores and no sweat exuded to haul the feed and sweep the crib, it also meant, as the contrasting line affirms, that productivity would remain low since only *"the strength of an ox"* (usually a young bull, castrated to keep him docile) would multiply the farmer's effort and produce *"much increase"* (income, productivity, or fruit; Heb. root describes what "comes in" to the coffers or granary). Increase of income calls for nothing less than increase of output. The farm beast has to be purchased, fed, equipped, and tended—all of which take goods and labor. Where the output is seen as investment, the prudent farmer will make it. And, having made it, he will care well for the animal as the key to an increased supply of food and material goods.

The second proverb seems to go a further step and teach kindness to 12:10 animals in view of providence.

> A righteous *man* regards the life of his animal,
> But the tender mercies of the wicked *are* cruel.
> *Prov. 12:10*

The two lines contrast sharply. The first pictures life in relationship. The *"righteous"* person understands how he depends on and what he owes to God, neighbor, and created possessions; his attitude toward his domestic beast (*"animal"*; see Gen. 8:1; 34:23; Lev. 11:2; Deut. 5:14) whether ox, milk cow, sheep, goat, or donkey is described as "regard" (knowing all about, caring thoroughly for; see Ps. 1:6; Amos 3:2, for this use of the verb "know"); it is a word of relationship, built on the animal's relationship to the Creator and the subsequent human regard for the Creator's gift and handiwork. The *"wicked"* persons (the noun is plural), to the contrary, pursue life in rebellion against the goodness of God and the creation. So out of phase are they that the most *"tender mercies"* (the word suggests the lower abdomen where physically our deepest feelings cluster; the Hebrew root means "womb") they can muster are branded *"cruel"* (11:27; 17:11; 27:4; the word can mean "deadly" like poison; Deut. 32:33).

Few proverbs silhouette more sharply the teachers' passion for seeing life whole. The animal world is not detached from the covenant, because it too was placed on earth by divine fiat. To be a biblical person means to see God's creatures through eyes of kinship and gratitude. To ignore that is to join the ranks of the wicked who do not admire what God did on history's first six days and add no "amen" in their living to God's verdict, "Very good!"

Implicit in these sayings is a call to be part of God's providence in guarding creation well. Ecological concerns will not be well served in our day if they are spearheaded by romantics who bow at nature's feet while turning their backs on nature's Source. Nor will gain come from aficionados of Eastern religions whose thirst for oneness with nature drives them to Buddhist or Hindu wells. Biblical people must provide a balance between adoration and exploitation. The whole creation and we human beings especially have as a first purpose to chant the glory of the Creator-Redeemer (Ps. 19:1). Our particular human role is to represent the Creator in the care of the creation (Gen. 1:28). The animal world, these proverbs suggest, is a good place to start. Animal abuse is as unchristian as animal worship or obsession with pets. Hunting for love of violence and thrill of the kill rather than for physical need is a violation of our divine commission (Hab. 2:17). God's ultimate covenant will bring peace between humankind and the world of beasts (Hos. 2:18). We wait for that peace with hope. Meanwhile we work toward it with kindness.

CHAPTER THIRTEEN

Violence and Hope

Proverbs 13:1–25

We have learned enough about the teachers' list of values to know that violence ranks low among their cherished attributes. Control of temper, speech, and action is important to them; violence disrupts their sense of poise and equilibrium. Genteel and modest use of power is a virtue with them; violence vitiates the mood of balance and proportion that marks authority when it is well employed. Stability in community life is a desideratum for them; violence explodes the networks of peace and goodwill that enable communities to function. In a half-dozen places the subject comes up and brings with it notes of warning, sighs of anguish, threats of disaster.

The teachers' realism about violence did not squeeze out their expectations of future blessing. Their commitment to an order, established and maintained by God, that promised not only survival but success to those who walked the right path gave them vision and courage to hold out hope to their pupils. The idea of hope is present wherever positive rewards are offered even though the word itself appears only rarely.

THE DANGERS OF VIOLENCE

Violence may be simply defined: the deliberate, willful effort to inflict harm on others by whatever means are available. The Hebrew terms (*ḥāmās* or *shōd*) reek with destruction. They describe what hostile armies do to helpless cities or what malicious men do to naive neighbors. Blood, smoke, and pain are the mix of violence no matter how artfully and shamelessly they may be disguised. The sages' treatment of it in Proverbs breaks down like this:

The forms of violence
    Speech   13:2

The forms of violence	
Speech	13:2
Deception	16:29–30
Oppression	28:3
Bloodshed	21:7; 28:17; 29:10
The targets of violence	
The poor—vulnerable and needy	28:3
The neighbor—gullible and trusting	16:29–30
The blameless—innocent and undeserving	29:10
The outcomes of violence	
Certain retribution	13:2, 19
Complete deprivation	28:3
Total destruction	21:7
Utter abandonment	28:17

Violence comes in many shapes and sizes. Like counterinsurgency, it may vary in technique from quiet infiltration, through guerrilla warfare, to massive demolition. It is a terrorist tactic in a peaceful community, whatever form it takes.

> A man shall eat well by the fruit of *his* mouth,
> But the soul of the unfaithful feeds on violence.
>
> *Prov. 13:2*

Treacherous speech (*"unfaithful,"* lying, deceitful people) is not the least of the types of violence. We are not told its precise form—false witness in court, empty gossip in the community, misrepresentation in a business transaction, placing a curse on an innocent victim? What we are told is that people have to eat their words (*"the fruit of his mouth"*). If those words are good, generous, kind, true, the person *"shall eat well"*; the good things spoken shall return to sustain him. If the person's speech reflects the treachery of his inner life, then *"violence"* will be his menu. *"Soul"* here should be translated as "gullet" or "appetite" and refers to what a violent man "craves" (NIV) or "desires" (NASB) and what he gets in retribution as his bitter diet.

Subtle deception is another form of violence. It is viewed as particularly loathsome when the neighbor is its object.

> 16:29 A violent man entices his neighbor,
>   And leads him in a way *that is* not good.
>   30 He winks his eye to devise perverse things;
>   He purses his lips *and* brings about evil.
>
> *Prov. 16:29–30*

Again we can only guess at the precise nature of the crime. *"Entices"* points to false promises, slick blandishments, artful lies by which he *"leads"* the friend to engage in conduct that will result in harm or even death—*"a way that is not good"*: not good in its practice, not good in its result. It may be complicity in a crime like those plotted by the perverse chaps of 1:10–19, participation in a crooked business scheme, or a pledge of guarantee for a loan that the violent borrower has no intent of repaying (see on 6:1–5 and "Rash Pledges" in chap. 11). Whatever the scam is, it is frightful: *"perverse things"* means the whole value system is turned upside down; *"evil"* suggests that the crime both inflicts deadly harm and will receive painful punishment. The neighbor's gullibility is implied in the failure to read the telltale signs of the schemer's body language: blinking, darting, shifty eyes and nervous pursing, puckering, and probably licking of the *"lips."* The neighbor's naiveté is added evidence of the violent person's criminality. He has taken ruthless advantage of one too simple to have known better.

Perhaps even more shameful than such deception is the oppression inflicted on the poor.

> A poor man who oppresses the poor
> *Is like* a driving rain which leaves no food.
> *Prov. 28:3*

The perpetrator is more likely to be a person of power, a leader or principal figure in the community than a fellow son of poverty. The first *"poor"* in the sentence should be changed slightly in Hebrew spelling to mean "head," "chief," or "foremost." The metaphor suggests irresistible, unrelenting power of one person over the other like the power of *"a driving rain"* which batters the grain into the ground, chokes out its life, leaves the field desolate. For other proverbs that express concern for the poor, see chapter 22 on "Crimes of Injustice."

> A man burdened with bloodshed will flee into a pit;
> Let no one help him.
> *Prov. 28:17*

It comes as no surprise that the violent person will not shrink from *"bloodshed."* The single-minded intensity at making gain despite the cost to others has already shown how cheaply he values human life. It is only a small step from fraud to murder, and another small step from murder to inevitable judgment where all aid and respite (*"help"*) are prohibited.

> The bloodthirsty hate the blameless,
> But the upright seek his well-being.
> *Prov. 29:10*

This is particularly true when the violent (*"bloodthirsty"*) comes into conflict with the *"blameless"* (or "complete," "perfect" like Job in 1:1) person. The clarity and purity of the one life serves as a mirror to expose the perverseness and corruption of the other. It is easier to shatter the mirror than to change the wretched face. Only those who are *"upright"* (innocent of violent plans and deeds) are free enough from envy and guilt to promote (*"seek"*) the *"well-being"* of the well behaved.

The terror of this violence is documented in subjects singled out as targets: the poor, vulnerable and needy and powerless to resist oppression, long on exploitability and short on advocacy in the community (28:3); the neighbor conditioned to trust and share by virtue of the interdependence of life in the villages and towns of Israel and perhaps by the coolly calculated "friendly" comportment of the crook prior to the crime (16:29–30); the blameless, innocent and undeserving, ripe to be exploited because exploitation is so far removed from their ways of acting and thinking. Nothing unmasks the meanness of the violent more than the nature of their hit list. It is a who's who of the undeserving. It combines the names of those who are least suspecting, most readily violated, and least apt to have the will or the means of retaliation.

But what the violent failed to take measure of was that life itself, ordered by a just and powerful Creator, would see that their crimes received a fitting outcome. Their retribution was certain. What they fed others—whether blessed helpful words or violent, harmful words—was what they had to eat (13:2). The boomerang character of reward or punishment was something that the violent—rendered blind and mindless—by their savage greed failed to take stock of. Like enraged bulls, they charged madly at their targets with no sense that behind the red flag lurked the sword of death.

Deprivation will be the certain lot of those who store up gain by depriving others of their goods. The picture of the driving rain demonstrates this (28:3). Oppression of the poor not only deprives the poor of sustenance, it also, in the long run, robs the oppressor of the goods that the poor would produce and of the means that the poor may garner to buy products from the affluent. When oppression washes out the entire crop, the oppressor may suffer hunger along with the poor. An imbalance where some have almost all of the wealth and others have none will in the end prove hurtful to the "haves" whose ultimate welfare is dependent on the abilities of others both to produce and to purchase agricultural crops and manufactured goods. An illustration opposite to that of exploitation is Henry Ford's revolutionary decision to pay laborers in the auto industry the then unheard of sum of $5 a day, which enabled them in time to buy the cars they helped to make.

Violence, as a pattern of injustice, may result in destruction.

> The violence of the wicked will destroy them,
> Because they refuse to do justice.
> *Prov. 21:7*

It breaks the rules and shatters the norms of society. In so doing, violence compromises its right to fair trial, due process, or leniency because of unusual circumstances. Refusing *"to do justice"* makes it hard, especially in tribal societies like Israel's, to insist on receiving justice. Community wrath rises to fever pitch in the face of flagrant oppression, and destruction of the oppressors is often the result. Marie Antoinette may have reflected on that reality as she placed her head on the block and waited for the guillotine to fall. And even where the masses are crushed beyond any ability to retaliate, justice will usually win in the end, given God's relentless commitment to it and his vehement resistance to all who violate it. That divine passion for justice is reflected in *"will destroy them,"* where the imagery, if the picture of fishing in Hab. 1:15 (which uses the same Hebrew word *gārar*) carries over to the proverb, is of being caught up and carried away in a fishing net, perhaps a net of their own making.

Utter abandonment seems to be the outcome featured in 28:17 (see above), which departs from normal proverbial form and sounds quite like a legal pronouncement. *"Burdened"* (or *"oppressed"*) with *"bloodshed"* seems to describe an awesome, inescapable load of guilt from which a person cannot escape, short of the *"pit,"* the grave, or death. Like Cain's fate as a fugitive and wanderer, the lot of the violent would be an unremitting pilgrimage toward death. Divine justice was not to be denied. In fact, whereas Cain's banishment included a command that no one should harm him, this pronouncement concludes with an order that no one should try to *"help him."* The implication is that no one would be able to provide rescue or relief even if he or she did try, so set was God on just retribution for the taking of life.

The heart of these lessons on violence is, of course, the sanctity of human rights—rights of reputation, rights of possessions, rights of protection, rights of life. The sternness of the proverbs with their harsh promises of retribution is cogent evidence of God's concern for the welfare of all persons, as creatures of his care, and for the stability and safety of the communities in which he has placed them. No society can be called decent that does not understand and convey that concern to all its citizens.

THE SIGNIFICANCE OF HOPE

The psychology of expectation was well understood by the sages. They knew the need for hope.

> Hope deferred makes the heart sick
> But *when* the desire comes, *it is* a tree of life.
> *Prov. 13:12*

They understand that *"hope"* is the strong line that pulls us out of the pit of boredom or despair. We can cope with the emptiness or anguish of today because we know that better things will come our way in due season. We are willing to work hard and live frugally during days as college students or newlyweds because we know that our sacrifice will be rewarded with promotion and prosperity down the line. When that hope is not rewarded on some reasonable schedule, we become sick of heart. Depression moves in and brings its roommate along—hopelessness. Such is the lot of thousands of persons today in their twenties and early thirties who are victims of what one observer has labeled "postponed adolescence." Raised in the 1960s, ebullient with hope for personal growth, prosperity, and power to bring social change, they have found themselves under-employed for their educational level, bored with a ho-hum lifestyle, intimidated by the harshness of their lot, and frustrated by the lack of opportunity. Deferred hope has literally made their hearts sick.

But the second half of the proverb is also true. The *"desire"* is the good things longed for, the hope whose postponement brought such agony. When it *"comes"* it brings complete revitalization. Acceptance to medical school, a positive answer from a sweetheart who had been previously indecisive, an extraordinary return on an investment, a loved one restored to health when all seemed bleak— these all are expressions of desire come true, with its life-giving powers. Nothing about us is more human than our ability to imagine the future and to be distressed or blessed by its outcome. One of the great gifts of the gospel is its hope which never lets us down (Rom. 5:5).

The wise teachers knew the satisfaction of hope as well as the need for it.

> A desire accomplished is sweet to the soul,
> But *it is* an abomination to fools to depart from evil.
> *Prov. 13:19*

"*Soul,*" as in 13:2, means "gullet" or "appetite." The metaphor is concrete: hope realized is like honey or sugar in its delight to the palate of our emotions. The second half of the verse seems only loosely connected to the first. Commentators frequently link 13:19a with 13:12 and 13:19b with 13:18. If we assume a tie between the two halves of 13:19, that tie may be sketched as follows: "*fools*" can never taste the sweetness of realizing positive goals because they are compulsively, "religiously" (as "*abomination*" suggests) attached to their "*evil*" ways. Since they will not "*depart*" or "turn away" from their shameful behavior they disqualify themselves from any blessing for which they brashly hope.

CHAPTER FOURTEEN

Fear of the Lord and Control of the Self

Proverbs 14:1–35

"Fear of the Lord"—like the four notes that mark the theme of Beethoven's Fifth Symphony, these words are pounded out at the beginning of Proverbs (1:7), at the end of the wisdom speeches (9:10), and periodically through the rest of the book. Its repetition never lets us forget the theological and spiritual meaning of wisdom. Its recurrence means that we can never slip into secular definitions of insight or prudence; we can never view wisdom as mere cunning or skill. "Fear of the Lord," sprinkled as it is throughout the text, salts the whole collection and preserves it from becoming tainted with flatly humanistic or plainly pragmatic approaches to wisdom.

Coupled in this chapter with the major theme of Fear of the Lord is the counter melody of Control of the Self. To be a God-fearer suggests not only devotion but discipline. It insists that all of life be kept in check—harsh speech, lustful appetites, violent actions, and above all fierce tempers. Long before the apostle Paul grouped self-control with the fruit of the Spirit (Gal. 5:23), Israel's wise had extolled it as a virtue deeply to be cherished by all persons, especially those to whom others looked for leadership and on whom they depended for guidance.

REVERENT OBEDIENCE

An outline by which to organize the sayings on fear of the Lord might look like this:

Understanding the fear		
a straight walk	14:2	
a humble ear	15:33	

a tender heart	28:14
a cleansed life	16:6
Valuing the fear	
its worth	15:16
its satisfaction	19:23
its safety	29:25; 14:26
its vitality	10:27; 14:27; 22:4

To understand the fear of Yahweh is to know it not as a fleeting emotion or a passing notion but as a habit, a straight walk.

> He who walks in his uprightness fears the LORD,
> But *he who is* perverse in his ways despises Him.
> *Prov. 14:2*

"Walks" and *"ways"* both testify to a continued pattern, a constant commitment to *"uprightness,"* a life marked by integrity, transparency, and sound behavior. "What you see is what you get" is one description of it. To be *"perverse"* is to follow the opposite track—crooked, deceitful, and underhanded. There are certainly social ramifications to such conduct, as the teachers frequently point out. But here the sage highlights the ultimate obscenity of life without integrity—it treats God with scorn (*"despises"*) and is a brand of blasphemy.

True fear is mediated through sound teaching, and a humble ear is its necessary prerequisite.

> The fear of the LORD *is* the instruction of wisdom,
> And before honor *is* humility.
> *Prov. 15:33*

Though there may be mystical elements in our prayer lives, our sense of Christian call, our day-by-day appreciation of God's presence, the content of our faith is usually conveyed by teaching and preaching. *"Instruction of wisdom"* (see on 1:2–6 for both nouns) comes to us through preachers and teachers whose grasp of God's ways and word enables them to open their insights to us and us to their insights. And before we can be accorded any *"honor"* or "glory" for either wisdom or obedience, we have to sit in *"humility"* before that instruction, with a clear openness and a deep sense of neediness which are prime ingredients of humility. Our generation so exalts good communication that virtually all the weight for getting the point across rests on the speaker. This is neither fair nor realistic.

The learner has a clear obligation as well—an obligation to recognize the need to learn and to do everything possible to aid that learning.

A tender heart is comrade to a humble ear.

> Happy *is* the man who is always reverent,
> But he who hardens his heart will fall into calamity.
>   *Prov. 28:14*

By this beatitude (see on 3:13; 8:32–34), the teacher is not touting compassion, as "tender heart" connotes to our ears, but obedience, a pliable will that is *"reverent"* (lit., "fearing") toward God and makes its decisions at his beckoning. *"Hardens his heart"* is a phrase for the willful stubborn disobedience that made Pharaoh infamous in Moses' day (Exod. 7:13–14). No beatitude (*"happy"*) is pronounced on him; only the *"calamity"* of unleashed waves and raging waters.

No saying may plumb the depths of what the wise meant by the fear of the Lord more than this picture of a cleansed life:

> In mercy and truth
> Atonement is provided for iniquity;
> And by the fear of the LORD *one* departs from evil.
>   *Prov. 16:6*

The synonymous parallelism tells us that *"fear of the Lord"* is marked by the attributes of *"mercy"* (Heb. ḥesed) and *"truth"* (Heb. ʾemet), qualities that characterize God's person and are what He desires in His covenant people. Without this aim to be like God and emulate His virtues, religious acts and rituals are empty deeds of human effort. *"Atonement"*—God's dealing with sin so that judgment is avoided—*"for iniquity,"* a concept commonly found in the instructions for sacrifice of Exodus and Leviticus, is possible only when the heart of the worshiper is contrite and obedient (Ps. 51:15–17; Hos. 6:6). Such obedience—fear of the Lord—leads one away from the harm or disaster (*"evil"*) that judgment for iniquity would necessarily entail. Nowhere is the faith of the teachers closer to the faith of the prophets and the psalmists than here.

Having caught something of the meaning of fear of the Lord, we turn to passages which expound its value. Its basic worth is featured in this comparison:

> Better *is* a little with the fear of the LORD,
> Than great treasure with trouble.
>   *Prov. 15:16*

The saying has no intention of devaluing wealth; the proverbs deal frequently with its advantages and its significance as a possible sign of divine blessing. The teacher's goal is to extol the *"fear of the Lord"* as a way of life to be treasured beyond measure. Even wealth with all that it signifies and affords is to be counted as nothing in comparison. Paul's words are a New Testament comment on the sense of this proverb: "Indeed I also count all things loss for the excellence of the knowledge of Christ Jesus my Lord" (Phil. 3:8).

The satisfaction it gives is another aspect of its value:

> The fear of the LORD *leads* to life,
> And *he who has it* will abide in satisfaction;
> He will not be visited with evil.
>   *Prov. 19:23*

"Life" in the biblical sense embraces much more than survival, though it certainly includes that concept. Here it is described as *"satisfaction,"* all basic needs met, nothing missing that would contribute to well-being. One result of fearing the Lord is the ability to sleep well. *"Abide"* means to *"pass the night."* God-fearers know that their deepest needs have been and will be met. Their righteous obedience is itself a safeguard against the calamities (*"evil"*) that may stalk the nights of those who run counter to God's will.

This theme of safety is sounded in two other proverbs.

> In the fear of the LORD *there is* strong confidence,
> And His children will have a place of refuge.
>   *Prov. 14:26*

The total provision of 19:23 is matched by the total protection of this verse. Fearing the Lord is the distinguishing mark of God's family. To revere and obey Him is to become *"His children,"* full of *"confidence,"* *"trust,"* and *"certainty"* that He cares and His care is as effective a shelter as a military fortress (*"refuge"*) would be. The mention of refuge or fort in Ps. 46:1, which uses the same Hebrew word as Prov. 14:26, sparked Luther's heart and pen with the theme song of the Reformation:

> A mighty fortress is our God
> A bulwark never failing.

The contrast between the value found in trusting God and trusting human beings is made clear in this proverb:

> The fear of man brings a snare,
> But whoever trusts in the LORD shall be safe.
>
> *Prov. 29:25*

Snare (see also 14:27; the word may mean "trigger-bar," the piece of wood or metal that holds the bait and releases the trap when pushed or stepped upon), trap, and pitfall are standard metaphors of unexpected calamity. Foolish persons are like dumb animals or unsuspecting birds when it comes to being trapped. *"Fear of man"* means crediting human beings, who are not God-fearers, with the power and wisdom to guide our lives. It means turning our pivotal decisions and basic values over to them and hence walking in their ways, not God's. It means trusting them when they are not trustworthy. It is the precise opposite of what we are commanded to do in Prov. 3:5–6.

> 3:5 Trust in the LORD with all your heart,
>   And lean not on your own understanding;
>   6 In all your ways acknowledge Him,
>   And He shall direct your paths.
>
> *Prov. 3:5–6*

Let people play god for us and the results cannot help but be disastrous. Dependence on the Lord and His guidance is the only safe route to travel.

The vitality produced by the fear of the Lord is its final value extolled by the sages. The general principle is stated in these contrasting lines:

> The fear of the LORD prolongs days,
> But the years of the wicked will be shortened.
>
> *Prov. 10:27*

One lesson from the antithetical parallelism is that the opposite of God-fearer is *"wicked."* And there can be no permanent category in between. The difference between the two ways of life is so vast, so total, that it affects the length of life. To live in utter disregard of God and in basic violation of His will is so to disrupt the normal flow of things that health itself may well be jeopardized. Stress, anxiety, conflict, dissipation all take their toll on human vitality and longevity. And where violence is a life habit the risks are even greater. Modern medicine and psychotherapy may have alleviated the impact of sin and extended life in spite of it. But they have eliminated neither it nor its results. The principle holds, though its application to individual lives may vary.

That principle is stated in a powerful mixed metaphor:

> The fear of the LORD *is* a fountain of life,
> To turn *one* away from the snares of death.
> *Prov. 14:27*

"Death" is the persistent hunter, trailing the unwary and silently coaxing them to make decisions that will catch them in his snares (see above on 29:25)—decisions about companionship, work, relaxation, diet, personal habits that violate God's will. The fear of God, like a ceaseless *"fountain"* provides both refreshment and persistence to enable us to quell death's plot.

The positive value of biblical obedience is summed up simply in these synthetic lines:

> By humility *and* the fear of the LORD
> *Are* riches and honor and life.
> *Prov. 22:4*

The combination of hard work and careful stewardship leads to *riches* not poverty. Riches is, of course, a relative term. Here and elsewhere in Proverbs (see chap. 19 on "Advantages of Wealth") it means something like having enough material goods to care for one's own family and to give generously to those around you who may be in want. Such wealth along with upright behavior and regard for the welfare of neighbors in the community promotes *"honor"* not shame. Honor refers to personal reputation and esteem. It literally conveys the sense of carrying weight, being regarded as a substantial person among the circle of acquaintances. *"Life"* here is longevity, preservation from illness or misfortune that would shorten the days of the wicked according to 10:27.

PERSONAL DISCIPLINE

The correlative topic of this chapter may be presented in a form something like this:

Introductory theme   13:16
The signs of self-control
  Discipline of personal appetites

craving for liquor	20:1
longing for luxuries	21:17, 20
wallowing in envy	14:30
Buoyancy under stress	15:13, 15; 17:22; 18:14
Openness to counsel	18:1
Constraint of temper	
As a normal pattern	12:16; 14:17, 29; 15:18;
	16:32; 19:19
As a response to attack	17:13, 14; 19:11; 20:3
The sources of self-control	
Correction in one's youth	20:30
Counsel from a profound person	20:5
Comradeship of a controlled person	27:19

Biblical wisdom is full of checks and balances. It shuns excesses; it avoids compulsiveness. It calls for total allegiance to Yahweh and freedom from all other forms of thralldom, especially thralldom to one's own basic urges. The teachers admired frankness and honesty but warned against sharp tongues impelled by hot tempers. They treasured the good life as a mark of divine blessing and argued that such blessings be neither hoarded nor squandered. They viewed the fruit of the vine as God's gift and chided those who abused it by overconsumption. They would have appreciated the words of "America the Beautiful."

> Confirm thy soul in self-control,
> Thy liberty in law.

The teachers marked a basic difference between the mastery of life that characterized the wise and the total loss of control exhibited by the foolish.

> Every prudent *man* acts with knowledge,
> But a fool lays open *his* folly.
>   *Prov. 13:16*

An alternative translation of the first line (supported in the Syriac and Vulgate versions) makes *"every"* the object of *"acts"*: *"a prudent man does everything with knowledge."* Such a person is in full control of his words and actions. He demonstrates a competence and quickness that leads to success, while retaining a canny subtleness that does not make a show of his capabilities (on "prudent," Heb. ʿārûm, see 12:16, 23). The self-control is prompted and guided by *"knowledge"* of what God is and what God wants (see 1:2, 7). In contrast the fool makes public display (*"lays open"*) of his folly. His talk and manner shout what he is to all the world. "Lays open" translates a verb (Heb. *pāraś*) that may describe the spreading of a net as though to catch others in his foolishness (Hos. 5:1; 7:12) or the setting out of wares for sale in the marketplace (see McKane's support of B. Gemser's suggestion). So out of control is a *"fool"* that he becomes either malicious in trying to trap others or stupid in thinking that his wicked nonsense is of public use.

The signs of self-control are sprinkled throughout the book. Israel's potential leaders were well informed by their mentors of the marks of discipline in habits, values, attitudes, and relationships. Self-control is an important attribute of anyone who wants to belong to a community, but it is an indispensable part of the equipment of any leader.

One clear sign of self-control is discipline of personal appetites. In a graphic saying drunkenness is singled out for the way in which it takes possession of persons, dictates their behavior, and robs them of the capacity to act wisely:

> Wine *is* a mocker,
> Strong drink *is* a brawler,
> And whoever is led astray by it is not wise.
> *Prov. 20:1*

By treating *"wine"* and *"drink"* as persons—the one a *"mocker"* (an object of frequent disdain in Proverbs; virtually the ultimate fool; see 1:22; 3:34; 9:7–8), the other a *"brawler"* (engaging in rowdylike conduct; see 7:11; 9:13)—the proverb dramatizes their impact on the intemperate person. They take charge and so control behavior that those under their influence (*"led astray"*) lose all ability to behave the way wise persons should. Wine is both valued and feared in Proverbs: Wisdom serves it at her banquet (9:2) as a mark of her elegant hospitality; Lemuel's mother warns her royal son against its power to muddle the mind and thus pervert the course of justice (31:4–9; see also 23:19–21, 29–35). *"Strong drink"* translates the word used (Heb. *shēkār*) for all alcoholic beverages besides wine, especially date liquor or beer (see 31:4, 6). The specific point of the final line is not that it is unwise to drink but that drink, when we are in its grips, renders us unwise.

Another expression of the highlife is to be avoided, the longing for luxuries.

He who loves pleasure *will be* a poor man;
He who loves wine and oil will not be rich.
                                            Prov. 21:17

The combination of hard work and divine blessing that may produce wealth is too important, too sacred, to allow its fruit to be squandered. Wealth is for security, independence, and charity, not for self-indulgence. Moreover, love of goods—like *"wine"* and *"[olive] oil"*—which bring pleasure rather than sustenance will rob us of the wealth we have acquired and make us *"poor"* in the end, as we expend our money on frills not essentials.

There is desirable treasure,
And oil in the dwelling of the wise,
But a foolish man squanders it.
                                            Prov. 21:20

Where such delicacies (*"desirable treasure"*) have been garnered they should be used sparingly. *"Oil"* especially had a valuable multiple use in Israel's homes—hygiene, medicine, fuel for lamps, condiment for cooking. Only a fool would squander (lit., "gulp it down") such a useful product that could be obtained only by the hard work of the farmer who grew, picked, and pressed the olives, and then hauled the oil to market in skins or clay jars. Whatever the "Lifestyles of the Rich and Famous" may look like in our day, the teachers' emphasis on diligence and stewardship rather than idle consumption is a lesson worth noting.

Wallowing in envy is another appetite that has to be curbed.

A sound heart *is* life to the body,
But envy *is* rottenness to the bones.
                                            Prov. 14:30

We are not to indulge in personal extravagance nor are we to be jealous (as *"envy"* literally means; see Eccles. 4:4) of those who seem to have money to burn. The *"sound* [or "healthy"] *heart"* which is envy's opposite in the proverb is the ability to make good decisions in the use of what we have. Those decisions become, then, a source of *"life"* to our *"body"* (lit., the "flesh"); they sustain us and keep us content with our lot. The alternative is to make ourselves bitter, unproductive, even sick with the lust for what we do not have—a condition so debilitating that it undercuts our stability and mobility like a severe case of osteoporosis (*"rottenness of the bones"*).

Buoyancy under stress is another sign of self-control.

A merry heart makes a cheerful countenance,
But by sorrow of the heart the spirit is broken.
Prov. 15:13

All the days of the afflicted *are* evil,
But he who is of a merry heart *has* a continual feast.
Prov. 15:15

A merry heart does good, *like* medicine,
But a broken spirit dries the bones.
Prov. 17:22

The spirit of a man will sustain him in sickness,
But who can bear a broken spirit?
Prov. 18:14

The ability to take what life sends and stay on the bright side was a trait the teachers treasured. They were utterly realistic about the amount of pain that life inflicted on the average person. But they also knew what a difference the right attitude could make. In 17:22 they played on the contrast between a *"merry* ["joyful"] *heart"* (15:13, 15) and a *"broken* ["beaten," "shattered"] *spirit."* One brought health like a good *"medicine"*; the other dehydrated the very *"bones"* of the sufferer. The medicinal effects of cheerfulness were explored by Norman Cousins in his famous experiment with comedy films and the therapeutic impact of laughter during his painful recovery from an inflammation of the nervous system. So dramatic were his findings that he has served on the faculty of the UCLA School of Medicine sharing his experiences with the neophyte physicians. His personal research anticipated the discovery of endorphins and other hormonal secretions which are the body's own pain blockers, released by the act of laughter and other expressions of hopeful, positive outlook.

Only the merry heart or spirit (18:14) can counteract the hardship (*"sorrow"* in 15:13) and *"sickness"* (18:14) that weigh us down and keep us from the complete emotional and spiritual collapse that *"broken spirit"* suggests. "Depression" is probably our modern equivalent. As the teachers knew, it was easier to prevent than to cure. Who can lift up (*"bear"*) a broken spirit once it sags to the bottom of hopelessness (18:14), inner disaster (*"evil,"* 15:15), and psychosomatic affliction? How important that we remind ourselves regularly of the resources available in our faith to stoke the fires of joy in hearts that burn low! And how helpful it is to have available in our day both the medical technology and clinical skills to mend the broken spirits! None of these, however, is a substitute for the healing of the soul's diseases that only the forgiving, sustaining grace of God can perform.

Openness to counsel is a vital sign of self-control. Self-control and self-sufficiency are two separate matters. The wise extol the former and decry the latter.

> A man who isolates himself seeks his own desire;
> He rages against all wise judgment.
>
> *Prov. 18:1*

Conning himself into thinking that he is self-contained, he *"isolates"* (*"separates"*) himself from the community and tries to live by his own intuitions, insights, and instincts (*"desire"*). He sees life from his angle only and pays no heed to the perspectives of his fellow citizens. In fact he is inclined to greet their helpful suggestions or sound decisions (*"wise judgment"*; see 2:7; 3:21; 8:14 for other uses of the Heb. word, *tushiyyāh*) with outbursts of anger and rejection (*"rages"*; the same word is translated *"start a quarrel"* in 17:14 and 20:3). The response is not only a symptom that self-control is lacking but that the person knows that it is lacking and that he is forced to rally all his defenses around an indefensible position. This turned-off dropout reminds me of his fellows in our own land during the 1960s. I asked one of them in the Haight-Ashbury district of San Francisco what he imagined himself doing twenty years from then. He flashed back at me, "I don't plan ahead, man, I don't plan ahead." Isolated, self-guided, and insulted by conventional wisdom, that young man was a symbol of a whole generation. But he was also a mirror image of a type known to wisdom's teachers from time immemorial.

The rage of the hermit was but one illustration of a failure of self-control in its most common form—failure of constraint of temper. A half-dozen sayings alert us to the explosive dangers of a short fuse and its incendiary impact on personal and community relations. The ability to bear conflict or abuse with poise was a cherished mark of the wise. As a normal pattern, they knew how to keep cool when the volcanic tempers of others erupted around them.

> A fool's wrath is known at once,
> But a prudent *man* covers shame.
>
> *Prov. 12:16*

The point of this saying is not cover-up but control. Let a fool be embarrassed, and his "irritation" ("*wrath*"; see 17:25; 21:19; 27:3) is disclosed immediately in both demeanor and speech. He leaves no space for a possible misunderstanding, no room for the one who offended him to apologize. He does not count to ten before he sounds off. The "*prudent*" person (Heb. ʿ*arûm*; see 12:23; 13:16; 14:8, 15, 18) is shrewd enough not to make a fool of himself in public. He absorbs the embarrassment ("*shame*"), retains composure, and averts further conflict.

Strong and silent, such persons merit the admiration of their friends. We feel safe with them. They will not bite our heads off if we say something wrong.

In contrast is this saying, whose synonymous lines describe a repulsive lack of control:

> A quick-tempered *man* acts foolishly,
> And a man of wicked intentions is hated.
> *Prov. 14:17*

Volatile ("*quick-tempered*") people seem to have evil schemes ("*wicked intentions,*" see 12:2) buried deep within them that spout forth like geysers when they are upset. We shun their company, feel relieved when no crisis is fomented when we have to be with them, and skittishly change the subject if they begin to look edgy. "*Hated*" sounds like a strong word for our reactions but it captures the realism of our instinctive aversion to people whose tempers are out of control.

The value to society of people who keep tight rein on their tempers is obvious.

> He who is slow to wrath has great understanding,
> But *he who is* impulsive exalts folly.
> *Prov. 14:29*

They are models from whom we can learn a lot about insight and "*understanding*" (for Heb. *tᵉbûnāh*, see 2:2, 3, 6). We need them since so many around us are "*impulsive*" (short of spirit) and "*exalt*" folly like a king to the throne of life.

> A wrathful man stirs up strife,
> But *he who is* slow to anger allays contention.
> *Prov. 15:18*

They are also peacemakers, these restrained folks. They quiet down ("*allay*") the tendency to quarrel and argue ("*contention*"). What the "*wrathful*" (heated-up) person splashes with kerosene to inflame they douse with the fire extinguisher of their self-control. Hot tempers take their toll on the whole society.

> A *man of* great wrath will suffer punishment;
> For if you rescue *him,* you will have to do it again.
> > *Prov. 19:19*

The wrathful have to pay the fine or penalty ("*punishment*") for their wrongdoing. Impulsively they attack other persons and land in court. Angrily they cut in on another driver or try to beat her to a parking place and cause an accident; clumsily they jump all over an innocent bystander at work and cause chaos in the company. All of this wastes time, energy, morale, and money. It can be especially costly to those who bail them out ("*rescue*") whether literally or figuratively. Since the behavior is a habit, the act of rescue can become habit forming— "*you will have to do it again*" and, perhaps, again.

The superlative value of constraining anger is affirmed in a better proverb, that makes its point by an intentionally extreme comparison:

> He *who is* slow to anger *is* better than the mighty,
> And he who rules his spirit than he who takes a
> > city.
> > *Prov. 16:32 (see also 25:28)*

The true heroes of society, say the teachers, are not the military champions who march to conquer cities ("*mighty*" means "warrior") but you who, as Kipling put it:

> —keep your head when those around you
> are losing theirs
> and blaming it on you.

Roger Voskuyl served as president of Westmont College as I began my career as a teacher. I once asked him, impulsive young faculty member that I was, how he could maintain such poise and patience when things weren't going well, took so long to fix, and he got much of the blame. His answer was simple: "I can take you to the chemistry lab at Harvard and show you the glass slivers in the wall where every experiment of mine for six months straight blew to smithereens."

He learned patience from chemistry and taught me patience along the way. No one can lead well without it.

Constraint of temper gains its highest marks when it is in evidence as a response to attack. The range of behavior patterns in our communities is appallingly wide. Two sayings mark the size of the gulf:

> Whoever rewards evil for good,
> Evil will not depart from his house.
> *Prov. 17:13*

> The discretion of a man makes him slow to anger,
> And his glory *is* to overlook a transgression.
> *Prov. 19:11*

On the one side are those whose values are so skewed, whose ability to respond sensibly to others is so distorted that *"good"* deeds are reimbursed (*"rewards"*) by hurtful (*"evil"*) ones. On the other side are those whose forbearance is so strong, so Godlike if you will, that even crimes (*"transgressions"*; Heb. *pesha‹*; see on 10:12; 12:13; 17:19) can be overlooked (lit., passed by, passed over; the word virtually means "forgive" in Amos 8:2). The rewards promised are appropriate to the behaviors contrasted: *"glory"* or "beauty" (the Hebrew word describes wisdom's crown in 4:9) to the one who absorbs the wicked blow; disaster (*"evil"*) as the permanent occupant of his *"house"* (or "household") for the one who rewards blessing with malice.

Persons who keep their tempers in check not only refuse to start quarrels no matter how badly they are baited, but they also are ready to intervene the instant someone else ventures to start one.

> The beginning of strife *is like* releasing water;
> Therefore stop contention before a quarrel starts.
> *Prov. 17:14*

> *It is* honorable for a man to stop striving,
> Since any fool can start a quarrel.
> *Prov. 20:3*

There is no such thing as a tiny quarrel, anymore than there can be just a small leak in a dam. Once that negative energy is released it flows harder and faster until all restraint is washed away. The time to plug the dam is before the *"water"* starts to gush through the gap; the time to stop the argument is before the quarrel begins. It is halting the conflict (*"striving"*) that is worthy of commendation ("honorable"), since "any fool" has more than enough talent to start one.

Three sources of self-control may be discovered in proverbs that describe sound behavior. The first source is correction in one's youth. Physical discipline to the point of pain is featured:

> Blows that hurt cleanse away evil,
> As *do* stripes the inner depths of the heart.
> *Prov.* 20:30

The comparison is between outward punishment and inward change. The pain, disgrace, and instruction of the discipline can have a maturing and purging influence on the inner chambers ("*depths*") of a person's emotions and choices. "*Heart*" here is literally "belly" and points to a deeper, more affective area of personhood than would *lēb*, the normal word for heart as the center where choices are made and thinking is done. We should read these words not as a hunting license to beat our kids but as a reminder of the importance of instruction, correction, and discipline. The punishment aims to shape their maturity not release our anger. No one can teach self-control while out of control. But every home needs its system of rewards and penalties to encourage the deep inner growth necessary for poised and mature living.

Counsel from a profound person is another source of self-control:

> Counsel in the heart of man *is like* deep water,
> But a man of understanding will draw it out.
> *Prov.* 20:5

"Still water runs deep" is our equivalent of the first half of this saying. The "*deep water*" of profound wisdom contrasts with the gushing water of strife that marked the comparison of 17:14. People who lack self-control are often ready, even before you ask, to give you advice you don't need and can't use. The wise, quiet person may wait for you to ask twice before she or he says anything. One definition of "*understanding*" (on *tᵉbûnāh* see 14:29) is to know who is wise enough to help you and how to be both probing and patient enough to gain access to that wisdom.

The comradeship of a controlled person is the final source of self-control. We are known by the company we keep. Even more, we become like the company we keep. This seems to be the point of a brief and puzzling proverb:

> As in water face *reflects* face,
> So a man's heart *reveals* the man.
> *Prov. 27:19*

Since *"reveals"* is not found in the Hebrew form, which is verbless, we have to struggle for the precise meaning. In his notes on this text William McKane cites a paraphrase from the famous Oxford scholar G. R. Driver: "As a man sees his own and no other face reflected in the water, so he will see his own nature and no other reflected in his companion's heart." Self-understanding is greatly enriched by the love of a kindred soul who plays back to us our thoughts in tunes composed by her or him. This interplay among persons committed to each other is part of what God uses to give us the insights necessary for poise and balance in everyday behavior. An alternate interpretation would place the emphasis on introspection not fellowship. The second line in that case would refer to one person not two, one person who would search his own inner self (*"heart"*) for the clues to growth and maturity.

The two themes of this chapter—fear of the Lord and control of the self—are the warp and woof of the fabric of Christian discipleship. They put proper emphasis on the vertical and horizontal dimensions of biblical living, and they capture the equal attention given to outward act and inward motivation. The perceptiveness of Israel's wise is indeed astonishing. How clearly they caught the tensions and turmoils of human existence and the divine help available to cope with them! How hard we modern folk have to run to catch up with their ancient wisdom!

CHAPTER FIFTEEN

Prudent Speech and Fervent Prayer

Proverbs 15:1–33

This chapter points us toward the heart of our humanity. It highlights what it means to be persons, capable of thinking, feeling, knowing, loving, and speaking. Speech and prayer are the two most obvious external signs of what it means to be made in God's image. They enable us to live life in relationship with the Lord and with each other. They allow us to express thought, pose questions, suggest answers, share needs, and voice thanksgiving—all essential factors in human existence. Israel's wise grasped this and included in their collection dozens of sayings directed toward the art of wise speaking.

With a battery of proverbs to hurl at their students, we can imagine how they monitored the classroom conversations and the reports of the ways that fledgling administrators handled their professional encounters. One helpful exercise in studying Proverbs is to reconstruct imaginatively the kinds of mistakes or successes that lie behind the tightly compressed and artfully composed sentences. Proverbs are birthed in pain, with the students' behavior acting as midwife, and proverbs are bathed in laughter, with the eager pupils playing the jester's role. Learning to speak wisely is a lifelong task for each of us. And learning to pray fervently takes even longer. We do well to put ourselves under the teachers' tutelage, test our speech and prayer before them, and let them zing us with their proverbs as they have been doing to God's people for three thousand years. Their words are seasoned, and ours need help, whether we talk to God or each other.

EFFECTIVE CONVERSATION

Speech and community go hand in hand. Community depends on communication—upon information and attitudes shared in common.

That was true in antiquity when only a small percentage of the populace could read and write. Business dealings, sales reports, contracts, land and water agreements and thousands of daily transactions were handled by word of mouth. Children were coached in the arts of work, play, and prayer by relatives who had only their own examples and spoken words as tools of education. And the situation is not all that different today. Menus, instruction books, newspapers, message boards, and church bulletins are symbols of our dependence on reading. But no product of modern technology—not the computer, not the copying machine, not the magnetic price scanner—has rendered obsolete a single saying in the Proverbs. Speech has as much power to help or hurt today as it ever had. It lies so close to the center of human life that it is still the most important art for each of us to master.

Within each person "heart" and "mouth" are tied together. The Bible, as poetic parallelism suggests (see 10:20; 15:7, 26, 28; 16:21, 23; 17:20), sees the connection as intimate. The mouth (or lips or tongue) is the channel of the heart, and the heart is the reservoir of the mouth. Thought and choice take place in the heart; we make them known only through the mouth. Speech, for the wisdom teachers, gained its importance because it was the conduit from one heart to another. It connected the depths of one person to the depths of others and conveyed woe or happiness, wisdom or folly, blessing or curse, counsel or confusion, truth or falsehood, love or hate. Purity of tongue was proof of purity of heart; hardness of heart spilled out in harshness of tongue (10:20). The teachers had no clearer test for distinguishing the wise from the fool than the litmus of speech.

Prudent speech begins with restraint in communication (10:19–20; 12:23; 13:3; 15:2, 28; 17:27–28).

> In the multitude of words sin is not lacking,
> But he who restrains his lips *is* wise.
>
> *Prov. 10:19*

Guarded, measured, almost reluctant to open are the *"lips"* of the truly *"wise."* An unchecked flow of words gives opportunity for misleading information, thoughtless advice, and just plain personal hurt. *"Sin"* (lit., *"transgression," "rebellion,"* or *"crime"*; Heb. *peshaʿ*; see 10:12; 12:13) describes the potential harm done to others when we *"mouth off"* mindlessly. *"Restrains"* is the same Hebrew word as *"spares."*

> He who has knowledge spares his words,
> *And* a man of understanding is of a calm spirit.
> > *Prov. 17:27*

Whether the object of the verb is *"lips"* (10:19) or *"words"* (17:27), the result is the same: control of speech is a prime mark of wisdom and understanding. Those who have mastered this art possess a *"calm* [lit., *"cool,"* as in the *"cold water"* of 25:25] *spirit"*; no steam or smoke obscures their speech. They say what they mean and mean what they say.

And they do this out of respect for themselves as well as others.

> He who guards his mouth preserves his life.
> *But* he who opens wide his lips shall have
> > destruction.
> > *Prov. 13:3*

Eating words does not make for a pleasant diet. They can, in fact, be poisonous—life-threatening in the guilt they generate in us and the hostile recriminations they spark against us. Guarding the *"mouth"* is an act of self-preservation. To open *"wide the lips"* (the verb suggests distortion at best and obscenity at worst; see Ezek. 16:25 for its use in a vile description of Jerusalem spreading her legs like a prostitute) is to court *"destruction"* (or *"utter ruin"*; see 10:14, 15; 14:28; 18:7; 21:15 for other uses in Proverbs). Measured speech not only cuts the risk of hurting oneself, it increases remarkably the odds that what we say will be beneficial to others.

> The tongue of the wise uses knowledge rightly,
> But the mouth of fools pours forth foolishness.
> > *Prov. 15:2*

> The heart of the righteous studies how to answer,
> But the mouth of the wicked pours forth evil.
> > *Prov. 15:28*

"Knowledge" (see 1:2–7) is viewed as a precious resource not to be wasted; we need to make good use of it (use it *"rightly,"* 15:2). We do this best if we study *"how to answer"* (lit., *"meditate"* on our response; 15:28). The alternative is unacceptable: it wastes words by letting them *"pour forth"* (15:2, 28) like a fountain polluted and out of control that soaks us with stagnant water when all we needed was a swallow of fresh. *"Foolishness"* and *"evil"* are the descriptors of what fools

splash on those around them. Time-wasting nonsense it may be or even worse, falsified facts, dangerous opinions, perverted advice, or ill-gotten gossip. No good can come from any of it.

> Even a fool is counted wise when he holds his
>   peace;
> *When* he shuts his lips, *he is considered* perceptive.
> > > *Prov. 17:28*

If a *"fool"* were able to grasp the situation, he would change his behavior, remain silent (*"hold his peace"*) and seal shut *"his lips."* That silence is at least ambiguous. People may give him the benefit of the doubt and deem him wise. If he speaks in his usual rash, brash pattern he will at once remove all doubt and be branded the fool he is.

The hip-shooting, hair-trigger tendency of fools stands in sharp contrast to the sealed lips of the prudent (shrewd, skilled) person: the former shouts out his folly—"proclaims" is the same Hebrew word used of wisdom's call for disciples:

> Does not wisdom cry out,
> And understanding lift up her voice?
> > > *Prov. 8:1*

The latter covers it up ("conceals"), waiting to be sure that he knows what he needs to say, to whom to say it, and when the time is ripe.

> A prudent man conceals knowledge,
> But the heart of fools proclaims foolishness.
> > > *Prov. 12:23*

In sizing up people as potential participants in the life of Fuller Seminary, whether as administrators or trustees, I observe carefully their patterns of speech. Obviously, what they say needs to make sense. But I watch for much more than that. Do they wait their turn? Do they step on the lines of others? Do they have a need for the last word? Do they try to top everyone else's stories? Do they sound off in their areas of incompetence? Can they say, "I don't know"? Do they repeat themselves badly or wonder aimlessly through their subject matter? Persons with these and other verbal liabilities do not usually make it to my team. They are not sensitive enough, not succinct enough, not modest enough, and not gracious enough to work well with others. They waste time, hurt feelings, and shatter morale. They, with the rest of us, need to sit further at the wise teachers' feet and learn that restraint in communication is essential to prudent speech.

Such restraint can lead us to recognition of consequences of rash conversation (10:13–14, 21, 31; 11:11; 12:18; 14:3; 15:4; 16:27–28; 17:4, 20). The proverbs seem franker than usual in driving home this point. It is as though the teachers want to grab their students by the nape of the neck and shake good sense into their mouths and tongues.

> Wisdom is found on the lips of him who has
>   understanding,
> But a rod *is* for the back of him who is devoid of
>   understanding.
> > *Prov. 10:13*

Stern discipline, even corporal punishment, may be necessary to head off these traits of foolish speech as they crop up in the young. I can still taste the Fels Naphtha soap that was my mother's antidote to foolish or improper language. One route to the *"lips"* was through the *"back"* to which a *"rod"* was applied to drum in a modicum of understanding. Early correction with adequate explanation is an approach that teachers of all eras have found useful.

> In the mouth of a fool *is* a rod of pride,
> But the lips of the wise will preserve them.
> > *Prov. 14:3*

"Rod of pride" may also be a reference to discipline since "pride" and "back" resemble each other closely in Hebrew. If "pride" is correct, then the tongue is seen as a rod or shoot (see Isa. 11:1) whose roots grow deep in the foolish heart. If "back" is preferred, self-punishment, even self-destruction, is pictured as the outcome of foolish speech.

The theme of self-destruction as a consequence of imprudent speech is well documented.

> Wise *people* store up knowledge,
> But the mouth of the foolish *is* near destruction.
> > *Prov. 10:14*

Whereas the wise *"store up knowledge,"* guarding it like an investment that will pay them regular dividends, the foolish mouth is close to *"destruction"* (see at 14:3) as though it held a lighted cherry bomb between the lips.

> The mouth of the righteous brings forth wisdom,
> But the perverse tongue will be cut out.
>   *Prov. 10:31*

The metaphor changes only slightly here as recrimination against
the *"perverse"* (totally distorted, upside down; see on 2:12, 14; 8:13)
speaker takes the harsh form of cutting out the tongue. Menaces to
public health have to be treated like cancer: extreme means may be
our only recourse to safety and stability. The least that can be done
is ignore the person's words and warn others against them. That is a
less bloody excision of the tongue than knife or scalpel would render. But it does preserve the peace and stability of the society.

> He who has a deceitful heart finds no good,
> And he who has a perverse tongue falls into evil.
>   *Prov. 17:20*

In the long run life itself, with its inbuilt system of rewards and
punishments, has a way of evening the score by depriving the
crooked (*"deceitful"*) *"heart"* of the desired blessings (*"good"*) and
seeing to it that the person of *"perverse* [see above at 10:31]
tongue"—we have already noted the intimate link between heart
and tongue—*"falls into"* hardship (*"evil"*), whatever form that hardship may take. One probable form is loss of credibility, respect, and
standing in the community, a bitter disaster indeed for one who
craved influence and prestige and was willing to lie, connive, and
mislead to get them.

Self-destruction was only part of the consequence; even more
dangerous was the damage done to others by the forked tongue of
the fool.

> The lips of the righteous feed many,
> But fools die for lack of wisdom.
>   *Prov. 10:21*

One danger was that other fools would listen, dependent on what
they hoped to be morsels of *"wisdom,"* and then *"die"* of starvation.
Their fate recalls the pitiful story of the desperate mother who tried
to save money by buying a powdered coffee creamer instead of
milk. Day after day she added water to the creamer, poured the mix
in the baby's bottle, and watched her suck it down. The baby nearly
died of malnutrition before the mother awakened to the fact that
what she thought was milk had almost no food value to it. The

contrast between the starved disciples of the fool and the well-fed followers of the *"righteous"* is startling and profound.

Sometimes the pain of foolish speech stings more and faster than the prolonged ache of starvation.

> There is one who speaks like the piercings of a
>   sword,
> But the tongue of the wise *promotes* health.
>   *Prov. 12:18*

Like *"the piercings of a sword,"* ill-chosen words stab their victims and leave them maimed and bleeding. Not so *"the tongue of the wise"* which carries healing (*"health,"* see on 4:22; 6:15) in its touch. A sword to jab, a swath to soothe—the tongue can be either (15:4 speaks of a "wholesome [healing] tongue").

> An ungodly man digs up evil,
> And *it is* on his lips like a burning fire.
>   *Prov. 16:27*

It can also be a bitumen torch fueled by the tar of *evil* which the person finds within himself and which he *digs up* in the community by grubbing for scandal and harrowing for gossip.

> A wholesome tongue *is* a tree of life,
> But perverseness in it breaks the spirit.
>   *Prov. 15:4*

Perhaps *"breaks the spirit"* is the clause that best captures the injurious impact of *"perverseness"* (or deceit; Heb. *seleph*; see also 11:3). Lying makes it almost impossible to trust either the liars or those they lie about. A complete breakdown of morale, a form of emotional depression, is the result. Where trust is absent, *"life"* (note honesty as a *"tree of life"* in 15:4a) becomes intolerable.

Indeed the social hurts of fools' talk are one of its monumental consequences.

> A perverse man sows strife,
> And a whisperer separates the best of friends.
>   *Prov. 16:28*

Gossip seems to be the crime. *"Whisperer"* is more forcefully translated "slanderer," a word used only in Proverbs (18:8; 26:20, 22). Its parallel is the familiar *"perverse"* (see on 10:31–32; 17:20), the person who deliberately gets everything wrong and then says it that way too. *"Strife"* in the community (note how this was decried as the climax of the seven deadly sins in 6:19) and separation of *"best [most intimate] of friends"* are the inevitable result of such intentional malice.

> An evildoer gives heed to false lips;
> A liar listens eagerly to a spiteful tongue.
> *Prov. 17:4*

Furthermore, *"a liar"* is encouraged by such false reports. Dangerous as typhoid carriers are these gossips; they infect other evildoers with their prevarications and start epidemics (*"spiteful"* speaks of *"destruction"*; see 19:13) of tale bearing.

The morale and stability of a whole town can be overthrown by such meanness.

> By the blessing of the upright the city is exalted,
> But it is overthrown by the mouth of the wicked.
> *Prov. 11:11*

"The mouth of the wicked" does not have to engage in espionage and the selling of secrets to an enemy to do this. It can counter the *"blessing of the upright,"* which contributes to the city's success and standing and which is the result of good deeds for and good wishes to others, by doing the opposite: bad-mouthing the leaders, misleading the population, and predicting calamity for the community. Misguided prophecies seem to possess greater power to fulfill themselves than oracles of truth. Rumormongers can fill auditoriums, while truth tellers can fit their audience into a toolshed.

Regard for its contribution is the final step in our understanding of the centrality of prudent speech to our biblical discipleship. The fitness of our speech and its freshness are two factors that determine what gifts of life and love we bring to others by our words.

Chapter 15 records a quartet of criteria that make for fitness, and other chapters add an equal number. We can but list them here with brief comments.

Fit speech is calming to those on the brink of anger.

> A soft answer turns away wrath,
> But a harsh word stirs up anger.
> *Prov. 15:1*

When accosted in *"wrath"* (lit., "heat"), we respond best with a *"soft,"* gentle, fragile, vulnerable answer ("soft" is used of a weak child or a pained man in Gen. 33:13; 2 Sam. 3:39). To follow our natural inclination and snap back with a harsh word (one that causes "pain"; see Gen. 3:16 for the Heb. word as a description of labor pangs) is to fuel the fires of *"anger."* Helping their students contain damage, defuse explosive situations, break the cycle of violence was a passionate desire of the teachers. Their words aim constantly at peaceful outcomes of dispute. Their confidence in the irresistible power of soft speech was voiced in the graphic line "and a gentle tongue breaks a bone" (25:15).

Wise speech is informing.

> The lips of the wise disperse knowledge,
> But the heart of the fool *does* not *do* so.
> *Prov. 15:7*

As farmers scatter (*"disperse"*) seed and the whole community benefits from the crop, so the *"knowledge"* of God's will and ways (as Heb. *da'at* means; see on 1:2–7) is sown in the soil of society by *"wise"* persons in a way that foolish people (*"fool"* translates a plural Hebrew word) have neither means nor desire to accomplish. *"Heart"* reminds us that wise speech is not a matter of verbal fluency but of inner goodness and integrity given expression through the *"lips."* The role of the heart in the task of communicating is central.

> The wise in heart will be called prudent,
> And sweetness of the lips increases learning.
> *Prov. 16:21*

What we say must make sense (one meaning of *"heart"*) to others for them to trust our words as *"prudent"* (understanding, insightful) persons. And how we say it is also vital to getting the point across. *"Sweetness,"* like honey, whets the appetite of the hearers and enables them to take in the *"learning"* or "teaching" (see on 1:5; 4:2) we convey. It is the spoonful of sugar that helps the medicine go down.

> The heart of the wise teaches his mouth,
> And adds learning to his lips.
> *Prov. 16:23*

The link of *"heart"* to *"lips"* is depicted most winsomely in this saying, where the heart carries its skillful understanding (*"teaches"*) to the *"mouth"* and *"adds"* the art of effective teaching (*"learning"*; see 16:21) to the lips. Only when mind (heart) and mouth sing "Blessed be the tie that binds" is powerful communication possible.

Timing is part of effective speech.

> A man has joy by the answer of his mouth,
> And a word *spoken* in due season, how good *it is!*
> > Prov. 15:23

The rightness of our advice depends partly on its timeliness. Sensing when people are ready and seizing the moment is a hallmark of wisdom. *"Due season"* means the right time. We have to guess at it before; we know for sure afterward, if we feel glad (*"has joy"*; *"how good!"*) about what we have said and how the other person received it. We had just finished a long conversation in my office. As my friend, who had driven several hours for the meeting, placed his hand on the doorknob, I asked him how his wife was doing. His answer was candid: "I am not sure how she feels about my switch of priority from business to more direct Christian service, and I don't know how much of my new life to share with her." My answer was direct and simple: "All of it." He paused a moment, squeezed my hand, and said, "Those last words were worth the whole trip!" Both my answer and timing seemed right. Would that such were always the case! There is great joy in experiencing the truth of the proverb, even though, thanks to our bungling ways, the occasions may be far rarer than we would like.

One of the sterling qualities of suitable speech is its uplifting character. Though we moderns may talk more openly and frequently about depression, we did not invent the experience nor do we have a monopoly on it. Saul, Elijah, Jeremiah, and the psalmists all record episodes where their spirits sagged to the point where their abilities to function were virtually paralyzed. The sages recognized how such things happened and wherein lay the cure.

> Anxiety in the heart of man causes depression,
> But a good word makes it glad.
> > Prov. 12:25

"Anxiety," in Ezek. 4:16, describes the panic in the hearts of Jerusalem's population when bread will become so scarce that it has to be rationed by weight. Depression translates a root that means "to sink." Its uses in Ps. 44:25 and Lam. 3:20 describe persons who have hit bottom in their emotional despair. The "it" in *"makes it"*

glad according to the Hebrew grammar is *"depression,"* which is a
feminine word, not *"heart"* which is masculine. The key to the
change of mood is a *"good"*—that is, kind, gracious, generous—
"word." The role of loving reassurance in the face of hopelessness is
one of the standard tools of modern psychology. Wise parents, loving spouses, and sensitive friends have intuitively employed it
through the ages.

> Pleasant words *are like* a honeycomb,
> Sweetness to the soul and health to the bones.
> *Prov. 16:24*

"Pleasant" is virtually a synonym for good and the metaphor of
"honeycomb" adds the sense of "delightful" to the taste and therapeutic (*"health"*) to the body. *"Soul"* and *"bones"* both describe the whole
person and are coupled as ways of expressing the self whose pain is
eased by the fitting words from a caring person. Honey is an ancient
remedy for quieting a cough, soothing a throat, or boosting the level
of energy. A total pickup is the idea. Kind words from a respected
person are a prescription of incredible effectiveness, as tailored to
the nature of depression as is quinine for malaria or vitamin C for
scurvy.

Saying the right thing is a rewarding enterprise.

> A man will be satisfied with good by the fruit of
>   *his* mouth,
> And the recompense of a man's hands will be
>   rendered to him.
> *Prov. 12:14*

We speak good things to others and are *"satisfied"* (fulfilled) by that
very act. But more than that we are repaid by the good which others
say to us in return. Consideration begets consideration; kindness
spawns kindness. This is true of both the spoken word—*"fruit of his
mouth"*—and the activities of a *"man's hands."* How we behave will
in large measure dictate how we are treated. Reaping and sowing
are social as well as agricultural patterns.

Finally, fit speech is pleasing to the Lord. Again the tongue is
seen as the messenger of the heart. In Prov. 15:26 below, "thoughts"
("plans," "deliberations") is in parallel to "words." What we think and
what we say are a seamless garment. The one will ultimately reveal
itself in the other. To catch the meaning of the Hebrew text we need
to revise slightly the translation of NKJV:

> An abomination to the LORD are the thoughts of a
>   wicked person,
> But pure are the words of pleasantness.
>
> *Prov. 15:26*

"Pure" and *"abomination"* are the first contrast. The language sounds like descriptions of acceptable (*"pure,"* "clean") and unacceptable (abominable, totally rejected) sacrifices or offerings. *"To the Lord"* casts its light on the second half of the proverb as well as the first: "pure to the Lord" is the intent of that line. *"Wicked"* and *"pleasantness"* are the second main contrast. "Wicked" or "evil" suggests a will to harm, to defraud, to degrade another person. "Pleasantness" is tantamount to kindness, the will to help, to encourage, to convey regard. The proverb draws us up short with its declaration that our thoughts and speech have the same significance to God as do our most devout religious acts. We draw careful lines between the sacred and the secular realms of our existence, and God grabs a proverb like this and uses it as a cosmic eraser to rub out those lines and mark all of life as divine territory.

> The lips of the righteous know what is acceptable,
> But the mouth of the wicked *what is* perverse.
>
> *Prov. 10:32*

Though the Lord's name is not mentioned, his participation may well be implied. *"Acceptable"* or "pleasing" frequently is used in relationship to our conduct before God, especially our sacrifices and offerings. *"Know"* suggests "caring about," "being concerned with" as in Ps. 1:6: "For the Lord knows the way of the righteous." *"Perverse"* is the opposite of acceptable. It means saying things in deliberately distorted, backward, or upside-down ways. Lying, cursing, slandering, and misleading would be its most common forms.

The positive contribution that prudent speech can make is contained in its freshness as well as its fitness. Two sayings signal the amazing impact that good news has on those who receive it.

> The light of the eyes rejoices the heart,
> *And* a good report makes the bones healthy.
>
> *Prov. 15:30*

Even the countenance of the messenger, eyes alight with the glow of the news and the expectations of its reception, *"rejoices the heart"* of the recipient. Body language—shining face, downcast

eyes, posture erect or slumping—is used to convey mood in biblical
literature just as it is in modern drama or cinema. Any parent can
tell the kind of day a schoolchild has had by the way she walks in
the door. When the *"good report"* (or news) is actually uttered, the
whole person is revived—*"makes . . . healthy"* translates the same
word that describes the anointing of the head with oil in Ps. 23:5.
"Bones" is not just a description of the human frame or skeleton but
of the entire person, the inner of the self. The impact of good news
is profound and thorough, not superficial or partial. A comparison
captures its effect on the hearer in 25:25.

> *As* cold water to a weary soul,
> So *is* good news from a far country.
> *Prov. 25:25*

It is as refreshingly bracing to the hearer as is *"cold water"* to a person who feels *"weary"* or "faint." The point of the proverb is sharpened by two adjectives: (1) the water is cold, a luxury indeed in a
land where water supplies turn tepid in a hurry and where any kind
of potable water is a treasure—anyone who has spent an afternoon
in the oppressive heat of the Dead Sea or has rambled around the
caves and digs of Qumran for a hour or two will swear to the value
of cold water; (2) the good news has traveled *"far"*—like letters from
home to a missionary in Timbuktu.

We can only guess at the content of the good news—an exile planning to come home, a foreign investment proving successful, an ill
relative recovering health, a diplomat reporting a positive reception
in a potentially hostile land. Any of these and a hundred other examples may account for this refreshment. Happy the bearer, happy
the hearer, of such tidings! If human messages produced these joyous results, think what a privilege it is to declare and receive the
ultimate good news. Getting it right, announcing it clearly, delivering it faithfully to those who need it most are responsibilities both
delightful and awesome.

Again, the value of prudent speech is distilled like fine perfume
in these words:

> The tongue of the righteous *is* choice silver,
> The heart of the wicked *is worth* little.
> *Prov. 10:20*

In Israel's earliest days *"silver,"* especially highly refined specimens
as *"choice"* suggests, was rarer and more valuable than gold (see 2:4;

8:10). The contrast, then, between *"the tongue of the righteous,"* those loyal to God's ways, and *"the heart* [or "mind"] *of the wicked* [the violently, turbulently out of control]" is extreme: the difference between very great worth and virtual worthlessness (*"worth little"*). We use silver-tongued to describe eloquence, a gift of gab polished to a high gloss of rhetoric. The biblical teachers knew better: they knew that integrity, tact, kindness, and encouragement were what made speech truly sterling—not just the ability to string words together in artistic sentences.

Prudence supplied its own polish; polish without prudence was not worth the bother. Prudence is always welcome even when the news is good. There are better and poorer ways of delivering eagerly awaited messages. But the real role of prudence, when its precious quality is fully valued, is when the news to be disclosed is bad. The pathology is positive; the tumor is malignant; the chromosome count indicates Down's syndrome; the auto accident was fatal; your job is being eliminated; the evidence is clear that the loved one is guilty as charged; your mother and I cannot afford to send you to that college. We people of God, commissioned to develop prudent tongues, would do well to study, sweat, pray, and bleed over our methods of telling people what is both utterly necessary and bitterly painful. The art of doleful disclosure may be the acid test of a silver tongue.

DEVOUT WORSHIP

Proverbs cannot be described as a handbook on worship. It can never replace Leviticus or Psalms with their instructions in and examples of public adoration of God. The proverbs neither compete with nor substitute for the practice of formal, communal worship that centered in the Jerusalem temple. A prime assumption of our understanding of the sages is that they followed the pattern of their exemplars, David, Solomon, and Hezekiah, in combining the practices of covenantal piety with the skills of proverbial wisdom. Almost all the time it is that wisdom which shines forth. But on select occasion they apply that wisdom to reinforce the practice of public worship and to alert their students to certain priorities and pitfalls in matters of organized religious life. (See Eccles. 5:1–6 for a clear example of this.) They did not focus on fine points of interpretation as did the priests. Rather they directed the observations gained from their experience to basic abuses in matters of devotion to God. Their care for right behavior in this area is as passionate and practical as in any other realm of life. Wholeness was their aim; successful living was their goal. If the path of prayer is crisscrossed with obstacles, that wholeness and that success become impossible.

The dangers of empty sacrifice are as much a menace to the wise as they are to the psalmists (Ps. 51:16–17) and the prophets (Hos. 6:6; Amos 5:21–24).

> The sacrifice of the wicked *is* an abomination to the
>   LORD,
> But the prayer of the upright *is* His delight.
>   *Prov. 15:8*

For people of proven and persistent disloyalty (*"the wicked"*) to assume that they could gull God or his faithful ones into accepting them as loyal worshipers by offering sacrifices was a religious outrage (*"abomination"*) to the Lord. The attitude in which sacrifices are offered is a central condition of their acceptance. The *"upright"* validate their sacrifices by the loyalty of their lives and the sincerity of their *"prayer."* God takes *"delight"* (or *"acceptance"* or *"pleasure"*; see above on 15:26 and 10:32) in prayer, which discloses the devotion of the worshiper, more than in the mere act of sacrifice. With the wicked, both the *"sacrifice"* and the words that accompany it are suspect at best, because they do not flow out of a life obedient to God. With the upright, prayer is utterly congruent with the daily walk in the right path.

> The sacrifice of the wicked *is* an abomination;
> How much more *when* he brings it with wicked
>   intent!
>   *Prov. 21:27*

The rhetorical question or exclamation in the second half of this verse underscores the importance of attitude and motivation in worship. The *"wicked"* is disqualified and not accepted both because of the habitual wrongness of his life and because even his *"intent"* in going through the forms of sacrifice is *wicked* (for *zimmāh* as "wicked scheme," see 10:23; 24:9).

The importance of faithful prayer is further highlighted in 15:29.

> The LORD *is* far from the wicked,
> But He hears the prayer of the righteous.
>   *Prov. 15:29*

The contrast between *"the wicked"* and *"the righteous"* (see chap. 10 for a discussion of these categories) is expressed in terms of distance from (*"far"*) and nearness to (close enough so that He *"hears"*) *"the Lord."* Physical or geographical distance is not the point, though it serves to sharpen the issue. Intimacy or familiarity are what nearness entails. The wicked are so distantly related to God through creation that they have no real claim on His grace or blessing. The righteous, in comparison, are loyal sons and daughters of the covenant. They know God in the intimacy of redemption. They belong to Him as His sheep, His subjects, His children. He hears their prayer and takes great delight in doing so. They respond regularly to the invitation:

> Seek the LORD while He may be found,
> Call upon Him while He is near.
> *Isa. 55:6*

And they experience regularly the promise:

> And He will have mercy on him—
> For He will abundantly pardon.
> *Isa. 55:7b*

The role of realistic vows has to be understood if prayer is going to have the fervor God desires. Vows were a standard component in prayers of complaint or supplication. The sufferers would pledge themselves to offer sacrifices and to pay public tribute to God's redemptive grace if He would solve their problems, whether of illness, financial disaster, maligned reputation, heinous sin, or false accusation of crime. The Book of Psalms abounds in illustrations:

> But as for me, I will come into Your house in the
>   multitude of Your mercy;
> In fear of You I will worship toward Your holy
>   temple.
> *Ps. 5:7*

> For You, O God, have heard my vows;
> You have given *me* the heritage of those who fear
>   Your name.
> *Ps. 61:5*

My praise *shall be* of you in the great assembly;
I will pay My vows before those who fear Him.
The poor shall eat and be satisfied.

                                        Ps. 22:25–26a

That last line reminds us that vows were important to the community
as well as to the Lord. The meat from the thank offering (Lev. 7:12–
15; 22:29) had to be eaten the same day and therefore was shared
with other members of the community, especially the poor.

It is a snare for a man to devote rashly *something*
    as holy,
And afterward to reconsider *his* vows.

                                        Prov. 20:25

"Devote rashly" seems to be the key to the proverb. The verb is used
of speech out of control in Job 6:3. It indicates a wild promise made
under pressure, a foxhole pledge that the vower later realizes was
extreme and reexamines (*"reconsider"*) to seek ways to evade it. See
Matt. 15:4–6 and Mark 7:10–13 for similar but not identical tactics.
"Make only vows that you can keep" is the nutshell form of the
saying.

The centrality of devotion to law is the final thought in this inventory of pious acts:

Where *there is* no revelation, the people cast off
    restraint;
But happy *is* he who keeps the law.

                                        Prov. 29:18

Since *"revelation"* is literally *"vision,"* the proverb seems to acknowledge the period toward the end of the Old Testament when prophetic
vision (see 1 Sam. 3:1) began to wane. The discipline that the words
of the prophets brought to Israel's moral and social life was in danger
of going lax (*"cast off restraint"*; Lev. 10:6 uses the same verb to describe hair hanging loose, letting your hair down, as we would say).
The God-given means of maintaining discipline was the *"law."* The
one who *"keeps"* it is protected from corruption, foolishness, and
rebellion. It supplies divine direction and with it happiness (see
Psalms 1, 19, and 119).

Those who forsake the law praise the wicked,
But such as keep the law contend with them.

                                        Prov. 28:4

"Law" here (as in 29:18) probably refers to the Mosaic law rather than to the general instruction in wisdom and piety which is also described as *tôrāh* (1:8; 3:1; 4:2). Devotion to the law dictates how we react to the *"wicked."* If we *"forsake"* (or "abandon") it, we salute the lawbreakers and cheer them on (*"praise"*); if we obey (*"keep"*) it, we enter into spiritual combat (*"contend"*; see Deut 2:5, 25 for the military sense of the verb *gārāh*) *"with them."* Probably nothing gives us clearer clues of our innate human perverseness than our persistent temptation in drama, cinema, or literature to root for the bad guys. Hiding the law in our hearts is the best way to deal with this.

CHAPTER SIXTEEN

The Lord's Eyes and the King's Face

Proverbs 16:1-33

From the beginning God's people have lived under the authority of the King and the kings. Dual authority we recognize—divine sovereignty and human government. Dual authority but not equal authority. The students in Proverbs needed to mark that difference. They were confronted regularly, as budding leaders, with the competence and caprice of monarchs. During Judah's heyday they watched the pendulum swing from righteous kings to foolish ones, from rulers who trusted God to those who tested Him. When the Babylonians crushed Jerusalem under Nebuchadrezzar in 586 B.C., Judah's king was dragged off to the banks of the Euphrates, and the political authority was vested in a foreign governor. The Persians, after 539 B.C., maintained the same system but with more class and less cruelty. Throughout this entire period, the time when the proverbs were part of the curriculum for training government administrators, the young officials had to be submissive to the central authority that regulated their labors. Apparently, they found the teachers' maxims were applicable in almost any political context.

Happily, necessarily, the sages, as true members of the covenant community, had incorporated in the collections a whole set of sayings that dealt with the authority that outranked royal rights. Side by side with proverbs that taught respect and regard for the earthly sovereign were those that focused on the power and glory of the heavenly Sovereign. The checks and balances were thus in place for the leaders of a people that for almost all the time from the Babylonian Exile to the establishment of the modern state of Israel in 1948 has lived in the tension between God and Caesar, the tension of which Jesus spoke so plainly when He gave His prescription for dealing with dual authority (Mark 12:13–17; Matt. 22:15–22;

Luke 20:19–26). Proverbs 16 more than any other section of the book brings together the two types of sayings—those that describe proper royal behavior and correct comportment of the ones who serve the kings and those that depict the King of kings, always to be reckoned with in His ultimate authority and hegemony in human affairs. Israel's young leaders, like all who wield authority in any place or time, lived under the eyes of their Lord and before the face of their king. How they did so is the subject of this chapter.

DEPENDENCE ON GOD

What has bubbled under the surface of this collection of Solomonic sayings beginning at 10:1 has now erupted with the prominence and power of Yellowstone's Old Faithful geyser. All along we have been noting that the key assumption of Proverbs is that wisdom is discoverable and teachable because Yahweh has built order and purpose into the creation. The sages' task is to discover it, frame it in memorable words, and set it before their pupils. But much of the time until chapter 16, the divine presence has been implicit, except in those places that call on the hearers to do their living in fear of Him. The necessity and the meaning of that fear become clearer here than ever before. Fearing God is necessary because His sovereign presence hovers over all of life to determine the success or failure of human plans and programs. Fearing God is meaningful because those who do so can count on His care in any circumstance they meet. "The Lord's eyes" is a shorthand way to express the dependability of His presence and the versatility of His care. That presence and that care, according to our catalog of the proverbs, find Yahweh at work in the following ways:

Exercising surveillance
    over our outward conduct   15:3
    over our inner life   15:11
Exhibiting sovereignty
    in justice   16:4
    in direction   16:9; 20:24
    in destiny   16:1, 3, 7, 33; 19:21; 21:30, 31
Affording security
    from danger   18:10
    in confidence   20:12
    in defense of truth   22:12
    in conscience   20:27; 22:2; 29:13

Employing scrutiny
   with accuracy   16:2; 21:2
   with blessings   16:7
   with thoroughness   17:3
   with compassion   17:5
   with justice   17:15; 19:3; 21:3

These twenty-five sayings comprise a curriculum for studying God's activity as the wise ones understood it. They are a collection of profound comments on God's engagement in the daily activities—whether intellectual, political, social, economic, military, or religious—of His people. They witness to how different life would be if we truly believed that it goes on, every bit of it, under the eyes of the Lord.

The proverbs on divine surveillance serve as general introduction to the subject.

> The eyes of the LORD *are* in every place,
> Keeping watch on the evil and the good.
> *Prov. 15:3*

> Hell and Destruction *are* before the LORD;
> So how much more the hearts of the sons of men.
> *Prov. 15:11*

They show us that God's vigilance is (1) inescapable, reaching *"every place"* where human beings are present; (2) inclusive, embracing the behavior pattern of the entire populace, whether the people are *"good,"* responsible and generous members of the community, whether they are *"evil,"* troublemakers for themselves and others, or whether they are anywhere in between (the contrasting words may describe not only the poles of conduct but everything between them as well, this literary device is a *merism*); (3) penetrating, piercing any barriers we raise to shield our inner thoughts (*"hearts"*), which are surely easier for God to see than the dark mysteries of *"hell"* (lit., Sheol, the grave or the abode of the dead, see on 1:12; 5:5; 7:27) and *"destruction"* (lit., Abaddon, the place, principle, or spirit of destruction that God alone understands):

> Sheol *is* naked before Him,
> And Destruction has no covering.
> *Job 26:6*

Like Sheol, *Abaddon* represents a realm too grim and dismal for mortal contemplation; no one had been there and come back to describe it; the only thing that the wise could opine about it was that its appetite was too voracious to be satisfied:

> Hell and Destruction are never full;
> So the eyes of man are never satisfied.
> *Prov. 27:20*

Abaddon, along with Death, began to be personified in Job 28:22, where they hear rumors of wisdom but find its meaning and source beyond their powers. The personification becomes complete when *Abaddon* is described as "the angel of the bottomless pit," called *Appollyon* in Greek (Rev. 9:11). These extensive comments are necessary background but should not seduce our attention from the major point: our hearts stand ever and always open to the Lord's all-seeing eye (Heb. 5:13). His surveillance is not an academic exercise in garnering information. It is the basis of His judgment—both in reward and punishment. He not only sees all, He acts on what He sees.

Divine sovereignty is part of what the "eyes of the Lord" signify.

> The LORD has made all for Himself,
> Yes, even the wicked for the day of doom.
> *Prov. 16:4*

That sovereignty shows itself in the way He has *"made"* the world and shaped the way it works. Balance and order seem to be what this proverb is teaching. *"For Himself"* does not convey the idea of the Hebrew text, whose word signifies either "for his purpose" (from a verb to "exert oneself," "exercise oneself," "to be busy with"; see Eccles. 1:13; 3:10; 5:19) or "with its answer" (from a more familiar verb; see Prov. 1:28; 15:28). If "purpose" is the intent here, then the *"wicked"* man represents the extreme example—even he has a purpose, namely, to reveal God's justice at the time (*"day"*) when *"doom"* ("evil" or "harm") overtakes him. If "answer" (see 16:1) is the meaning, as I would suggest, then R. B. Y. Scott's translation "counterpart" renders it well, conveying the notion that God has built balance into the structure of reality so that each behavioral pattern has its appropriate "answer" or "counterpart" in the results of that pattern. The "counterpart" effected by Yahweh for a wicked person is the day of doom, when he will receive the appropriate "answer" to his defiant conduct.

Divine direction is an absolute necessity, given life's complexity and human frailty. Left to our own devices, we can not find the path in the light let alone the dark. In the parallelism, "the Lord" and "man" are the focal points of contrast in the two lines, translated here literally:

> A man's heart plans his way,
> But the LORD directs his steps.
> *Prov. 16:9*

> A man's steps *are* of the LORD;
> How then can a man [Heb. ʾādām] understand his
>   own way?
> *Prov. 20:24*

God's sovereignty is pictured here in the full dress of transcendence, free from all that limits human perception and discernment. The least that this means is that we cannot pick our own values, set our own standards, or depend on our own judgment. Our perceptions have a certain validity because the instruments of seeing and hearing are God's creation (20:12; see below). But they also have sure limitations, since God alone knows what is good and how to attain it.

It is in determining the outcome or destiny of our schemes and plans that divine sovereignty shows itself most clearly.

> The preparations of the heart *belong* to man,
> But the answer of the tongue *is* from the LORD.
> *Prov. 16:1*

The distinction made is between human plans—*"preparations"* suggest making careful arrangements, tidily putting all our "ducks in a row"—and the divine *"answer."* As Today's English Version puts it, God "has the last word." The outcome is decided by His *"tongue"* not our considerations.

> Commit your works to the LORD,
> And your thoughts will be established.
> *Prov. 16:3*

This being the case, we need to *"commit"* (lit., "roll") our chosen tasks and efforts (*"works"*) on the Lord, since He already has clear charge of them. Only then can what we devise, dream of, and hope for ("*thoughts*") take on solid reality ("*be established*"). God is in no sense obligated to do what we want—divine freedom is the central theme of these sayings—but we have no hope at all of seeing our plans take shape unless we depend on Him for grace and guidance.

> When a man's ways please the LORD,
> He makes even his enemies to be at peace with
>   him.
>
> *Prov. 16:7*

One outcome of this dependence—the only way to "*please the Lord*"—is social harmony. The true disciple is a peacemaker as Jesus taught His followers to be (Matt. 5:9). He or she (the subject of the second line is not the Lord but the person who pleases Him) cares so much about "*peace*" that all quarrel is avoided, even with those who behave hostilely ("*enemies*") toward the godly person. This saying needs to be heard as part of the transition between the earlier definition of biblical regard, "You shall love your neighbor as yourself" (Lev. 19:18), and the ampler one yet to come, "Love your enemies, bless those who curse you, do good to those who hate you" (Matt. 5:44). Jesus' acknowledgment that some of His countrymen interpreted the command to love the neighbor as a license to hate the enemy shows that they had lost sight of the description of godliness embedded in Prov. 16:7.

> The lot is cast into the lap,
> But its every decision *is* from the LORD.
>
> *Prov. 16:33*

So great is God's sovereignty that even the casting of a "*lot*"—probably a stone or clay object with a "yes" side and a "no" side, like the head and tail of a coin, used in deciding whether or not a contemplated decision had God's blessing or not—was under His control. This method was neither mechanical nor magical, but a way of allowing God to lead by a specific test set up to determine His will. The Urim and Thummim of Israel's high priest (Exod. 28:30; Lev. 8:8) were so used (Num. 27:21; Deut. 33:8, 10; 1 Sam. 23:9–12). This practice of divining God's will persisted into the New Testament, where a lot was used to choose Matthias not Justus as successor to Judas in the apostolic company (Acts 1:21–26). Luke's story may illustrate the point of the proverb: the lot may or may not truly discover God's "*decision*" (lit., "judgment" in Prov. 16:33), but in the long run God's decision will prevail however the lot may fall. Paul, not Matthias, was selected to complete the Twelve. The lot had given one answer; God's sovereign work in history gave another. God has freedom to use or not use the lot, but He will see to it that His will is done. Thanks to the completion of Scripture, the example of Christ, the witness of the Spirit, and the wisdom of fellow Christians, we have better ways of finding God's will than dropping a marked stone into our laps.

> There are many plans in a man's heart,
> Nevertheless the LORD's counsel—that will stand.
> *Prov. 19:21*

A clutch of sayings outside of chapter 16 carry on this line of thinking. The big vote belongs to the Lord no matter how *"many plans,"* thoughts, and strategies swirl in the human mind (*"heart"*). Because the outcome is His to determine, especially in the major political and military decisions in which the pupils were being coached to participate, *"the Lord's counsel"* is what they should seek to find because it alone *"will stand"* when human schemes have fallen flat on their faces and toppled the schemers with them.

> *There is* no wisdom or understanding
> Or counsel against the LORD.
> *Prov. 21:30*

In this saying that is really one long line, not two, this point is restated: no human intellectual skill can guarantee the success of a venture when the Lord is set against it. To be wise and to oppose God is a contradiction in terms.

This pivotal proverb applies to a military setting all that has been said about God's sovereignty over the outcome of human plans.

> The horse *is* prepared for the day of battle,
> But deliverance *is* of the LORD.
> *Prov. 21:31*

The *"horse,"* ever in Scripture a symbol of military action, not transportation or recreation, sums up all that battle strategy, preparation, and equipment entail: manpower, weaponry, field tactics. None of this is really the means of *"deliverance"* (lit., *"salvation"*; see 11:14; 24:6). That art belongs to God alone. It was the failure of Israel's wise to heed these sayings that sparked the ire of prophets like Isaiah

(30:1–5) and Jeremiah (8:8–9) against the political decision-makers of their day: "[They] devise plans [Heb. *ʿēṣah*, the very word used in Prov. 19:21 for counsel], but not of My Spirit" (Isa. 30:1).

The security God provides is a parallel theme in Proverbs to the sovereignty He wields and the surveillance He exercises.

> The name of the LORD *is* a strong tower;
> The righteous run to it and are safe.
> *Prov. 18:10*

Safety in danger is what He offers as well as deliverance in battle. His very *"name,"* that is, His person revered for majesty, power, and truth, is like the *"strong tower"* of a fort. Those who are loyal to His will and ways (*"the righteous"*) eagerly *"run"* to that name and find themselves as *"safe"* as though they were surrounded by high, insurmountable walls. This metaphor for dependence on God is colorful indeed in the context of a tiny land, always vulnerable not only to threat of major powers from the valleys of the Nile or the Tigris-Euphrates but also to opportunistic neighbors like Edomites and Philistines. A secure refuge in times of assault was indispensable. Whatever attack life hurled at them could not threaten the strong name of the everlasting Lord.

Confidence in God was never misplaced.

> The hearing ear and the seeing eye,
> The LORD has made them both.
> *Prov. 20:12*

That confidence could also extend to the powers of observation and understanding that we possess as gifts of God, *"the hearing ear and the seeing eye."* Though human perception is no match for divine wisdom, it can be relied on in many situations not because of human ingenuity but because of divine creation: *"The Lord has made both of them."* Wisdom and insight derived from our perception should be neither undervalued nor overvalued. They should, rather, be checked by the observations of wise counselors and tested by the will of God as revealed in Scripture. The wrong kind of pride will lead to the perversions of arrogance. The wrong kind of humility will produce the distortions of self-deprecation. Dependence on God is, in part at least, dependence on the gift of evaluation and analysis with which the Creator has endowed us. Devaluing them does no honor to Him.

God provides security as He acts in defense of truth.

> The eyes of the LORD preserve knowledge,
> But He overthrows the words of the faithless.
> *Prov. 22:12*

His *"eyes"* spy out the difference between true *"knowledge"* of His provisions and His requirements (see on 1:2–7), on the one hand, and lies uttered about them, on the other. The knowledge He stands watch over and guards (*"preserve"*) with all the tenacity of soldiers protecting their young. The lies of the *"faithless"* ("deceitful," "treacherous," see at 2:22; 11:3, 6), who subvert His truth, He brings to ruin (*"overthrows"*) with all the ferocity of troops assaulting an army that had raped their women. The passion for truth which gleams in the Lord's eyes should govern both how we speak and to what we listen.

> The spirit of a man *is* the lamp of the LORD,
> Searching all the inner depths of his heart.
> *Prov. 20:27*

The Lord's legacy to His human creatures extends to the planting of His *"lamp"* within them in the form of conscience. *"The spirit* [or "breath" or "soul"] *of a man"* harks back to the dramatic moment of creation when the breath of God transformed the molded clay into a living person (Gen. 2:7). That spirit has a perception about human duty beyond anything found in the animal realm; it has such an otherworldly quality to it that it is named the *"lamp of the Lord."* It brings sufficient light to the *"inner depths"* ("hidden chambers") of our thoughts and intentions (*"heart"*) to give us virtually a heavenly perspective on our own behavior. That power of self-transcendence is almost an out-of-body experience. We see ourselves from heights far taller than we can climb on our own; we see ourselves with inner eyes much sharper than even 20/20 vision can afford. Part of wisdom's task is to remind us not only of the outward experiences whose meanings we observe but of the inner lamp in whose light we read ourselves. The Lord's eyes are above us, and His lamp is within us. Together they impart to our conduct, our words, our thoughts, and our attitudes a sense of secure guidance that helps us discern the significance of our humanity.

> The rich and poor have this in common,
> The LORD *is* the maker of them all.
> *Prov. 22:2*

The pain and privilege of conscience are available to *"rich"* and *"poor"* alike. They overarch the differences in class, station, and wealth. They are of the essence of what defines our nature. They remind us—the Lord's eyes and the Lord's lamp—of the essential unity of the human family. They witness to the dominant truth of all mankind: *"The Lord is the maker of them all."* Whatever else may appear to separate us—language, culture, race, religion—this truth we hold *"in common"*: we all come from the Lord and are accountable to Him.

That accountability seems to be the point of 29:13.

> The poor *man* and the oppressor have this in
>   common:
> The LORD gives light to the eyes of both.
> *Prov. 29:13*

Here the matched pair are not the poor and the rich but *"the poor man"* and *"the oppressor,"* who takes advantage of the poor by various means of extortion. What brings them together and causes them to have a *"common"* meeting ground is that the Lord illumines (*"gives light to"*) *"the eyes of both."* Conscience or consciousness is the result of this illumination: the poor man, who is the victim, has light to see that he belongs to God despite the evil treatment; the oppressor, who is the culprit, has light to see that he has violated God's will and God's creature by his extortions.

I sat enthralled as I listened to Benjamin Mays. The distinguished preacher-educator and president of Morehouse College in Atlanta described his pilgrimage from the fields of South Carolina to the halls of Academe. What helped the young black child, born in the last century, gain perspective on himself in a time and place when second-class status was the best that a kid like him could hope for? His Sunday school teacher had told him that he was made in God's image, and he sensed at that tender age that he was as good as anybody else no matter what the practices and practitioners of segregation said about him. The lamp of the Lord burned bright within him, and in that light he lived his long, full life, as he taught thousands of African-Americans to live the same way.

The scrutiny God employs is a substantial subject in Proverbs. The accountability which governs the lives of Jacob's sons and daughters—thanks to the law, the teachings of the sages, and the lamp of conscience—is enforced in the end by the judgment of the just and holy Lord.

Divine scrutiny is marked by accuracy. Conscience is a useful human tool but is bent somewhat out of shape by our sin which often prejudices our judgment in our own favor.

> All the ways of a man *are* pure in his own eyes,
> But the LORD weighs the spirits.
>
> *Prov. 16:2*

Our patterns of conduct (*"ways"*) appear *"pure"* ("clean," "uncontaminated"; see Prov. 20:11; in Exod. 30:34 the word describes the finest frankincense) to us. But the Lord is the best and last judge. He has superior measuring equipment (*"weighs"*), and can examine motives, affections, attitudes, desires and all the other inward considerations embraced in the word *"spirits"* (16:2). The need for God's accurate scrutiny is underscored in 21:2, a proverb almost identical to 16:2.

> Every way of a man *is* right in his own eyes,
> But the LORD weighs the hearts.
>
> *Prov. 21:2*

"Right" (or "upright") means about the same thing as "pure," and *"hearts"* is synonymous with "spirits" in this context. The act of weighing, found in both sayings, is often compared with the Egyptian hieroglyphics that picture the human heart being weighed on one scale of the balance against the feather of truth on the other. The Hebrew concept is less mechanical and more personal. The Lord Himself is both the standard of righteousness and the One who flawlessly measures our performance.

> When a man's ways please the LORD,
> He makes even his enemies to be at peace with
>   him.
>
> *Prov. 16:7*

When the outcomes of the weigh-in bring a smile (*"please"*) to the Lord, divine blessing is one result. An ordered life may be impressive even to a person's *"enemies."* Influenced by the disciple's graciousness and by the divine favor that shines through his circumstances, the person inclined toward jealousy, acrimony, and hostility may be constrained by what he sees to stay *"at peace"* (to refrain from disturbing the well-being) of the godly neighbor.

The thoroughness of God's scrutiny is pictured in an apt comparison.

> The refining pot *is* for silver and the furnace for
>   gold,
> But the LORD tests the hearts.
>
> *Prov. 17:3*

Just as the clay crucible (*"refining pot"*) and the charcoal-heated *"furnace"* (see 27:21, for both terms) made of clay, stone, or bronze are the suitable agents for melting *"silver"* and *"gold,"* allowing the dross and other bits of extraneous ore to bubble to the surface and be ladled off, so God performs that same smelting process (*"tests"*; see Zech. 13:9 for the metallurgical use of the verb *bāḥan*) on human hearts. Genuineness, integrity, consonance between what we profess and what we are, comprise the pure metal which the Master Refiner is seeking.

The Lord's eyes employ their scrutiny with compassion for the oppressed and the suffering.

> He who mocks the poor reproaches his Maker;
> He who is glad at calamity will not go unpunished.
>
> *Prov. 17:5*

God takes personally all joy that is gained at the expense of another. To *"mock"* or jeer at a poor person is tantamount to taunting or reviling (*"reproaches"*) God Himself, since God is the one who made him. Every person has infinite value and deserves dignified treatment not because of wealth or achievement but because he or she bears the very image of God. To demean neighbors by being *"glad"* when they experience *"calamity"* (or "disaster"; the word describes Job's plight in 18:12 and Moab's destruction in Jer. 48:16) is to prove oneself guilty of making sport of God's handiwork. No one can do that and escape the consequences (*"go unpunished"*).

Most important, justice shapes the style of God's scrutiny. This is especially true when God calls to account the judges who are commissioned to do His work in society.

> He who justifies the wicked, and he who condemns
>   the just,
> Both of them alike *are* an abomination to the LORD.
>
> *Prov. 17:15*

Whether they acquit (*"justify"*) the constant troublemakers (*"wicked"*) or pronounce guilty verdicts (*"condemn"*) on the innocent (*"just"*), their evaluation by God is the same: they are so despicable to Him (*"abomination"*) that He wants nothing to do with them. An important word was this to young people being groomed to be part of the judicial system of the nation. No language was too strong to express the moral outrage done to a society and to the Lord who cared about that society, when justice was turned topsy-turvy. Justice, at bottom, is not just a matter of custom or culture, of law or regulation, of power or authority. It is an expression of God's will to be done on earth as in heaven. Failure to maintain it—whether in ancient Israel or modern America—is to profane the heavenly Father's hallowed name.

Yet perversion in human acts and decisions is at least as much a reality as righteousness.

> The foolishness of a man twists his way,
> And his heart frets against the LORD.
> *Prov. 19:3*

"Foolishness" gets life backward. The feet that were made to go straight walk so crookedly that their tracks can be traced only with a corkscrew (*"twists"*; *"misleads"* or *"ruins"*; see 13:6; 22:12). The heart, made to love and praise the Lord, *"frets"* (or *"rages"* like Jonah's sea, 1:15) against God's commands and warnings. The Lord's eyes miss none of this; they will see that justice is done.

And they will look for the practice of rightness and justice (for the definitions, see on 2:4) on the part of God's people.

> To do righteousness and justice
> *Is* more acceptable to the LORD than sacrifice.
> *Prov. 21:3*

This concern for the needs and rights of others—a special duty of the royal court and its representatives (Ps. 72:2)—was the preferred (*"acceptable"* or *"chosen"*) expression of spiritual devotion. Without it, even the ritual of *"sacrifice"* lost its meaning. Amos has close ties to Proverbs in many features of content and style; none is closer than his declaration of Yahweh's utter rejection of all aspects of public worship and all forms of sacrifice so long as justice and righteousness are treated as dirt.

> You who turn justice to wormwood,
> And lay righteousness to rest in the earth!

> I hate, I despise your fast days,
> And I do not savor your sacred assemblies.
> Though you offer Me burnt offerings and your
>   grain offerings,
> I will not accept *them*
> Nor will I regard your fattened peace offerings.
> Take away from Me the noise of your songs,
> For I will not hear the melody of your stringed
>   instruments.
>
> Do horses run on rocks?
> Does *one* plow *there* with oxen?
> Yet you have turned justice into gall,
> And the fruit of righteousness into wormwood.
>
> *Amos 5:7, 21–23; 6:12*

RESPECT FOR THE KING

Political protocol was part of the teachers' curriculum. Their pupils had to be familiar with both the duties and the desires of the monarchs whom they served. Much of their counsel in these matters seems pragmatic. They understood the ways of kings and the dangers inherent if those ways were treated lightly. Yet fundamental to their sayings was a conviction of the God-given guidelines for ruling. Part of the Creator's providence for human society was the responsible exercise of human authority. Kings, whether Israelite or Persian, served His purposes—especially when they exercised their power in ways congenial to Him. Since abuse of power comes easier to most than responsible use, the limits of human authority had to be clearly understood, as the warnings of Moses (Deuteronomy 18) and Samuel (1 Samuel 8) make clear. Their double theme—the importance and dangers of kingship—is sounded again in these sayings. A summary of the advice about kings and how to deal with them may look like this:

Introduction—the king's influence	16:15
How kings behave	
Justly	16:10, 12; 20:8, 26
Demandingly	16:14; 19:12; 20:2
Appreciatively	20:28
Truthfully	17:7
Humbly	21:1
What kings expect	
Effective service	14:35
Truthful reports	16:13

As the chief figure of authority in Israel's society the king had a parental power to bring blessing or distress to others by the cast of his countenance alone.

> In the light of the king's face *is* life,
> And his favor *is* like a cloud of the latter rain.
> *Prov. 16:15*

Filled with *"light,"* it shone its delights on courtier and commoner alike, infusing them with an invigorating appreciation akin to *"life"* itself. The parallelism shows that "light" means "favor" or approval. The *"face"* could convey less welcome messages as well: rejection—the person turns away or hides the face (2 Chron. 29:6; Ps. 102:2); hostility—the person sets the face against someone else (Jer. 21:10). *"Favor"* carries refreshment to the approved person as treasured as the spring (*"latter"*) *"rain"* that cheers the farmer's heart and gives the crops their final boost in March and April to ready them for summer harvest. The lit-up face speaks volumes to me. My dad was bald and could smile in a northerly direction from mouth to eyes to forehead to pate and almost down to the nape of his neck. That incandescent smile with the words "There's my big boy" welcomed me home regularly to the year he died. His middle name was King. And he knew the importance of royal blessings to us who looked up to him.

How kings behave, or should behave, to be true kings is the subject of a cluster of proverbs.

> Divination *is* on the lips of the king;
> His mouth must not transgress in judgment.
> *Prov. 16:10*

Acting justly is a requirement set forth more than once. Because kings were believed to have special access to God—the power of *"divination,"* the ability to receive oracles which helped them shape their political decisions and judicial verdicts—they had a special obligation not to be unfaithful (*"transgress"*) to the requirements of justice (as *"judgment"* is better read). NIV has caught the sense of the saying:

> The lips of a king speak as an oracle,
> and his mouth should not betray justice.

What is wrong for a king to commit is also wrong—abominable, in fact—for him to allow. To catch the force of the Hebrew we need to insert "for anyone":

> It *is* an abomination to kings [for anyone] to commit wickedness.
> For a throne is established by righteousness.
>
> *Prov. 16:12*

The reason is clear: *"righteousness"* is the only sure support or foundation (*"established"*) *"for a throne."* Both the divine order in creation and the divine vigilance over history are geared, sooner or later, to topple unrighteous kings from their royal seat. Enforcing justice is virtually an act of regal self-preservation. Whatever threatens the stability of his hegemony has earned the sovereign's ire.

Twice the enactment of judgment (the Heb. root is *dîn,* the act of making decisions in court) is compared to winnowing wheat from chaff.

> A king who sits on the throne of judgment
> Scatters all evil with his eyes.
>
> *Prov. 20:8*

> A wise king sifts out the wicked,
> And brings the threshing wheel over them.
>
> *Prov. 20:26*

"Scatters" (20:8) and *"sifts"* (20:26) render the same Hebrew word. In the first instance, an uncanny perception is accorded the wise king to spot *"evil with his eyes"* and scatter it to the wind by judging the evildoer and thus dissipating evil's influence. In the second instance, the king's judgment is likened to a *"threshing wheel"* (the same word used for the famous wheels in Ezekiel's visions; chaps. 1 and 10). In either case the troublemakers are crushed and scattered.

The wheel in this metaphor was probably a cartwheel used in threshing large sheaves of grain by running over them repeatedly on the stone threshing floor until the stalks were chopped and the kernels separated from their husks (Isa. 28:27–28). The king's face had to be dead set against evil or it would devastate his kingdom like the plague.

It was partly the passion for justice and partly the desire for achievement that prompted kings to behave demandingly.

> As messengers of death *is* the king's wrath,
> But a wise man will appease it.
>
> *Prov. 16:14*

"The king's wrath" (lit., *"heat"*) is like *"messengers* [or angels] *of death,"* that is, servants commissioned either to announce a death sentence or to enforce it. The *"wise"* person has the prudence not to incur such wrath: he does the king's bidding, accomplishes his tasks, and accurately reports the results. If some mishap has occurred, he has the skill to explain it, the grace to apologize for it, and the resolve to do better the next time. All of these help to *"appease"* the anger, that is, to turn it aside as a well-motivated sacrifice turns aside the wrath of God. "Appease" might be translated "atone."

Powerful persons have great capacity to hurt or heal, frighten or comfort, refresh, or depress.

> The king's wrath *is* like the roaring of a lion,
> But his favor is like dew on the grass.
>
> *Prov. 19:12*

"The king's wrath" (or *"rage"*) is as terrifying as a lion's roar. Amos found the epitome of uncontrollable fright in the sudden roar of a lion (Amos 3:8). Lions were at home in Palestine from earliest times to the end of the Crusades, about A.D. 1200. Samson (Judg. 14:5), David (1 Sam. 17:34–35), and Benaiah (2 Sam. 23:20) all did battle with them. The contrasting line of our proverb takes its imagery not from the animal world but from the weather. The king's approval (*"favor,"* "pleasure") is compared to the *"dew"* that refreshes the *"grass"* and all the vegetation. Between the rainy seasons, the contribution of dew to irrigation in Palestine is utterly essential to the growth of grass for grazing animals and leafy vegetables for the people. For dew as blessing, see Ps. 133:3.

> The wrath of a king *is* like the roaring of a lion;
> *Whoever* provokes him to anger sins *against* his own
>   life.
>
> *Prov. 20:2*

The first line of 20:2 is virtually identical to that of 19:12—only the word for *"wrath"* ("terror," "dread," Gen. 15:12; Josh. 2:9) is different, the third such word translated "wrath" in the three proverbs just studied, a reminder of the range of forms and intensity of feeling kings can muster when their noses are out of joint. The final line of 20:2 shows how anger kindled violence. A king out of control is more dangerous than anyone else. He becomes a law to himself and can threaten the *"life"* ("soul," "person") of anyone who crosses or *"provokes him."* Henry VIII, fuming at the pope for blocking his plan to divorce and remarry, was neither the first nor last illustration of raging, royal anger.

Though the monarchs were tempted to put high demands on their court and give vent to anger when let down or betrayed, at their best they learned to live appreciatively.

> Mercy and truth preserve the king,
> And by lovingkindness he upholds his throne.
> *Prov. 20:28*

They had God's covenant love (*"mercy"*; Heb. *ḥesed*) and faithful reliability (*"truth"*; Heb. *ᵉmet*) to stand guard (*"preserve"*) over them. And when they did what God and the people expected of them, they showed their gratitude by exercising grace ("loving-kindness"; again *ḥesed*), though the LXX "righteousness" suggests Hebrew *ṣedeq* may have been the original word, thus avoiding duplication. The meaning would be about the same, since *ḥesed* and *ṣedeq* both describe doing toward others what the covenant demands. Responding faithfully to God's grace by extending it to others is the solid rock on which a wise king supports and sustains (*"upholds"*) *"his throne."*

Rulers and nobles behave well by speaking truthfully.

> Excellent speech is not becoming to a fool,
> Much less lying lips to a prince.
> *Prov. 17:7*

As a *"fool"* never looks more foolish than when he jabbers at length on matters beyond his understanding, trying to make his words sound *"excellent,"* so a *"prince"* or noble gentleman is never so ignoble as when he stoops to *"lying."* Common people in that day had no press corps to investigate the truth of royal pronouncements; they had to be able to trust the words of their governors. When Jimmy Carter, as a presidential candidate, promised never to lie to the people, he had grasped the irreplaceable importance of truthfulness as a duty of government. As hard as that duty is to fulfill, no responsible public servant can ever treat it lightly. The Profumo scandal in

Britain's House of Commons centered not so much in the cabinet member's sexual immorality, bad as that was, but in the fact that his public failure to come clean destroyed the credibility of his word and disqualified him from government service.

Despite the lofty station, the wise king knows the importance of behaving humbly.

> The king's heart *is* in the hand of the LORD,
> *Like* the rivers of water;
> He turns it wherever He wishes.
> *Prov. 21:1*

Every turn of the king's mind (*"heart"*) is in Yahweh's control (*"hand"*). The Lord is pictured like a farmer directing the flow in the various irrigation canals (*"rivers"*) that water the land. He can dam one stream and release water to another. So Yahweh guides the thoughts, plans, strategies, and success of the most powerful monarch. The eyes of the Lord control the face of the king. People at court, both the ambitious and the intimidated, needed to know that.

What kings expect is the second dominant theme of the royal axioms. To would-be servants and administrators for the court, effective service is the first expectation.

> The king's favor *is* toward a wise servant,
> But his wrath *is against* him who causes shame.
> *Prov. 14:35*

On such service depends the king's disposition, whether *"favor"* (see 19:12) or *"wrath,"* yet a fourth Hebrew word suggests a fiery, burning disposition (see on 16:14; 19:12; 20:2). *"Wise"* or skillful (on *maśkîl*, see 1:3; 10:5) conduct is contrasted with causing *"shame,"* failing in ways that embarrassed the sovereign with loss of face. Surprising the boss or letting her down in public is not a trait appreciated in modern business or political life either.

Hand in hand with effective service goes truthful reporting.

> Righteous lips *are* the delight of kings,
> And they love him who speaks *what is* right.
> *Prov. 16:13*

"Righteous lips" seem to describe messengers who get the facts correctly or ministers of state who grasp the full picture and relate it accurately (*"what is right,"* upright, or straight) to the king. It seems

that such reporting is both essential and rare; *"delight"* ("favor" or "pleasure"; see at 14:35) and *"love"* convey the king's enthusiasm with exceptional force. This saying recalls a comforting moment in my own life. I had finished three jam-packed days of board meetings and then presided over our lengthy commencement service. Hungry for solitude I took refuge in a tiny Chinese restaurant. The egg-flower soup, deep-fried shrimp, and chicken chow-mein with soft noodles were as good as usual. The message in the fortune cookie was even better: "From now on you will play with a full deck." That is every leader's dream—to have all the facts and have them straight!

Special favors apparently played a role in court protocol.

> A man's gift makes room for him,
> And brings him before great men.
> *Prov. 18:16*

The *"gift"* that *"makes room"* for the giver and provides access (*"brings"* or "leads") for him into the presence (*"before"*) of people of stature and influence is not, in this text, an intellectual, musical, or artistic gift. It is a gift of money, handcrafts, spices, or perfumes like the gifts of the Magi which Matthew records. It is not considered bribery, whose purpose is not to encourage favor or friendship but to influence judicial or administrative decisions (Exod. 23:8; Amos 5:12). Such gifts were undoubtedly subject to abuse. But that is not the teachers' point here. What is encouraged are acts of courtesy and thoughtfulness that pay honor to important persons and mark the donor as a person of taste, breeding, consideration, and tact, worthy of association with the prominent citizens of the land.

Obedient respect for the station and training of those who rule seems to be the point of 19:10.

> Luxury is not fitting for a fool,
> Much less for a servant to rule over princes.
> *Prov. 19:10*

The literary form parallels 17:7 and suggests that the major point is found in the second line. The proverb is not primarily about a *"fool"* who bathes in *"luxury"* and, not knowing how to do so, gauchely splashes his wealth around, offends others with it, and finally squanders it on trivia. That truth is the obvious one, as any person of grace and taste will witness. What is more incongruous is for a slave (*"servant"*), who was not even a full citizen, to usurp the right of high government leaders—*"princes"* are not restricted in the Old

Testament to the bloodline of the king, who are more normally called the king's sons—and to exercise authority over them without training, experience, or talent. The message to the pupils was plain: do not strive for power beyond your reach, but work and wait until those who merited it are willing to share it.

A concluding note about the king's success: it is utterly dependent on the support of followers. Israel's history documented that from the beginning when Saul's women fans began to forsake him and laud the exploits of David whose fallen enemies outnumbered Saul's by a multiple of ten (1 Sam. 18:7). Without the combination of charisma, ability, and integrity no one can stay in power long.

> In a multitude of people *is* a king's honor,
> But in the lack of people *is* the downfall of a prince.
> *Prov. 14:28*

"Lack of people" who believe in a leader and trust him is the first stage in the ruin (*"downfall"*) of a prominent official (*"prince"* or *"dignitary"*). In the long run all government is *"of the people"*; what they do not respect they will in the end discard, despite the entrenched power of those who govern. All this is a reminder of what governments are for—the people. Kings at bottom are public servants as are all government officials from dogcatcher to chief justice of the Supreme Court. Remembering that is their best key to continuing in office. Expecting that is our best way to support their leadership.

The Lord's eyes and the king's face. Having regard for each but always knowing the difference is an essential achievement of biblical discipleship. Romans 13 shows us the importance of respecting our government. Revelation 13 shows us the dangers of worshiping our government. Peter's proverb tries to put all our basic loyalties in perspective and sets our priorities:

> Honor all people.
> Love the brotherhood.
> Fear God.
> Honor the king.
> *1 Pet. 2:17*

Fear of God outranks our honor of the king, just as our love of fellow Christians is a more intimate bond than our honor of all persons outside of Christ.

Happily, in our society, we can keep all four of these commands without tension or conflict most of the time. Where tension may arise we give first place to the eyes of the Lord while still understanding the importance of human government. Thomas More made the right choice in 1535 when he felt that to say yes to God was to say no to Henry VIII, who craved Sir Thomas's support of the proposed divorce. In Robert Bolt's *A Man for All Seasons*, More approached the executioner's block with these words:

> I die his majesty's good servant
> but God's first.

CHAPTER SEVENTEEN

Family Ties and Friendly Bonds

Proverbs 17:1–28

The incentives to seek wisdom turn intimate in this chapter. Not wealth, not power, not station are the motivations proposed by the teachers, but welfare of parents and friends. Folly would be deplorable if its damage were restricted to the fool himself. But when loved ones are affected by churlish conduct—and when aren't they?—the results are detestable. The close-knit structures of the ancient oriental families made the suffering unbearable. Put yourself in King David's sandals. He grieves first over the sins of his sons and then over their calamitous deaths (2 Samuel 13–18): Amnon sins by raping his sister Tamar, and David is angry; Absalom slays Amnon with vile vengeance, and David weeps; Absalom tries to snatch the throne from David, and David is angry; Absalom dies fleeing from David's man, and David weeps. The sons' wicked folly has cost their father dearly.

Next to fear of the Lord, honor of parents may well be the sages' highest value. Parents themselves, they knew the joy and pain which children's behavior can engender. They also knew that God's promise of longevity and peace in the land was attached to only one of the ten commandments: "Honor your father and your mother, that your days may be long upon the land which the Lord your God is giving you" (Exod. 20:12). Their concern for the welfare of the nation helped focus their attention on the ways that the wisdom or folly of young people impacted the lives of their parents.

If they willingly admitted that blood was thicker than water, that kinship was the primary tie, they also recognized that water was essential, that the bands of friendship contributed beyond words to personal success and social stability, the twin aims of wisdom. After all, they had before them the sterling example of David's love for Jonathan as witness to the possibility and importance of friendship as a consolidating force when the unity of the kingdom was put to severe test.

In both these themes—family ties and friendly bonds—relationship is paired with achievement. The latter at the price of the former has always been a poor bargain. The cluster of sayings in chapter 17 and elsewhere in Proverbs has much insight to offer a generation blind with greed and drunk with ambition. No persons in any era or setting can deem themselves wise if they neglect to understand the effect of their drives and decisions on the people closest to them.

HONOR TO PARENTS

The thirteen sayings in this category, of which four are found in chapter 17 (vv. 2, 6, 21, 25), seem to line up under four major headings.

The joy wisdom brings	27:11; 10:1; 15:5, 20
The pain folly inflicts	17:21, 25
The forms dishonor takes	
Mistreatment of parents	19:26; 20:20
Misbehavior in public	28:7; 29:3
Misuse of inheritance	17:2
The gift the generations give	
Glory	17:6
Ruin	19:13

The strong family life pictured in Scripture entailed vulnerability as well as intimacy. What happened to one member flowed into the lives of every other member. The family, in fact, was almost like one person in its capacity to experience joy or pain, guilt or forgiveness, shame or honor. They were the keepers of their kin, as Cain's negative example taught them and us. They did not compartmentalize their lives and insulate themselves by the forms of individualism that characterize our society.

In my graduate school days in St. Andrews, Scotland, I made the acquaintance of a physician from Calcutta, India. He was pursuing advanced research in medicine, and for a summer we lived in the same student residence. Our friendship gave us opportunity to explore the differences between Indian and American cultures. Night after night—literally morning after morning, since our confabs usually began at 1:00 or 2:00 A.M. after we had finished our evening's study—I enjoyed his hospitality: tea and peanuts. Each time I would thank him, and he would tease me by saying, "Thank you for thanking me." To his way of thinking, our friendship had passed the point where the formalities of verbal thanks were required. Once he chided me, "I bet you would thank your own brother for doing you a favor." "Of course I would!" was my abrupt reply. "I don't want to take another person for granted." His words were full of shock and dismay. "Your brother, another person?" No sentence before or since has helped me more to understand the way in which Orientals view the intimate ties of kinship. Dr. Roy's perplexed question was a whole curriculum to me in biblical thinking about family life.

The joy wisdom brings to other family members and especially to parents is exhibited as a key lure to the young persons for whom the proverbs were originally intended. Though indirectly these words may remind parents of the consequences of raising children well or badly, their primary purpose is to inform the young that they have a lot more to think about than just themselves. That point is plain in the only admonition found in the proverbs that deal with family ties.

> My son, be wise, and make my heart glad,
> That I may answer him who reproaches me.
> *Prov. 27:11*

The two imperatives, *"be wise"* and *"make glad,"* put the onus squarely on the shoulders of *"my son."* The second line shows us that scoffers were ready to make hay when their enemies had difficulty with their offspring. Of course, the parent wanted the youth to act responsibly for many reasons, but for none more than his ability to protect his reputation against the one who was geared to point out his shame and make fun of him (*"reproaches"*).

The normal sayings, where the grammar is indicative and not imperative, do not need such reasons.

> A wise son makes a glad father,
> But a foolish son *is* the grief of his mother.
> *Prov. 10:1b*

> A wise son makes a father glad,
> But a foolish man despises his mother.
> *Prov. 15:20*

These maxims merely point out in sharp contrasts the benefits of wisdom and the damages of folly: gladness to the *"father"* and *"grief"* (or *"affliction"*; see 14:13; 17:21) to the *"mother."* In 15:20, the first line of 10:1b is echoed, and two words are changed in the second: *"son"* becomes *"man"* and *"grief"* is replaced by *"despises"* with *"foolish man"* as subject. These changes seem to put more responsibility on the son who is mature enough to be called a man and culpable enough not only to bring grief but deliberately to treat his mother with spite.

> A fool despises his father's instruction,
> But he who receives correction is prudent.
> *Prov. 15:5*

Both grief and spite can be avoided if a son will receive and guard his *"father's instruction"* (or *"discipline"*; see on 1:2–6) and especially the *"correction"* which is one of wisdom's chief functions (1:23, 25, 30; 15:10, 31–32). Ability to take correction, even rebuke, and learn from it is a prime trait of the *"prudent,"* skillful or cunning (Heb. root ʿrm; see 19:25 for the verb as here; see 12:16, 23; 13:16; 14:8, 15; 22:3; 27:12 for the adjective).

The pain folly inflicts is described in two synonymous sayings which do not contain the contrasts found in 10:1; 15:5, 20. The first (17:21) borrows the language of 10:1 to make its point and reinforce it.

> He who begets a scoffer *does so* to his sorrow,
> And the father of a fool has no joy.
> *Prov. 17:21*

"Sorrow" is the same word translated as *"grief,"* and *"has joy"* is the verb read as *"makes glad."* *"Scoffer"* and *"fool"* are synonyms, *"scoffer"* being the most common word for fool in these sayings. The synonymous form does not choose to mention the mother but uses a synonym, *"He who begets,"* for *"father."* Two new words are introduced to describe the parents' pain in 17:25

> A foolish son *is* a grief to his father,
> And bitterness to her who bore him.
> *Prov. 17:25*

"Grief" means *"vexation,"* even *"anger,"* an appropriate response to foolish rebellion, as indicated by God's anger which Jeroboam's sin provoked (1 Kings 15:30); *"bitterness,"* a Hebrew word used only here but related to both the familiar waters of Marah (Exod. 15:23), whose bitterness gave them their name and to Naomi's adopted

name, after her lot changed from sweet to bitter (Ruth 1:20).
"Mother" here is paraphrased *"her who bore him,"* a precise parallel
to the "he who begets" of 17:21. The longer Hebrew form may help
to balance the length of the poetic lines by adding one more syllable
than would be present in "to his mother."

The forms dishonor takes are manifold. Most outrageous is the
direct mistreatment of parents.

> He who mistreats *his* father *and* chases away *his*
> mother
> *Is* a son who causes shame and brings reproach.
> *Prov. 19:26*

"Mistreats" suggests violence, even destruction. *"Chases away,"* literally "causes to flee," pictures a son old enough and strong enough to
commandeer the parents' household and physically eject them. The
New Testament son took his share and played the fool by abandoning his family and squandering his resources (Luke 15). This Old
Testament fool is much more to be censured; he has confiscated his
parents' holdings and cruelly sent them packing. Their inward pain
is amplified by horrible *"shame"* and *"reproach"* (see 27:11), since the
whole affair has been placarded in their community.

The maliciousness of all this is compounded by the act of cursing
the parents.

> Whoever curses his father or his mother,
> His lamp will be put out in deep darkness.
> *Prov. 20:20*

"Cursing" implies the wish and threat that all blessings be cut off,
all mercy withdrawn, and all harm invoked upon them. Parents
have become the worst possible enemies, and no evil is deemed too
terrible to bring down on their heads. Here the folly has reached
the point where dire judgment is called for. The focus is not on the
parents' grief, pain, or shame but on the fool's destruction. He has
shattered the command to honor those who begot and bore him. He
has removed the lamp of their presence from their household and,
in just retribution, his own *"lamp will be put out in deep* [like the
darkness of the iris of the eye] *darkness."* The extinguished lamp is
an image of death (see 13:9; Job 18:6; 21:17), perhaps related to the
description of David's offspring as a lamp before Yahweh in Jerusalem (Ps. 132:17; 1 Kings 11:36; 15:4), whose extinguishing would
mean the loss of light to Israel (see W. McKane, p. 405).

Misbehavior in public is another form that dishonor of parents may take. Two proverbs, identical in structure, call attention to specific acts of prodigality to which the young men were prone that brought grievous hurt to parents. Both acts involve hanging out with the wrong crowd ("companion"), a familiar theme of the sages (see on 1:10–19; 4:14–17).

> Whoever keeps the law *is* a discerning son,
> But a companion of gluttons shames his father.
> *Prov. 28:7*

One group includes persons who like lavish, frivolous living (*"gluttons,"* see Titus 1:12), drowning themselves in undisciplined excess that stands diametrically opposed to the instructions (*"law"* here is not the decalogue but the codified teachings of the wise; see on 3:1) that help make a *"discerning"* (insightful, understanding) person. The consequence of mixing with carousers is shame (see also 25:8) to the *"father."* Both the acts themselves and the results produce shame: wastrels are on the path to poverty (23:20–21). The other group is comprised of harlots (see on 6:26; 7:10ff.).

> Whoever loves wisdom makes his father rejoice,
> But a companion of harlots wastes *his* wealth.
> *Prov. 29:3*

"Wastes" (destroys or loses) *"wealth"* is the dreaded result here, a reminder that spendthrift behavior causes financial pain as well as emotional to the parent who would much prefer to *"rejoice"* in the child's love of *"wisdom."*

The third form which dishonor of parents may take is misuse of an inheritance. So valued is wisdom, so despised is folly, that possessing the one and not the other turns the whole socioeconomic system upside down.

> A wise servant will rule over a son who causes
>   shame,
> And will share an inheritance among the brothers.
> *Prov. 17:2*

A clever (*"wise"*; on *maśkîl*, see 1:3; 10:5; 14:35) *"servant"* or slave will gain authority (*"rule"*) over a *"son"* who brings *"shame"* (embarrassment, loss of face) to the family. The slave may replace the foolish son as one of the heirs who *"share"* (or divide) the *"inheritance,"* which by law and custom went to the *"brothers"* (13:22; Lev. 25:46). A monumental threat this is to family stability as well as to the welfare of the disinherited individual. That threat is the point of the saying: it is directed to the son and brothers to warn them against shameful behavior, not to the slaves to encourage them to gain wisdom and thus assure their futures. Nevertheless for us as Christians, the thought that slaves may be adopted in the family and share the inheritance of the blood members is one of the marvelous hopes of the gospel, as the apostles never tired of affirming (Rom. 8:17; Gal. 5:21; Eph. 5:5; 1 Pet. 1:4).

The gift the generations give is stated in both negative and positive terms.

> Children's children *are* the crown of old men,
> And the glory of children *is* their father.
> *Prov. 17:6*

Positively, the gift is *"glory"* and it flows two ways: from the grandchildren (*"children's children"*) to the grandparents (*"old men"* or elders) and from the *"father,"* which could mean any male ancestor, to the children, who could also be grandchildren or great grandchildren. *"Crown"* and *"glory,"* the two words which convey the value of the relationships, are a fixed pair, words commonly coupled in Hebrew parallelism (see on 4:9). They refer literally to headdresses or garlands that mark people as worthy of respect, admiration, and affection. Honoring ancestors and appreciating offspring brings meaning and dignity to life more than any other act save worshiping God. And no worshiping of God has full validity if it is devoid of piety in family relationships.

Negatively the gift is ruin.

> A foolish son *is* the ruin of his father,
> And the contentions of a wife *are* a continual
>   dripping.
> *Prov. 19:13*

This painful saying describes the vulnerability of a person to the mayhem caused by foolishness, whether the fool is a *"son"* or a spouse, in this case, as is usual in Proverbs, *"a wife."* *"Ruin"* is literally *"destruction"* (see on 17:4). *"Contentions"* are arguments about decisions to be taken, criticisms of every word and deed. In the case of the foolish son, the picture is of devastation as an army would inflict on an enemy town; in the case of a foolish wife, the image is of the nagging, persistent (*"continual"*) *"dripping"* of a leaky roof, nerve-racking if not soul destroying.

Intimacy entails vulnerability. It subjects us to roller-coaster emotions. Our spirits are so intertwined with those of our parents and children that what happens to them happens to us. Their highs are ours, and so are their lows. Their behavior is the barometer of our well-being. Nothing sparks joy so much as their love and goodwill; nothing triggers pain like their rejection and rebellion.

Because the proverbs are directed to the younger generation, the major emphasis in maintaining family ties is the honor due parents from their children. The parents' responsibilities of discipline will be touched upon in chapters 20 and 29. We need to apply the proverbs in the light of the New Testament which portrays both Jesus' revolutionary regard for children (Mark 10:13–16) and the apostolic constraints placed on parents who were forbidden to abuse the honor due them and warned not to "provoke your children, lest they become discouraged" (Col. 3:21).

LOVE OF FRIENDS

Grounded as they were in the covenantal traditions which featured a personal relationship between a loving God and a needy people, the teachers did not neglect the subject of love. Along with their efforts to keep family ties tight by getting children to weigh the contribution made to their parents' well-being by their behavior, they stress the stability and security brought to society by bonds of friendship bound tautly between persons who care for each other. Seven sayings on the subject of love call for attention here. They divide into three main headings:

Love forgives	10:12; 17:9; 21:10
Love rewards	11:17; 15:17
Love perseveres	7:17; 18:24

How love forgives is stated starkly.

> Hatred stirs up strife.
> But love covers all sins.
> *Prov. 10:12*

The saying is antithetical: the contrast is between *"hatred"* and *"love"*; the point is the impact of each on personal relationships. Like a stubborn dog, hatred digs up every possible bone of contention, worries it with relish, parades it around in its snarling snout, and drops it messily on the carpet where it causes nothing but consternation. Love, on the other hand, like a prudent squirrel, hides the morsels of scandal in a secret place where the light of exposure never reaches. *"Stirs up"* means to arouse what ought to be left in quiet repose, as its frequent use in the Song of Solomon indicates (Song of Sol. 2:7; 3:5; 8:4, 5). It is the exact opposite of *"cover"* which suggests letting something lie out of sight where it is neither disturbed nor disturbing. *"Sins"* ("transgressions" or even "crimes"; see on 17:9, 19) are faced realistically. Our best friends may fail the Lord, themselves, others, and us. The difference between love and hatred is how that failure is handled. Hatred wants to draw it into the public eye, debate it, quarrel over it (*"strife"*), come to blows if necessary to see that every angle of the scandal is exposed and every last drop of shame drawn from the face of the offender. Love accepts the contrite repentance of the wrongdoer and seeks to contain the damage to him, his loved ones, and the larger community. Peter had this proverb in mind when he urged his cadres of believers stretched around the Mediterranean to keep their love fervent in whatever difficulties they found themselves, "for 'love will cover a multitude of sins'" (1 Pet. 4:8). Not that our love atones for sin, only Christ's can do that, but that our love helps us overlook the sins of others and not let strife be the outcome.

Love that forgives keeps quiet about a transgression. That is what "cover" means in 17:9.

> He who covers a transgression seeks love,
> But he who repeats a matter separates friends.
>   *Prov. 17:9*

Silence is never more golden than when we refuse to make personal capital by gossiping about the failings of a friend. *"Seeks love"* points to pursuing the best way to show love and to keep the loving friendship sound by not betraying its confidences. Its stupid and deadly opposite is *"repeats a matter,"* a sure way to breakup (*"separates"*) friendships, whether with the offender or between the offender and someone else.

The healing, bonding role of forgiveness looms even larger when we contemplate the terrible alternative.

> The soul of the wicked desires evil;
> His neighbor finds no favor in his eyes.
>   *Prov. 21:10*

"Evil" which the wicked person yearns for *("desires")* in his very core *("soul")* is hurt to others. This may be vengeance in place of forbearance; it may be just plain malice, totally unprovoked. In any case, it leaves no room for mercy, grace, or charity, for kindness or consideration. Nothing the *"neighbor"* can do will ease the wicked person's urge to be mean.

My friend from India, Dr. Roy, whose understanding of family ties I noted earlier in this chapter, frequently described his friends as *"well-wishers."* The wise teachers of Jerusalem would have embraced this term. Loving friendships, for them, meant wishing friends the best even though they had done the worst. The purveyors of wickedness, in contrast, could not wish others well if his or their life depended on it.

Love rewards the one who does the loving. This point needs making, since the one who receives love obviously gets some benefit from the care and concern of others.

> The merciful man does good for his own soul,
> But *he who is* cruel troubles his own flesh.
> *Prov. 11:17*

Loving is pictured as an act of self-benefit and cruelty as an act of self-punishment. *"Merciful"* is the Hebrew *hesed* and describes the person who extends to another the same kind of loyalty and kindness that God showed His people by making covenant with them. Such a person renders a positive payment *("does good"*; see 3:30; 31:12) to himself by exercising kindness to others. His opposite, the *"cruel"* person (see 5:9; 12:10; 17:11), brings *"trouble"* or sorrow (see 11:29; 15:27) to himself in a deep and personal manner *("his own flesh"*; see 5:11). This contrast is another example of the blessing that comes from our behaving in ways God intended us to follow and the harm that befalls us when we don't.

The benefits of love outstrip the value of hatred by any comparison you can name.

> Better *is* a dinner of herbs where love is,
> Than a fatted calf with hatred.
> *Prov. 15:17*

The "better" form of proverb sets up the sharpest kind of contrast—here the difference between a simple *"dinner"* (portion or allowance) of vegetables *("herbs"*; see Deut. 11:10) and one that featured a *"fatted calf,"* force-fed and not toughened by work. The former would be the standard fare of every peasant; the latter, a banquet fit for a king (see Solomon's menu in 1 Kings 4:23). The one, most people would eat daily with a bit of bread on the side; the other, most people would never have eaten, since meat in large quantities was not affordable to any but the rich. The very scarcity of access to meat served to point up the value of *"love"* which outranked *"hatred"* farther than *"a fatted calf"* outdistanced a dish of herbs.

For nearly forty years Ruth and I have enjoyed the friendship of an Armenian family that lived in Pasadena. To plan for their financial future they invested all they had to build a small store building on the street front behind which they lived. They shared with us the extent of their sacrifice, when they gave up eating meat for more than a decade in order to make mortgage payments on the building. "No kebab for ten years" was the way they put it. They lived on bread and vegetables till the mortgage was paid down. They could do that because love was present at every meal, and they knew that it alone was what really counted.

Love perseveres is the final theme. Succinctly and graphically it is stated in a saying that extols friendships that last, especially through adversity.

> A friend loves at all times,
> And a brother is born for adversity.
> *Prov. 17:17*

"At all times" admits no exceptions, no mitigating circumstances. The parallel line is synonymous and seconds the proposition stated in the first line by an even more dramatic affirmation: *"a brother,"* whether by blood or covenant, knows that the very reason for his life (*"is born for"*) is to stand by a friend and help him in difficulty and hardship (*"adversity"*). Foul-weather friends are the only ones worth having. More important to the point of the proverb, they are the only ones worth being. The text is not about gaining a stalwart friend. It is about being one.

> A man *who has* friends must himself be friendly,
> But there is a friend *who* sticks closer than a
> brother.
> *Prov. 18:24*

The second line of this saying encourages such perseverance by describing a *"friend"* who is glued (*"sticks"* or cleaves) to another person with more tenacious loyalty than would be expected of a *"brother."* And 17:17 has already told us about the toughness of brotherly love. The first line apparently stands in contrast to the second but is much harder to decipher. Modern translations usually take two different tacks, neither of which follows the New King James. The problem is the phrase *"must himself be friendly"* which renders a difficult Hebrew word. Some versions connect the word with a root meaning "destroy" or "ruin" and read it, "A man of many companions may come to ruin" (NIV; so also NASB; JB omits "many" which is not in the Hebrew text).

Others interpret it as a form of "shout" or "chatter" in reference to superficial conversation: "Some companions are good only for idle talk" (NEB; see also RSV: "pretend to be friends"). The issue is too technical to be debated here, but NEB'S reading makes excellent sense. In either interpretation the contrast is the same: superficial friendships *cannot* be counted on and should be avoided, since what we really need are not more casual acquaintances who have no stake in our welfare but a few, perhaps only one, true friend to stand by us through thick and thin. "Friendship inflation" was how a friend of mine, a Greek scientist raised in Germany, labeled our American habit of making lots of friends quickly and then dropping them lightly. The bonds that tie persons together in friendship are too precious to be made of the cheap material of convenience. Choosing such a friend and being such a friend are among life's major decisions. Happy are those who treat that decision with high respect.

As important as are success and achievement, relationship outranks them by several steps. The grand commands of Scripture spotlight this: Love God; love your neighbor; love one another as I have loved you. Loving outweighs doing, as important as doing may be. Israel's neophyte leaders had to be taught this or they would fail in their governmental and familial responsibilities. This side of Christ's incarnation we know even more of the centrality of love for family and friends. As Christians we have joined a community of which brotherly-sisterly love is the hallmark. *Philadelphia* was what the Greeks called it. William Penn gave that name to a town he thought would mark a breakthrough in community life. Only a few of us may live in that city. But all of us by God's grace can inhabit that state.

CHAPTER EIGHTEEN

Peace in Society and Purity in Speech

Proverbs 18:1–24

A prime task of leaders is to avert conflict when they can and resolve it when they cannot avert it. Conflict hurts individuals, drains away needed energy, and threatens the covenants that hold families and societies together. No wonder Israel's young leaders needed help in dealing with conflict and received it from their teachers in ample and frequent doses. The two topics of this chapter go well together: of the many things that can ruffle the peace of a society, nothing is more effective than cruel or thoughtless speech. Chapter 18 highlights the dangers and offers good help in avoiding them.

PEACE IN SOCIETY

The proverbs assume a stable society and aim to keep it that way. The prophets dealt with upheaval; they shouted warnings to a people that was undermining the covenant foundations on which its life depended. The psalmists lived on the edge of calamity if not in the midst of it; they lifted to God their complaints about disasters—personal, natural, historical—that jeopardized their welfare and even their lives. But the sages treasured stability and argued against any behavior that rocked the boat of Israel's time-tested patterns and traditional values. Keeping life the same was their agenda, not effecting drastic change. Refining the honored ways of safe conduct was their goal, not designing new paths of human comportment.

They knew both the price of discord—how it ruins fellowship (17:1), loses status (11:29), invites destruction (17:19)—and the knack of concord—how to settle disputes early (18:18–19), how to deal with troublemakers toughly (22:10). This knowledge they eagerly conveyed to their pupils who, as they assumed responsibilities in government and commerce, were to hold the peace of society in their hands.

> Better *is* a dry morsel with quietness,
> Than a house full of feasting *with* strife.
> *Prov. 17:1*

Discord ruins fellowship—this was the plain message of one of the famous "better" proverbs. It contrasts *"strife,"* argumentative, contentious quarreling with *"quietness,"* carefree tranquillity (see 1:32 for a negative use of the same Hebrew word, *shalwāh* which can also mean apathetic carelessness). Appropriately the setting is a mealtime, and wisely the point is made: what counts is the mood not the menu. Dinner is for fellowship more than nutrition. More than once I have thrown up a meal consumed (I do not say "enjoyed") in a fine hotel under circumstances that were taut with hostility or heated by friction. The infinite difference between quarrel and quiet is signaled by the dramatic contrast between *"dry morsel"* and *"house full of feasting,"* literally "sacrifices," a clue that animals were often slaughtered as sacrifices and then devoured in a festal setting.

Dry morsels were an everyday occurrence in Palestine where the desert air desiccates anything that contains a drop of moisture, especially when modern means of packaging are not available. (I once carried sandwiches from Jerusalem to the Dead Sea. When lunchtime came they were so parched by the arid atmosphere that I did not know whether to eat them or carbon-date them.) Feasting with meat, on the other hand, was a rare privilege, one that many peasants in ancient Israel may have experienced only a handful of times in their life. Barley bread and cooked vegetables were their normal fare. Dry morsels were the peanut butter sandwiches of their day. Given the chance to tie-in to a rump roast or a leg of lamb they should have jumped with joy. Not so, say the wise. The value of the meal is in the quality of the fellowship. Where the conversation is upbeat and the mood supportive, the crusty bread tastes like a royal banquet. Where they are not, rack of lamb turns to chalk in the eater's throat. There ought to be special kinds of indigestion reserved for people who spoil a meal for others by their cantankerous conversation. And we need to be wise enough to schedule tense meetings for empty stomachs.

Discord loses status for those who promote it.

> He who troubles his own house will inherit the
>   wind,
> And the fool *will be* servant to the wise of heart.
> *Prov. 11:29*

Stern penalties are prescribed to one who *"troubles,"* disturbs, or brings sorrow (see 11:17; 15:6, 27) to his own household (*"house"*; 11:29). Simply put, he will forfeit his share of the family inheritance and *"inherit"* only *"the wind,"* a symbol of nothingness, used frequently in Ecclesiastes (2:26; 4:4). Furthermore, such a troublemaker (*"fool"*) will end as *"servant,"* not master, to the one so *"wise of heart"* as not to cause dissension in a family or community. These social entities are fragile in their strength and delicate in their toughness. The love and loyalty that make them function well also make them vulnerable to disruption. They are based on trust and covenant, bound together by gossamer not cowhide. Attacked, tampered with, stretched beyond their bearing, these ties may snap and let the community fall apart. Fools indeed are we to value so lightly the concordant consensus that allows a community to nurture, support, and restrain those who call it home.

Discord invites destruction both for the rebels and for the communities they disrupt.

> He who loves transgression loves strife,
> And he who exalts his gate seeks destruction.
> *Prov. 17:19*

Those so given to violating the rules of society that they do it deliberately (*"transgression"*) with relish and zest (*"loves"*) also must have an appetite for *"strife"* (quarrel or contention; see 13:10). Solid, stable families, churches, or larger communities have a low kindling point when it comes to tolerating dissent. They are not used to coping with bad behavior. Like the universities that were turned into armed camps by the student revolts of the 1960s, they hardly know how to respond to angry rule breaking (on the relationship of transgression and anger see 29:22) and may move from underreaction to overreaction as the 1970 shooting of the four young people at Kent State illustrates. Taking the law into our own hands, as transgressors do, carries with it the real risk of so riling a society that the response may be larger than the rebels ever bargained for. "You asked for it" was what Israel's teachers were telling their pupils when their transgression spawned strife.

The second line of 17:19 is not easy to link to the first. One difficulty is the meaning of *"exalts his gate."* Does this clause describe a pretentious, showy house that seeks to one-up the neighborhood and thus invite community outrage that can lead to the owner's *"destruction"*? Or is the doorway built high up so as to be inaccessible and unwelcoming, a mark of deliberate unfriendliness in a society that gave high marks to hospitality (see R. B. Y. Scott, Anchor Bible, p. 111)? Again, is *"gate"* a metaphor for *"mouth,"* projecting the picture of arrogant, haughty speech? Whichever reading we follow, and I lean toward the first, the point seems to be the dangers of lofty isolation and self-centeredness which break fellowship and ultimately shatter (as *"destruction"* can be translated) the person who has so little regard for the community as to ride roughshod over its mores in the first place.

When it came to the knack of concord—how to retain harmony in a world threatening to fly apart—two bits of advice were offered. The first was settle disputes early.

> 18:18 Casting lots causes contentions to cease,
> And keeps the mighty apart.
> 19 A brother offended *is harder to win* than a
> strong city,
> And contentions *are* like the bars of a castle.
> *Prov. 18:18–19*

"Casting lots" may be a mechanical way of settling quarrels (*"contentions"*) but it does far less damage to all concerned than throwing punches. Picture two powerful people arguing about who is right, who has the better idea, who is responsible for damage done to one of them. The issue is far from clear or the quarrel would not have reached fever pitch. The voices rise, the faces flush, the fists clench, inch by inch they edge toward each other until they stand toe to toe. That is an excellent moment for one of them or an outsider to say, "Let's draw straws or flip a coin." Such a move *"keeps the mighty apart,"* reminds them that there is probably some truth on both sides, that there are more ways than one to do a thing right, and that winning is not worth the price in most debates.

The consequences of letting the argument boil over are noted forcefully in 18:19. The image drawn is of a fortified *"city"* or a *"castle"* with *"bars"* to secure the gates. Defensiveness is the best way to sum this up. Arguments alienate brother from brother. Each becomes more convinced of the rightness of his position or more reluctant to back down. The issue is no longer truth but winning. All energy goes into making the city *"strong"* or keeping the castle's bars in place. No vitality is available to reexamine the issues, take stock of what the battle has cost, or develop a conciliatory strategy. Avoiding the impasse of mutual defensiveness needs to be a high aim if the peace of our societies is to be preserved. "Settle quickly and be willing to lose a little" is the sage advice in these two sayings.

A litigious society like ours needs to hear them. One of my friends who is both a theologian and a lawyer had dedicated his ministry to the amicable settling of disputes. I asked him why this mission had such high priority for him. His answer was simple: "The standard pattern of taking conflict to court forces one party to win big and the other to lose." As a law school professor and professional arbitrator he works night and day to change the climate of our society so that the courts will become the last, not the first, resort for settling disputes. He cares about the peace of our society.

Deal with the troublemaker toughly was what the wise counseled when stubborn persons persisted in quarrel and strife, when they refused to cast lots or shape some other compromise.

> Cast out the scoffer, and contention will leave;
> Yes, strife and reproach will cease.
>
> *Prov. 22:10*

The command could not be sharper: *"Cast* [or *"drive"*] *out the scoffer"* (22:10). The latter term is probably the strongest word that wisdom has to describe wicked stupidity. Scoffers or scorners (see Ps. 1:1) are persons so entrenched in foolish and spiteful behavior that they make sport of those who try to do right (see on 1:22; 3:34; 9:7–8). The very word suggests persistence and incorrigibility. No finesse will change them. They are beyond being shamed. Gentle persuasion falls on their deaf ears. Firm measures are utterly necessary. They must be cut off from the fellowship of the community lest their disruptive influence become permanent. Their absence eases each pressure which their presence produced: *"contention"*—the quarrel or argument which they never allowed to ease up; *"strife"*—the conflict over decisions in which the rest of the community thought their opinion dead wrong; *"reproach"*—the shame that the scoffers by their nasty talk and insolent slurs heaped on their neighbors during the disputes.

"Time out" it is called. Parents and teachers are using it effectively with their children. A kid who is stubbornly dominating a game, speaking meanly to the others, or physically abusing a playmate is forced to sit or stand alone, apart from the group, for a period of time. Thus cast out, he or she has opportunity to cool down, break the pattern of aggressiveness, feel the pain of discipline, and get ready to resume normal relations. Troublemakers need such isolation, and groups need such relief. The well-being of a community is essential if it is to afford the strength, support, and direction that we require to live fruitfully as persons within our circles, societies, and neighborhoods.

INTEGRITY IN CONVERSATION

We have met this subject in chapter 15 under the rubric of "Prudent Speech." It is a theme so prominent and persistent in Proverbs that we will look at it again in chapter 25. The ten sayings surveyed here can be discussed under the following headings:

Theme verses	18:2; 19:1
Characteristics of pure speech	
Blessing consistently	18:4
Reporting accurately	18:8; 20:19
Listening carefully	18:13
Questioning pointedly	18:17
Incentives to pure speech	
Peacefulness	18:6–7
Fruitfulness	18:20–21
Richness	20:15
Freedom	21:23
Acceptance	22:11

Better *is* the poor who walks in his integrity
Than *one who is* perverse in his lips, and is a fool.
Prov. 19:1

The first theme verse states simply the wretchedness of the person whose habits of speaking ("*lips*") are "*perverse*" (twisted or crooked). "*Better*" off and of more good to society is the one who is "*poor*" and yet makes a practice ("*walks*") of "*integrity*" (wholeness, completeness) in deed and word. Impure, meanly intended, slanderous speech is a hallmark of a "*fool*"—a far worse lot than poverty. The power of the comparison expressed in this "better" saying is found in the importance which the teachers attached to prosperity (see chap. 10 for the exhortations to hard work as escape from poverty and chap. 19

for their teaching on the advantages of wealth). They encouraged
their students to be generous to the poor (see chap. 11) and to remember God's concern for the poor as the One who created them
(see chap. 16), but they never urged their disciples to admire or emulate the poor. Yet they esteemed poverty as sheer blessing if the alternative was the folly of corrupt speech. In form, 19:1 bears a close
resemblance to 28:6, but there the comparison is between the poor
wise person and the rich fool:

> Better *is* the poor who walks in his integrity
> Than one perverse *in his* ways, though he *be* rich.
> *Prov. 28:6*

The similarity has encouraged some scholars to emend the Hebrew of
19:1 to match the parallelism of 28:6 so that the "fool" is changed to
"rich," a reading already found in the Syriac translation. But the Hebrew is clear enough to make its point effectively: integrity outshines
folly no matter what the economic status of the person may be.

The second theme verse pictures a blabbermouth.

> A fool has no delight in understanding,
> But in expressing his own heart.
> *Prov. 18:2*

Deep insight ("*understanding*"; Heb. *tᵉbûnāh*, see 2:2–3, 6) into life's
issues is of no concern to the "*fool*," who is thus deprived of the
"*delight*" or pleasure that so enriches the life of the wise. Instead,
he finds perverse delight in exposing the vast inventory of foolishness that his mind ("*heart*") contains by spilling out his heedless
words without restraint of any kind. A public act of indecency is
how the text describes this: "*expressing*" is a verb form used elsewhere in the Old Testament only to depict Noah's drunken naked-
ness (Gen. 9:21).

The characteristics of pure speech are traits as admirable today as
they were in the courts of the ancient Jewish kings. The first is its
gift of blessing consistently.

> The words of a man's mouth *are* deep waters;
> The wellspring of wisdom *is* a flowing brook.
> *Prov. 18:4*

"*Deep waters*" seems to suggest profundity of wisdom, the ability to
verbalize complex ideas and pose solutions to puzzling questions.

The second line completes the thought rather than contrasting with it. It extends the metaphor of *"waters"* with further descriptions: *"flowing brook"* and *"wellspring of wisdom."* The *"is"* supplied in NKJV should be omitted. *"Words"* is the only subject of the sentence, which is synthetic parallelism. The *"man"* is obviously a wise person, knowledgeable, articulate, and thoughtful. The whole picture is replete with blessing and refreshment. "Waters," "brook," and especially "wellspring" all speak of life. Note "well of life" or its equivalent, in 10:11; 13:14; 14:27; 16:22. Grasping the importance of water in the Scripture calls for us to place ourselves in arid contexts, deprived of the benefit of regular rain, well-stocked reservoirs, and the abundance of water taps that release instant refreshment into our homes and gardens. In a Palestinian setting there can be no higher tribute to helpful speech than to liken it to water, deep at its source, abundant and incessant in its flow.

Reporting accurately is the thrust to be noted in the identical warnings against the "talebearer" (slanderer, a term occurring only in Proverbs: 16:28; 26:20, 22; the root means "backbite").

> The words of a talebearer *are* like tasty trifles,
> And they go down into the inmost body.
> *Prov. 18:8*

> The words of a talebearer *are* like tasty trifles,
> And they go down into the inmost body.
> *Prov. 26:22*

The danger lies in the combination of attractiveness (*"tasty trifles"*) and penetration (*"inmost body"*; lit., "the chambers of the belly"). Our mouths water to savor the latest gossip and then we find that the *"words"* stay with us a discomforting length of time. We keep remembering the vicious rumors, toying with the possibility that they are true, delighting in them and despising them at the same time. And we become angry with ourselves for listening and with the *"talebearer"* for feeding us such tangy, yet indigestible stuff. We were served chocolate mousse at a recent banquet. A friend of mine, conscious of calories, contrasted the tempting taste of mousse with the lead weight it became in his stomach. You will judge the gustatory accuracy of his evaluation of mousse, but that description is precisely how the teachers viewed the impact of gossip.

Even keeping company ("associate") with such types is frowned on.

> He who goes about *as* a talebearer reveals secrets;
> Therefore do not associate with one who flatters
>   with his lips.
>
> *Prov. 20:19*

They are not to be trusted with confidentialities (*"secrets"*) because their whole bent is to make them public (*"reveals"*). They are especially dangerous, these blabbermouths (*"talebearer"* or slanderer, a different Hebrew term from that in 18:8; see 11:13), because they combine undisciplined gossip with winsome, seductive flattery. Like a Venus flytrap they lure friends into their grasp and then devour them by betraying their secrets. Their destructive example reminds us not to trust them or imitate them. Their speech embodies everything that biblical honesty opposes. Reporting accurately only what we have a right to report is a practice passionately to be cultivated.

Listening carefully is an equally admirable trait.

> He who answers a matter before he hears *it*,
> It *is* folly and shame to him.
>
> *Prov. 18:13*

Bluntly put, the crime is to *"answer"* a *"matter"* (lit., a *"word"*) before we *"hear"* it (18:3). What is a fairly regular habit with many of us is called *"folly"* and *"shame"* (or *"insult"*). Folly it is, because we are not God; we have no power to read hearts. Shame it is, because we have treated the other person as an inferior; we have assumed that we are smart enough to know what she will say before she says it; we have treated her as less than a full person and have shamed and insulted ourselves by revealing our insensitivity and ignorance. Flashy communicators may hone their skills by practice speaking; mature communicators do so by careful listening.

Questioning pointedly is a valuable component of sound speech.

> The first *one* to plead his cause *seems* right,
> Until his neighbor comes and examines him.
>
> *Prov. 18:17*

Its primary use is in legal contexts, as *"plead his cause"* suggests. The scene was the town gate, where the elders convened to hear grievances among neighbors and to sort out the truth and error of charge and countercharge. The first neighbor speaks and his case seems eminently plausible (*"right"*; lit., *"righteous"*). Then comes the second *"neighbor"* and *"[cross-]examines"* him. Additional facts come to light; another side to the story surfaces. The elders have to revise their initial opinion in view of what the questioning has revealed. The applications of this principle are legion. It still plays a vital part in our judicial processes; it is standard practice in our daily work as administrators; our children use it to dispense justice to their children. Given human biases and sinful prejudices, we are seldom near the truth of an issue until we hear all sides. Pointed questioning is almost always the best way to do that.

The incentives to pure speech are as durable as the characteristics. Peacefulness is valued in its absence in two sayings that capture the disturbance that unguarded, ill-considered speech can foment.

> 18:6 A fool's lips enter into contention,
>   And his mouth calls for blows.
> 7 A fool's mouth *is* his destruction,
>   And his lips *are* the snare of his soul.
> *Prov. 18:6–7*

The first saying pictures the fool's tendency to pick a quarrel (on *"contention,"* Heb. *rîb*, see 17:1) with his words (*"lips"* and *"mouth"* stand for what they say) that ultimately has to be settled with his fists (*"blows"*; see 19:29, *"beatings"*). Lack of manners and absence of wisdom are a dangerous combination as verse 7 attests. The results are virtually suicidal. *"Destruction"* is an active participle better read *"his destroyer,"* while *"snare"* (Heb. *môqēsh*; see 12:13; 13:14; 14:27) is the trigger-bar of a trap that holds the bait and, when touched, releases the nets to clutch the victim, in this case the soul or *"life"* (as Heb. *nephesh* can mean) of the *"fool."* Lethal words indeed, destroying the peace of the community and the life of the fool who utters them.

Fruitfulness and productivity were featured as rewards of fine speech in a land that treasured its agricultural output and often pictured true success in terms of fruit-laden trees or well-stocked vines (see Ps. 1:3). Reliable speech was virtually a guarantee of financial stability since it contributed so much to the worker's success on the job.

> A man's stomach shall be satisfied from the fruit of
>   his mouth;
> *From* the produce of his lips he shall be filled.
> *Prov. 18:20*

Wholesome *"fruit"* of the *"mouth"* or *"produce"* of the *"lips"* was the key to a *"satisfied"* stomach (18:20). Professor William McKane takes

276 PEACE IN SOCIETY AND PURITY IN SPEECH

the meaning a step further in his observation that speech was not an end in itself but achieved fruitful, constructive results in society and thus brought satisfaction both to the speakers and their neighbors.

This social application seems to catch the force of 18:21.

> Death and life *are* in the power of the tongue,
> And those who love it will eat its fruit.
>
> *Prov. 18:21*

"Death and life" refer to the impact (*"power"*; lit., "hand") of speech on others. They are extreme ways of describing the harm and blessing of what we say. Moreover death and life mark the poles of human existence and include everything in between. We call this rhetorical device a *merism*; it states the boundaries and embraces all the territory marked off by them. To *"love"* the tongue (*"it"*) means to understand this power and to use it with great care. The results (*"fruit"*) of solid, sensible, sensitive speech will be both satisfying and sustaining (*"eat"*). Good communicators know this. Would that we always behaved on what we know!

The richness of knowledgeable speech is part of what draws us to develop it.

> There is gold and a multitude of rubies,
> But the lips of knowledge *are* a precious jewel.
>
> *Prov. 20:15*

"Lips of knowledge," lips that are adept at sharing not just helpful information but insights into and experience of God's ways (see on 1:7), outrank both *"gold"* and *"rubies,"* which may mean "coral" (see on 3:15; 8:11). Such lips and the speech they pour forth are one of life's true treasures, as rare and valued as a costly, *"precious jewel."* Prospectors battle heat, drought, flies, snakes, and thieves in the remote areas of the world from Cripple Creek, Colorado, to Kalgoorlie, Australia in the hope of striking it rich. The grand nugget, the magnificent gem, is their driving hope. And it can be found on the front of our faces if we have the sense to seek it there. We grasp immediately the power of speech when we are asked, "Would you trade the Gettysburg Address for the Mona Lisa, the Lord's Prayer for the Hope Diamond?" Valuable as great works of art may be, they cannot compare in magnificence of contribution to the words that carry the knowledge of God's will to the human family.

Freedom from trouble is another gift of pure speech.

> Whoever guards his mouth and tongue
> Keeps his soul from troubles.
> *Prov. 21:23*

That awesome power of life and death that resides in the tongue (18:21) makes it literally a lethal weapon—to others and ourselves. To guard *"mouth and tongue,"* therefore becomes a prime duty to others and a prudent service to oneself, since not to do so exposes us to a potential host of *"troubles."* The almost endless varieties of distress that our foolish speech can inflict on us—from guilt, to shame, to anxiety, to pride—are strong arguments for studied restraint in what we say and how we say it.

Acceptance in high places is the last reward to be considered.

> He who loves purity of heart
> *And has* grace on his lips,
> The king *will be* his friend.
> *Prov. 22:11*

Integrity and sensitivity are the indispensable requirements for those who would serve well in positions of leadership. Talent and skill, brilliance and alertness, eloquence and energy are not enough. The problem is not just getting work done but building relationships which set the mood and context for effective service. *"Purity of heart"* and *"grace on his lips"* are the accurate and descriptive terms for integrity and sensitivity (22:11), while friendship with the *"king"* depicts the importance of the relationship. It is hard to serve well people we do not like and who do not like us, and it is almost impossible to like someone whose motives and words we cannot trust. To say what we mean and mean what we say demands a cooperation between *"heart"* (thought, will) and *"lips"* (words, speech) akin to the teamwork between catcher and pitcher on a well-coached baseball team. Let one zig while the other zags, and the game is up. If Judah's young administrators were willing to discipline themselves to please their king, what should be our commitment who are stewards to the King of kings?

CHAPTER NINETEEN

Open Ears and Full Hands

Proverbs 19:1–29

Heeding instruction and handling wealth were two essential responsibilities of Israel's cadre of young leaders. Like the Yuppies of our generation, they were talented, confident, assertive, ambitious, and affluent—or about to be. Their personal skill, administrative responsibility, and social influence needed outside help if they were to be well used. Yet the very poise and pride that contributed to their success made them susceptible to arrogant self-sufficiency. Coming from landed families as many of them did, they were used to wealth and in danger of not appreciating its purposes, risks, and obligations.

The curriculum of the teachers did not overlook these subjects. Had it done so, it would have failed the students. They and their successors right down to our day have learned that the ability to heed instruction is prerequisite to the ability of giving instruction. We become good shepherds to others by first being good sheep to those who lead us. We become good stewards of material goods by first respecting what it takes to garner wealth and how difficult it is to use it wisely. Neither open ears nor full hands come automatically. Hence the importance of the proverbs that deal with these subjects. Their very number—more than thirty that call for sensitivity to instruction and over twenty that treat the implications of wealth (sixteen of which are discussed here and the rest in chap. 28)—underscores their ancient and modern importance.

HEEDING INSTRUCTION

Many of us are not famous for taking instructions. Just ask our spouses. I tear open packages of cereal at the wrong end, open milk cartons from the back side, and look at the assembly guide sheet only when I am already in trouble in putting our grandsons' toys together.

While I am confessing, I must add to the list my reluctance even to seek instruction when I am lost, especially if Ruth is with me. Somehow the gas station attendants, traffic cops, and taxi drivers all look like temptations to be skirted, not resources to be consulted.

There's a lot within us that resists advice, that says, "You can do it on your own, you don't need help, you can sail through the uncharted waters, or at least muddle through. Don't bother anybody else, don't depend on outsiders. Do it yourself, do it your own way." The wise teachers understood these feelings and hammered hard to counter them. Especially dangerous, in their view, was the tendency of their young friends to resist correction. There is something that makes us resent most what we most need to hear—what we have done wrong and how we can do better next time.

This theme is sounded in 13:1, which reduces to its essence the importance of seeking and heeding correction or instruction (for Heb. *mûsār*, see on 1:2–6).

> A wise son *heeds* his father's instruction,
> But a scoffer does not listen to rebuke.
> *Prov. 13:1*

A hallmark of the *"wise son"* or daughter is the ability to accept even stern or painful advice with open ears. The *"scoffer"* of the contrasting line is so attached to foolish behavior, so well defended against changing his ways, so skeptical of the values of the community that he will *"not listen"* to any *"rebuke"* (see on 13:8; the word is translated "threat" at Isa. 30:17). Cocksureness and stupidity are soul mates just as are humility and wisdom.

Some implications of this theme are unpacked in the following discussion which can be outlined like this:

Introduction
    verbs of passion
    nouns of correction
Barriers to listening
    stupidity   12:1; 26:11
    cynicism   14:6; 19:25; 21:11
    pride   13:10
Benefits of listening
    direction   10:17; 15:10; 19:27
    reward   13:13
    wisdom   12:15; 13:20; 14:8; 15:31–32; 17:10; 18:15;
                             19:20

success	10:8; 15:22; 20:18; 13:18; 16:20
companionship	14:7; 15:12; 27:17
life	13:14; 15:10; 19:16; 29:1
Conclusion	
obedience and prayer	28:9

The seriousness of the subject can be garnered from a look at the verbs and nouns that anchor these sayings. The verbs capture the intense passion, the focused commitment, expected of wise disciples. The frequent contrasts between the positive terms that urge attention and the negative actions of those who turn deaf ears to wise advice serve only to heighten the passion by reminding us that for the teachers neutrality was nonexistent:

keep	(or guard) suggests the value of instruction, a treasure to be retained and protected; its opposites are *"refuse"* (or abandon, 10:17), *"disdain"* (or neglect, 13:18 where "keeps" is translated *"regards"*), and *"is careless"* (or despising, 19:16).
love	(12:1) implies that wisdom is worth caring about, investing oneself in; *"hate"* is its appropriate opposite (see also 15:10).
hear	(listen or heed, 12:15; 13:1; 15:31–32; 19:20, 27) describes an attention so riveted on the teaching that its impact can be channeled to the heart; not to listen is to deem oneself *"right"* in one's *"own eyes"* (12:15), to *"disdain"* (or neglect, 15:32), and to *"stray"* from the true knowledge of God (19:27).
fear	(or revere, 13:13) means to treat truth with awe, mindful of the fearful results of disregarding it; *"despise"* is its antonym.
heed wisely	(or ponder, 16:20) is reinforced by *"trust"* in the parallel line; the combination implies that God's words are trustworthy and therefore worth close attention.
seek, acquire, and *receive*	(18:15), (10:8; 19:20; 21:11; two different Heb. words) underscore both the eagerness necessary to gain wisdom and the sure result with which that eagerness will be rewarded.

The fact that the lion's share of this list is in participle form indicates that these verbs are more than incidental activities. They describe, rather, persons whose chief characteristics, whose personal attributes, are keeping, loving, hearing, fearing, and heeding wisely the commands of the wise.

The nouns display the manifold nature of the advice to which the ears of the wise need to be open. We have met them before and list them here only to show their variegated character and their cumulative impact in this sampling of proverbs:

instruction	correction for the sake of discipline (10:17; 12:1; 13:1, 18; 15:10; see 1:2–3, 7–8).
reproof	argument to prove someone wrong (12:1; 13:18; 15:10, 31–32; see on 1:25, 30).
rebuke	reprimand of unacceptable behavior (13:1; 17:10 ["reproof"]).
knowledge	especially of God's will and ways (12:1; 14:6–7; 18:15; 19:27; 21:11; see on 1:4, 7).
commandment	specific direction so essential for well-being that it becomes a mandate not an option (10:8; 13:13; 19:16; see on 2:1; 3:1).
word	the teaching of the wise viewed in its power to effect good purpose (13:13).
law	instruction in right and wrong based on an understanding of God's will (13:14; see on 1:8; 3:1; "law" in 28:9 seems to be the Lord's direct law like the commands of the Pentateuch).
counsel	advice that leads to successful plans (12:15; see on 1:30; 8:14; in 15:22 a second Hebrew term is used which suggests a "counsel" that delves into problems so obscure as to be classified as secrets or mysteries).

Barriers to listening are pictured in no-nonsense terms. Our modern theories of communication and our desire to be polite and take responsibility for breakdowns in understanding may be well taken. But listeners have obligations too. No amount of graciousness, patience, or artistry in our teaching will work without deliberate concentration on the part of the hearers. The sages minced no words. Failure to keep open ears was a badge of stupidity. Actually that word is too weak to catch the full force of the Hebrew in the following proverb:

> Whoever loves instruction loves knowledge,
> But he who hates correction *is* stupid.
>
> *Prov. 12:1*

"Brutish" may be better. To hate *"correction"* puts one in the category of a stubborn mule that won't move no matter how hard the tug, how sharp the whip. The comparison between an unheeding fool and a dumb animal is made graphic in these words (see also 2 Pet. 2:22):

> As a dog returns to his own vomit,
> *So* a fool repeats his folly.
> *Prov. 26:11*

The verse highlights the importance of hearing the second time even if we miss the point the first. *"A dog"* seems not to discern its own stupidity and *"returns"* to lap up the foul residue of what its stomach rejected in the first place. Human beings in contrast should have the capacity to rise above their patterns of life and decide to make deliberate changes in behavior which has proved harmful. None of us will get everything right the first time. To catch the meaning the second time marks off the wise from the fool and demonstrates our wonderful human gift of changing even long-grooved patterns of conduct.

Cynicism may be an even uglier barrier to listening than stupidity.

> A scoffer seeks wisdom and does not *find it,*
> But knowledge *is* easy to him who understands.
> *Prov. 14:6*

The *"scoffer"* is the cynic par excellence (see on 1:22; 3:34); he scorns all sound advice, probing it for loopholes, jeering at the motives of the teachers, mocking the naiveté of those who try to do right. His search (*"seeks"*) is a farce. He finds no wisdom because he does not believe there is any and cannot recognize it when it stares him in the face. His opposite, the one *"who understands,"* has insight into the character of wisdom, has a good eye for it and finds it an easy (light, simple) task to spot it. We are reminded of an eagle-eyed caddie who finds golf balls that we duffers have almost stepped on and not seen.

> Strike a scoffer, and the simple will become wary;
> Rebuke one who has understanding, *and* he will
>   discern knowledge.
> *Prov. 19:25*

So hardened is the cynicism of scoffers that even physical punishment (*"strike"*) or the exacting of a fine (as "punished" seems to imply in 21:11; see 27:12) will not change their behavior.

> When the scoffer is punished, the simple is made
>   wise;
> But when the wise is instructed, he receives
>   knowledge.
>
> *Prov. 21:11*

Nevertheless such punishment must take place for the wariness (or shrewdness, 19:25) and wisdom (21:11) that the naive person (*"simple"*) may garner from the scorner's painful example. In contrast, punishment becomes a means of instruction and improvement for the *"wise"* (21:11) and discerning (*"has understanding"*; 19:25) person who is humble enough to accept correction, acknowledge wrong behavior, and learn from the whole experience.

Pride is the third barrier to listening.

> By pride comes nothing but strife,
> But with the well-advised *is* wisdom.
> *Prov. 13:10*

The proud one is insolent (the Hebrew word crops up at 11:2; 21:24), a know-it-all. The result of trying to teach such a one is *"contention"* or quarreling (see 17:19). No docility or teachability is present. Every point the teacher serves up is slapped back with speed and spin and the whole encounter becomes a ping-pong game. Not so with the *"well-advised."* They are open to counsel, receptive to instruction. They are like wide receivers in football; they can hardly wait to catch words of *"wisdom"* and run with them.

The benefits of listening are given much more attention than the barriers.

> He who keeps instruction *is in* the way of life,
> But he who refuses correction goes astray.
> *Prov. 10:17*

Direction is one of them. The *"way of life"* is the path that leads to fruitful, effective, and successful living. To stay on it one must guard closely the teachers' *"instruction"* even though it may take the form of reproof or *"correction."* Not to do so is to wander aimlessly (stray) from the path like a drunken vagabond or a lost animal (for stray and "lead astray" see 12:26; Hos. 4:12).

> Harsh discipline *is* for him who forsakes the way,
> *And* he who hates correction will die.
> *Prov. 15:10*

The dangers of such straying are pointed out when *"harsh discipline"* is necessary for those who abandon (forsake) *"the way"* of right living. *"Harsh"* (lit., "bad" or "evil") as the *"correction"* may be, it is much preferred to the alternative: death awaits those who refuse to let correction nudge them back to the true path. *"Will die"* may be intended literally, given the dangers of foolish behavior, or figuratively to describe a life emptied of meaning and blessing.

> Cease listening to instruction, my son,
> And you will stray from the words of knowledge.
> *Prov. 19:27*

Keeping one's bearings takes constant *"listening,"* the kind a pilot does to stay on course during a storm-laden cross-country flight. To *"cease listening"* is to court disaster. Like the bleeps of a homing signal, *"words* [or sayings] *of knowledge"* are indispensable to reaching the target. To close an ear to them will leave us to *"stray"* like lost sheep (Ezek. 34:6 uses the same Hebrew word).

Reward is the all-embracing benefit promised in 13:13.

> He who despises the word will be destroyed,
> But he who fears the commandment will be
>   rewarded.
> *Prov. 13:13*

Success, a good life, acceptance in the community, favor with God are probably all components of the reward. The opposite fate, *"will be destroyed,"* is not so clear in Hebrew and may mean something more general like "will pay for it." If taken literally, "will pay for it" may describe a court procedure where misconduct leads to the payment of a fine or the holding of the criminal as pledge until the damage can be paid for.

Wisdom is the benefit most commonly listed.

> The way of a fool *is* right in his own eyes,
> But he who heeds counsel *is* wise.
> *Prov. 12:15*

It is an acquired not an innate blessing. The *"fool"* may ride through life like a lone ranger and make huge blunders by doing what *"is right in his own eyes"* (see Judg. 21:25); true wisdom comes by listening to sound advice.

> He who walks with wise *men* will be wise,
> But the companion of fools will be destroyed.
> *Prov. 13:20*

Heeding instruction in a consistent pattern calls for keeping regular company ("*walks*") with the "*wise.*" What they are rubs off on us. We learn their ways, follow their example, and reap their rewards. The opposite kinds of "*companions,*" the "*fools,*" produce the opposite results in us—harsh, destructive, even evil outcomes (see 11:15 for another use of the Hebrew word translated "*will be destroyed*").

> The wisdom of the prudent *is* to understand his
>   way,
> But the folly of fools *is* deceit.
> *Prov. 14:8*

"*Wisdom*" and "direction," discussed above, are virtual synonyms in 14:8. Wisdom is the lamp that helps us read the compass and stay on course. "*Folly,*" on the other hand, deceives the fool into thinking he is headed straight when he is wandering aimlessly and dangerously without knowing it.

The joys and dangers of listening or not listening are set back to back in 15:31–32.

> 15:31 The ear that hears the rebukes of life
>   Will abide among the wise.
>   32 He who disdains instruction despises his own
>   soul,
>   But he who heeds rebuke gets understanding.
> *Prov. 15:31–32*

"*Rebuke*" is to be heard both because it is life-renewing and because hearing it is a membership card that allows a person to have a home (abode) "*among the wise*" (15:31). To reject wisdom as costing too much or inflicting more pain than we can handle—when it comes in the forms of correction ("*instruction*") or rebuke—is to pay a much higher price: the loss of self-respect, described in this proverb as despising one's own soul. Self-rejection is emotional suicide. We should spare no price to obtain the wisdom that will protect us from that.

> Rebuke is more effective for a wise *man*
> Than a hundred blows on a fool.
> *Prov. 17:10*

Wisdom and perfection are not synonyms. Even the *"wise"* need strong *"rebuke."* What proves their wisdom is the way they take it: they allow it quickly to penetrate their hearts and goad them to repentance and change (see 21:11); the *"fool,"* on the other hand, may have truth pounded into him and still not get the point. *"Effective"* can mean "penetrate deeply"; the Hebrew word describes the action of an arrow in Ps. 38:2.

Though wisdom has God's grace as its source, it is not an instant, automatic gift.

> The heart of the prudent acquires knowledge,
> And the ear of the wise seeks knowledge.
> *Prov. 18:15*

It has to be pursued with both *"ear"* and *"heart."* One has to listen, ponder, and then apply the *"knowledge"* which is acquired. Persistence is inferred from the tenses of the verbs: they are imperfect in Hebrew and suggest ongoing action—*"acquires"* means "keeps on acquiring" and *"seeks"* means "does not stop seeking."

> Listen to counsel and receive instruction,
> That you may be wise in your latter days.
> *Prov. 19:20*

The importance of persistence—with the length of it—shows up *"in your latter days"* of 19:20. The promise is profound: one can attain the title of *"wise."* But the cost of doing so in patient obedience to the commands *"listen"* and *"receive"* (take in) must be fully reckoned.

Success in carrying out life's aims is another fruit of listening.

> The wise in heart will receive commands,
> But a prating fool will fall.
> *Prov. 10:8*

The *"prating fool"* (lit., "a fool in lips") talks much and listens little. Left to his own devices he and all he plans come to ruin (*"will fall"*; see the same Hebrew verb in Hos. 4:14). Success is impossible because his thinking—in contrast to the wise in heart, the one who makes wise decisions that lead to success—is limited to his own resources and not enriched by the *"commands"* of the prudent people around him. Success depends on listening. That is made even more clear in this saying:

> Without counsel, plans go awry,
> But in the multitude of counselors they are
>   established.
>
> *Prov. 15:22*

Where *"counsel"* (especially from those who know us intimately and understand us personally, as the Hebrew word suggests) is absent, *"plans"* are frustrated and break down (*"go awry"*). When our perspective is enlarged by input from a number (*"multitude"*) of caring, experienced and honest advisers (*"counselors"*), the plans will stand up (*"established"*) to any normal test put to them. Practically speaking, I have found it useful to have counselors who know me well, from whom I have very few secrets, but who also have wide-ranging experience in the areas where I need help. Obviously, some of our trustees play this role. But so do my coworkers, some of whom I supervise. Their knowledge of me and their intimacy with the situations I face combine to provide admirable advice. Foolish are the ministers who do not listen to their assistants; dangerous the pastors who do not seek the counsel of their secretaries.

> Plans are established by counsel;
> By wise counsel wage war.
> *Prov. 20:18*

What applies to church leaders must apply in spades to politicians and military officers. To *"wage war"* is always harmful and dangerous; to do so on bad advice is a heinous crime. *"Plans"* for force or violence of any kind need checking and rechecking with the wisest resources available.

One badge of success, as the teachers saw it, was honor.

> Poverty and shame *will come* to him who disdains
>   correction,
> But he who regards rebuke will be honored.
> *Prov. 13:18*

To guard and cling to (*"regards"*) *"a rebuke"* was not grounds for shame but for respect and even material reward. The Hebrew root for "honor" can mean both glory and wealth. To welcome reproof and let it change our ways is a mark of maturity that people will admire and that may make our work more effective and perhaps more profitable. To disdain correction, in contrast, abandons us to our own resources, severs us from the wisdom and regard of our

associates, and may well lead to *"poverty and shame."* Poverty here
implies losing wealth that one had earlier acquired and losing it by
making bad decisions based on ignoring (*"disdains"*) sound correction. In such circumstances—though certainly not in all circumstances—the poverty would inevitably lead to shame.

As honor was the external badge of success, happiness was its
internal seal.

> He who heeds the word wisely will find good,
> And whoever trusts in the LORD, happy *is* he.
> *Prov. 16:20*

This proverb is virtually a beatitude, though the declaration *"happy
is he"* is its climax not its beginning (for the normal pattern see 3:13).
"Happy" and *"good"* are synonyms here and must refer to a general
well-being, a sense of being cared for and encouraged. The synonymous parallelism tells us something else: the proverbial *"word"* of
line one is viewed in its truth as coming from *"the Lord."* To heed it
"wisely" was the direct equivalent of *"trust"* in Him.

Companionship is another benefit of listening and an aid to it
as well.

> Go from the presence of a foolish man,
> When you do not perceive *in him* the lips of
>   knowledge.
> *Prov. 14:7*

In fact, companionship is so influential on our lives that we
deliberately *"go from the presence of a foolish man,"* whose ways are
hazardous, whose reputation is shameful, and whose *"lips"* lack
"knowledge." If you can help such a one, fine! But the odds are long,
the wasted time is precious, and the risks of being influenced are
considerable (see on 13:20 above).

> A scoffer does not love one who corrects him,
> Nor will he go to the wise.
> *Prov. 15:12*

The *"scoffer"* we have already met in this chapter (14:6; 19:25;
21:11). He is incapable either of going *"to the wise"* for counsel or
appreciating (*"love"*) anyone *"who corrects him"* by showing where
and why he is wrong. Spending time with him is utterly useless,
perhaps downright dangerous. Sowing good seed on bad soil

makes no sense to the sages or to our Lord Himself (see Mark 4:20; Luke 10:10–12).

> As iron sharpens iron,
> So a man sharpens the countenance of his friend.
>   *Prov. 27:17*

The positive impact of companionship seems to be the point of 27:17, although a precise translation is not easy to come by. My literal rendering is this:

> Steel by steel is sharpened,
> And a man is sharpened [by] the face of his friend.

This reading treats the verbs alike and makes them passive or stative. It also carries forward the preposition "by," which is attached to *"steel,"* and makes it modify "face" (*"countenance"*) as well. The picture seems to be of a friendship so intimate and so honest that the person's judgment is sharpened and the thinking honed, as in the whetting of a knife, merely by the reactions of the other person's face. My late friend and associate at Fuller, Dr. Glenn W. Barker had such a face. I could tell in mid-argument whether I was on track or not by the lift of an eyebrow, the curl of a corner of the mouth, the query of a tongue inside the cheek, the glowing brow of affirmation. Not that he kept silent long! But his facial clues more than once were enough to make me either drop or reinforce my point. Happy the person who has friends like that!

Life is the ultimate blessing of good listening.

> The law of the wise *is* a fountain of life,
> To turn *one* away from the snares of death.
>   *Prov. 13:14*

"Life" and *"death"* in proverbs like this may be intended as literal, figurative, or both. It is not always easy to tell and, in a sense, does not matter. There can come a point when life is so drained of purpose, fellowship, and joy that it is a walking death and a prolonged experience of that walking death can bring on physical destruction itself. Listening to the *"law* [instruction] *of the wise"* was life-bringing like having an artesian well (*"fountain"*) in your garden. Its affirmed task was *"to turn"* the pupils *"away from the snares of death."* The mixing of the metaphor from refreshment in drought to rescue from hunters serves only to heighten the impact of the *"law."* With it

comes refreshment and safety; without it, dehydration and captivity—complete debilitation and loss of all freedom that life provides (see on 15:10 above).

> He who keeps the commandment keeps his soul,
> *But* he who is careless of his ways will die.
> > *Prov. 19:16*

A less poetic form of 13:14 is found in 19:16 where keeping (or guarding) *"the commandment,"* the binding words of the wise, is tantamount to guarding one's own life (*"soul"* or person or self), while carelessness (or disdain) in following the right paths (*"ways"*) has death as its outcome.

> He who is often rebuked, *and* hardens *his* neck,
> Will suddenly be destroyed, and that without
> remedy.
> > *Prov. 29:1*

The connection between obstinacy and disaster centers in the *"neck"* according to 29:1. The figure is of a stubborn animal, an ox or a donkey, refusing to be guided by a driver's tug at yoke or bridle. All attempts to correct (reprove) the unruly beast are resisted and it fixes its neck (*"hardens"*) in an immovable position. The hardened neck describes an intransigent Israel in Deut. 31:27 and Exod. 32:9 (cf. also the *"stubborn calf"* in Hos. 4:16). *"Destroyed"* is literally *"broken"* and seems to carry on the picture of the stiff neck. Refusing to bend, it is broken either by the frantic pull of the frustrated farmer or by the animal's own pell-mell plunge into pit or crevice. In any case, the result is damage beyond anyone's ability to heal (*"without remedy"*)—a sharp reminder that refusal to keep an open ear to counsel, correction, or censure carries with it the seeds of its own judgment.

Even more dire are the results of spiritual deafness described in a proverb which may serve as a summary conclusion to this whole topic.

> One who turns away his ear from hearing the law,
> Even his prayer *is* an abomination.
> > *Prov. 28:9*

If hearing the advice of the wise is vital to successful living, how much more crucial is *"hearing the law."* The mention of *"prayer"* in the synthetic parallelism which completes the verse suggests that "law" here, in contrast with 13:14, may refer to the Lord's law revealed in the Pentateuch. We cannot be dogmatic about this, however, since we are not told to whom the prayer of the spiritually deaf is *"an abomination"* (see on 3:32; 13:19; 29:27). If Yahweh is the outraged party, then His law is what is going unheeded. If, on the other hand, it is the members of the community who were gravely offended, then law is probably the counsel of the wise. The intent of the proverb in that case would be to teach that acts of piety cannot compensate for refusal to face sound advice, since, in a sense that the wise clearly understood, sound advice was based on God's way of doing things. If we refuse to hear God's voice when it comes to us in the wisdom of friends or parents, how can we expect Him to hear our pleas and bail us out of the troubles in which our own foolishness has ensnared us? So do the teachers press upon their pupils the importance of the open ear.

HANDLING WEALTH

All the way through Proverbs there runs the assumption that the audience will and must deal with wealth. There are probably two reasons for this: (1) most of the students must have come from landed or moneyed families in order to have the background for their administrative responsibilities; (2) the wisdom that they were garnering was key to retaining or accumulating a measure of affluence. Full hands were a reasonably predictable result of open ears. Listening to solid advice even when it hurt was crucial if one were to get and keep the resources that the blessing of God made available.

What do prudent people do about budgets, investments, and the use of material means? That question is still the central one for all boards of trustees of churches, schools, and other corporations. There is no way we can always be right: the markets, economies, and local circumstances can do curious and hurtful things. In twenty-five years of managing finances and properties I have acquired a huge inventory of scars from doing what I thought was right and having it turn out wrong. Seeking the best possible counsel does not make us foolproof. But the surest way to prove we are fools is not to seek expert counsel, not to solicit and heed the advice of prudent persons, especially those that both know their business and care about God's mission. The following outline highlights some themes that recur among the sayings that deal with wealth:

How wealth is made
   By human labor without dishonesty   10:16; 13:11
   By divine blessing without sorrow   10:22
   By personal righteousness without trouble   15:6
How wealth is used
   For family inheritance   13:22
   For personal security   10:15; 18:11
How wealth works
   Positively
      For encouragement of friendship   14:20; 19:4, 7
      For exercise of power   18:23; 22:7
   Negatively
      No substitute for righteousness   10:2; 11:4, 28
      No excuse for pretense   13:7
      No protection against abuse   13:8

The three clues as to how wealth is made combine major themes of Proverbs: hard work, divine grace, and righteous behavior.

> The labor of the righteous *leads* to life,
> The wages of the wicked to sin.
> *Prov. 10:16*

How literally to read 10:16 is not easy to decide. Its basic contrast is between the reward for a righteous person's *"labor"*—the word can mean not only the work itself but the fruits of the work whether reward (Isa. 40:10) or punishment (Isa. 65:17)—and the *"wages"* of a wicked person's life. At a flatly literal plane the meaning would be that the diligent toil of the upright brings sufficient income to sustain *"life"* at a level of abundant satisfaction, while wickedness is so unproductive that it leads to the emptiness and even death that are sin's payoff. In any case *"sin"* must mean punishment for sin (see Zech. 14:19). If 10:16 does not deal with material rewards, then it probably should be grouped with the general sayings that describe the benefits of righteousness and the hazards of wickedness (see chaps. 10 and 28).

How wealth is gained was important to the teachers.

> Wealth *gained by* dishonesty will be diminished,
> But he who gathers by labor will increase.
> *Prov. 13:11*

Cause and effect were tightly linked in their minds. Good ends do not justify bad means. Get-rich-quick schemes were outlawed in their textbooks. *"Dishonesty"* (lit., *"vain"* or *"empty methods"*; the Heb. is Ecclesiastes' favorite term *"vanity")* may promise lavish and rapid returns but they shrink (*"be diminished"*) before our eyes as the assets of gullible people disappear in the brown paper bag of the bunco artists. The result proves as unreliable as the method. Even winners may become losers on the timeless principle of "easy come, easy go." *"Labor"* (lit., *"by hand")* is slower and harder but is infinitely more dependable. The lotteries in most of our states may well create a mood of easy expectation that undercuts the importance of personal effort, especially among those whose environment has not encouraged them to be hard workers. Such silent lessons in the curriculum of indolence may outweigh whatever good the public schools receive from their modest percentage of the lottery "take."

As strongly as the teachers urged hard work as a key to prosperity, they knew that the ultimate source of material success was the enriching grace (blessing) of the Lord.

> The blessing of the LORD makes *one* rich,
> And He adds no sorrow with it.
> *Prov. 10:22*

Who else sent the rain for the crops, protected the ships that carried the goods, gave the wisdom and energy that made productivity possible? Blessings accrued from other sources were always mixed. Gifts carried obligations; shady transactions prompted guilt; gain at the expense of others triggered vengeance. But *"no sorrow,"* pain, or hardship (see Gen. 3:16 for the Heb. word) were packaged in the divine generosity. God's grace is the only unmixed blessing in our human experience.

Treasure (see 27:24) or trouble (see Gen. 34:30) is the choice offered here:

> *In* the house of the righteous *there is* much treasure,
> But in the revenue of the wicked is trouble.
> *Prov. 15:6*

The *"righteous"* person (see chap. 10), thanks to God's blessings of both effort and motive, has goods to store up for rainy days, future needs, and family care. The income of *"the wicked"*, in contrast, is either too uncertain or too tainted to provide confidence and comfort. Instead it leads to disarray and confusion. Whatever it may promise, it ultimately will not or cannot be enjoyed.

How wealth is used is given a double answer. Family inheritance is one that is featured:

> A good *man* leaves an inheritance to his children's
> children,
> But the wealth of the sinner is stored up for the
> righteous.
>
> *Prov. 13:22*

The *"good"* person, the word means both generous and righteous, is prosperous and prudent. He does well financially and stewards his goods carefully. At least two generations—*"his children's children"*—are the beneficiaries. The *"sinner"* is neither upright nor prudent. He wanders from the path of the wise and squanders what he has earned or has to give back what he has stolen. Either way, his *"wealth"* ends in the treasuries of the *"righteous"* (here synonymous with *"good"*), with the clear implication that his offspring go empty handed.

Personal security is another by-product of wealth fairly gained and soundly used.

> The rich man's wealth *is* his strong city;
> The destruction of the poor *is* their poverty.
>
> *Prov. 10:15*

> The rich man's wealth *is* his strong city,
> And like a high wall in his own esteem.
>
> *Prov. 18:11*

Twice the picture of a *"strong* [well-fortified] *city"* is used to emphasize the protection from calamity which financial resources (*"wealth"*) may provide. The enduring quality of the impregnable walls is contrasted in 10:15 with the inevitable financial *"destruction"* that comes to those whose lot is *"poverty."* They are left defenseless when calamity strikes. Three lessons for us may lurk in these two sayings. First, hard work and careful stewardship do give us a measure of protection that others may not have. Second, to live in community means to be concerned for the poor as well as the affluent and to do what we can to help buffer them against the onslaughts of disaster. Third, we need to be grateful for the measure of affluence we have while not deceiving ourselves into thinking it makes us impregnable. God is our true refuge and strength (Ps. 46:1). Our defensive preparations do not ultimately determine the outcome of battle; His will does (Prov. 21:31). The phrase *"in his own esteem"* (18:11) may be designed to tweak the conscience of the overconfident. Note the NEB reading of the last line, "A towering wall, so he supposes."

How wealth works is described both positively and negatively.

> The poor *man* is hated even by his own neighbor,
> But the rich *has* many friends.
>
> *Prov. 14:20*

> Wealth makes many friends,
> But the poor is separated from his friend.
>
> *Prov. 19:4*

> All the brothers of the poor hate him;
> How much more do his friends go far from him!
> He may pursue *them with* words, *yet* they abandon
> him.
>
> *Prov. 19:7*

For one thing, wealth encourages friendships, not so much because of the rich person's largess but because the rich make no material demands on their friends. The opposite is true of *"the poor"* as all three sayings agree. Twice *"hate"* (14:20; 19:7) is the strong word used for the intensity with which persons, even *"brothers"* (19:7) shun the needy. The aversion is keen. Along with hate, *"is separated"* (or divided, 19:4) and *"go far"* (or put distance between, 19:7) show how unwelcome are the poor as friends or companions. Why? We cannot be sure. Do they make demands? Are their appearance and manners distasteful? Does their presence induce guilt in those who are better off? Some combination of these and other responses is probably the answer. The third line of 19:7 is a rare exception to the two-line pattern of sayings in 10:1–22:16. It may be an attempt to amplify the problem of strained relationships between the poor and their brothers and friends, as the NKJV interpretation suggests. Virtually any reading of that line is based on a reconstruction of a cryptic clause which may describe the poor person dogging (*"pursue"*) his *"friends"* and *"brothers,"* begging them for help in pleading *"words"* and getting no response in return.

These verses should be read as descriptions of how we human beings do behave, not as prescriptions of how we should behave. James's words about taking initiative to help widows and orphans (1:27), welcoming poor people in church (2:1–17), and paying them

fair wages at work (5:4) are to set the pace for our walk with God in
this matter more than these proverbs, important though they be as
windows on human conduct and incentives to emerge from poverty
if we possibly can.

Wealth almost automatically conveys certain powers, especially
the power to set the terms of any bargain.

> The poor *man* uses entreaties,
> But the rich answers roughly.
> *Prov. 18:23*

> The rich rules over the poor,
> And the borrower *is* servant to the lender.
> *Prov. 22:7*

Whether in personal conversations or in economic dealings the one
who possesses material goods seems to dominate the exchange. A
friend of mine was once invited into the office of a business execu-
tive who was both influential and eccentric. Stretching from the en-
trance to the desk was a long strip of red carpet. The walk seemed
almost endless and my friend experienced the vivid sensation of
shrinking several inches with every stride, as the desk and its awesome occupant grew to massive proportions the nearer my friend
approached. Wealth and eminence have that effect on both sides of
a desk. In conversation, the *"poor"* person has to resort to begging
(*"entreaties"*) based on the hope of mercy or compassion; the same
Hebrew word translates as "supplication" in the Psalms (see Pss. 6:9;
55:1; 119:170). The *"rich"* person need respond only with a blunt,
curt (*"roughly"*) answer that makes further plea futile. How much the
teachers commend this type of behavior we are not given to know.
But freedom from having to beg is certainly an incentive to self-
reliance and careful spending.

The point is strengthened in 22:7, where the comparison is made
between the status of rich and poor: one *"rules"*; the other *"is servant."* Even when the entreaty of 18:23 is heeded, *"the borrower"* is
placed under heavy obligation *"to the lender."* Most of what he earns
he has to pay out to reduce the loan. Where he cannot repay he
may be forced to become a long-term slave to his creditor. Though
the Mosaic law forbade the charging of interest (Exod. 22:25), the
prophets like Amos (2:6–8) inform us that standard practice during
parts, at least, of Israel's history was to violate the rights of the poor
even to the point of selling them into slavery when they left unpaid

trivial amounts of fines or debts. The teachers knew a kinder way and one in keeping with Yahweh's own generosity:

> He who has pity on the poor lends to the LORD,
> And He will pay back what he has given .
> *Prov. 19:17*

Wealth may bring power, but happy is the person who uses it with tenderness and restraint. Wealth was to be valued but not overvalued. It was both blessing and temptation, and the wise issued their warnings as well as their promises.

> Treasures of wickedness profit nothing,
> But righteousness delivers from death.
> *Prov. 10:2*

> He who trusts in his riches will fall,
> But the righteous will flourish like foliage.
> *Prov. 11:28*

True prosperity is first loyalty to God—a shorthand definition of *"righteous"*—and then material reward if God so pleases. *"Riches"* without righteousness are hollow reeds on which we lean (*"trusts"*) only to *"fall"*; *"righteousness,"* whatever our economic status, produces a tree that will *"flourish"* and offer refreshment and shade through its abundant *"foliage"* (see Ps. 1:3).

> Riches do not profit in the day of wrath,
> But righteousness delivers from death.
> *Prov. 11:4*

"Righteousness" will also serve as a rescuer (*"delivers,"* "snatches") from premature *"death,"* since God's blessings of life and safety rest on those who trust Him. *"Riches"* (treasures) without righteousness yield no true *"profit,"* since they cannot buy the divine care which is the only guarantee of prosperity. Even more basic is the warning that riches cannot bribe or buy their possessors out of the grips of God's *"wrath"* when judgment is their due. Righteousness is their only rescue or ransom. We say, mindlessly mouthing the conventional wisdom, "the good die young." The Hebrew sages read life the other way around: the righteous may be snatched (delivered) from the jaws of death, but the wicked, no matter how rich, may face God's wrath and have their lives shortened. *"Day of*

wrath" may describe any kind of calamity—plague, accident, illness, attack—that suddenly and inescapably strikes a person who has violated God's plans and commands. Jesus' parable of the rich man and Lazarus (Luke 16:19–31) enacts the sentiment of these sayings.

A second warning is against pretense—a form of dishonesty of which both rich and poor may be guilty.

> There is one who makes himself rich, yet *has*
>   nothing;
> *And* one who makes himself poor, yet *has* great
>   riches.
>   *Prov. 13:7*

Posing (*"one who makes himself rich"*) as a possessor of wealth may deceive the community and demean those who have labored diligently for what they have. Worse still, it pretends to enjoy God's blessing of which wealth was viewed as evidence. Feigning poverty to mask the possession of *"great riches"* is equally contemptible. It provides an excuse for miserliness not generosity; it mocks those who are truly poor; it signals ingratitude to the Lord who has made wealth possible. How much better than pretense— which betrays a gross unease with our lot in life—is Paul's strong pledge of contentment *"in whatever state"* he finds himself whether full or hungry, abounding or suffering want. The wise teachers of Israel did not yet know *"Christ who strengthens me"* (Phil. 4:11– 13). They did, however, know that denying what God had given, or pretending to enjoy what He had not, smacked of lack of both faith and integrity.

Wealth carried a practical as well as a spiritual risk, it offered no protection against abuse.

> The ransom of a man's life *is* his riches,
> But the poor does not hear rebuke.
>   *Prov. 13:8*

Wealth made a person vulnerable either to blackmail or kidnapping through which an enemy might extort *"ransom."* The *"poor"* person, happily, is free from such a threat. He does not pay any attention (*"hear"*) to them. *"Rebuke"* (see 13:1; 17:10) here must mean either a personal threat or a legal accusation that has financial consequences like a lawsuit or claim of damages. Whatever the situation—whether "your money or your life" or "I'll sue you for all you're worth"—the rich not the poor are the prime targets. Even a blessing as highly touted as material wealth has its downside. It is not the poor who need walled compounds, burly bodyguards, and clever lawyers. The sages knew this and made sure that their young people, either raised with wealth or on their way to it, knew it as well. If God had gifted them with full hands, they surely needed the grace of open ears to keep life in balance.

CHAPTER TWENTY

Firm Hands and Fair Scales

Proverbs 20:1–30

Stability in the community—this was a basic concern of Israel's teachers. Without it, life would return to chaos, villages become jungles, and the covenant of neighbor love be shredded into tiny pieces. How children are raised and how business is transacted are two key factors in the solidarity or fragmentation of a community. *Fiddler on the Roof* reminded us of that. Tevye sparked a roisterous argument among the citizens of Anatevka when he baited two of them about the age of a horse they had traded. Was it six years old or twelve? Who had cheated whom? And Tevye felt the pain of daughters whose choices seemed to be beyond his control. Could he bend far enough to accommodate their challenges to tradition or would he break?

Simply put, the sages who taught the proverbs urged parents to use firm hands and merchants to use fair scales. The welfare of the community and the good pleasure of God were on the line. Guidelines to sound living in both these areas appear in ample number for us to catch their importance.

DISCIPLINE OF CHILDREN

Almost nothing gets us on edge quicker than children who obviously despise the authority of their families and the society around them. Our anxiety, frustration, rage—however we brand this inner tension—are well taken. We know that all social units are only a generation away from disruptive change. In my own lifetime every decade has brought a significant difference in how our children behave. In the 1930s the great depression shaped our attitudes—fear of not having enough, drive to succeed in education, profession, or business to make sure that we could put those weary years of want behind us. In the 1940s war clouds darkened the horizon and our children, many of them raised with fathers in distant and dangerous places, often reacted to the uncertainty and neglect in ways we call delinquent. In the 1950s peace and prosperity encouraged complacency and some laziness at the same time that the "cold war" was threatening to vaporize us in a mushroom cloud of atomic fission. In the 1960s our children called for free speech, smoked pot and dropped acid, marched for civil rights, and stormed police barricades to scream for peace in Vietnam. In the 1970s, a return to rugged individualism prompted our young to think about jobs, careers, material possessions, and their own personal survival rather than the welfare of the oppressed or the ultimate survival of the world. In the 1980s outbreaks of violence in our cities have brought us again to the brink of anarchy. On our Southern California news broadcasts, we hear of a daily toll of gang shootings, often drug related. Last night the total was five. We are reaping bitter fruit grown from several seeds—poverty, prejudice, selfishness, alienation, and especially lack of discipline. Given the rapidity of change in our society, the words of the wise need to be taken to heart as keenly in our days as ever in history.

Five topics may be identified in their sayings on the need for firm parental hands (see chap. 29, for an additional list):

Safeguards in discipline	
innocence is impossible	20:9; 16:2
vengeance is unthinkable	20:22
inconsistency is ineffective	20:7
Necessity of discipline	
the heart is perverse	22:15
the habits are persistent	22:6
Timeliness of discipline	
memory is short	13:24
hope is fleeting	19:18
Evidence of discipline	20:11
Fruit of discipline	20:29

Discipline and cruelty are not the same thing. In fact they are opposites. To change bad behavior and not reinforce it, parents have to understand a trio of safeguards.

> Who can say, "I have made my heart clean,
> I am pure from my sin"?
>
> *Prov. 20:9*

One is not to parade one's own innocence. We have to call our children to account but as we do it is good for us to remember that the answer to the rhetorical question in this saying (20:9) is an emphatic "No one." The emphasis here may be on original sin, our human incapacity since Adam's fall to do anything that would qualify us for fellowship with and approval by God. What Paul stressed in his epistles (Rom. 3:23) is not a major emphasis in Old Testament wisdom literature. More likely the focus in Proverbs is on our human inability to read our own motives. Only the Lord can do that:

> All the ways of a man *are* pure in his own eyes,
> But the LORD weighs the spirits.
>> *Prov. 16:2*

"Sin" (20:9), then, would be a misreading of the reasons for the decisions made by the *"heart."* *"Clean"* (see Pss. 51:7; 73:13) and *"pure"* (see especially its use in Leviticus 12–17) have to do with meeting God's standard. No one, not even the wisest, kindest parents can do that either in action or motive. Biblically guided mothers and fathers know that and let their kids in on the truth of human imperfection. Parents also do well to check their own motives, even though the check is not 100 percent accurate, before they lash out in punishment.

Another safeguard is to throttle all temptation to see discipline as taking revenge (*"recompense evil"*).

> Do not say, "I will recompense evil";
> Wait for the LORD, and He will save you.
>> *Prov. 20:22*

Discipline, often called *"instruction"* or *"correction"* in Proverbs (see on 1:2–3), is for the sake of the child not the parent. It is designed not for the relief of the enforcer but for the maturity of the recipient. Vengeance is an activity too hot for any of us to handle. Its motivation is selfish; its execution is usually extreme; its result is to accelerate conflict not to slow it down. In short, vengeance is God's business not ours (Deut. 32:35; Rom. 12:19; Heb. 10:30). All human sin is sin against Him, so He is the ultimate victim; only He can judge accurately the damage done; only He can distribute fairly the blame; only He can exact freely the proper penalty. We are not entitled to *"play God"* at any time, least of all when our children are involved. We stand so close to them, we are so emotionally entangled with them, we feel so guilty at their failings, we are so tempted to overblame them for our guilt that we dare not exercise discipline without giving ourselves a chance to cool down and get our facts and feelings straight. *"Wait"* with confidence and hope (Heb. *qāwāh* is a verb of patient yet high expectation, frequent in Psalms like 25, 27, 40, but found only here in Proverbs) is much better advice than counting to ten, although that will certainly help in a pinch. *"For the Lord"* tells us why biblical waiting is so worthwhile. The very act of waiting places matters in better hands. The Lord has the power and perspective to set matters right. *"Save"* means both getting us out of any predicament in which others have placed us and also clearing our reputations which we have such a brash desire to defend.

The third safeguard that parents need to observe in rearing their young to fear God, respect the rights of others, and contribute to the well-being of their communities is to avoid inconsistency. Discipline is gained by quiet demonstration as much as by vocal instruction.

> The righteous *man* walks in his integrity;
> His children *are* blessed after him.
>   *Prov. 20:7*

Cause and result seem to be the intent of the two lines in the synthetic parallelism. *"Walks"* translates a participial form of a Hebrew stem that suggests a pattern of life, a constant way of comporting oneself. The first line virtually echoes God's command to Abram: "Walk before Me and be blameless" (Gen. 17:1). The verb stems are identical, and the "blameless" is the same Hebrew root (*tmm*) as *"integrity"* in the proverb. This consistent loyalty to God and His people (Heb. *ṣaddîq*, *"righteous man"*) bears results that are like a beatitude. The beneficiaries of the happiness (*"blessed"*; 3:13; 8:32, 34) are the *"children."* Day by day, year after year they have seen consistent integrity at work in their family. It is coded into their bones from their father's walk with God. And in addition, the material fruits of God's blessing survive as part of their inheritance.

The necessity of discipline is taken for granted by the wise. The world we live in and the kinds of persons we are demand it. No parent who understands life from a biblical perspective need ever be surprised at the frequency and intensity with which discipline is required. No person who has an inkling of self-understanding doubts the central role that instruction with correction plays in human nurture. "No pain no gain" is not the first rule of physical fitness only; it applies equally to moral and spiritual development.

The human heart (see on 2:2) is perverse.

> Foolishness *is* bound up in the heart of a child,
> The rod of correction will drive it far from him.
>   *Prov.* 22:15

We are born not knowing how to make sound choices. Our instincts run toward self-centeredness not toward cooperation with others. Our bent is to assert our own rights whatever that assertiveness may do to those around us. Such selfishness is branded *"foolishness"* (Heb. *ʾiwwelet*; see on 5:23; 12:23; 14:1, 8, 24) by the teachers. It is not the stuff of which strong families and close communities are built. Yet it is so integral to human life that it is described as *"bound up in the heart"* as tightly as Rahab's scarlet cord was tied to her window in Jericho (Heb. *qāshar*, Josh. 2:18, 21). Strong leverage like the *"rod of correction"* (*mûsār*, the standard noun for discipline and instruction; see on 1:2–3) is needed to pry it loose, toss *"it far from"* the child, and give *"the heart"* room to wrap itself in wisdom. 'Rod' is certainly to be understood literally, but not only literally. It can stand for any discipline that inflicts sufficient pain to discourage bad behavior and encourage good. Discipline, not mere physical beating, is the cure for folly. Without it, the cords that bind foolishness to our hearts become only tougher as the years go by.

One way that the heart's perversity can be restrained with wisdom is by encouraging good habits that are persistent.

> Train up a child in the way he should go,
> And when he is old he will not depart from it.
>   *Prov.* 22:6

To *"train"* (Heb. *ḥānak* means to "initiate" or "dedicate" as Solomon did the Temple, 1 Kings 8:63; Jews today preserve the word in their Feast of Hanukkah celebrating the rededication of the Temple after Antiochus Epiphanes defiled it in 167 B.C.) *"a child"* is not to convert her or him but to initiate and continue a pattern of correction that will curb the heart's perversity and free the youngster to grow up and even to grow *"old"* without turning aside (*"depart"*) from the *"way"* (Heb. *derek*; see on 1:19, 31; 2:12–13), the pattern of obedience and righteousness required for effective participation in human society. This proverb states an accurate principle; it does not offer an absolute promise. Good training almost always brings beneficial results; bad habits almost inevitably spell trouble for those who have acquired them and for those around them. In pastoral ministry we may use this verse to encourage Christian parents whose young people are going through stages of carelessness or rebellion. We ought not to use it to guarantee an automatic return to obedience and faith. Much of the time that will happen through faithful prayer and steady love. Tragically, there are exceptions; they call for special sensitivity toward the despair and disillusionment of disappointed parents.

Wise persons stress the timeliness of discipline.

> He who spares his rod hates his son,
> But he who loves him disciplines him promptly.
> *Prov. 13:24*

Even more they see in promptness (*"promptly"*) an act of love. Memories are short: parents who delay can forget to punish and leave their children with feelings of guilt or with a false sense of righteousness—after all their behavior must not have been too bad since their parents did nothing about it; or the young ones can forget why they are being punished and judge their belated punishment as harsh and arbitrary. The time for correction is when the wrong deed is discovered. Then the situation is clear, the feelings intense, and the opportunity for learning is most available. Withholding needed punishment (*"spares his rod"*) is a sign of hate not love: bad behavior is rewarded by neglect, the opportunity of teaching an important lesson is lost, and the dignity of both child and parent is tarnished.

Timeliness is valued also because hope is fleeting.

> Chasten your son while there is hope,
> And do not set your heart on his destruction.
> *Prov. 19:18*

There may come a time when it is too late to correct (*"chasten"*—the same Hebrew root used in "discipline" or "instruction," *yāsar*). The foolish patterns have been grooved beyond change, or, worse still, the inevitable destruction—the Hebrew is even stronger, "the causing of his death"—may have taken place. No wonder regular correction is viewed as an act of love. To withhold it is to rob a child of all hope of change and blessing. Lax parenting is a virtual death sentence given the fact that we have only a handful of years during which we have *"hope"* of helping our children govern their habits, shape their values, and learn the joy of doing God's will. Once they have left our homes we surround them with prayer and ask God to send positive influences into their lives. But our opportunity to do what is needed ourselves flees all too quickly. We dare not waste an hour of it.

Evidence of discipline is available to all who know what to look for.

> Even a child is known by his deeds,
> Whether what he does *is* pure and right.
> *Prov. 20:11*

Good *"deeds"* (the Hebrew word describes a wide range of activities whether in the religious, moral, social, economic, or political spheres) are self-evident and allow *"even a child,"* a youth or adolescent, to be recognized (*"is known"*) as a worthy member of society and a credit to the family. Though good deeds were seen as an expression of good inward decisions made by a pure heart, the pure heart alone was not enough. Goodness was inward, of course, but never only inward. To be true biblical goodness (*"pure,"* clean, and clear, see 21:8; *"right,"* upright, full of integrity, see 2:21) it had to demonstrate itself through daily actions in every relationship and arena of life (Matt. 7:20).

The fruit of discipline is long life and the respect and reputation that come with it.

> The glory of young men *is* their strength,
> And the splendor of old men *is* their gray head.
> *Prov. 20:29*

Disobedience leads to destruction; obedience, to longevity. So goes the thinking of Israel's teachers. The *"strength"* and vitality that mark the *"young,"* the choice samples of society, are their ornaments (see 4:9) of *"glory,"* their badges of pride and beauty. Like Olympians they draw our admiration and applause. They run fast, jump high, play well, work hard. Yet at least as much honor or *"splendor"* is to be accorded to the *"old"* whose *"gray"* hair, the crown of experience, suffering, wisdom, and blessing, heralded God's reward of their righteousness and uprightness. Whatever their physical strength may have been, their spiritual and moral strength led them to persevere and to testify to the goodness of God's will and the rightness of God's ways. If we applaud the strong youths, we should bow before the noble aged. Growing old is not for sissies, and every gray hair is a sermon in which to read of God's providence toward those who depend on Him. The good may sometimes die young. But more often than not their abstinence from foul habits, their freedom from guilt and frustration, their quiet joy in God's goodness are a fountain of youth beyond Ponce de León's fondest dreams. And behind most of their stories we can spot the firm hands of parents or grandparents who cared enough and dared enough to discipline them.

HONESTY IN BUSINESS

Honest business practices are as vital to the well-being of a society as are sound patterns of raising children. Our communities whether rural, urban, or suburban are networks of commerce. We all buy from one another; we all sell to each other. Scour our continent and it would be hard to find any family that is self-contained, that grows and makes all it needs and has no surplus to trade with others. Exchange of skills, services, goods, and time is what makes our society tick and enables each of us to contribute something to others and in turn gain something from them. For this essential system to work well, justice and equity must be at its heart. The law of neighbor love (Lev. 19:18; Matt. 22:39) must govern not only our deeds of charity and our leisure activities but also our economic systems. A cluster of proverbs remind us of this. They focus on four types of unworthy business activities:

Crooked weights	11:1; 16:11; 20:10, 23
Secret bribes	15:27; 17:8, 23
Slick bargaining	20:14
Subtle lies	20:17; 21:6
Summary	20:21

Four sayings deal with weights and balances, the standard instruments for measuring gold or silver payments. Amos describes a threefold approach to cheating, "Making the ephah [the standard measuring basket] small and the shekel large, / Falsifying the scales by deceit" (Amos 8:5). Overcharging and undersupplying was the nature of the compounded crime. The weight and the measure were featured in Proverbs:

Diverse weights *and* diverse measures,
They *are* both alike, an abomination to the LORD.
Prov. 20:10

The weight could be skewed in two ways: an overweight shekel on one side of the balance called for a surplus of gold to be placed by the customer on the other; if the balance itself was bent slightly out of kilter, the customer could be bilked even more.

What we must not miss is that *"the Lord"* is pictured as having a keen interest in the pricing transaction in all four sayings.

> Dishonest scales *are* an abomination to the LORD,
> But a just weight *is* His delight.
> > *Prov. 11:1*

This verse is antithetical in parallelism and contrasts *"dishonest"* (deceitful, totally misleading; see the Hebrew word in 12:9, 17) and *"just"* ("complete," "intact"; the same root as *shālôm*, peace). A second contrast is in the Lord's reaction: *"abomination"* (see 3:32) or *"delight"* (see 8:35). The words are strong ones and bring a distinct religious tone to the marketplace. "Delight" speaks of God's acceptance of sacrifices and the one who offers them (Exod. 28:38; Lev. 1:3); *"abomination"* describes what horrifies God so that He turns His back and will not receive the person (Lev. 18:22, 26, 29–30). Three times *"abomination"* underscores what a horrible act God deems cheating to be (11:1; 20:10, 23).

> Honest weights and scales *are* the LORD'S;
> All the weights in the bag *are* His work.
> > *Prov. 16:11*

Here the form is synonymous parallelism, both lines are positives. *"Weights"* [lit., "scale pointers"; see Isa. 40:12] *and scales"* are matched by *"weights in the bag,"* while *"are the Lord's"* is paired with *"are His work."* The picture of God's involvement is heightened. Not only is He a spectator who is outraged or pleased by the accuracy of the transaction, but He is ultimately the owner and manufacturer of the equipment and the master of the market. That being the case, *"honest,"* *"fair,"* accurate equipment are His stock in trade. Woe to His people who use anything else!

> Diverse weights *and* diverse measures,
> They *are* both alike, an abomination to the LORD.
> > *Prov. 20:10*

The Hebrew for *"diverse"* is graphic: it is expressed by repetition, literally *stone stone, ephah ephah.* That is first one sized stone then another, a regular ephah (about 2/3 of a bushel; the standard measure of grain) and then a smaller one. Anything short of constant dependability is a source of horror (*"abomination"*) to the Lord.

The final saying drums the point home:

> Diverse weights *are* an abomination to the LORD,
> And dishonest scales are not good.
>
> *Prov. 20:23*

"Diverse weights" is like 20:10 and *"dishonest scales"* like 11:1. The new element is *"not good,"* where Hebrew *tôb* must mean "pleasing," "welcome," "acceptable" as did "delight" in 11:1. *"To the Lord"* probably carries over to the second line as well. "Not good" is not a general but a specific verdict expressing God's dislike in parallel to the strong *"abomination."* "Not good" then is total rejection by the divine Inspector.

In California we have a State Board of Equalization responsible for just weights and measures. Merchants whose equipment is sloppy or whose motives are greedy are subject to fine or imprisonment. Christians in business are accountable to an even higher authority. Our devotion to God must include his ownership of our business, and our conformity to the Owner's standards.

Bribery is described in three proverbs, each pointing to a different aspect of its role. Seen from the view of the recipient it promises prosperity.

> A present *is* a precious stone in the eyes of its
>   possessor;
> Wherever he turns, he prospers.
>
> *Prov. 17:8*

He panders influence *"wherever he turns"*—the very clause suggests instability and manipulation—and imagines that *"he prospers,"* that his shrewdness (see 1:3; 10:5 for the same Hebrew word translated "wisdom" or "wise") has truly paid off. The bribe (*"present"* here is too bland; 17:23 translates the same word "bribe") is so attractive that it is viewed (*"in the eyes"*) of the *"possessor"* (lit., "its owner" or "master") as a *"precious* [lit., "graceful"] *stone."* Such fantasied prosperity is not the accurate perspective on bribery at all.

That comes only when bribery is viewed for what it truly is: inordinate greed that has trouble as its chief result.

> He who is greedy for gain troubles his own house,
> But he who hates bribes will live.
>
> *Prov. 15:27*

Rather than a source of prosperity "the master of the bribe" becomes the one "*who troubles his own house,*" the one who brings sorrow to his whole family. To be "*greedy for gain*" (the Hebrew reinforces the idea by repeating the root *bāṣaʿ*) is to be susceptible to all manner of corruption like the stock manipulators who sought to beat the market by using insider information. The boomerang nature of justice brought their greed back on their hearts. Prov. 1:19 could be the epitaph of those who live by greed in any age:

> So *are* the ways of everyone who is greedy for gain;
> It takes away the life of its owners.

The only sure defense against destructive greed is to hate it in all its forms, especially in the form of "*bribes.*" "*Will live*" promises survival rather than shame, punishment, or destruction. In a world where divine justice will settle all accounts, righteousness is the only reliable key to life.

Bribery's motive may be greed; its personal result may be trouble; its social impact is even worse—injustice.

> A wicked *man* accepts a bribe behind the back
> To pervert the ways of justice.
>
> *Prov. 17:23*

It rots the soul of its practitioner and undermines the foundations of society. Bribery necessarily favors the haves against the have-nots because only the affluent can afford it. If "*the ways of justice*" are put to auction, the poor will always be outbid. The greedy is branded as "*wicked*" (see 2:22; 10:30), as fierce a word as Hebrew possesses to indicate the turbulence and violence of behavior run amok. No petty crime is this when one person cozies up to another and slips a bag of gold into a fold at the front of the garment just above the belt (see Exod. 4:6–7 where the Hebrew is read "bosom"). No private transaction is this: the flywheel of society—the pursuit of "*justice*"—is thrown off center and all of life will feel the wobble.

Slick bargaining also comes in for fire.

> "*It is* good for nothing," cries the buyer;
> But when he has gone his way, then he boasts.
>
> *Prov. 20:14*

The proverb is actually a vignette. It pictures a scene in the bazaar in which a *"buyer"* chisels down the price of an article—say a pot or a blanket—by bad-mouthing it: "Bad, bad" is what he *"cries."* You can see the scowl on his face and the gesticulating of his hands as he inspects and criticizes the proposed purchase. In despair the seller lowers the price to an indecent level, and the buyer reluctantly shells it out still protesting the highway robbery. Once out of sight, his tone changes. He floods himself with self-centered *"boasts."* See 25:14; 27:1 for other instances of the same word, which means "to flaunt one's own accomplishments." Bargaining has been part of Middle Eastern culture for ages. Both buyers and sellers grow skilled at it. Our niece Isomi is Japanese and was raised in a climate of fixed prices. Sometime ago she participated in a rummage sale at our seminary. She was overwhelmed by the negotiating prowess of the African students and disappointed in the amount of her take for the day. Such business takes practice. Our proverb, however, seems to picture a transaction shocking even by the norms of its culture. The buyer has played the game unfairly, insulted the seller, taken advantage of the financial exigency that forced him to sell cheaply, demeaned a product that in fact the buyer cherished, and then gloated over his greed and the pain it caused the seller. No sense of fairness present here, no law of neighbor love at work! It was a business practice in which the tongue was as false as the balances decried in the other proverbs, and the spirit was as undersized as the shrunken ephah measure (20:10).

Subtle lies are often a tool in crooked business practices.

> Bread gained by deceit *is* sweet to a man,
> But afterward his mouth will be filled with gravel.
> *Prov. 20:17*

The results are usually short-lived, though they may be *"sweet"* at first like stolen *"bread."* But conscience-driven guilt, anxiety over fear of being caught, and uneasiness in the presence of the person cheated—these all conspire to replace sweetness in *"his mouth"* with *"gravel,"* about as unpalatable a menu as one can imagine.

Lying is a quest for death, says this proverb in even stronger language.

> Getting treasures by a lying tongue
> *Is* the fleeting fantasy of those who seek death.
> *Prov. 21:6*

Its result is not only an unchewable product that longs to be spat out, but a futile *"fantasy"*—the word is translated "vanity" in Ecclesiastes and means "bubble," "vapor," "fleeting breath"—that ends as a kind of death wish. In a society where citizens cheat on income taxes, employees pad their expense accounts, hospitals tend to overcharge their patients or their insurance companies, upright people pocket their change when the cashier has made an error in their favor, *"getting treasures by a lying tongue"* is fast becoming a national trait. What we need to recognize is that the shadow of *"death"* hangs thicker than smog over all who relish such behavior.

The summation of these warnings applies to all get-rich-quick schemes, whether perpetrated by sellers as in most of the sayings or by buyers (as in 20:14 above).

> An inheritance gained hastily at the beginning
> Will not be blessed at the end.
> *Prov. 20:21*

"Inheritance" applies primarily to money or property passed down the family line. *"Gained hastily"* suggests the recipient was youthful and not mature enough to appreciate the value of the wealth and to use it wisely. *"Blessed"* here means something like *"get full benefit from,"* the implication being either that the inheritance will be squandered or that the owner will take no great satisfaction from what he has not worked and waited for. The saying in 13:11 is cousin to this one (see chap. 19).

> Wealth *gained* by dishonesty will be diminished,
> But he who gathers by labor will increase.
> *Prov. 13:11*

As contemporary Christians we seem to pay more attention to the firm hands of this chapter than to the fair scales. The Old Testament has a lot to say about business practices that are just and equitable. I am not sure we give them their due in pulpit or classroom. Browse through your local Christian bookstore and count the volumes that offer help in raising children and building stable families. Then look for books that deal with business ethics, responsible consumerism, or integrity in the getting and spending of money. "Firm hands" outnumbers "fair scales" on a ratio of at least twenty-to-one. I once gave a radio series on "Right Living in a World Gone Wrong." I covered subjects that dealt with Christian sexuality, Christian responsibility to government, and Christian behavior in the marketplace. The talks were offered to our listeners in booklets that contained three or four messages on each of the major themes. Requests for the section on sexuality flooded our mailroom. Letters asking for the series on government flowed at a steady rate. Correspondence on the topic of Christian business practices trickled in—a card or two at a time. I am still baffled as to how people who treasure the Bible and respect its authority can be heedless of a subject about which the biblical authors cared so deeply. God help us to mend our ways and mind our ethics—starting with how we do business.

CHAPTER TWENTY-ONE

Rewards of Conduct and Problems of Pride

Proverbs 21:1–31

Choices—the wise teachers bring us back to that familiar theme: the choice between wise behavior and foolish, between righteous conduct and wicked, has consequences that boggle the mind. Spotlighting the importance of those choices is as central to their curriculum as outlining the specific issues involved in each choice. Motivation to choose correctly was as much their mission as was detailed instruction in each type of choice. Simple numerical count makes that plain. In chapter 10 we surveyed over fifty sayings that deal with the rewards or outcomes of conduct, and here we shall look at nearly forty more. And that will still leave nineteen proverbs to be treated in chapter 28.

Since the discussion in chapter 10 dealt with the nature of human choice—the freedom to decide, the faithfulness to God expressed in sound choices and the fellowship in community that influences responsible decisions—we shall focus here mainly on the results of our choices, especially the wrong ones. Duplications in vocabulary between the earlier chapter and this one make it convenient to use cross-references and avoid the redundancy of explaining repeated terms twice.

It seems appropriate to couple this survey of the rewards of conduct with a look at the teachers' words on the problems of pride. A dozen sayings drive home the truth that arrogance is self-deceptive, demeaning of neighbors, and abhorrent to God. It is the essence of folly because it disregards our creatureliness, our commonality with other human beings made by God, and our utter dependence on God's grace and goodness for all that we are and have. Nothing should push us more to seek, cherish, and practice wisdom than a clear recognition of our inability to discern God's ways without God's help.

RISKS OF FOLLY

If pride prompts us to miss that point and sail through life on our own steam, the results will be just the kinds of disasters against which the proverbs warn us with their proddings about the consequences of bad conduct. One measure of the lure of folly and our proneness to chase it is the incredible tenacity with which the teachers try to head us away from it. All of us as communicators know that some subjects demand constant repetition. For Israel's communicators this topic was number one: go wisdom's way and gain blessing; walk folly's path and face tragedy. The facets of that tragedy shape the outline of our discussion:

Loss of personal satisfaction	14:14, 33; 19:8
Loss of social reputation	11:23; 14:10, 18–19, 22, 24, 34; 18:3; 6:33; 21:8
Loss of mental discernment	14:13; 15:14, 21; 16:8, 16, 22, 25 (14:12); 17:16, 24
Loss of self-control	17:12; 21:22
Loss of political freedom	17:11; 19:29
Loss of divine favor	14:9; 15:9; 21:12
Loss of life	11:27; 13:21; 14:11, 32; 15:24; 16:17, 31; 21:15, 16, 18, 21

The doctrine of the two ways—the two ways to choose and the two utterly different ends to such choices—is the dominant motif through all the proverbs treated in this section. Loss of personal satisfaction is the keynote in three of them.

> The backslider in heart will be filled with his own
> ways,
> But a good man *will be satisfied* from above:
> > *Prov. 14:14*

The chief contrast in 14:14 is between the persons described: the *"backslider in heart"* we meet only here in Proverbs; his mind, thought, and choices (on *"heart"* see 2:2, 10; 3:1) move away from God not toward him (see use of Heb. *sûg* in Pss. 53:3; 80:18); the *"good man"* does things right, seeks God's ways with devotion to Him and kindness to others. Each feeds on the results of his conduct: one has to be satisfied (*"filled"*) with the junk food of his *"own* [rebellious] *ways"*; the other, with the delicious diet that comes from pursuing the "paths" of righteousness. "Paths" in my reading is a necessary emendation of the word translated *"from above"* in NKJV.

The Heb. *ma ʿgal* is frequent in Proverbs (2:9, 15, 18, etc.), closely resembles the word for "from above" and is appropriately parallel to the *"his own ways"* of the first line (see NIV). *"Will be filled"* carries over to the second line. Each will be filled with the results of his choices, but the difference is as wide as that between chalk and cheese.

> Wisdom rests in the heart of him who has
>   understanding,
> But *what is* in the heart of fools is made known.
> *Prov. 14:33*

"Fools" have no shot at the personal satisfaction that *"wisdom"* (see 1:2–6) brings, because it finds no place of rest or comfort within them (*"heart"* here is a Hebrew word that means "middle" of the body). The second line needs retranslating:

> Wisdom is not acquainted [made known] with the
>   inward parts of fools.

"Not" is found in Greek and Syriac manuscripts and was apparently dropped accidentally from the Hebrew. The second line then is a clear antithesis of the first which describes wisdom as completely at home (*"rests"*) in the *"heart"* (the familiar word *leb* as in 14:14) of the person whose life is marked by *"understanding"* and insight (the root is *byn*; see on 1:2–6).

> He who gets wisdom loves his own soul;
> He who keeps understanding will find good.
> *Prov. 19:8*

What fools lack in ultimate satisfaction, the one *"who gets* [acquires so as to own and possess] *wisdom* [here, lit., "heart" as the seat of insight]" and *"keeps* [or guards] *understanding* [on *tᵉbûnāh*, see 1:2–6]" will gain in lavish measure a sense of self-worth described as *"loves his own soul"* (or self) and a sense of genuine well-being called by the all-purpose word *"good,"* blessing from God and admiration from others. While 14:14, 33 are contrasting in form as is characteristic of the sayings in chapters 10–15, 19:18 is synonymous and aims to underscore the benefits of wisdom.

The loss of personal satisfaction was matched by a loss of social reputation. Neither wisdom nor folly was viewed as a private attribute. Both were as much outward actions as inward attitudes.

> The desire of the righteous *is* only good,
> *But* the expectation of the wicked *is* wrath.
>
> Prov. 11:23

The point of the contrast between *"the righteous"* and *"the wicked"* persons (see chap. 10) is in the outcome of their longings. *"Desire"* and *"expectation"* (or "hope") are synonyms, expressing what such persons would really like to happen to them as the result of their conduct. *"Only good,"* generous treatment at divine and human hands, is the lot of the loyal, while *"wrath"* sparked by darkened hopes, bitter frustration, and public embarrassment is the fate of the wicked. In the highly verbal society of ancient Israel neither the expectations nor the wrath would have been kept secret.

> A soft answer turns away wrath,
> But a harsh word stirs up anger.
>
> Prov. 15:1

And in a context where soft answers (15:1) were admired, public wrath would have been a source of shame.

Not that Israelites were not entitled to emotional privacy.

> The heart knows its own bitterness,
> And a stranger does not share its joy.
>
> Prov. 14:10

Feelings too deep for public sharing were part of their experience along with the rest of us. The feelings swept across the whole range, from *"bitterness"* (the same root as the waters of Marah in Exod. 15:23) to *"joy."* And, as the contrast suggests, both may have been present at once in any possible combination. Bittersweet comes in many different flavors, and the extremes of bitterness and joy are probably a *merism*, the literary device that names the opposite poles with the aim of covering everything between them.

> The simple inherit folly,
> But the prudent are crowned with knowledge.
>
> Prov. 14:18

Private emotions may be concealable especially where they lie so deep that we barely understand them ourselves (14:10), but *"folly"* (on this basic word, found exclusively in Psalms and Proverbs, see 5:23) and *"knowledge"* (which may mean "knowledge of God"; see on

1:7) are matters of public record. The *"simple"* (see on 1:4) may be merely naive, and thus vulnerable to folly or amenable to knowledge depending on the quality of their choices. Left unmotivated and untutored, they will automatically display their folly, since knowledge is so much harder to come by. *"Inherit"* should be translated "adorned" from a root *hlh* found in words like "necklace" or "pendant" in Prov. 25:12 and Song of Sol. 7:2. It stands in parallel to *"crowned"* and highlights the public way in which the naive, bereft of instruction, will placard folly, while the *"prudent"* (on Heb. ʿārûm see 12:16, 23), schooled in the knowledge of God's ways, will be as readily recognizable as though they wore royal turbans.

The note of public embarrassment that plagues the foolish is heightened in the picture of utter public subjection that will be their lot.

> The evil will bow before the good,
> And the wicked at the gates of the righteous.
> *Prov. 14:19*

The implication is that the folly of *"the evil"* (see on 1:16, 33) and *"the wicked"* (2:22; 3:25) will so backfire on them that they will lose their homes, lands, and goods and be reduced to servitude in which *"the righteous"* and *"good"* (or generous) members of society will be their masters before whom they *"bow"* in supplication and submission.

As we treat others so are we treated, most of the time at least.

> Do they not go astray who devise evil?
> But mercy and truth *belong* to those who devise
>   good.
> *Prov. 14:22*

Those who fashion or craft (*"devise"*) *"evil"* gain the results of their malevolent workmanship. The question form of the lead line calls for the strong answer—Yes. Having tied their lives to what is malicious, mean, and damaging to their community they craft for themselves failure, even more, lostness as *"they . . . go astray,"* wandering from the path that leads to fruitful, productive living. Nor does their behavior warrant intervention or rescue at the hands of their neighbors. The artisans (again "devise," the verb of craftsmanship; see Gen. 4:22; 1 Kings 7:14, for literal uses; see Prov. 3:29; 6:14, 18 for figurative) of *"good,"* which means plans, intentions, actions which are both right and generous, and hence beneficial to the whole community, receive the finest responses possible from their friends and neighbors: (1) *mercy,* loving-kindness, covenant loyalty; (2) *truth,* faithfulness, reliability (for the pair *ḥesed* and *ᵓᵉmet,* see 3:3; 20:28).

> The crown of the wise is their riches,
> *But* the foolishness of fools *is* folly.
> *Prov. 14:24*

This saying replays the picture of 14:18: the results of conduct whether of *"wise"* persons or of *"fools"* are displayed as prominently in public as the *"crown"* (turban) of nobility or the wreath of special recognition. *"Riches"* are the manifestation of wisdom here as "knowledge" was in 14:18. "Fools" have replaced the "simple" or "naive" in the contrasting clause, as though to suggest that the apprenticeship in folly is completed and the subjects of public disdain are journeymen fools (Heb. *kᵉsîlîm;* see 1:22; 3:35). They are so marked by wearing their blatant stupidity (*"folly,"* see 5:23) on their heads like a "wreath," as *"foolishness"* should probably be translated (see 1:9; 4:9 for the Heb. word for "wreath" or "ornament" that closely resembles "foolishness"). Note "chief ornament" in NEB. The parallel of "wreath" to "crown" completes the balance of the two lines and replaces the awkward redundancy of NKJV'S *"foolishness of fools is folly"* with the clearer *"the wreath of fools is folly."*

The same principle holds on a national scale.

> Righteousness exalts a nation,
> But sin *is* a reproach to *any* people.
> *Prov. 14:34*

"Righteousness," loyalty to covenant relationships both to God and neighbor (8:18, 20), *"exalts"* or lifts to prominence and respect a *"nation"* or people (Heb. *gôy,* "nation" in general, not *ʿam,* the special word for Israel). *"Sin,"* the deviation from the course or target of God's will (5:22), is a source of shame or disgrace (*"reproach"* translates *ḥesed* whose negative force is attested in Lev. 20:17) to any social or tribal entity. *"People"* describes the populace of an area more than its political systems (11:26; 14:28; 24:24). The national application is indeed an appropriate reminder to the young persons into whose hands would fall the political, moral, and administrative leadership of Israel's tribes.

When the wicked comes, contempt comes also;
And with dishonor *comes* reproach.

Prov. 18:3

This saying is synonymous in structure, the second line reinforces the first. The emphasis is on the negative reception (*"comes"*) accorded what is patently and crudely "wickedness." (The parallelism with *"dishonor"* suggests that the Hebrew means "wickedness" not *"wicked"* person.) Its very presence ushers in an aura of *"contempt"* (on *bûz* see 12:8) that leads more sensible people to despise it. The second line shows how inevitably disgraceful behavior (*"dishonor"*; see 13:18) is viewed as *"reproach,"* that is, totally shameful conduct (6:33) which deserves eradication lest the whole community lose face. The double point of all this should not be missed: wickedness damages the reputations of the culprits and those of their families and fellow citizens. "Peer pressure" is a familiar term in our generation, a frequent reason why people adopt bad habits or engage in wicked acts. What we need is the peer pressure toward righteousness that the wise of Israel so valued and encouraged.

Transparency versus tortuousness seems to be the contrast in this saying.

The way of a guilty man *is* perverse;
But *as for* the pure, his work *is* right.

Prov. 21:8

The second line is clearer in Hebrew than the first. What the *"pure,"* straightforward, guileless, person (see 16:2 and esp. 20:11, where the gist is essentially the same as 21:8) does as a pattern of life (*"work"*) is marked by uprightness and integrity (*"right"*; Heb. *yāshār*, 2:7, 21). On the contrary *"the way"*—here parallel to *"work"* as a reminder that both words speak of the sum of conduct, the style of life—*"of a guilty man,"* or "criminal" or "liar" (the Hebrew word occurs only here in the Old Testament and has to be interpreted in the light of its Arabic cognates) is corkscrew-crooked. *"Perverse"* translates an odd word expanded for emphasis by the repetition of the last two consonants (*haphakphak* from *hpk* to "change" or "turn"). The repetition tells us how extraordinarily crooked the "criminal's" path has become.

This interesting subcollection of sayings tells us that the conduct of the sons and daughters of Israel was, by and large, observable to the general populace both in its character and its consequence. Secret sins there may be but they are far fewer than their perpetrators imagine. The truth will out eventually, if not sooner. We need to choose our daily deeds on the assumption that they will be exposed—either for good or for ill.

An equal number of sayings describe the loss of mental discernment that stalks the tracks of the foolish. Rather than learning from their mistakes they are apt to ignore them and grow increasing blind to what is highly apparent to those around them.

> Even in laughter the heart may sorrow,
> And the end of mirth *may be* grief.
> > *Prov. 14:13*

The teachers knew that emotions may be mixed, that we may not be able to discern all that we feel because feelings swirl within us in complex patterns. *"Laughter"* and *"sorrow"* can be present at the same time in the same *"heart."* And what begins as unsullied joy (*"mirth"*) may at *"the end"* be exposed as *"grief"* (see 10:1; 17:21).

But it is not this kind of emotional ambiguity that is their main theme.

> The heart of him who has understanding seeks
> > knowledge,
> But the mouth of fools feeds on foolishness.
> > *Prov. 15:14*

It is the blandness, even blindness of judgment, that makes unsightly choices seem handsome and tasteless decisions delectable: *"The mouth* [reading here with the traditional Hebrew pronunciation; the consonantal text has *"face"*] *of fools* [see on 14:24] *feeds on foolishness."* Folly creates an appetite for more of itself and corrupts our mental palate so that we crave what harms us. At the turn of the century my mother had to hide the boiled potatoes from her diabetic mother lest she literally eat herself into a coma. The *"heart"* of the person with *"understanding"* (Heb. *nābôn;* see on 1:5) makes better choices: *"knowledge"* (of God, see on 1:7) is the object of the appetite, a diet in which overeating is an impossibility.

> Folly *is* joy *to him who is* destitute of discernment,
> But a man of understanding walks uprightly.
> > *Prov. 15:21*

This saying mirrors 15:14 by reversing the order of the lines. The fool, *"destitute of discernment"* (lit., of a *"heart"* that makes right choices), finds unbridled *"joy"* in rebellious stupidity (*"folly"*; a word found twenty-three times in Proverbs). His opposite, the *"man of understanding"* (*t*ᵉ*bûnāh;* see at 2:2 and eighteen other times in Proverbs) eschews all giddiness and pursues a life (*"walks"*) of simple integrity (*"uprightly"*; root *yāshār;* see 21:8). What you see in him is what you get.

Our incredible human ability to distort our value system so that good things look bad and bad things good helped to generate a whole family of sayings that began with "better" (lit., "good-from" which equals "better-than" in Hebrew).

> Better *is* a little with righteousness,
> Than vast revenues without justice.
> *Prov. 16:8*

Each of these sayings contrasts something that we ordinarily relish with something that we may undervalue and yet is counted of magnificent worth to the wise teachers. What we value is *"vast revenues"* (lit., "produce" or income of any kind; see 3:14, 19). We can do so much with them: support ourselves, engage in philanthropy, enlarge our businesses, bequeath estates to our offspring, give substantial offerings to the Lord's work. Who can call such income anything but good? And the wise ones would agree—unless those revenues become a substitute for *"righteousness"* and *"justice"* (on this word pair see 1:3; 2:9; 21:3). Then meager holdings (*"a little"*) outweigh any amount of revenues. The *"better"* formula here is striking: in a book that puts high premium on the garnering and use of wealth (see chaps. 19 and 28), "righteousness" and "justice" so outrank it as to reduce it almost to the inconsequential. Wealth is what God has and bestows on us according to His good pleasure; "righteous" and "just" are what God is and insists that His people emulate in all their dealings with others.

> How much better *to get* wisdom than gold!
> And to get understanding is to be chosen rather
>   than silver.
> *Prov. 16:16*

For the same reason *"wisdom"* outweighs *"gold,"* and *"understanding"* or insight (Heb. *bînāh;* see 1:2; 4:1) is preferable to *"silver,"* as scarce and valuable as silver was in ancient Israel (see 2:4). *"To get"* in both lines reminds us that wisdom and understanding were not innate gifts, like absolute pitch in music, which some are born with and the rest of us cannot acquire. The purpose of such sayings is to motivate us to work and strive for what we do not have and yet can acquire by listening to our teachers, learning from our mistakes, and seeking God's guidance through the Scriptures as the Holy Spirit helps us respond to them. We look around us at the captains of industry, the investment bankers, the doctors, lawyers, and engineers—many of them working almost fiendishly to acquire gold and silver. How much sweat, blood, and tears are we expending for the infinitely ("*how much*") "*better*" gifts of wisdom and understanding?

> Understanding *is* a wellspring of life to him who
>   has it.
> But the correction of fools *is* folly.
> > *Prov. 16:22*

The importance of "*understanding*" (Heb. *śēkel* here, as in 3:4; 12:8; 13:15) is elevated by its comparison with a "*wellspring of life*," an artesian fountain that provides a constant supply of life-giving water (10:11). One who owns ("*him who has it*") such a source of mental and spiritual blessing need never fear the dry periods that hamper those who do not have wisdom in plentiful supply. The "*fools*" (for *ᵉwîlîm* see 1:7; 7:22), on the other hand, neither possess understanding nor have any capacity to acquire it. "*Correction*" ("instruction" or "discipline"; see *mûsār* at 1:2, 3, 7) is wasted on them. So perverted is their perspective that what the wise call "correction" they call "folly." And whoever wastes time trying to correct them engages in an act of folly. Fools are worse than horses; they cannot even be led to water, let alone forced to drink.

> There is a way *that seems* right to a man,
> But its end *is* the way of death.
> > *Prov. 16:25*

This saying (found verbatim in 14:12), puts the matter in the strongest possible form. What some think to be the "*right*," straight, direct way of life leads inexorably to "*death*." "*Way of death*" may be intended either literally or figuratively: "death" may be a life emptied of all meaning and purpose, devoid of God's blessing—a fate as least as doleful as physical death. The "*man*" who misreads the path is patently a fool, though not so named. The overall point is that without the insights of God-fearing teachers any one is capable of making the tragic and ultimate mistake. As Luther put it, "the arm [or mind!] of flesh will fail you, ye dare not trust your own."

The wise of Israel pondered questions as well as posed answers.

> Why *is there* in the hand of a fool the purchase
>   price of wisdom,
> Since *he has* no heart *for* it?
>
> *Prov. 17:16*

One question was prompted by their observation that the *"fool"* who may have possessed the tuition to pay for instruction (*"the purchase price of wisdom"*) did not have the brains (*"heart"* often stands for mind or brain) to absorb it. The corollary was probably equally obvious though it went unstated: persons capable of quickly grasping the basics of wisdom may not have been able to afford its cost. Stable societies have long recognized this inequity and provided subsidized instruction through taxes or scholarships.

Loss of mental discernment shows itself in failure to focus on the tasks at hand.

> Wisdom *is* in the sight of him who has
>   understanding,
> But the eyes of a fool *are* on the ends of the earth.
>
> *Prov. 17:24*

The one *"who has understanding"* (Heb. *mēbîn,* as in 8:9; 17:10; 28:2), perceptive insight, got that way and stays that way by keeping his mind fixed on *"wisdom,"* that is, on the topics and issues that will add to his store of wisdom. Not so the *"fool"* whose *"eyes"* roam from subject to subject, place to place, as far away from the intellectual target at hand as are *"the ends of the earth."* A few geniuses there may be who can master large areas of truth in a hurry and skip from one subject to another. To imitate the Thomas Jeffersons without their exceptional ability is the height of folly. Most of us do well to focus on narrower topics and gain some measure of mastery by such concentration.

Loss of self-control is another result of folly.

> Let a man meet a bear robbed of her cubs,
> Rather than a fool in his folly.
>
> *Prov. 17:12*

The comparison in 17:12 is about as violent as the Old Testament can get. The *"bear robbed of her cubs"* (lit., "bereft") is a symbol of high ferocity. God describes Himself as executing judgment as a bereft bear that will rip open Israel's chest cavity (Hos. 13:8). In other words *a fool* living in the grips of *his folly* is viciously unpredictable. Wise persons will give him wide berth personally and try to contain the harm he may do in their community.

Fools may be violent, but they are also vulnerable.

> A wise *man* scales the city of the mighty,
> And brings down the trusted stronghold.
>   *Prov. 21:22*

The calm, collected tactics of the *"wise"* one can penetrate the defenses of the *"city"* manned by crack troops (*"the mighty"*; see on Eccles. 9:11) who have falsely *"trusted"* their fortifications (*"stronghold"*; see 10:15) rather than the wisdom of the God who is their true fortress (Ps. 46:1) and who makes those who fear Him strong fortresses for their families (14:26).

Loss of political freedom is a price some persons pay for their folly.

> An evil *man* seeks only rebellion;
> Therefore a cruel messenger will be sent against
>   him.
>   *Prov. 17:11*

Where *"an evil man,"* intent on doing severe harm, *"seeks"* to disturb the peace of his community, tribe, or nation by fomenting rebellion, the leaders of the society have no choice but to use harsh measures. *"A cruel* [or merciless; see Jer. 6:23] *messenger,"* that is, an official dispatched to rebuke or apprehend the culprit (the Hebrew word for *"messenger"* is often used for *"angel"*), will be commissioned (*"sent"*) to enforce the will of the leaders. Punishment of some kind is in view which will jeopardize the rebel's role in the society. Since prisons were few, banishment or even death could be the evildoer's fate. This stern proverb would have warned young officials as to both their duties as emissaries of the crown and their liability should they themselves be tempted to defy their authorities.

> Judgments are prepared for scoffers,
> And beatings for the backs of fools.
>   *Prov. 19:29*

"Judgments" probably means *"penalties"* exacted as judgments, as the parallel *"beatings,"* a standard ancient form of civil or criminal punishment (see 2 Cor. 11:23–25), suggests. *"Scoffers"* (see on 1:22;

9:7–8) and *"fools"* describe here the moral dregs of the society who contribute nothing worthwhile and make sport of those who do. So childish is their behavior that they have to be reprimanded with rods as do wayward schoolboys (see on chap. 20).

More serious than any other of these negative results, in the minds of Israel's wise, is the loss of divine favor.

> The way of the wicked *is* an abomination to the
>   Lord,
> But He loves him who follows righteousness.
>   *Prov. 15:9*

To the ultimate Judge of all our conduct, the life path (*"way"*) *"of the wicked"* (see 2:22; 3:25, 33) is an intolerable insult, a shameless act of sacrilege (*"abomination"*; see 3:32). Since its opposite in the text is *"loves,"* *"abomination"* can mean nothing less than "hate." Wickedness is the studied, premeditated pursuit of disobedience as surely as following *"righteousness"* is the relentless quest to be found loyal and faithful to the covenant Lord in all we say and do. The intensity of the divine emotions—love and hate—shows how crucial is our choice.

The abomination felt by God in 15:9 expresses itself in action in 21:12.

> The righteous *God* wisely considers the house of the
>   wicked,
> Overthrowing the wicked for *their* wickedness.
>   *Prov. 21:12*

"The wicked" not only violate God's ways; they outrage His very character as the righteous God, who is always true to His own person and faithful to those who trust in Him. The very households, including the families, as *"house"* here must mean, come under God's careful scrutiny and are tagged for ruinous judgment (on *"overthrowing,"* see 13:6; 19:3; 22:12).

A further reason for God's displeasure toward the wicked is their impenitent attitude

> Fools mock at sin,
> But among the upright *there is* favor.
>   *Prov. 14:9*

Though this is a difficult saying to translate (note the variety of readings among the standard versions and commentaries), NKJV has caught its basic gist. The form is antithetical, *"fools"* and *"upright"* (Heb. *yāshār*, see 2:7, 21) are contrasted, as are *"sin"* and *"favor."* The precise crime of the fools is harder to discern: (1) what they *"mock"* or scoff at (the verb is linked to the familiar pejorative noun, "scoffers" may be any sense of sin or more precisely "guilt," as Hebrew *ʾāshām* may mean; in this case they are downplaying their own wickedness and rationalizing it as normal, acceptable behavior); (2) sin ("guilt") may be understood as the offering required in public worship to atone for sin (translated "trespass offering" by NKJV in Lev. 5:15; 7:14, etc.). While the first reading seems more likely, the second has some support in the use of *"favor"* (Heb. *rāṣôn*) which is a technical word for "acceptance" of offerings in Hebrew law (see Lev. 22:20–21). This raises the question of what is meant by "favor" and from where does it come. It may be human approval accorded the upright by their fellow citizens as NIV's "goodwill" seems to indicate. It may be "divine favor," as Scott (Anchor Bible) reads it. Perhaps it is deliberately ambiguous to extend its positive affirmations over the total range of conduct and sharpen the contrast between the wretched mockery of the fools and the total sense of well-being and acceptance of those who take sin seriously and seek every means, including contrite sacrifices (15:8; 21:27), to deal with it.

A dozen other sayings pick up this theme of ruinous judgment without necessarily naming Yahweh as the agent. Loss of life is the final price exacted by persistent folly. Paul's profound understanding of the wages of sin (Rom. 6:23) captures precisely the teachings of the wise. "Seek and you will find," was Jesus' promise (Matt. 7:7). His emphasis was on the positive. Our proverb says, "what you seek is what you'll get both positively and negatively."

> He who earnestly seeks good finds favor,
> But trouble will come to him who seeks *evil.*
> *Prov. 11:27*

"Seeks" here means "make it your life's aim to obtain something"— whether *"good"* or *"evil,"* both terms are general and wide-ranging, covering a whole landscape of righteous or wicked ambition. *"Favor"* is the positive result; it describes the good will and approval of the whole community. *"Trouble,"* perhaps better, *"disaster,"* is the negative outcome; it pictures a calamity which publicly exposes wicked behavior and implies both loss of face and loss of support in the community—a fate akin to death.

> Evil pursues sinners,
> But to the righteous, good shall be repaid.
>   *Prov. 13:21*

This theme of retribution is sounded crisply in the line *"evil* [i.e., "disaster" or "calamity"] *pursues sinners,"* as the hounds harry the stag. The conduct of wicked persons inexorably returns to haunt and destroy them. So God has geared the universe to trap those who go against Him and to reward (*"repaid"*) with *"good,"* all kinds of generous blessings including His favor, those whose loyalty to and trust in Him is constant (*"the righteous"*).

> The house of the wicked will be overthrown,
> But the tent of the upright will flourish.
>   *Prov. 14:11*

"House" and *"tent"* are synonyms describing all personal circumstances of goods, property, and family. The power of the saying rests not in these synonyms but in the antonyms, especially the verbs. The reward for the *"wicked"* is utter devastation, the Hebrew root *shāmad* (*"overthrown"*) being one of the strongest of the large family of words that signify "destruction." See Deuteronomy 9 for a half dozen instances of its use. The reward for the *"upright"* will be a household that will *"flourish,"* a horticultural term that speaks of effusive blossoming (11:28; Song of Sol. 6:11; 7:12).

> The wicked is banished in his wickedness,
> But the righteous has a refuge in his death.
>   *Prov. 14:32*

The first line makes clear the fate of the *"wicked"* man: he is pushed down or out (*"banished"*; for characteristic uses of the verb, see Pss. 118:13; 140:4), by his "evil behavior" (*"wickedness"*; two different Hebrew roots are translated as "wicked" or "wickedness" in NKJV; the first is *rāshā'*, the usual word for turbulent, violent misbehavior; the second is *rā'āh* the more general term for "evil"). "Evil" may be chosen here as a deliberate ambiguity, since the same word may describe the "evil activities" that bring the downfall (as most translations assume) or the "evil results" that form the judgment on the wicked man. In the first case the preposition *"in"* would mean "because of"; in the second, "into." The second line contrasts its subject and verb with those of the first line in the usual manner of antithetic proverbs. The contrast of the prepositional phrases, *"in his*

death" with *"in his wickedness,"* is more baffling. Three interpreta-
tions are offered: (1) "his" of *"his death"* is the wicked man's so that
"the righteous has a refuge" both in a relief from oppression and a
sense of vindication when the wicked man's evil catches up with
him; (2) "his" is *"the righteous man"* whose *"death"* is *"a refuge"* because it takes him out of the perils of this world into the safety of
God's eternal care; (3) the Hebrew word for *"his death"* should have
two letters reversed (*bmtw* to *btmw*) and thus be read "in his innocence" or "perfection" as the Greek translation has it. The first option disturbs the contrast by bringing mention of the wicked into
the second line which would normally refer only to the righteous.
The second option points to a view of death as blessing and hints at
a concept of eternal life not usually found in the Old Testament. The
third reading is probably the best since it preserves the balance of
the two lines, has attestation in ancient versions, and is readily ex-
plicable as a switch in spelling (see Anchor Bible and NEB).

> The way of life *winds* upward for the wise,
> That he may turn away from hell below.
> *Prov. 15:24*

The poetic form is synthetic in order to make explicit the life-
preserving role of wisdom. *"Upward"* and *"below"* mark choices between a successful life and the grave, as hell or sheol connote (see
1:12; 7:27; 9:18). One important result of the upward path is the distance that it puts, the margin of safety it effects, between the *"wise,"*
shrewd or intelligent person (see *maśkîl* at 10:5; 14:35) and the threat
of death that ever hovers over the fool's head. It would not be far-
fetched to hear an inkling of a doctrine of afterlife—heaven and
hell—in the contrast between upward and below, though the full
implications of those realities were yet to be revealed.
   Wisdom is again valued as a lifesaver.

> The highway of the upright *is* to depart from evil;
> He who keeps his way preserves his soul.
> *Prov. 16:17*

Wisdom directs us unfailingly to the *"highway"* (here only in
Proverbs; see Isa. 40:3; 62:10 for its use as a major artery along
which multitudes travel) that leads away (*"depart"*) *"from evil"*—
again (see 14:32) the ambiguous term suggests both wrongdoing
and the harmful consequences of such behavior. One definition
of *"upright"* (see on 2:7; 3:32; 8:9) is to keep or guard the path of

conduct as avidly as a sentinel stands watch over his station. Life itself is at risk, as *"preserves* [or *"protects"] his soul,"* his very person (see 3:22), points out.

> The silver-haired head *is* a crown of glory,
> *If* it is found in the way of righteousness.
> *Prov. 16:31*

Gray hair, *"the silver-haired head"* (see 20:29), is a banner that testifies to a lifelong walk in *"righteousness"* (Heb. *ṣᵉdāqāh;* see 8:18, 20). It crowns the loyal, obedient, godly person with *"glory,"* as a costly ornament dresses up an elegant costume (for Heb. *tiphʾeret,* 4:9; 17:6). We note that the Hebrew text has no *"if"* at the beginning of line two. The gray-crowned head is assumed by the teachers and their followers to be the sign of divine blessing that accompanies and enables long life. In short the second line gives the reason for the first, in this sample of synthetic parallelism.

Righteous (*"just"*) living pays off in the present as well as the future.

> *It is* a joy for the just to do justice,
> But destruction *will come* to the workers of iniquity.
> *Prov. 21:15*

It is not a grim grind, endured by a set-jawed people. It is full of *"joy."* Seeing that order, equity, protection of rights, and redress of grievances are practiced in a community—all are facets in *"justice"* (see on 1:3; 2:9)—is a delight indeed. It means that human life takes on a godly character, shines with a holy light, and mirrors something of God's own nature. The righteous person (*"just"* is Heb. *ṣaddîq;* see 2:20; 3:33) brings joy through justice and receives joy through divine blessing. The opposite happens to *"the workers of iniquity"* (see on 10:29), whose mayhem knows no bounds either in form or ferocity: they work *"destruction"* by opposing, undermining, and scorning justice and gain destruction (*mᵉḥittāh,* a favorite word in Proverbs for ruin and the terror it brings in its wake; 10:14, 15, 29; 13:3; 14:28; 18:7).

> A man who wanders from the way of
>   understanding
> Will rest in the assembly of the dead.
> *Prov. 21:16*

The fate of the fool—the *"man who wanders from the way of under-standing"* (Heb. *śekel*, the prudence that is marked both by shrewd-ness and effectiveness; see on 3:4)—is expressed in a dramatic clause found only here: he *"will rest in the assembly* [Heb. *qāhāl*, the standard word for Israel's gathering together in official meetings; 5:14; Joel 2:16; Deut. 9:10; 10:4] *of the dead."* *"Dead"* is literally *"shades"* or *"spirits"* of deceased persons (Heb. *rᵉphā'îm*; see 2:18; 9:18; Isa. 26:14, 19), a reflection of the Hebrew belief that those who died were *"gathered to their people"* (Gen. 25:8; 49:29). Something more than mere burial must be meant by this, but it is not neces-sarily a clear intimation of afterlife, though the literature of Israel's northern neighbors in Ugarit on the Syrian coast contains descrip-tions of shades assembled in the nether world. Premature, untimely death may be part of what the saying pictures. It is clearly not a happy, welcome state, whatever it may mean. The wanderers from their teachers' paths have left the land of the living and become part of the company of the departed; even their memory will be tinged more with regret than with blessedness.

> The wicked *shall be* a ransom for the righteous,
> And the unfaithful for the upright.
>> *Prov. 21:18*

The synonymous lines of this saying put across a single point: what a *"wicked"* or treacherous (*"unfaithful,"* untrustworthy deceiver, Heb. *bôḡēḏ*; see on 2:22; 11:3, 6) person plots for a *"righteous"* and *"upright"* person returns as his own fate. He, in fact, becomes *"a ransom,"* that is, a "substitute" (Heb. *kōpher*, lit., "atonement"; see Exod. 21:30) for his intended victim. So turn the wheels of divine justice, as Haman learned when they hanged him *"on the gallows that he had prepared for Mordecai"* (Esther 7:10; an illustration of Prov. 21:18 first proposed by the Jewish rabbi and master commen-tator, Rashi).

> He who follows righteousness and mercy
> Finds life, righteousness and honor.
>> *Prov. 21:21*

This saying is the opposite of 21:16. Both are synthetic in form—the first line describing the conduct, the second stating the conse-quences. The negative biography of the wanderer is the theme of verse 16; the positive story of the one who *"follows* ["pursues," "hunts down"; Heb. *rādaph*; see 28:1] *righteousness and mercy* [Heb. *ḥesed*, covenant loyalty, behavior that is both kind and reliable; see on 3:3; 14:22]" is featured in verse 21. The rewards are long *"life"* (see on 16:31; 20:29), prosperity (as the second *"righteousness"* should be understood; see NIV), and prestige or good repute (*"honor"* is *"glory,"* lit., carrying *"weight"* in the community; see on 3:2, 16). Again the seeking-finding note anticipates Jesus' beatitude on those who *"hunger and thirst for righteousness"* (Matt. 5:6), though the material and social benefits promised by Israel's teachers give way to the spiritual understanding of righteousness in the words of our great Teacher.

It is fitting that this survey of sayings on Rewards of Conduct end not on a tragic but on a positive plane. That, after all, was the intent of the wise: not to mock the fate of fools but to encourage wise, loving, loyal, responsible behavior with every tool in their workshop. That their sayings survived and were incorporated into Jewish and Christian Scripture is ample proof of their effectiveness in fulfilling their intent. We do not canonize prescriptions that lead their followers to failure.

GAINS OF HUMILITY

Pride is pagan behavior. It should have no place in the lives of God's people. Israel's teachers, psalmists, chroniclers, and prophets were unanimous on that point. Pride was, for them, a rejection of creatureliness, a declaration of independence from God if not an announcement of war against Him. Pride drew God's scorn, sparked His ire, and guaranteed His judgment. Moreover, it did not make friends for the haughty nor raise their esteem in their communities. Hard it is to love our neighbor as ourselves when we have an exaggerated sense of our own importance. We can easily sop up our total supply of love for our own needs, given our exalted ideas of how lovable we are.

The sayings in Proverbs hit hard against pride and hammer home the importance of humility. We sketch their teachings under headings like these:

Introduction	
The choice: humiliation or honor	29:23
The certainty of pride's punishment	16:5, 18–19; 18:12
The dangers of pride's presumptuousness	
No prospect	26:12

No power	27:1–2
No prestige	21:24
No protection	15:25
The futility of pride's perspective	21:4
Conclusion	
The choice: shame or wisdom	11:2

What goes up must come down; what bows down will be lifted up.

> A man's pride will bring him low,
> But the humble in spirit will retain honor.
>   *Prov. 29:23*

In a nutshell that is what the wise taught about God's dealings with the proud and the humble. *"Pride"* (Heb. *g'h* is the root here and in 15:25; 16:18, 19) is derived from a word meaning "high." It suggests elevating ourselves, looking down on others, seeking to lord it over them. In the long run, it is Tower-of-Babel behavior that says, "Let us be like 'a tower whose top is the heavens; let us make a name for ourselves'" (Gen. 11:4). God's response to arrogant ambition is ever the same: He thwarted the plan and confused the planners. What started with high hopes ended in deep chaos. *"Low,"* which here implies abject humiliation, is a literal term which may describe bowing in humility before elders or superiors or being forced to bend low in shame to masters or even to God (25:7; Job 5:11; 2 Sam. 6:22; Mal. 2:9). The Hebrew root *shaphal* occurs in the geographical name of the "lowlands"—*shephelah*—that bridge the hills of Judah to the coastal plain of the Philistines (Deut. 1:7; 1 Kings 10:27). *"Humble* [lit., "low"] *in spirit"* is the direct opposite of *"pride"* and depicts the person who does not overvalue himself and consequently devalue his fellows. Starting low means there is no way to go but up. Modesty gains *"honor"* by not threatening the neighbors; when worn well, it retains, *"clutches," "holds fast"* (3:18; 4:4 for the Heb. *tāmak*) the honor, the weighty respect, because no one is tempted to snatch it away.

Though God may level us in our pride as the Babel story teaches, our family, friends, and foes may also do it without direct divine intervention. There is something about the arrogance of others that challenges us to topple them from their lofty, self-assigned status. We are eager to expose their ignorance, call their bluff, prove their limitations. Pity the team that mocks its opponents to the press! The locker room bulletin board will cry out for revenge, and as often as not the high are brought low. The beatitudes that encourage us to be *"poor in spirit"* and *"meek"* (Matt. 5:3, 5) are direct descendants of this proverb. They too assume that we have a choice and that choosing wrongly always brings results diametrically opposed to what we ask for. "Seek and you shall find" is trustworthy only when we seek what God deems right.

The certainty of pride's punishment rings loud and clear:

> Everyone proud in heart *is* an abomination to the
>   LORD;
> *Though they join* forces, none will go unpunished.
> *Prov. 16:5*

The fate of the *"proud"*—again the root idea is "high" (Heb. *gbh;* 16:18)—is to be hated (*"abomination,"* as despicable a term as Heb. has; 3:32; 6:16) by *"the Lord."* So horrified is Yahweh that He personally sees to it that no proud person will *"go unpunished"* or "deemed innocent" (see 6:29; 11:21; 17:5; 19:5, 9; 28:20). The punishment is guaranteed by an oath whose nuance NKJV has not caught: *"though they join forces"* does not give the sense of the Hebrew "hand to hand." The phrase describes a "handshake" or some other gesture where two parties join hands to seal an agreement or strike a bargain (see 11:21). "Be sure of this:" (NIV) is the correct rendering, which conveys the intensity of the divine abomination and the certainty of the retribution.

> 16:18 Pride *goes* before destruction,
>   And a haughty spirit before a fall.
>   19 Better *to be* of a humble spirit with the lowly,
>   Than to divide the spoil with the proud.
> *Prov. 16:18–19*

This is one of the few occasions in 10:1–22:16 where sayings treating the same topic are placed back to back. Verse 18 is synonymous in form and makes clear the inevitable consequences of *"pride"* (again "high"; Heb. *gᵊh;* see 29:33) also described as *"a haughty* [another word for "high"; Heb. *gbh;* see 16:5] *spirit,"* whose opposite is the "humble ["low"] in spirit" of 29:23. "Spirit" in both instances describes the totality of inward attitudes which reveal themselves in outward signs, words, and actions. The results of lofty self-exaltation are calamitous: a total shattering of what the person has and is (*"destruction"*) and a crashing down as from a cliff or high place (*"fall,"* lit., stumbling off the edge of a bank or precipice). The attitude itself is viewed as working these consequences, since God is not mentioned in the text as He was in 16:5.

In form, verse 19 is a *"better"* comparison saying. Its message underscores the dangers of pride by amplifying the teaching of verse 18. So dangerous is pride that it is infinitely better for a person to retain *"a humble spirit"* (see 29:23) and keep company *"with the lowly"* (or *"poor"*; see 3:34; 14:21) people of the land who have no claim to goods or fame and live in day-by-day dependence on God than to hobnob with the *"proud,"* who may be financially successful—though not always by legal or ethical means—and to share in the division of their ill-gotten loot (*"spoil"*). The spoil which the proud *"divide"* is not ultimately a worthwhile contribution to their fellows. Their pride itself is contagious, and, hence, their very company—rewarding though it may seem—is a menace to sound living and thinking.

> Before destruction the heart of a man is haughty,
> And before honor *is* humility.
>
> *Prov. 18:12*

The first line of 18:12 repeats the calamitous notes of 16:18: *"destruction"* translates the same Hebrew word (*sheber*, breaking or shattering). The act of pride here is centered in a *"haughty* ['lifted up"; Heb. *gbh* as in 16:18] *heart."* It pictures a person whose thoughts and decisions are both selfish and unrealistic. He sees himself larger than life, imagines he can accomplish more than he can, and fantasizes that others will rally to his greatness. When none of these things comes true, his life breaks into pieces with no one to care, let alone to rescue. His destruction evokes more scorn than sadness. *"Humility,"* devout and pious dependence on God and concern for the well-being of others (for the Heb. *ᶜᵃnāwāh*, see 15:33; 22:4; Zeph. 2:3), in contrast, leads to *"honor"* or glory (*kābôd*, lit., *"weight"*) in the community. People trust its selflessness, are attracted to its esteem of others, and hold no fear of threat or ambition from it.

Pride's presumptuousness risks a cluster of dangers in addition to the clear-cut punishment threatened in the sayings above. No prospect is the first.

> Do you see a man wise in his own eyes?
> *There is* more hope for a fool than for him.
>
> *Prov. 26:12*

"Wise in his own eyes" is an apt depiction of pride. It is a solitary act of self-evaluation, a motion seconded by no other party. It is the verdict of a lonely unrelated ego utterly heedless of the opinions of others. If

"there is more hope" (Heb. *tiqwāh,* the word of confident, patient expectation; 10:28; 19:18) of reform and blessing *"for a fool,"* it is only because the fool is less defended by his own self-aggrandizement, less resistant to the counsel or correction of others. The point, of course, is not the tractability of the fool; we have ample evidence that he does not change readily. It is the incorrigibility of the proud, who is dead wrong in his understanding of himself and dead set against any correction to that misunderstanding.

No power is a second danger faced by the proud.

> 27:1 Do not boast about tomorrow,
>   For you do not know what a day may bring
>   forth.
>   2 Let another man praise you, and not your own
>   mouth;
>   A stranger, and not your own lips.
>   *Prov. 27:1–2*

Verse 1 reminds them that they are powerless to predict their future (*"tomorrow"*) exploits. On *"boast,"* whose root means "praise," see 20:14; 25:14. The idea is clearly an act of bragging about what one will achieve, or where one will go, as though the future were in human not divine control. The command (*"Do not boast"* is a jussive form in Hebrew, akin to the imperative in giving orders), followed by *"for,"* marks the saying as an admonition reinforced by a motivation that "for" introduces. Ignorance of *"what a day may bring"* should promote humility not presumptuousness as James's strong words indicate: "Instead you ought to say, 'If the Lord wills, we shall live and do this or that.' But now you boast in your arrogance. All such boasting is evil" (James 4:15–16).

Verse 2 suggests that we lack power to evaluate as well as predict. The synonymous lines both underscore the fact that we stand far too close to ourselves to see clearly either our strengths or weaknesses, our virtues or vices. Sound evaluation can come only from others— and they ought not to be too close to us; *"another man"* suggests an outsider, even a foreigner (Heb. *zār;* see 6:1 for masculine use; 5:3, 20 for feminine); *"stranger"* (Heb. *nokrî;* masculine 5:10; feminine 2:16) underscores the sense of distance. Neither friend, neighbor, nor family member would be described in such terms. Outsider *"praise"* (Heb. *hll,* the root for praise in the Psalms and the base of the familiar "Hallelujah") may not always be accurate but it is always more seemly than self-praise which shades over into the boasting described in verse 1.

Pride leaves the haughty (see Hab. 2:5 for the other use of Heb. *yāhîr*) person with no prestige.

> A proud *and* haughty *man—"Scoffer" is* his name;
> He acts with arrogant pride.
>
> *Prov. 21:24*

The very status that pride presumes for itself is that of which pride robs itself. Others name the *"arrogant"* man (Heb. *'ebrāh* from a root expressing *"anger"*; see 11:4, 23; 22:8) *"scoffer,"* as demeaning a title as the Hebrew tongue can spit out at another person (Heb. *lēṣ;* see in 1:22; 3:34; 9:7–8). *"Pride"* here may translate the strongest Hebrew word for presumptuousness (*zādôn;* see 11:2), a word used to describe Babylon as the epitome of pride in Jer. 50:31–32.

> The LORD will destroy the house of the proud,
> But He will establish the boundary of the widow.
>
> *Prov. 15:25*

The contrast here is deliberate and powerful. *"Proud"* persons will find their whole estate (*"house"* here means dwellers, buildings, and holdings) wiped out because of their lofty claims of worth, achievement, and invulnerability. When *"the Lord"* marches to *"destroy,"* they who thought so highly of themselves will have nothing left. Their presumptuousness means no protection. The Lord has become their enemy. On the other hand, the Lord has become the Guardian of *"the widow"* (used only here in Proverbs), the symbol of the defenseless, powerless persons in Israel's society (Deut. 10:18; Ps. 68:6). Her territory (*"boundary"*; see 22:28; 23:10) will be kept inviolate by the righteous Judge of all the earth, while neither God nor man will intervene when judgment strikes the proud.

> A haughty look, a proud heart,
> *And* the plowing of the wicked *are* sin.
>
> *Prov. 21:4*

This baffling saying seems to speak of the futility of pride's perspective on life. Its structure is synthetic, and its climax is the verdict *"sin."* So understood, it condemns as misdirected and therefore futile three gestures made by or to the proud. The first two gestures are clear enough: *"haughty look"* (lofty, exalted eyes), *"proud heart"* (a wide, broad way of thinking about oneself; see 1 Kings 5:9; its opposite is "lacking in heart" or intelligence as in Prov. 6:32; 7:7; 9:4). The meaning here has turned pejorative and mental prowess has become mental hubris (as in Ezek. 28:2–3). These are fresh ways of describing the self-aggrandizement and disdain of others which are the themes of this whole section of sayings treated as Problems of Pride. They are clearly viewed as *"sin"* (on Heb. *ḥṭ*, see 1:10; 5:22; 10:10; 13:6). The third clause is more difficult and is rendered with considerable variety: One approach follows the Greek translation and reads *"plowing"* (Heb. *nîr*) as "lamp" (Heb. *nēr*):

> Haughty eye, proud heart
> lamp of the wicked, nothing but sin.
> JB; see also NIV

Another tack is to emend *nîr* to *neder:*

> Because of their pride and arrogance
> The vow of evil men is a sin.
> Scott, Anchor Bible

Other versions use broad paraphrases to try to catch the sense:

> Haughty looks and a proud heart—
> These sins mark a wicked man.
> NEB

> Wicked people are controlled by their conceit
> and arrogance, and this is sinful.
> TEV

If we stay with the Hebrew text, as NKJV has attempted, then "plowing" (see 13:23) should be read as an "effort to cultivate." The meanings then would come out something like these, as McKane has suggested: (1) striving to cultivate (educate) the *"wicked"* is a thoroughly futile task and therefore is just as much a misdirection of time and energy as are haughty looks and proud hearts; (2) to educate (cultivate) the wicked produces even more sin in their lives and should not at all be encouraged. In either case the wicked are beyond educating, bound as they are in scornful, shameful pride which either keeps them from learning or puts their learning to further evil uses.

> When pride comes, then comes shame;
> But with the humble *is* wisdom.
> Prov. 11:2

This saying faces the fledging wise of Israel—and us with them—
with another ultimate choice. In 29:23, it was humiliation or honor.
Here it is *"shame"* or *"wisdom." "Pride"* (Heb. *zādôn;* 13:10; 21:24;
Deut. 18:22; Jer. 49:16; Obad. 3—the latter two verses describe
Edom's vaunted arrogance and highlight again how pagan at heart
is human pride) does not walk alone. Its inevitable companion, lurking in its shadow, moving surreptitiously but always there, is *"shame"*
(3:39; 6:33; 13:18), the lightweight, worthless opposite of honor or
glory. *"Humble"* people (Heb. *ṣᵉnûᵊîm;* used only here in the Old
Testament) recall the demand of Yahweh in Mic. 6:8 to "walk humbly
[Heb. *ṣnᵊ*] with your God" and find a different kind of fellow-
traveler—wisdom. Their humility teaches them the limits of strength
and knowledge, opens them to learn all they can from trustworthy
teachers and companions, and casts them on the mercy and support
of God whom to fear is to begin to gain knowledge.

> The fear of the LORD *is* the beginning of knowledge,
> *But* fools despise wisdom and instruction.
>
> *Prov. 1:7*

Each choice is two choices: choose your stance—whether pride or
humility—and you have chosen the companion who will either drag
you into shame or lead you into wisdom.

To catch fully the terror of pride, we have to hear Isaiah's words
denouncing, in Yahweh's name, everything that exalts itself in competition with the covenant Lord.

> For the day of the LORD of Hosts
> *Shall come* upon everything proud and lofty,
> Upon everything lifted up—
> And it shall be brought low—
>> cedars . . . oaks . . .
>> high mountains . . . hills *that are* lifted up . . .
>> high tower . . . fortified wall
>> ships . . . sloops.
> The loftiness of man shall be bowed down,
> And the haughtiness of men shall be brought low;
> And the LORD alone will be exalted in that day.
>
> *Isa. 2:12–17*

CHAPTER TWENTY-TWO

Cautious Conduct and Passionate Justice

Proverbs 22:1–16

The lengthy garland of sayings that form the centerpiece of Proverbs comes to its end in this chapter. From 10:1 to 22:16, we can examine each individual flower—375 in all—of this massive, variegated, multihued bouquet of wisdom. At 22:17 the scene, setting, and style will change, though the theme of wisdom will continue. Two topics call for comment in these final sixteen verses. They describe ingredients essential to the stable community life which the sages cherished and to which they constantly encouraged their pupils: (1) behavior that measures each step with prudence and avoids the rashness of quick decision or hasty action; (2) justice that spares no effort to treat all members of society with fairness and to redress all grievances caused by greed or cruelty.

Like all portions of Scripture, these sayings have to be heard first in their ancient setting. They served as guidelines for fruitful living in a culture both agrarian and urban, as directions for the leaders who had the authority and responsibility to shape the tone and structure of their society. Yet more than some portions of Scripture, they speak directly and universally to our present social needs. Rash action and disdain of justice are as endemic to human behavior today as they were three millennia ago. They are part of the chronic ailments of civilization like high blood pressure and stomach ulcers. The prescriptions of Israel's teachers are both tested and timely. We do well to take them regularly and in adequate dosage.

The lead verse of chapter 22 serves as an effective introduction to both topics.

> A *good* name is to be chosen rather than great
>   riches,
> Loving favor rather than silver and gold.
> *Prov. 22:1*

It reminds us of the personal reward of good behavior in any form. The esteem of the community—*"a good name"* ("good" is supplied here to clarify the meaning; see Eccles. 7:1 where "good" appears in the Hebrew)—is one of wisdom's highest prizes. It describes trustworthiness, gratitude, and enduring remembrance. It cannot be demanded, only proffered. It is not a right but a gift, offered on the basis of a lengthy history of reliable contributions to the lives of others. It is an act of love in response to a life of love. *"Loving favor"* is literally "good grace" and shows the warmth and regard bestowed on the wise person by fellow citizens. More than anything else, Proverbs is about relationships built on integrity. Nothing can compare in value with that—not *"great riches,"* not *"silver and gold"* (see on 2:4; 8:10; 11:22). Solomon rightly chose wisdom and with it came a good name and *"loving favor."* When wisdom failed him in his religious compromises and his oppressive use of power, not even his immense riches could salvage his name.

DISCIPLINING OURSELVES

We shall meet this central topic again in chapter 26. No definition of prudent living can be complete without it. Its several expressions can be summarized like this:

Weighing words	14:15
Avoiding temptation	14:16; 21:29; 22:3, 5
Resisting haste	19:2; 21:5
Easing anger	21:14

Trust is a virtue; credulity is not. Naiveté may not be as wicked a disposition as deceitfulness, but it is no less dangerous.

> The simple believes every word,
> But the prudent considers well his steps.
> *Prov. 14:15*

The *"simple"* person lacks worldly wisdom, *"believes every word"* said to him by any person, and is readily taken in. Gullibility leaves him open to manipulation, disappointment, and a dozen other painful fates. Not so with the shrewd, experienced, *"prudent"* person (see on Heb. ʿārûm at 12:16, 23). Fully aware (*"considers well"* is to have "insight" or "understanding"; Heb. *byn*, see at 2:5) of the potential deception or misinformation in human conversation, he takes pains to "verify" what he is told. *"His steps"* should perhaps be read to "verify" or "confirm" it, based on one Aramaic meaning of the consonants *ʾšr* which NKJV has read as "steps." Clear and common examples of this caution are our constant need to check out rumors and hear both (or more) sides of any story. As pastors, teachers, and administrators we have ample scars to display from our failure to use care in the weighing of the words we hear.

The biblical person shows caution by avoiding temptation.

> A wise *man* fears and departs from evil,
> But a fool rages and is self-confident.
> *Prov. 14:16*

This saying echoes Job 1:1 in its picture of the *"wise"* person who *"fears and departs from evil."* Here it is not God that is the object of fear as in Job; it is the *"evil"* itself, to be feared and shunned because it is both wrong and dangerous. Its risks outweigh any possible gains. If a wise person gives evil a wide berth, *"a fool rages"* out of control (the verb suggests an erratic disposition especially given to anger; see 20:2; 26:17) and rushes rashly (*"self-confident"*) into situations and relationships fraught with evil. Jesus, the greater Sage, knew our propensity to rashness when He taught us to pray:

> And do not lead us into temptation,
> But deliver us from the evil one.
> *Matt. 6:13*

Part of the temptation from which we need rescue is the tendency to pretend to be what we are not, to feel what we cannot, and to mean what we do not.

> A wicked man hardens his face,
> But *as for* the upright, he establishes his way.
> *Prov. 21:29*

Bluffing, posturing, faking—these are the actions of one who *"hardens* [lit., "causes to be strong, firm, set"] *his face."* That visage may be useful in a game like poker, but it makes no contribution to honest, upright, caring relationships. Indeed it is a trait of the *"wicked"* person to try to deceive others by a look, since superficiality and pretense are his standard equipment. With the *"upright"* person, however, reality outranks sham; the genuine is valued, the counterfeit despised. The upright lives not by a false face but by a solid, well-marked, tested path ("*way*")—a pattern of life that is plain, tried, and trustworthy.

Foresight is a virtue in dealing with temptation.

> A prudent *man* foresees evil and hides himself,
> But the simple pass on and are punished.
>
> *Prov.* 22:3

Part of the power of this saying is a pun: a "*prudent*" person (see on 14:15) "*foresees evil*"—the Hebrew is *rā'āh rā'āh* (the two words sound almost alike). We deal with *rā'āh* ("*evil*," disaster, harm) by *rā'āh* (open-eyed spotting of the risks and consequences). And that foresight enables the shrewd, crafty person to hide himself as he would from highway robbers or wild animals. "*The simple*," who live unguardedly and throw caution to the winds, keep right on going ("*pass on*") into the jaws of danger and pay the consequent penalty ("*are punished*"; lit., "are fined"; see 17:26; 21:11; 27:12).

> Thorns *and* snares *are* in the way of the perverse;
> He who guards his soul will be far from them.
>
> *Prov.* 22:5

"*The perverse*," the deliberately rather than naively wayward (see 2:15; 8:8; 11:20; 17:20; 19:1; 28:6), also dash headlong into dangers—whether natural bramble bushes ("*thorns*") that choke their paths, tearing their clothes and flesh, or man-made bird traps ("*snares*"; see Amos 3:5; Ps. 124:7) that clap together when triggered and capture their prey in their netted frames. The rashness of the perverse, who cares nothing for the welfare of himself or his neighbors, is countered by the constant vigil ("*guards his soul*," his entire person whether viewed physically, morally, or spiritually) of the cautious person who walks not on the edge of dangers but at a great distance ("*far*") from the thorns and snares. A wise word this is for those of us who flirt with temptation like school kids tottering on a narrow ledge, virtually daring ourselves to fall.

Haste may be the ultimate enemy of caution.

> Also it is not good *for* a soul *to be* without
>   knowledge,
> And he sins who hastens with *his* feet.
>
> *Prov.* 19:2

Rushing recklessly into dangerous situations ("*hastens* [21:5; 28:20; 29:20] *with his feet*"), dashing off the proven path is a clear sign that

the person is *"without knowledge,"* as the synonymous poetry indicates. "Without knowledge" means ignorance, at least; it may go further to suggest disobedience to the information and requirements
that God has made known (see Heb. *da'at,* 1:2, 4, 7). *"Not good"*
is further defined as *"sins,"* an apt word in this context since the
Hebrew *ḥṭ'* suggests losing the path, straying from the destination,
or missing the target. *"Soul"* (Heb. *nephesh*) in this saying may mean
"vitality," "strong feeling," or "drive" (see Gen. 23:8; 2 Kings 9:15). If
so, the contrast is between energy hastily expended ("zeal," NIV) and
knowledge carefully employed. The one without the other can derail
us from God's chosen course.

> The plans of the diligent *lead* surely to plenty,
> But *those of* everyone *who is* hasty, surely to
>   poverty.
>
> *Prov. 21:5*

"Haste makes waste" is the traditional equivalent of this saying. The
"diligent" person (see 10:4; 12:24, 27; 13:4) not only works hard but
plans well, measuring each step in the process and then carefully
implementing the strategy. The result is *"plenty"* (see 14:23; Eccles.
3:19), an excess over what is needed, an advantage that the careless
do not have. The *"hasty"* settle for an approach that is quick and
dirty, sloppily planned and halfheartedly implemented. Their accomplishment is *"poverty,"* the lack of all the basics needed to support life adequately. To be cautious and to be casual are not the same
thing. Most ministers and Christian leaders in my acquaintance plan
too little or too quickly and then are utterly baffled at the poverty of
their results. This saying (21:15) will tell them why.

> A gift in secret pacifies anger,
> And a bribe behind the back, strong wrath.
>
> *Prov. 21:14*

These synonymous lines contain an answer to anger. They should
not be read as justification for bribery, which is condemned elsewhere in Prov. 15:27; 17:23. The context of 21:14 is not a court of
law or a delicate financial transaction. It is a case of ruptured relationships, personal misunderstandings that have left someone blazing with *"anger"* and *"strong wrath."* The cautious person *"pacifies,"*
turns aside, averts (Heb. *kph,* only here in the Old Testament) those
intense feelings by offering a *"gift"* or a "present" (*"bribe"* is a misleading translation here; 1 Kings 15:19; 2 Kings 16:8; Prov 17:8) as

an expression of friendship and an overture of peace. *"In secret"* and *"behind the back"* (better translated "in the chest-high front fold of the garment"; 16:33; 17:23) do not intimate crookedness but privacy; the giver's desire is not to embarrass the angry companion but to give space for the anger to abate unnoticed by outsiders. An act of kindness or generosity quietly rendered can be one of the soft answers that turn away wrath (15:1).

DEFENDING OTHERS

Justice is a cause on which every portion of Scripture is insistent—law, history, prophecy, psalms, apocalyptic, gospels, epistles, and certainly wisdom. Given who God is and how He cares for the human family, it would be unthinkable for injustice to be condoned or even tolerated. Whenever the subject arises, as it does in prophets like Amos and Micah, the volume is turned up and the music is transposed to a higher key. The call to justice is not only a rational set of instructions to do right wherever one can, but it is a passionate cry to stamp out wrong wherever one finds it. A half dozen sayings in Proverbs catch that cry and pass it on. No definition of wisdom in Israel—or anywhere else—can be complete without a stern denunciation of injustice and a strong plea for justice to "run down like water" (Amos 5:24). These headings give us a handle on the way the wise responded to the cry:

The fact of injustice	13:23
The plot of injustice	12:5
The prevention of injustice	17:26; 18:5
The fate of injustice	22:8, 16

Injustice takes many forms and can have any person or segment of society as its target. The Proverbs reflect this range of forms and targets. There is concern for the poor who are always vulnerable to exploitation (13:23; 22:16), for the innocent (righteous) whose very uprightness lures the wicked to connive against them (12:5; 17:26; 18:5), for the nobility (princes) whose exercise of authority makes them susceptible to accusation or attack (17:26). The marketplace (13:23; 22:16) and the city gate where courts of law were convened (18:5) and political debates were held (12:5; 17:26) were the chief arenas of injustice. Controlling them was a prime concern of prophets and sages.

Injustice was not a trivial deviation from society's norm but a matter of life and death, especially for the poor, and more especially where food supply was the issue.

> Much food *is in* the fallow *ground* of the poor,
> And for lack of justice there is waste.
> *Prov. 13:23*

In stressing the fact of injustice, this proverb seems to contrast the bountiful crops (*"much food"*) grown by *"the poor"* in their plowed land (*"fallow ground"*; Heb. *nîr;* see on 21:4; also Hos. 10:12; Jer. 4:3) with the meager amount they are allowed to keep. *"There is waste"* is literally "it is swept away," suggesting that the landowners took an unjust (*"lack of justice"*) share of the produce and left the poor, who had tilled the fields as sharecroppers with almost nothing for themselves. Both Amos (5:11) and James (5:4–5) decry the cruel and wicked unfairness of owners who garner wealth at the expense of the workers who grew the crops. Whatever else justice may mean in the Old Testament, it calls for the rights of every sector of society and all parties in any transaction to be safeguarded.

> The thoughts of the righteous *are* right,
> *But* the counsels of the wicked *are* deceitful.
> *Prov. 12:5*

Here we are reminded that while injustice may at times be due to oversight, it may more often be the fruit of plots (*"counsels"*) of wicked people. They seem deliberately to lay *"deceitful,"* treacherous, and fraudulent (Heb. *mirmāh;* see 11:1) plans to cheat their neighbors and undercut the stability of the community. The *"thoughts,"* reckonings, or calculations (Heb. *maḥshābôt;* 6:18; 15:22, 26) of the *"righteous,"* who care about community loyalty and neighbor love, *"are right."* "Right" means more than correct or accurate. It translates the Hebrew *mishpāṭ,* "justice" and suggests that the righteous have in mind what is fair and equitable for every one. Deceitful selfishness stamps the plans of the *"wicked"*; passionate justice motivates the thoughts of the loyal sons and daughters of the covenant. They aim to block the plot of injustice and to see God's will done on earth as it is in heaven.

Doing justice entails the prevention of injustice.

> Also, to punish the righteous *is* not good,
> *Nor* to strike princes for *their* uprightness.
> *Prov. 17:26*

Two parallel instances are featured in 17:26. *"Also"* may hint that this proverb was once part of a list of sayings that dealt with unjust behavior. Here, however, it seems unconnected to 17:25 and the other sayings that precede it. To fine (as *"punish"* means here; see 21:11; 22:3) innocent, guiltless (so *"righteous"* frequently means) persons is against upright or correct practice (*"not good"*). It discourages integrity and rewards deceit. The same is said of inflicting undeserved lashings (*"strike"*) as penalty on officials (*"princes"*; n^edîbîm, see 8:16; 17:7; 19:6; 25:7; Song of Sol. 6:12; 7:2) whose *"uprightness"* is judged perversely. Both acts shred the fabric of justice which holds the society together.

Due process and equitable sentences are hallmarks of a decent legal system.

> *It is* not good to show partiality to the wicked,
> *Or* to overthrow the righteous in judgment.
> *Prov. 18:5*

"Partiality [lit., *"*paying attention to the face or appearance of the person"] *to the wicked,"* that is, the obviously *"*guilty," since the context implies a legal situation, cannot be tolerated (see on 24:23–26). Judicial decisions must follow, as closely as possible, the ways of the divine Judge who is *"*no respecter of persons," as the AV has traditionally rendered the phrase (Acts 10:34; see 2 Sam. 14:14). The setting of 18:5 seems to suggest that the *"wicked"* were wealthy or influential and therefore able to exercise undue and intimidating influences on the legal process. The innocent (*"righteous"*) parties, in contrast, were probably vulnerable to exploitation and had no strong advocates to prevent the *"overthrow"* of their case when it came to court (in justice). The point is plain: nothing but the facts and merits of the cases should influence the verdicts—not the prominence or obscurity of either plaintiff or defendant.

The law of cause and effect is held by the wise to be fully operative in the area of justice.

> He who sows iniquity will reap sorrow,
> And the rod of his anger will fail.
> *Prov. 22:8*

The fate of injustice is like that of any act of folly: it gets precisely what it deserves. Two metaphors in this saying describe that fate. From the realm of agriculture comes the familiar combination of *"sow"* and *"reap"* (11:18; Gal. 6:7–8). The seed here is *"iniquity"* (on

Heb. ʿawlāh, in Proverbs only here, see Hos. 10:13), perverseness, deviation from the right path is the sense, at times with overtures of violence as in Hab. 2:12 where it parallels "bloodshed." The crop is "sorrow" (Heb. ʾāwen; see 6:12, 18) or, even stronger, "calamity," "emptiness," "annihilation." The second metaphor comes from the realm of discipline or corporal punishment. The offender's "rod" with which he would unjustly flog another person will turn to "strike him." This is a better reading than "will fail" and involves the change of only one Hebrew letter. It preserves the boomerang force of the saying which is clearly established in the first line. The rod symbolizes anger or perhaps "arrogance" as the Hebrew word ʿebrāh means in 21:24. Proud disdain with which we batter the rights of others comes back to flay us. Wicked one-upmanship causes the underdogs who have chafed beneath it to unite and pool their energies to pommel the pride out of us. And if others do not tackle that task, God will, as chapter 21 has taught us.

> He who oppresses the poor to increase his *riches,*
> And he who gives to the rich, *will* surely *come* to
>   poverty.
>
> *Prov. 22:16*

This proverb applies the principle of cause and effect to the field of economics. The divine order will produce the opposite of what the unjust person intends. The one who oppresses (Heb. ʿāsaq; 14:31; 28:3; see also Amos 4:1; Mic. 2:2), exploits, or extorts from the "poor" will only "increase his [the poor person's] riches"; in turn, the one who "gives" money, whether ill-gotten gain or bribe, to the "rich" person ultimately contributes to the rich one's "poverty," lack or want (maḥsôr, 6:11; 11:24; 21:5). God protects the abused poor and punishes the greedy rich, by allowing him either to develop extravagant tastes that spend him into insolvency or to make foolish investments which deplete his wealth.

Biblical justice is anything but blind. Though it does not show preference to the prominent or powerful, it does face human sin and greed with both eyes open. When oppression dogs the poor or rigged verdicts plague the innocent, the God of justice expects His people to act and is Himself prepared to act where they do not. "With liberty and justice for all" is the climactic ending of our American pledge of allegiance to the flag. If we are to be "one nation under God," we had better mean what we say.

Words of the Wise

Proverbs 22:17–24:34

CHAPTER TWENTY-THREE

Words of the Wise:
First Collection

Proverbs 22:17–24:22

The editor of Proverbs has clearly signaled that we have left one section of the book—10:1–22:16—and entered another. Here he makes no reference to Solomon (see 1:1; 10:1; 25:1) but labels the section "words of the wise" in the first line of the text, 22:17. We know for sure that this is a section title when we come to 24:23 and read: "These things also belong to the wise."

The two collections, one longer (22:17–24:22) and one shorter (24:23–34), are distinguished by their form as well as their titles. They resemble the teachings of chapters 1–9 more than the two-line sayings of 10:1–22:16. The teacher-student or parent-child relationship is prominent again as the frequent use of "my son" and the first-person speech of the teacher—"my knowledge," "have I not written?" (22:17, 20)—suggest. Calls to attention are prominent, as "hear" or "listen" or "be wise" dot the pages (22:17; 23:19, 22, 26) as they did in the first section of Proverbs. The instructions vary in length and several verses may cluster together around one theme. The dominant proverbial form is admonition, marked by imperative verbs, direct address, and motivation clauses which list the benefits of following ("for") and the risks of not following ("lest") the commands. The topics vary, many of them featuring familiar themes of the teachers but cast in form different from their earlier settings in the book.

Most modern translations agree that "excellent things" in 22:20 should be translated "thirty sayings" (NIV, NEB, Anchor Bible, "thirty precepts"; JB, "thirty chapters"). There is, however, no clear agreement on where the exact divisions lie. My approach identifies some of the calls to attention as separate sayings to be counted among the thirty. The often-debated relationship between these sayings and the thirty chapters of the Egyptian wisdom document named after

Amenemope is discussed in the *Introduction*. It is clear that the materials, whatever their original source, have been thoroughly revamped in terms of Israel's covenant faith and conformed carefully to the belief that Yahweh is Lord of life.

SAYING 1. CALL TO ATTENTION TO THE VALUE OF WISDOM

22:17 Incline your ear and hear the words of the wise,
    And apply your heart to my knowledge;
 18 For *it is* a pleasant thing if you keep them
        within you;
    Let them all be fixed upon your lips,
 19 So that your trust may be in the LORD;
    I have instructed you today, even you.
 20 Have I not written to you excellent things
    Of counsels and knowledge,
 21 That I may make you know the certainty of
        the words of truth,
    That you may answer words of truth
    To those who send to you?

Prov. 22:17–21

The teacher who has lain low during our lengthy journey through the first collection of Solomon's sayings (10:1–22:16) now returns to prominence, speaking to the student directly, intently, and personally as the pronouns *"you"* and *"I"* indicate. Nothing less than full attention will do. Note the imperatives (vv. 17–18): *"incline,"* tilt your head so you don't miss a word; *"hear,"* take it all in and ponder it; *"apply,"* let your whole intellect grasp the meaning and decide how to put it to work; *"let them be fixed,"* build them into your speech with all the firmness of a palace foundation. And note also the nouns (vv. 17–18): *"ear,"* the chief receptacle of wisdom; *"heart,"* the center of thinking, choosing, deciding; *"belly"* (*"within you"* is literally *"in your belly"*), the center of one's being where the emotions affirm the certitude of the decision made by the heart; *"lips,"* the vehicle of communication with which the cycle of learning is repeated, as the learner not only recites the lesson to the teacher but begins to instruct others.

This detailed account of the student's total engagement in the learning process is matched by the range and intensity of the teacher's pedagogy and subject matter. Note the verbs: *"I have instructed,"* have made you to know what I have learned from long experience; *"have I not written,"* taken pains to write them out so that you will have a verbatim list of the thirty sayings to memorize ("write" occurs three times in Proverbs; see also 3:3; 7:3, where the use is figurative—"write them on . . . your heart"; "hear," in contrast, occurs about thirty times); *"I may make you know,"* a repetition of the form used in "I have instructed," the causative use of Hebrew *yāda'* (see at 1:2; 3:6; 4:1).

Likewise, consider the nouns: *"sayings"* (*"words"*) *"of the wise,"* teachings worth learning and repeating because of the authority, ability, and integrity of those who have taught them; *"my knowledge,"* the special understanding based on the experience of how God works in human life; *"counsels,"* clever plans which have a positive connotation here in contrast to their negative use in 1:31: schemes or fancies; *"certainty,"* found only here in the Old Testament is akin to an Aramaic meaning "straightness" or "correctness"; "accuracy" may be the force here; *"words of truth,"* found twice, underscore the utter reliability of the teacher's sayings, a reliability to be matched in the student's recital of them when he is called to account.

The final line of verse 21 casts light on the background of the thirty sayings. *"Those who send to you"* should be read as "those who send you" (NIV's "him who sent" is curious given the plural form of the Heb. participle), that is, commission you to represent them in diplomatic, administrative, or mercantile activities. The student is clearly being trained for official responsibilities where he is not to freelance in the negotiations but to carry information verbatim from one party to another.

Yet even this faithful discharge of duty is not the primary motivation of the instruction. That is found in verse 19, where the punctuation of NKJV needs slight revising. There should be a full stop at the end of verse 18 and a comma after verse 19a. The first line of verse 19 then introduces the purpose of the instruction that follows: *"So that your trust* [Heb. *mibṭāḥ,* see 14:26; 21:22; 25:19] *may be in the Lord."* Crucial to the curriculum was the concern that *"knowledge,"* *"counsels,"* and *"truth"* be connected with the will of Yahweh. This saying is close kin to the stated theme of Proverbs: "The fear of the Lord is the beginning of wisdom" (1:7).

SAYING 2. ADMONITION ON CARE FOR THE POOR

22:22 Do not rob the poor because he *is* poor,
      Nor oppress the afflicted at the gate;

23 For the LORD will plead their cause,
   And plunder the soul of those who plunder
   them.

Prov. 22:22–23

Here the student's administrative duties blend with his commitment to obey the Lord. *"Gate"* puts the command in an official judicial setting, since legal transactions were carried out there. The verbs of exploitation are strong: *"rob"* means to tear possessions away from the owner in a most destructive fashion (28:24); *"oppress"* is literally to *"crush"* (its noun means *"dust"* in Ps. 90:3). *"Because he is poor"* underscores the wickedness of the injustice: the poor (Heb. *dal*, 10:15; 14:31) or *"afflicted"* (Heb. *ʿānî*, 15:15) are at the bottom of the social ladder, without power, recourse, or advocacy. To pick on them just because of their low status and without sound legal grounds is like kicking a sick dog.

It is much worse, in fact. It is a capital cause. Those without human advocates will have Yahweh by their side to press charges (*"plead their cause"* shows again the legal setting of this admonition; see at 23:11; 25:9; Mic. 6:2; 7:9) against their oppressors and to execute the verdict as is in His power. *"Plunder* [Heb. *qābaʿ* means to *"rob God"* in Mal. 3:8–9] *the soul"* or person seems to imply the taking of life. It is a just verdict according to the *lex talionis* (law of equality: eye for eye, tooth for tooth). To rob the poor by selling them as slaves to cover trivial debts (Amos 2:6), by taking an unfair share of the crops they raise (Amos 5:11), by keeping the garments they have pawned as pledge against debts they owe (Amos 2:8), or by confiscating the lands that were part of their family inheritance in order to foreclose on a mortgage (Mic. 2:2) is to rob them of life itself. A capital crime warrants capital punishment, and the Lord Himself will see to it. On the whole subject of injustice see chapter 22.

SAYING 3. ADMONITION ON ASSOCIATING WITH THE ANGRY

22:24 Make no friendship with an angry man,
      And with a furious man do not go,
   25 Lest you learn his ways
      And set a snare for your soul.

Prov. 22:24–25

Levelheadedness, control of temper, and patience are prime requisites for leadership. One way to cultivate these traits is to avoid *"friendship"* with those whose lives are stamped by fury and anger.

"An angry man" (lit., an "owner of anger") and *"a furious man"* (lit., a
"man of heats") are not persons who occasionally let off excess
steam. They are veritable steam engines with subnormal boiling
points and extra loads of fuel. Anger is their path of life (*"ways"*). To
walk that road with them is to put your whole stability and equilibrium in jeopardy, since their path is laced by traps which any
misstep will trigger. *"Snare"* is better read as "striker bar," the latch
that springs the trap. Here, in contrast to Saying 2, the punishment
is more a case of normal cause and effect than divine intention. But
it is no less dangerous.

SAYING 4. ADMONITION ON RASH PLEDGES

> 22:26 Do not be one of those who shakes hands in a
>   pledge,
>   One of those who is surety for debts;
>   27 If you have nothing *with which* to pay,
>   Why should he take away your bed from
>   under you?
>   *Prov. 22:26–27*

Again the admonition or prohibition is based on prudence and
experience. The background of the practice of guaranteeing the obligations of another person by a *"pledge"* of one's own assets as security has been treated at 6:1–5 in this commentary as well as in
chapter 11. *"Shakes"* or strikes *"hands"* suggests a formal agreement,
and the threatened penalty—removal of the *"bed"* while the guaran-
tor is resting on it (*"from under you"*)—pictures, with a touch of humor, the legal obligation. The least that is being said is that no one
should stand surety unless there are ample means to pay the bond if
the third party defaults. The assumption in this as in many of the
other sayings is that the students had the financial means, the reputation for integrity, and the generosity of spirit to be drawn into
such ticklish obligations. The admonition guarded them not against
their tendency to do evil but their temptation to do good glibly or
naively.

SAYING 5. ADMONITION ON MOVING BOUNDARIES

> 22:28 Do not remove the ancient landmark
>   Which your fathers have set.
>   *Prov. 22:28*

The legal expression of this prohibition is voiced in Deut. 19:14. The group in society most apt to suffer abuse in this matter were the poor—note the fatherless in 23:10—who were vulnerable to chiselers, cheats, or sharp traders. The young administrators were urged not to engage in such practices and to forbid others to do so. The instruction only hints at reasons that preclude such conduct: *"ancient"* recalls the parceling out of land as part of the tribal settlements in Joshua's day; *"fathers"* underscores those old agreements and confirms their binding authority. The *"landmark"* or boundary was central to the existence of each family. It symbolized the grace of God who portioned out the land; it represented their survival—no land, no livelihood; it assured their continuity, as vital to them as was their name. God's endorsement of this view comes clear in 23:11.

SAYING 6. QUESTION ON THE IMPORTANCE OF TALENT

22:29 Do you see a man *who* excels in his work?
       He will stand before kings;
       He will not stand before unknown *men*.
                                    Prov. 22:29

The interrogative form, though not clearly marked in Hebrew, seems to be the agreed way to punctuate the first line. The question serves to catch the attention of the hearer and make almost a game out of the proverb. Oral timing would put a space between lines one and two leaving room to guess at what comes next and heightening the suspense. *"Excels"* means sagacious, keen-witted, gifted for the chosen task (Heb. *māhîr* reads "ready" in Ps. 45:1, where the accompanying noun is "writer" or "scribe," an apt comment on the proverb). *"Work"* here speaks of a profession like scribe, courtier, or government official. The reward for the right combination of discipline and skill is access (*"will stand before"*) to *"kings,"* in high government service. The alternative to be avoided is working not merely for lesser lights but for obscure and low-ranked subofficials (*"unknown"*; Heb. *ḥašukkîm* used only here suggests people who work in the "dark") with no notoriety or publicity, the no-names of the bureaucracy. The proverb is geared to encourage diligence and practice by offering celebrity not obscurity as reward.

Saying 7. Admonition on Etiquette with Royalty

23:1 When you sit down to eat with a ruler,
Consider carefully what *is* before you;
2 And put a knife to your throat
If you *are* a man given to appetite.
3 Do not desire his delicacies,
For they *are* deceptive food.
Prov. 23:1–3

This admonition follows nicely the question of 22:29. If one is to stand before kings, one had better know how to behave. Rule one in this series is to control your *"appetite."* The steps for doing this are clear. First, *"consider carefully"* suggests understanding full well (Heb. root *bîn* appears twice for emphasis) the situation in which you find yourself. *"What is before you"* may include both the food served and the royal scene and personage that go with it. Such occasions are opportunities both to learn and to impress. Gluttony is never a virtue (23:21), much less in this lofty setting. Second, *"put a knife to* [or *"in"*] *your throat"* is a hyperbole that means take whatever drastic steps are necessary to curb your urges, especially if you are a noted trencherman (*"given to appetite"* translates literally *"owner of a ravenous gullet"*). Third, *"do not desire"* large quantities of the royal *"delicacies"* no matter how attractive they look nor how eager your palate is for them. The Hebrew for "delicacies" occurs only in this chapter (v. 6) and in Genesis 27 where it occurs as savory food in the account of the trick that Jacob and Rachel played on Isaac who thought he was eating Esau's gamy cuisine. *"Deceptive food"* may recall that story, but certainly speaks of the seductive nature of special dishes that lure us to eat more than is politic or healthful.

Saying 8. Admonition on Financial Ambition

23:4 Do not overwork to be rich;
Because of your own understanding, cease!
5 Will you set your eyes on that which is not?
· For *riches* certainly make themselves wings;
They fly away like an eagle *toward* heaven.
Prov. 23:4–5

The dangers of greed are well documented in Proverbs (see chaps. 11 and 25 on generosity and chaps. 19 and 26 on wealth). Here they are illustrated in what is almost a cartoon. The imperatives are apt and biting: *"do not overwork"* entails laboring to the point of collapse through fatigue—"burnout" in our jargon; *"cease"* means "stop right this minute" and for good reason—you yourself perceive sharply (*"understanding"*) the fleeting value of money. Now you see it, now you don't. Quicker than your *"eyes"* can flit to it (*"set"* really means "cause to fly") it disappears. *"Riches"*—the subject here carries over from the thought of the first line—have an uncanny ability to *"make themselves wings"* and head for the sky (*"heaven"*) with the alacrity of an *"eagle"* (the word can also mean "vulture"!). The simile recalls the comics of my youth. When a pitiful character wasted, lost, or was conned out of money, the balloon above his head inevitably pictured a bird with a dollar sign on the chest flapping its wings skyward.

SAYING 9. ADMONITION ON EATING WITH THE STINGY

> 23:6 Do not eat the bread of a miser,
>   Nor desire his delicacies;
>   7 For as he thinks in his heart, so *is* he.
>   "Eat and drink!" he says to you,
>   But his heart is not with you.
>   8 The morsel you have eaten, you will vomit up,
>   And waste your pleasant words.
>
> *Prov. 23:6–8*

Eat carefully with kings (23:1–3) but do not eat at all with *"a miser."* So goes the sage's advice on sociability. "Miser," literally an "evil eye" (28:22), implies more than stinginess. It suggests a wretchedly antisocial behavior that not only resents the *"delicacies"* (see on 23:3) a companion may consume but resents the companion as well, no matter how cordial his *"Eat and drink"* may try to sound. *"Thinks"* may mean "calculate" or "estimate" as though the bitter man were inwardly (*"in his heart"* or "soul") calculating the food consumed and the time wasted. His *"heart"* is not at all in his hospitality (*"with you"*). The tiniest *"morsel"* (the Hebrew root means "crumble") eaten under such emotional duress will make one sick, figuratively if not literally. *"Vomit"* (see 25:16) is the Hebrew verb that describes the fish's expulsion of Jonah (2:11). The whole event miscarries: the food does no good and all attempts at *"pleasant"* (or "sweet") conversation are wasted. The Greek translation is more graphic at verse 7. It likens the bad experience to swallowing a hair (Heb. "hair" and "thinks" in this text have the same consonants) and fighting the consequent irritation that can make one sick.

SAYING 10. ADMONITION ON WASTING WORDS ON FOOLS

> 23:9 Do not speak in the hearing of a fool,
> For he will despise the wisdom of your words.
> *Prov. 23:9*

This brief instruction picks up the theme of wasted words from verse 8. Time is precious, and speaking, especially in teaching or counseling, takes energy. The prudent, disciplined leader will guard both zealously. *"Wisdom"* (Heb. *śēkēl;* see on 3:4; 12:8), the art of making perceptive and successful decisions, is not a commodity to be wasted. Having another *"despise"* what you have worked hard to garner is an intolerable experience and more than adequate reason to avoid conversation with someone who has proven to be totally unappreciative or even thoroughly resentful of it.

SAYING 11. ADMONITION ON MOVING BOUNDARIES

> 23:10 Do not remove the ancient landmark,
> Nor enter the fields of the fatherless;
> 11 For their Redeemer is mighty;
> He will plead their cause against you.
> *Prov. 23:10–11*

The first line repeats the admonition of 22:28. The second line shifts the emphasis from "your fathers" and Israel's past history, when the land plots were assigned to the families, to *"the fatherless"* (orphans, here only in Proverbs; see Deut. 10:18; Jer. 5:28; Ps. 68:6) who had no human kin to stand up for their rights if their boundaries were invaded and their land used or confiscated. The motivation sentences (introduced by *"for,"* v. 11) add further to the thought of 22:28 and give the highest possible reasons for obeying the admonitions. *"Redeemer"* (see Heb. *gōʾēl,* Deut. 19:12; Ruth 2:26; 3:9, etc.) marks God as the near-kinsman who freely and forcefully defends (*"pleads"*) *"the cause"* (see 2:23, for legal use of *rîb*) of the helpless. Their cause becomes His. To pick on orphans is to risk the wrath of the *"mighty"* God (Heb. *ḥāzāq*, here only in Proverbs; see Job 5:15; also passages like Exod. 3:19 and Deut. 3:24 where it describes God's incomparable power to rescue His people with a lifted hand), whose redeeming strength was well attested in Israel's own experience.

SAYING 12. ADMONITION TO WISDOM

23:12 Apply your heart to instruction,
And your ears to words of knowledge.
Prov. 23:12

The wholehearted commitment to the teacher's lessons is called for once again (see 22:17–21), as the instructions or specific patterns of behaviors are underscored with a general command to give full attention. (On *"heart"* and *"ears"* as organs of heeding, obeying, and deliberately choosing see 22:17.) *"Knowledge"* serves as a summation of God's will and way (see on 1:2, 22:19–21). *"Apply"* implies deliberate discipline. Literally it says, Take your heart in hand and bring it into the presence of *"instruction."* The latter word pictures the cost of learning: correction, even punishment and pain (see Heb. *mûsār* at 1:2).

SAYING 13. ADMONITION ON DISCIPLINE OF CHILDREN

23:13 Do not withhold correction from a child,
For *if* you beat him with a rod, he will not die.
14 You shall beat him with a rod,
And deliver his soul from hell.
Prov. 23:13–14

That theme of painful *"correction"* (23:12) is amplified in an instruction that centers in corporal discipline of children; see chapters 20 and 29. This saying is a counsel to consistency. Correction is to be applied regularly as needed and continued until the child is fully grown. Hebrew *na'ar* covers an age range that includes what we would call *"young adult"*; Jeremiah used it to describe his youthfulness at the time of his call to prophesy (Jer. 1:6). It is also a counsel to restraint. Discipline with a stick (*"rod"*) is not designed to wound or maim but to teach lessons of care, caution, and obedience. Despite the yells, shrieks, and tears of the willful youngster, death will not be the result. *"He will not die"* in no way justifies child abuse. All that the proverbs teach would preclude that. Its point seems to be, "Don't let the young one bluff you to *'withhold correction'* by shouts, protests, or accusations. 'I hate you,' 'I'll never speak to you again,' 'I'm going to run away,' 'You're a bad daddy,' 'You're killing me'"—none of these outbursts is accurate under normal circumstances; they should not deter us from our parental duties to correct our children when they violate the rules of the household. Though rod is mentioned twice, the emphasis is on the firmness of the discipline not on the specific means. Suggestions of nonphysical yet very effective means of discipline are found elsewhere in the commentary (see "Firm Hands" in chap. 20).

The saying is also a counsel to concern. The parent personally is to administer the correction, as *"you,"* emphatic in Hebrew, informs us (v. 14). But the parent is to act not to vent her or his spleen at the young one's expense but in love to save (*"deliver"*) the child's life (*"soul"*) from the threat of an early death (*"hell"* is Heb. *sh°ôl*, the grave). Uncorrected waywardness leads to rasher acts of disobedience, which, if left unchecked, can be literally life-threatening. Parents who carelessly or fearfully turned their backs on substance abuse, on petty thievery, on modest acts of cruelty or violence, on companionship with unruly gang members have learned this lesson from a sheriff's phone call, a judge's verdict, or a coroner's report. Love may have to inflict moderate pain to *"deliver"* a child from ultimate pain.

SAYING 14. EXPRESSION OF HOPE BY THE TEACHER

> 23:15 My son, if your heart is wise,
> My heart will rejoice—indeed, I myself;
> 16 Yes, my inmost being will rejoice
> When your lips speak right things.
>> *Prov. 23:15–16*

This saying echoes the thoughts of Saying 1 (22:17–20) by emphasizing *"wise"* thinking and upright (*"right things"* suggests ethical integrity; Heb. *mêyshārîm*; 1:3; 23:31) speech. The call to attention in the earlier passage did not make explicit how much the teacher cared about the pupil's response. Here the whole relationship—like that of the parent and child in Saying 13 (23:13–14) is reciprocal. What happens to the one deeply affects the other. In fact, Saying 14 would serve well as a summary of the parental speech to the child about to be disciplined in Saying 13. The structure is chiastic (reversed order): the first and last lines picture the pupil's conduct in thinking (*"heart"*) and speaking (*"lips"*); the middle two lines describe the teacher's reaction—*"rejoice"* and *"exult"* or *"thrill with the joy of victory,"* as the second *"rejoice"* (Heb. ʿālaz; Hab. 3:18; Pss. 28:7; 60:6; 149:5) may be translated. The structure casts the spotlight on the pupil's behavior, mentioned first and last, and only secondarily on the teacher's intellectual (*"heart"*) and emotional (*"inmost being"* is literally *"liver,"* Heb. kilyāh used here only in Proverbs; for physical use, see Lev. 3:4; for figurative, see Ps. 16:7) reactions. The apostle John knew full well the meaning of this saying (3 John 4).

SAYING 15. ADMONITION ON FEAR OF THE LORD

23:17 Do not let your heart envy sinners,
　　　But *be zealous* for the fear of the LORD all the
　　　　day;
　18 For surely there is a hereafter,
　　　And your hope will not be cut off.
　　　　　　　　　　　　　　　Prov. 23:17–18

This admonition touches on a subject familiar to Israel's teachers: how should we react when persons who spurn God's way seem to get what they want and go unpunished (see Ps. 37:37)? In such cases we may be tempted to *"envy* ["be jealous of"; Heb. qānāʾ; 3:31; 24:1; 24:19, all negative in meaning] sinners" (see on 1:10), who while missing the mark of responsible conduct gain rewards that ought to be reserved for those who live in the *"fear of the Lord"* (see 1:7 and chap. 16). They are the ones to be envied, is the thrust of the Hebrew which assumes that the verb carries over to the second line in a positive use like that of Yahweh's envy, jealousy, or zeal for His land in Joel 2:18. *"All the day"* is counsel to patient and consistent obedience as the motivation in v. 18 makes explicit. *"Hereafter"* does not necessarily point to life after death, but to life further down the road when the sinners' missteps will catch up with them and the God-fearers' steadfastness will be honored. *"Hope"* (see at chap. 13)—maintained over the long haul—*"will not be cut off"* and be left frustrated. The justice of God will come to pass for those who obey (*"fear"*) Him and wait. Good counsel is all of this for a generation conditioned by the cheap, tricky, and instant solutions of television comedy (thirty minutes) or drama (sixty minutes).

SAYING 16. CALL TO ATTENTION

23:19 Hear, my son, and be wise;
     And guide your heart in the way.
                                              Prov. 23:19

Again the teacher pauses from the list of specific interactions to make sure he has the pupil's attention to and enthusiasm for the wisdom being purveyed (see 22:17–20; 23:12). To *"be wise,"* after all, is more than a series of admonitions on the details of conduct, though it is certainly that. It is nothing less than a *"way"* (see on 1:19, 31) of life whose every step one must *"guide"* (Heb. ʾashshēr; see Isa. 1:17; 3:12; 9:16), choice by choice, thought by thought, decision by decision (*"heart"*).

SAYING 17. ADMONITION ON TEMPERANCE

23:20 Do not mix with winebibbers,
        Or with gluttonous eaters of meat;
   21 For the drunkard and the glutton will come to
        poverty,
        And drowsiness will clothe *a man* with rags.
                                              Prov. 23:20–21

The imperative here is a simple warning against spending time (*"mix"* in Hebrew is simply *"be"*) with people who drink to the point of inebriation (*"winebibbers"*) or eat *"meat"* to the point of a debasing extravagance (28:7). On the peculiar temptation of young men to engage in these two excesses, see Deut. 21:20. Though both drunkenness and gluttony represented waste in an austere society where both wine and meat tended to be saved for religious offerings and festive meals, it is the lazy stupor they induce that causes them to be proscribed here. *"Drowsiness"* (only here as a noun; see Ps. 121:3–4 for verb) explains the *"poverty"* in the motivation sentences (v. 21; note *"for"*). And *"rags"* (bits of torn and shredded clothes; the word is used to describe the division of the prophet's mantle into twelve rags to symbolize the breakup of Rehoboam's kingdom; 1 Kings 11:30–31) dramatize the extent of the poverty. Anyone who has dealt with alcoholics can testify to the expense of the habit in money, in loss of focus on other aspects of life, and in the inability to work to one's potential with regularity. Administrators on whose reliability, accuracy, and alertness the people had a right to depend have no business aping the ways of lazy carousers.

SAYING 18. CALL TO ATTENTION TO WISDOM OF PARENTS

23:22 Listen to your father who begot you,
And do not despise your mother when she
is old.

23 Buy the truth, and do not sell *it*,
Also wisdom and instruction and
understanding.

24 The father of the righteous will greatly rejoice,
And he who begets a wise *child* will delight in
him.

25 Let your father and your mother be glad,
And let her who bore you rejoice.
Prov. 23:22–25

Commands, whether imperatives (2d person) or jussives (3d person) dominate this instruction. Verses 22, 23, and 25 are admonitions, while verse 24 serves as motivation, giving reasons to support the commands, though the usual "for" at the beginning is missing. Both parents are featured in the manner of 1:8, but with repetition and elaboration. The mentions of *"mother"* (vv. 22, 25) and *"her who bore"* (v. 25) suggest that the setting of this passage is the home not the school or the court. It may be, inasmuch as all parental references are in third-person form (in contrast, see chap. 4), that the teacher is reminding the pupil to pay respect to what he has been and is being taught at home.

Three implicit arguments support the commands to *"listen"* (1:5, 8) and not despise (1:7; 30:17). First, the intimate bond of procreation—*"who begot you"* (v. 22) and *"who bore you"* (v. 25)—calls for honor, respect, and appreciation; children's very existence derives from the parents. We cannot reject them without losing something of our own identity and dignity. Even *"when she is old,"* a victim of the aging processes that must have taken a cruel toll in antiquity, given numbers of pregnancies, arduous physical labor, and only primitive medical care, she was still the mother, still to be respected for the wisdom garnered at the price of stooped shoulders, gnarled hands, and wrinkled face.

Second, their teaching was to be treasured (buy and do not sell; 4:5, 7; 18:15) for its basic reliability—as *"truth"* (3:3; 8:7), as *"wisdom,"* as *"instruction,"* as *"understanding"* (1:2). The bunching of synonyms demonstrates the value and range of what they learned. It was the parents' greatest legacy to their children, more valuable through life than goods or lands. Third, obedience (see Exod. 20:12; Deut. 5:16 for the legal background of these proverbs) was a source of continual gladness and joy to the parents, whose children combined the loyal integrity of *"the righteous"* (2:20; chap. 10) with the God-fearing perceptiveness of the *"wise."*

SAYING 19. CALL TO ATTENTION

23:26 My son, give me your heart,
  And let your eyes observe my ways.
        Prov. 23:26

This call to full trust in and conformity to (*"give me your heart"*) the teacher's instruction is especially apt in light of the saying that follows. Some things may be learned for oneself with relatively little risk of serious damage. Dalliance with a harlot (23:27–28) is not an example of low-risk experimentation. Far better to learn painlessly from a wise teacher! The teacher's integrity and wisdom may be seen as well as heard. *"Observe"* means to watch over something with the vigilance of a sentinel. The call is not merely to see what the wise man does in his course of life (*"my ways"*) but to keep one's feet to that righteous and chaste path as well.

SAYING 20. DESCRIPTION OF A HARLOT

23:27 For a harlot *is* a deep pit,
  And a seductress *is* a narrow well.
 28 She also lies in wait as *for* a victim,
  And increases the unfaithful among men.
        Prov. 23:27–28

It is possible that Sayings 19 and 20 should be combined, with verse 26 conveying the general admonitions and verses 27–28 the specific motivation which gives the call to attention both its context and its reason. We return here to a theme well developed in the beginning instructions of Chapters 2, 5–7. The *"harlot"* (6:26) or *"seductress"* (2:16; 5:10, 20; 6:24; 7:5) is pictured as ineluctably dangerous in language borrowed from hunting. *"Deep pit"* (see also

22:14) translates the Hebrew used in Jeremiah's complaint at the plot of his enemies to capture him in 18:20, 22. The *"narrow well"* had steep sides and sloped outward from the smaller opening to the larger bottom, like the famous Bottle Dungeon beneath the castle in St. Andrews, Scotland, where the infamous Cardinal David Beaton imprisoned some of the Reformation leaders. The same Hebrew word depicts a place to capture or retain captured animals in 2 Sam. 23:20 (see also Jer. 38:6–8). Brigandage furnishes another word picture of the seductress' ploys. *"Lies in wait"* is *"*sets an ambush*"* (7:12), while *"victim"* (a Hebrew word used only here in Old Testament) more likely means *"*bandit*"* (NIV), since the verbal form reads *"*snatch away*"* in Job 9:12. The picture of thievery may continue in the last line if we slightly revise the Hebrew spelling along lines suggested by Mitchell Dahood: *"*She collects garments (Hebrew consonants are the same as those of unfaithful) from men.*"* *"Increases the unfaithful"* (or *"*treacherously deceitful*"*; see at 2:22), however, is a readily explainable summary clause of the harlot's devastation. Adultery is treachery to a spouse, and fornication, intercourse before marriage, is unfaithfulness, implicitly at least, to a future covenant partner. In either case, the emphasis of the whole verse is on the exploitive wiles of the harlot and the dreadful menace to the man who falls into her clutches. All that we have learned in our modern era about the social, emotional, and physical dangers of prostitution only confirms and enhances the wisdom of the Hebrew teacher.

SAYING 21. QUESTIONS AND ADMONITIONS ON DRUNKENNESS

23:29 Who has woe?
Who has sorrow?
Who has contentions?
Who has complaints?
Who has wounds without cause?
Who has redness of eyes?
30 Those who linger long at the wine,
Those who go in search of mixed wine.
31 Do not look on the wine when it is red,
When it sparkles in the cup,
When it swirls around smoothly;
32 At the last it bites like a serpent,
And stings like a viper.
33 Your eyes will see strange things,
And your heart will utter perverse things.

34 Yes, you will be like one who lies down in the
    midst of the sea,
Or like one who lies at the top of the mast,
    saying:
35 "They have struck me, *but* I was not hurt;
They have beaten me, but I did not feel *it.*
When shall I awake, that I may seek another
    drink?"

Prov. 23:29–35

The instructions return to the topic of Saying 17 (23:20–21) but
with different form and emphases. Earlier the focus was on the drinking companions and the economic consequences of inebriation. Here
attention is fixed on the lure of the *"wine"* itself and the mental delu-
sions of those held in the sway of its stupefactions. The form of Saying 17 is the simple combination of admonition (v. 20) and motivation
(v. 21), each with two parallel lines. The longer saying (vv. 29–35) is
an artful combination of questions (v. 29) and answers (v. 30) that
comprise something like a riddle (see Samson's example in Judg.
14:12–18) followed by a brief admonition (v. 31) and a lengthy motivation (vv. 32–35) that has no formal introduction, like "for" or "lest."

The riddle-questions serve to emphasize the benumbing and be-
fuddling affects of drunkenness. There are six of them, each beginning with *"who has,"* literally "to whom is" in Hebrew: (1) *"woe,"*
elsewhere in the Old Testament is an exclamation in the form of
"woe to . . ."; here it serves as a noun, synonymous with "trouble";
(2) *"sorrow,"* used only here in the Old Testament, seems also to have
been an exclamation, like "Alas!"; it voices the frustrations of life
gone wrong; (3) *"contentions"* (see 6:14) is a frequent word in
Proverbs to describe the feisty quarrelsomeness which is so disruptive to community; (4) *"complaints"* like those of Hannah's prayer
(1 Sam. 1:16) express anguish over one's lot in life; (5) *"wounds* [see
20:30; 27:6; and Lamech's song of vengeance in Gen. 4:23] *without
cause* [1:11, 17; 3:30]" are needlessly inflicted cuts and bruises, the
price paid for either losing motor coordination or picking fights with
others; (6) *"redness of eyes"* means "bloodshot" eyes (NEB, NIV, Anchor
Bible), "blackened eyes" (Byington in McKane, p. 393) or "lustreless"
eyes (McKane, p. 393); "redness" is derived from a root meaning
"dark" and serves as a compliment in Jacob's blessing on Judah
(Gen. 49:12):

His eyes are darker than wine.

The line in Proverbs, not at all intended to be complimentary, may be a sarcastic play on Jacob's metaphor.

The answer (v. 30) emphasizes the extent and intensity of the drinking bouts. *"Those who linger"* (or *"delay"*; see Eccles. 5:4) and *"those who go in search of"* (*"explore,"* 18:17; 25:12; 28:1) are both participial forms, implying continued or frequently repeated behavior. What is pictured is not a congenial glass of wine over a meal graced with cordial conversation. It is compulsive behavior on the part of those who linger to consume as much wine as possible and who dig into every opportunity to find and gulp down *"mixed wine,"* perhaps thinned with water and spiced with honey and pepper, a kind of mead apparently used in pagan religious ceremonies (Isa. 65:11).

The brief admonition (v. 31) warns against the hypnotic impact of *"wine"* on those who crave it. There is no way that they can gaze at it without craving it. Its *"red"* color, its *"sparkle"* (lit., *"its eye"*) as the light catches its bubbles, its smooth (*"straight,"* without interruption; Song of Sol. 7:9) swirling motions as one rotates its *"cup"*—all of these hold an irresistible fascination for the winebibber. *"Do not drink it"* would be wasted words, once the tempted person takes the first look and feels the caress of the cup in the hand.

Attractive at the beginning, but mind-addling *"at the last"*—so it goes with those who succumb to the temptation (v. 32). They are snake bit (v. 32), bleary eyed, and tongue unhinged. Dosed with the venom of the *"serpent"* and doused in the poisons that *"secrete"* (as *"sting"* should be retranslated) from a *"viper's"* fangs, the intemperate drinker is gripped in a toxic, catatonic stupor. Nothing works right (v. 33): *"your* [the personal tone continues from the imperative verb of verse 31] *eyes . . . see strange* ["foreign," "outlandish"] *things; your heart* [the ultimate source of all speech—the mind and will] *[speaks] perverse* [topsy-turvy, all-mixed-up (see Heb. *tahpukāh* at 2:12, 14; 8:13; 10:31–32)] *things."*

This delirium is aptly illustrated by a nautical scene (vv. 34–35). Disoriented like a sleepy, seasick sailor (*"midst of the sea"* implies a boat as the parallel line indicates), the drunk lies down only to feel the floor or ground heaving and falling under him like a storm-tossed skiff. Where on the boat he lies is not clear. *"Mast"* is variously translated "tackle" (McKane), "rigging" (NIV) or "lookout" (NASB note); the word seems to be related to the Hebrew for *"rope."* From the exclamations quoted in verse 35, we would guess that the ropes were on deck, perhaps coiled as "tackle," since the drunkard's sensation is not merely of swaying as on a tipsy mast but of being pummeled ("*struck*") and hammered ("*beaten*" is the same Hebrew word that describes Jael's deathblow against Sisera in Judg. 5:26). Yet like the stupefied sailor disoriented by *mal de mer*, the drunkard feels no great pain. His one thought is for his head to clear ("*awake*") so that he can have the concentration to go look for ("*seek*") "*another drink.*" Bleak humor this is, calculated in its pathetic ridiculousness to warn the student of the immense dangers of letting alcohol seize the upper hand. "Awake" in 6:22 marks the time to listen to the commands and teachings of wise parents. "Awake" in 23:35 signals the occasion to repeat the devastating cycle of drink and delirium. The contrast shows how treacherously alcoholism plays hob with every decent human value.

SAYING 22. ADMONITION ON ENVY OF EVIL PERSONS

24:1 Do not be envious of evil men,
Nor desire to be with them;
2 For their heart devises violence,
And their lips talk of troublemaking.
Prov. 24:1–2

The apparent freedom of "*evil men,*" especially those who flaunt the conventions of society and seem to get away with it, has a way of causing even the most staid of us to "*be envious*" (see at 23:17) at times. A great deal of modern entertainment—whether short story, novel, film, or ballad—is based on the celebration of the wickedly unconventional. It banks on the fact that we as audience members have a perverse attraction, even affection, for those who act out the mischief that we only dream of. This saying summarizes the thought of 1:10–19 and of Saying 15 (23:17–18). It differs from the latter by not stressing the fate of the wicked but by stating succinctly the evil of their ways and words: "*violence*" or "*destruction*" dominates the cogitations ("*devises*" is literally "meditate" or "murmur" 8:7; 15:28; Pss. 1:2; 2:1) of their "*heart*" and thus shapes all their plans and decisions; "*troublemaking*" (Heb. ʿāmāl is a favorite word of Ecclesiastes and has a range of meanings from "grueling labor" to "mischief," which is its force here) is the central theme of their conversations. They are bad company indeed for any who care for the welfare of society and want to see no effort spared to work for righteousness, peace, and stability.

SAYING 23. DESCRIPTIONS OF WISDOM'S IMPORTANCE

24:3 Through wisdom a house is built,
    And by understanding it is established;
  4 By knowledge the rooms are filled
    With all precious and pleasant riches.

  5 A wise man *is* strong,
    Yes, a man of knowledge increases strength;
  6 For by wise counsel you will wage your own
      war,
    And in a multitude of counselors *there is* safety.

  7 Wisdom *is* too lofty for a fool;
    He does not open his mouth in the gate.
                                    Prov. 24:3–7

While many commentators and versions, including NKJV, have divided these verses into separate sayings, I have chosen to treat them as a single saying in which the value of wisdom is applied to three central spheres of Israel's life: (1) the home (*"house"*) whose architecture and decor demonstrate the importance of wisdom (vv. 3–4); (2) the battlefield (*"war"*) where success is more dependent on prudence than on power (vv. 5–6); (3) the seat of governance (*"gate"*) in which issues of consequence must be settled by sagacious debate not by the prating of *"a fool"* (v. 7).

There are no admonitions here, only sentences which describe how wisdom works. Only by implication do they call for action, though verse 6 contains a motivation couplet similar to those that explain the commands of admonitions. The use of synonyms like *"understanding"* (v. 3; Heb. *tᵉbûnāh*, 2:2, 6 and seventeen other places in Proverbs), *"knowledge"* (vv. 3–5; Heb. *da'at*, 1:4, 7 and in three dozen other verses in Proverbs), and *"wise counsel"* (or "strategy," v. 6; Heb. *taḥbulôt*, 1:5 and four other uses in Proverbs) serve both to heighten the importance of *"wisdom"* (vv. 3, 5, 7) and to broaden the range of meanings it carries as the central factor in keeping stable the personal, social, and political life of the nation.

The house built *"through wisdom"* (v. 3) is not the allegorical structure that houses wisdom's banquet in 9:1–5. It is a wise person's house, gracefully designed, solidly erected (*"established"*), and beautifully furnished with *"precious"* (Heb. *yāqār*, 1:13; 3:15) and *"pleasant"* (lit., "sweet," "lovely"; Heb. *nā'îm*, 22:18; 23:8; Song of Sol. 1:16) objects that take wealth (*"riches"*; Heb. *hôn*, 1:13; 3:9) to acquire. The house itself and the bounty that fills its rooms are patent evidence that the owner's wisdom has been blessed of God. The sayings that forbid envy (23:17–18; 24:1–2; Pss. 37; 73) make clear that the teachers held no automatic and ironclad connection between wisdom and prosperity. They were very sure, however, that the odds of life, given the divine order that governs it, highly favored the wise over the fool who almost always lacked the skill, patience, discipline, and taste to build and equip a graceful dwelling. In a society that was still learning what it meant to walk by faith the tangible, present rewards were a keen incentive to follow God's ways.

The military sphere (war) is obviously the setting of verses 5–6. But the precise meaning of verse 5 is not so clear. Most commentators and many versions, following the Greek translation take it as a double comparison:

> Wisdom prevails over strength,
> knowledge over brute force.
>
> *NEB*

More literally the Hebrew text, which has to be slightly emended, reads like this:

> Mightier is the wise man than the strong one,
> and the man of knowledge than the one who
>   increases strength.

The motivations (note *"for"*) of verse 6 then bring the whole picture into focus by telling us how war is won: not by strength but by *"wise counsel."* *"Your own"* describes the wise leader's place in Israel's military strategy, as he fights a war that has great consequence for him and his comrades. *"Multitude of counselors"* (11:14) describes the group of planners whose agreement has devised the strategies that lead to *"safety"* (lit., *"salvation"*; Heb. *tᵉshûʿāh,* 21:31). The point is not merely the number of advisers but the consensus that they achieve.

The saying ends at the *"gate"* (1:21; 8:3; 22:22), where wisdom is supremely valued as the keystone of politics and jurisprudence (v. 7). The wisdom required to settle crucial community issues is simply beyond the reach (*"too lofty"*) of a fool. He can make no contribution to the discussion. Consequently, whether by intimidation, self-restraint, or by the insistence of the elders he keeps his mouth shut.

SAYING 24. DESCRIPTIONS OF THE EVILS OF FOLLY

24:8 He who plots to do evil
    Will be called a schemer.
  9 The devising of foolishness *is* sin,
    And the scoffer *is* an abomination to men.
                                            Prov. 24:8–9

This saying forms a virtual antithesis to Saying 23. There the multifaceted contribution of wisdom to personal prosperity, military success, and legal equity was celebrated. Here we leave the too lofty (v. 7) heights of wisdom and view the dregs of society. *"Plots,"* *"schemer"* (lit., *"master of schemes"*; on Heb. *mᵉzimmāh*, "schemes," "devices," see its positive use at 1:4; its negative, at 14:17), *"devising"* or "intrigue" (Heb. *zimmāh*, 10:2; 21:27) all imply willful, calculated, intentional malice. Nothing is explosive or spontaneous here. With gimlet-eyed intensity and cold-blooded reckoning (on "plots," Heb. *ḥāshab*, see 16:9; Hos. 7:15) these enemies of society have charted hurt to their neighbors and ruin to their communities. And at the bottom rung of the social order we find once more the *"scoffer"* (see 1:22; 3:34). He not only schemes in private but snickers and smirks in public, to the utter horror (on *"abomination,"* see 3:32) of the whole society (*"men"* translates *ᵓādām*, "human beings"). Since "scoffer" refers to a person, it seems best, with Greek and Latin versions, to give a parallel concrete meaning to *"foolishness"* and read *"the devising of a fool"* is *"sin"* (Heb. *ḥaṭṭāᵓt*, 5:22; 10:16), a complete missing of God's standards of justice and righteousness.

SAYING 25. DESCRIPTION AND ADMONITION ON HELPING OTHERS

24:10 *If* you faint in the day of adversity,
     Your strength *is* small.

   11 Deliver *those who* are drawn toward death,
      And hold back *those* stumbling to the
         slaughter.
   12 If you say, "Surely we did not know this,"
      Does not He who weighs the hearts consider *it?*
      He who keeps your soul, does He *not* know *it?*
      And will He *not* render to *each* man according
         to his deeds?
                                            Prov. 24:10–12

Our attention is turned back to the way wise persons ought to conduct themselves. Fools and cynics may hatch their plots to devastate their neighbor (Saying 24); the prudent behave otherwise. They stand ready to help, especially where the cause of justice is at stake. I take these three verses to be a unit, though many treat verse 10 as an independent saying. To relate it to what follows, we understand *"day of adversity"* (v. 10) to describe the circumstances of pending *"death"* and threatening *"slaughter"* posited in verse 11. The day is distressful (Heb. ṣārāh, constricting, narrowing, pressure-packed; see the *"narrow well"* in 23:27, for the literal use of the word) not only for the person addressed but for his neighbors who are being manhandled without the due process of law. Their adversity becomes the test of his *"strength"* (v. 10), both physical and moral. *"If you faint"* (Heb. *rph* in the form used here can describe slack, idle, disheartened, or dawdling behavior; 18:9; Josh. 18:3) you have demonstrated the *"small"* (lit., *"narrow"*; Heb. ṣar, a pun on ṣārāh, adversity, in line one) stuff of which you are made.

The admonition (v. 11) counsels courageous actions which are the opposite of fainting: (1) *"deliver"* (*"snatch,"* *"rescue"*) those who are being led away (*"drawn"*) *"toward death,"* whether literally as though accused of a capital crime or figuratively as if assigned to a soul-destroying oppression; (2) *"hold back"* [*"hang on to them to protect them"*; Heb. ḥśk; see 21:26; Gen. 22:12, 16 where Abraham did not withhold Isaac from being offered to the Lord] *those stumbling"* (lit., *"tottering"*), perhaps from being beaten or bound *"to the slaughter"*; again it may be figurative or literal.

The explanation or motivation (v. 12) makes clear that to deliver and to hold back (v. 11) were righteous acts and therefore utterly obligatory. They must have been attempts to (1) thwart oppression and exploitation of the poor, say, by taking their livelihood and selling them into slavery; (2) foil false arrests that could lead to harsh punishment without fair trial; (3) break up gang violence in the streets and thus save innocent citizens from physical harm. Officials had responsibility for justice and peace. They could not plead ignorance—*"we did not know this"*—of circumstances with which it was their duty to be familiar. They were accountable to the highest Authority, who knew their *"hearts"* and rewarded (*"render"* is literally *"cause to return"*) their *"deeds"* on a personal (*"each man"*) basis. God is not named, but the description of his activities—*"weighs* [or examines the inward motives according to his set standard; G. R. Driver in McKane, p. 402] *the hearts* [see 21:2 and 16:2 for identical or similar wording]" and *"keeps* [may be *"guards"* but here means "watches closely" so as to hold accountable] *your soul*"—leaves no doubt that the rewarding/judging official is the Lord of the covenant. He alone "perceives accurately" (*"considers"*; Heb. *byn*; see 2:5, 9); He alone will *"know"* what people do and why they do it. Earlier (chap. 22) the active quality of Hebrew justice was described. Nowhere in the Bible does that quality have clearer illustration than in this saying.

SAYING 26. ADMONITION ON THE DELIGHT OF WISDOM

24:13 My son, eat honey because *it is* good,
And the honeycomb *which is* sweet to your
taste;
14 So *shall* the knowledge of wisdom *be* to your
soul;
If you have found *it*, there is a prospect,
And your hope will not be cut off.
Prov. 24:13–14

This saying may contain a double message: (1) nutritional and gustatory value of *"honey"* (see 16:24; 25:16, 27; note the limits placed on the amount of honey in the last two verses) which for the ancients was the most handy source of sugar and the energy it supplied; (2) the delight and profit of *"wisdom"* which never disappoints in the rewards it offers. *"So"* (v. 14) makes clear that the second message is the primary one, with verse 13 functioning largely as a comparison. One reading of verse 14 is to carry over *"sweet"* (Heb. *mātôg*, 16:24) and *"good"* and have them modify *"knowledge"* and *"wisdom"*:

so is knowledge [sweet] and wisdom [good] for your
soul.
Anchor Bible

An alternate rendering would retain the imperative form of the Masoretic Text (somewhat obscured in NKJV):

So know that wisdom is [good and sweet] for your
soul.

In any case it is the rewards and results of wisdom that are the proof of the pudding: *"prospect"* (Heb. *'aḥᵃrît*) is what happens after a considerable span of time, which may be woe (14:13) or weal (23:18).

Here it is obviously weal as shown by the parallel note of imperishable (*"not be cut off"*) *"hope"* (see 10:28). Patient waiting for God to bring the blessings which are promised to those who go His way is made more than tolerable by the fact that wisdom is not a nasty-tasting medicine but a comb rich with honey.

SAYING 27. ADMONITION ON VIOLENCE

> 24:15 Do not lie in wait, O wicked *man*, against the
>   dwelling of the righteous;
>   Do not plunder his resting place;
>   16 For a righteous *man* may fall seven times
>   And rise again,
>   But the wicked shall fall by calamity.
>   *Prov. 24:15–16*

The long-range vindication and prosperity of the wise affirmed in Saying 26 is documented here. The motivation tells us how (v. 16). The *"righteous"* person, loyal to the Lord and His people, may come on hard times (*"fall"*) repeatedly—*"seven"* is a number symbolic of fullness or completeness—but each time he will *"rise,"* as the Lord, whose hand is at work though His name is not mentioned, vindicates him in due season (see the delayed timing of 23:18; 24:14). *"Wicked"* people (the noun is plural here, but singular in v. 15) are made to stumble (*"fall"* in v. 16 translates two different Hebrew words; the second, *kāshal* describes stumbling over an obstacle or being tripped up; 4:12, 19; see noun form at 16:18) and never get up. *"Calamity"* (Heb. *rā'āh*, evil or disaster) hits them as divine judgment and lays them low once for all.

All this being true, the wicked man is told that it makes no sense to set ambushes (*"lie in wait"*; 1:11; 23:28) against the *"dwelling"* or estate (Heb. *n°wēh* often means "pasture" and by extension the "home" where one eats and rests; 3:33) *"of the righteous person."* Nor is it profitable to vex him by making off (*"plunder"*) with goods or property from *"his resting place"* (again a word drawn from pastoral vocabulary: the place where sheep and cattle lie down to rest; Isa. 65:10). "Dwelling" becomes a figure for the security and relaxation due one in his own home. The unusual nouns for "house" seem to be deliberately chosen to show what a mindless thing it is to disturb the peace of those whose prosperity God will take endless pains to restore.

Saying 28. Admonition on Gloating over Enemies

24:17 Do not rejoice when your enemy falls,
　　　And do not let your heart be glad when he
　　　　stumbles;
　　18 Lest the LORD see *it*, and it displease Him,
　　　And He turn away His wrath from him.

Prov. 24:17–18

Both theme (the fate of an *"enemy"*) and language (*"falls,"* *"stumbles"*) connect this saying with the preceding one. This admonition seems to be one of the series of checks and balances characteristic of the teachings of Proverbs. Saying 27 made clear the permanent fall of the wicked. That fate is built into the very order of life as God has set it up. Yet the righteous person is not to *"rejoice"* or *"be glad"* at that fate, as though he could take credit for it or God was somehow obligated to take his side in all controversies. The Lord, who weighs and watches our hearts (24:12), will *"see"* our self-centered gloating, which will *"displease"* (lit., "and it will be evil in his eyes") him. Should He *"turn away His wrath"* (see Amos 1:3, etc., for similar language) from the enemy, He may well redirect it on the self-righteous gloater: "your glee may well be a more punishable sin than all the guilt of your enemy" (Kidner, p. 155). Humane treatment of a personal enemy—war does not appear directly as the background of any these statements—is a repeated biblical theme (Exod. 23:4–5; Prov. 25:21–22; Matt. 5:43–45).

Saying 29. Admonition on Envy of Evil Ones

24:19 Do not fret because of evildoers,
　　　Nor be envious of the wicked;
　　20 For there will be no prospect for the evil *man*;
　　　The lamp of the wicked will be put out.

Prov. 24:19–20

The familiar theme is sounded once again (23:17–18; 24:1–2). Here the motivation that discourages envy of *"evildoers"* who seem to prosper is the judgment that awaits them. In contrast to the righteous for whom the long-term *"prospect"* is full of hope no matter how harsh their present may be, *"the evil"* and *"the wicked"* persons have *"no prospect"* (Heb. ʾaḥʰrît; see 24:14) except for the strong possibility of premature death, expressed in the metaphor of their lamp being put out (see 13:9; 20:20; Job 18:6; 21:17). There is some possibility that the imagery of a continually burning lamp as a figure for life was drawn from the language of Israel's sanctuary where a light burned permanently to symbolize the Lord's presence and the vitality of His covenant (Exod. 27:20; Lev. 24:2). See McKane, p. 405, for further background.

The admonition (v. 19) is almost identical to Ps. 37:1. *"Fret"* (Ps. 37:1, 7–8) suggests getting hot under the collar from indignation and frustration about life's scales going out of balance. Those who ought to have do not; those who ought not to have do. The feelings of indignation over this injustice can readily coax one to *"be envious"* (Heb. *qānā*, 3:31; 23:17; 24:1). But both the heat and lust are wasted efforts; for the wise to indulge those dispositions is to play the fool by confusing their temporary lot with their permanent reward. The wicked will not win, as Scott notes (p. 147), because (1) they are detested by the Lord (3:32); (2) they are dangerous to society (24:2); (3) they are doomed to defeat and death (Pss. 37:2; 73:17–20).

SAYING 30. ADMONITION ON FEARING GOD AND THE KING

24:21 My son, fear the LORD and the king;
  Do not associate with those given to change;
 22 For their calamity will rise suddenly,
  And who knows the ruin those two can bring?
          Prov. 24:21–22

This is an apt conclusion to the chain of sayings and a fitting summation of much that Proverbs teaches in terms of *"the fear"* of *"the Lord"* (as Sovereign of all of life see chaps. 14 and 16) and respect for *"the king"* as the guardian of a stable social order (see chap. 16). For Israel's teachers, the path of wisdom and the path of rebellion against authority led in opposite directions. Wisdom leads to life— the whole thrust of Proverbs makes that point; rebellion leads to *"calamity"* (Heb. *ʾêd;* 1:26–27; 17:5) and *"ruin"* or *"decay"* (Heb. *pîd;* Job 12:5; 30:24; 31:29).

The gist of the saying is clear enough, though translations of the specific Hebrew forms vary widely. A key rub is the meaning of *"those given to change"* which seems too weak an idea, too trivial to warrant the promised *"calamity"* and *"ruin."* Two major suggestions for reading Hebrew *shônîm,* "those who change," may be noted: (1) with an Arabic root as clue, it may be translated "noblemen" (see

McKane, pp. 405–6), understood as noblemen who engage in intrigues against the throne, though the latter clause has to be supplied from the context; (2) on the basis of the final line, *shônîm* can be emended to *sh^enêhem*, *"those two,"* by adding an *h*; if this solution is adopted, as I suggest, then *"do not associate"* needs (by changing, *tit'ārāb* [14:10; 20:19] to *tit'abbēr*) to be read as *"do not be angry with"* or *"oppose"* (for this verb, see 14:16; 20:2; 26:17); both of these changes are based on the Greek translation and supported in the Anchor Bible and JB. The two lines of verse 21 are then parallel: the first encourages awesome respect (*"fear"*) for deity and ruler, the second forbids rebellion against them both.

The motivation (v. 22) then, also features the Lord and the king: *"their calamity"* is the calamity they bring on the disobedient, as the second line makes patent. Practical instruction in regard for and obedience to authority, both divine and human, is not restricted to Proverbs. Koheleth tries his hand at it as well (5:1–2, 4–6; 8:2–5). None of this means that monarch and deity are peers. The pairing of the two is a reminder, however, that human government is one means used by God to maintain justice and order in a fallen world. Even when Caesar has replaced the sons of David the mandate of respect is repeated (Matt. 22:21; Rom. 13:1–7; 1 Pet. 2:13–17).

CHAPTER TWENTY-FOUR

Words of the Wise: Second Collection

Proverbs 24:23-34

Four important topics crop up in this brief section, which is a supplement to the thirty sayings assembled in 22:17–24:22 and discussed in the previous chapter. The heading—"These things [or sayings] also belong to the wise"—complements "words of the wise" (22:17) and marks both the boundary and the connection between the two collections. The four topics seem deliberately chosen to touch areas of justice and wisdom not specifically dealt with in the thirty sayings: Partiality in Law (vv. 23–26); Sound Priorities (v. 27); Honesty in Court (vv. 28–29); Industry in Work (vv. 30–34).

These themes are not strangers to the pages of Proverbs. But their literary forms, in three cases at least, mark them off from the sayings of 10:1–22:16 and chapters 25–29 and link them to the longer, more developed instructions of 22:17–24:22. Saying 1 (vv. 23–26) begins and ends with a single line saying that encapsulates the message about the pronouncement of just verdicts in court: verse 23a does that literally, and verse 26 figuratively. Between are sandwiched antithetic verses which describe the curses directed toward crooked judges (v. 24) and the blessings poured out on honest ones (v. 25). Saying 2 (v. 27) is a threefold admonition with no motivation clause. Saying 3 (vv. 28–29) is a double admonition with what may be a motivation question in verse 28b. Saying 4 (vv. 30–34) is a first-person autobiographical reflection (vv. 30–32) that culminates in a proverb which contains a poetic description of laziness and its dire results (vv. 33–34; see 6:10–11). The artistry and subtlety of the four sayings are a good match for the wisdom and practicality of their messages.

SAYING 1. DESCRIPTIONS OF PARTIALITY IN LAW

24:23 These *things* also *belong* to the wise:

It is not good to show partiality in judgment.
24 He who says to the wicked, "You *are*
   righteous,"
Him the people will curse;
Nations will abhor him.
25 But those who rebuke *the wicked* will have
   delight,
And a good blessing will come upon them.

26 He who gives a right answer kisses the lips.
                                        Prov. 24:23–26

The passage begins as plainly, bluntly, and literally as any
proverb can. It sets the theme without any doubt. Partiality (see on
18:5 in chap. 22; also 28:21) is to "recognize faces" and therefore
give special breaks or exact unjust penalties according to how the
accused is liked or disliked. The crassness of partiality ("*not good*") is
illustrated in the following verse. It is nothing less than twisting the
verdict in court ("*judgment*" or "justice") by 180 degrees so that a
blatantly guilty party (so "*wicked*" means here) is declared "innocent"
("*righteous*"). That boldface lie rocks the community whose welfare
is based on sound legal processes, just verdicts, and equitable sentences and stirs an uproar among all who hear. "*The people*" is plural,
suggesting all kinds of groups within the society; "*nations*" also describes collections of citizens within the body politic. To show what
a horrendous crime partiality is, the nouns are deliberately inclusive
and all-embracing and the verbs sharp and condemnatory (for
"*curse,*" Heb. *qābab,* see 11:26 and especially Balaam's ill-fated attempts to curse Israel in Num. 22–24; for "*abhor,*" its synonym,
which can also mean "scold," see 22:14).

Where justice is present and "*rebuke*" ("reproof" or "punish"; see
3:12; 9:7–8) is the judicial action, the judges will find "*delight*" (2:10;
9:17) and "*blessing*" (see 10:6; 11:26) as their reward. The context
suggests that these are human accolades, but divine approval surely
lurks in the shadows.

"*Right answer*" (v. 26) seems to be the way in which the teacher
sums up an impartial verdict. Straight, reliable words (for Heb.
nᵉkōḥîm, see 8:9: "plain") in court have the same warming, comforting, reassuring impact on society that "*kisses*" on "*the lips*" have for
close friends. It would be hard to find a more apt figure to describe
how dearly justice must be valued in any community.

SAYING 2. ADMONITION ON PRIORITIES

24:27 Prepare your outside work,
   Make it fit for yourself in the field;
   And afterward build your house.
                                    Prov. 24:27

With their usual balance and comprehensiveness the teachers move from the larger canvas of the community and its passion for justice to the smaller frame of the personal household of their students. Public responsibility is best exercised by those whose daily lives are marked by personal prudence. The gist of Saying 2 is clear: develop the means of personal livelihood (*"outside work"*; *"fields"*) before investing in your own comfort (*"house"*). I was once taken around the perimeter of a massive and elegant wall in Scotland, a wall that encircled an estate that was never completed because the owner had spent too much on the wall!

We can probably read our proverb in enlarging concentric circles. The inmost is literal: cultivate your *"field,"* plant your crops, orchards, and vineyards; then construct the house where you will live. The picture assumes an extended family where the young person can reside with parents or relatives while he pursues the plan outlined in the proverb. The next circle interprets "house" as "household" or family (see 3:33 for this meaning of Heb. *bayit*); reading the text thusly the Stuttgart Hebrew Bible suggests the insertion of "take for yourself a wife and" between *"afterward"* and *"build."* The largest circle hears the instruction figuratively: make sure your economic base is solidly in place before you tackle other opportunities or investments. Such an understanding is like our interpretation of "people who live in glass houses should not throw stones" which is about houses and stones and a whole lot more. Scott (Anchor Bible, p. 149) compares verse 27 with Jesus' words on counting the cost before building the tower (Luke 14:28–32).

SAYING 3. ADMONITIONS ON
WITNESSING AGAINST A NEIGHBOR

24:28 Do not be a witness against your neighbor
   without cause,
   For would you deceive with your lips?

> 29 Do not say, "I will do to him just as he has
>   done to me;
>   I will render to the man according to his work."
>   *Prov. 24:28-29*

The key terms for grasping the meaning of this saying, which takes us back to the courtroom (or gate) of Saying 1, are *"without cause"* (v. 28) and *"just as."* Together they picture a case of false *"witness"* where the testimony is made out of whole cloth ("without cause") and the motive is a mean streak that itches for revenge ("just as") on a *"neighbor"* who has slandered the person now called to testify. Verbal deceit is what is forbidden in verse 28 (see Hebrew root *pth* in the intensive form; 1:10; 16:29). As we noted in chapter 12 (12:6, 17; 14:5, 25; 19:5, 9, 28; 21:28), Israel's judicial system depended for its fairness on the reliability of witnesses. Persons who for financial gain, self-aggrandizement, or vengeance offered testimony based on inadequate or fabricated evidence were a menace to society's health and, therefore, treacherous members of it, as the rhetorical question (v. 28b) indicates. The implied negative answer, "of course not," makes the question a negative motivation tantamount to "[lest] *you deceive with your lips."*

The cycle of revenge must be broken even as the accuracy of the legal process must be protected. That is the point of verse 29, with its pivotal "just as." Lying to punish liars continues a vicious chain of falsehood that will encumber to the point of paralysis the practice of justice. Both personal integrity and communal stability demand honesty even when reasons for cheating seem cogent. Nothing here is said about leaving vengeance in the Lord's hands, although that note is sounded strongly in 20:22 and may still be echoing in the distance.

SAYING 4. REFLECTION AND DESCRIPTION OF LAZINESS

> 24:30 I went by the field of the lazy *man,*
>   And by the vineyard of the man devoid of
>   understanding;
>   31 And there it was, all overgrown with thorns;
>   Its surface was covered with nettles;
>   Its stone wall was broken down.
>   32 When I saw *it,* I considered *it* well;
>   I looked on *it and* received instruction:

33 A little sleep, a little slumber,
   A little folding of the hands to rest;
34 So shall your poverty come *like* a prowler,
   And your need like an armed man.

Prov. 24:30–34

The teacher bases the validity of this saying on personal experience as all the "I's" in the first three verses tell us. The narrative style we have met before in 4:1–5 and 7:6–7. We shall meet it again in Ecclesiastes, where the feisty sage is forever looking at life for himself (1:14; 2:3, 13, 24; 3:10, etc.) and pondering his findings, which he then shares with his students. Here the lesson of the sage was discovered in *"the fields of the lazy man"* (Heb. *ʿāṣēl;* see 6:6, 9 and a dozen other places in Proverbs), which stand in sharp contrast with the "fit field" which the wise person is urged to prepare in Saying 2 (v. 27). The *"vineyard"* of the empty-headed man (*"devoid of understanding,"* lit., "heart," a common phrase for sheer stupidity; 6:32; 7:7; 9:4, 16; 10:13, 21; 11:12; 12:11; 15:21; 17:18) is also part of the classroom. The parallel between *"lazy man"* and *"devoid of understanding"* makes clear that the laziness in view was not the result of a weak back but a hollow brain. Not strength but will was the lack.

The threefold evidence of sloth is detailed in verse 31: (1) the land that should have been carefully cultivated and kept clear of foreign foliage was riddled with *"thorns"* or *"weeds,"* signs of dereliction and even judgment (Isa. 34:13; Hos. 9:6); (2) *"its surface"* (lit., "its faces") was shrouded with nettles, perhaps wild artichokes (Zeph. 2:9; Job 30:7); (3) its rough *"stone wall"* (see Num. 22:24; Ps. 80:12; Isa. 5:5) was torn down (11:11) and its fragments scattered. All this was an object lesson to be pondered carefully (*"I considered it well"* is literally "I put my mind/heart on the matter") to distill and express its meaning. The painful lesson (*"instruction"*; Heb. *mûsār,* see 1:2) came quickly and in a form already seen at 6:10–11, whose words are repeated almost verbatim.

Helpful commentary on this passage and on Saying 2 comes from Isaiah's song of the vineyard (5:1–6) where the careful steps necessary to prepare land for cultivation are outlined (v. 2) and the ways in which neglected land is ravaged are spelled out (vv. 5–6). The weight given to work as an expression of wisdom can be seen in chapters 10 and 27. Diligence was a virtue admired by the apostle as well as the sage. Citing his own example of labor and toil (1 Thess. 2:9), Paul urges the new believers "to work with your own hands" (4:11) and to obey the command, "If anyone will not work, neither shall he eat" (2 Thess. 3:10). Anything less than this ardor and constancy of labor violates the creative purposes of God, forfeits our role as coregents of His world (Gen. 1:28–29), and brands us as leeches on the society which we are obligated to support with the means, mind, and might which God has given us.

Proverbs of Solomon through Hezekiah's Scribes

Proverbs 25:1–29:27

CHAPTER TWENTY-FIVE

Righteous Rule, Wise Speech, Generous Heart

Proverbs 25:1-28

> These also *are* proverbs of Solomon which the men
> of Hezekiah king of Judah copied:
>
> *Prov. 25:1*

The title verse signals both the close of the two-part collection of Sayings of the Wise (22:17–24:22; 24:23–34) and the beginning of the final section of Solomonic proverbs (25:1–29:27). Unlike the heading at 10:1, where *"Solomon"* also is given top billing, *"men of Hezekiah"* (whose reign spanned 715–686 B.C.), undoubtedly wise men and scribes responsible for teaching Judah's administrators, are mentioned in a supporting role. This is evidence that this is of the key part played by the royal administration in the garnering, polishing, and transmitting of the wisdom sayings from generation to generation. *"Copied"* may picture a bevy of scribes taking turns transferring the text from worn out or faded manuscripts to new parchment or papyrus for use by generations following.

Judah's bureaucracy had been in place nearly three hundred years by Hezekiah's time (2 Kings 18–20). And a large and complex organizational structure it was. We gain numerous glimpses of its size and complexity in the Old Testament. We can cite here a few only: (1) the term "king's servants" embraces a wide range of offices from the soldiers who did escort duty (1 Kings 1:33), through the stewards that managed the household (1 Kings 10:4–5), to top officials like Jeroboam before his revolution (1 Kings 11:26); (2) the kings were invariably landowners whose staffs managed huge estates like those of Uzziah (2 Chron. 26:10) or Hezekiah (2 Chron. 32:28–29), a pattern reflected both in Ezekiel's program of the future (45:7; 46:16–18) and in Qoheleth's picture of Solomonic prosperity (Eccles. 2:4–7); (3) lists of senior officials (2 Sam. 8:16–18;

20:23–26) include commander of the army, commander of the guard, herald, secretary, as well as priest; no doubt each officer managed a staff of considerable size; (4) the huge labor forces must have required a substantial management team (1 Kings 9:15–19); (5) the division of the land into twelve districts, each with its own prefect to govern the affairs in the king's name (1 Kings 4:7–19) and to collect taxes in the form of food supplies, entailed a vast crew of trained and responsible lieutenants.

Virtually every one of these governmental posts required wisdom of its occupant. The appointment of Daniel and his three colleagues to Nebuchadrezzar's court gives us a window on the prerequisites for royal service: "young men in whom there was no blemish, but good-looking, gifted in all wisdom, possessing knowledge and quick to understand" (Dan. 1:4). This list of desired qualities draws heavily on vocabulary familiar to us in Proverbs: "gifted" is *maśkîl* (10:5); wisdom is the ever present *ḥokmāh*; "possessing knowledge" is literally "knowing knowledge," the double use of the Hebrew *ydʻ* (1:2, 7); "quick to understand" is "perceiving knowledge," combining forms of Hebrew *bîn* and *ydʻ*. What Daniel and his friends possessed were precisely those attributes that Israel's sages sought to inculcate in their students. And the closer they were to the king, the more they needed wisdom in its manifold forms.

The collection copied by Hezekiah's men (25:1–29:27) began with court life in view. It stressed respect for the king's role and dealt with a range of topics that may be organized like this:

Royal responsibility	
mastery of issues	25:2
majesty of perspective	25:3
mandate of righteousness	25:4–5; 28:15–16; 29:2, 4, 12, 14
Official response	
humility	25:6–7
diplomacy	25:15
patience	29:26

On the whole subject of Judah's kings, how they were to behave and how their servants were to deal with them, see chapter 16. Other key topics that crop up in chapter 25 are wise practices in speaking (see chaps. 15 and 18) and generous patterns of giving (see chap. 11).

Chapters 25–27 differ in form and style from the other Solomonic sections. The sayings tend to cluster by subjects so that several verses running may treat the same topic. Comparisons are frequent, especially those drawn from observations of the created order (what we in the modern, Western world call "nature"). The language is thus made graphic and some of the book's most memorable sayings are found here. The marks of an editor's hand are more clear in these chapters than in other sections since the sequence and grouping of the sayings seems to be the result of careful, intentional ordering of a kind not readily observable in 10:1–22:16.

RESPECT FOR THE KING'S RULE

The royal responsibilities are spelled out not primarily to remind the kings of what good conduct entails but more to instruct their court in what behavior to foster and encourage.

> *It is* the glory of God to conceal a matter,
> But the glory of kings *is* to search out a matter.
> *Prov. 25:2*

The theme verse (25:2) encapsulates the royal duty to gain a mastery (*"search out"*; 23:20; Ps. 139:1, 23) of the issues (*"matter,"* "word," "thing," or "act"'; Heb. *dābār*) in order to render sound decisions whether in politics, war, law, or economics. This investigative action takes place in a context of profound humility before the mystery of God's ways. Part of the *"glory"* and majesty of God is that His ways are past finding out; it is God's privilege to choose whether *"to conceal* [see "hid" in Exod. 3:6] *a matter* [again Heb. *dābār*]" or to reveal it, as He frequently did through the prophets (Amos 3:7). Order there will be in God's ways but always order with mystery. The king has both a special obligation to try to discern that order no matter how difficult the task, but at the same time he must live in the fear of the Lord who alone knows where wisdom in its fullness lies (see Job 28:20–28 for this rhythm of concealment and revelation).

Just as the king is subordinate to God in his assigned duties and his abilities to discover what is true and good and effective in life, so the king has a power and perspective that sets him above the rest of the citizenry.

> *As* the heavens for height and the earth for depth,
> So the heart of kings *is* unsearchable.
> *Prov. 25:3*

The comparative form of the proverb is cryptic—no "like" or *"as"* appears in the Hebrew. The two lines are flatly stated back to back:

> Heavens for height and earth for depth,
> And the heart [or "mind"] of kings there is no
>   searching.

The point is the king's majesty of perspective, which has height and depth to it that a commoner can compare only to the scope of creation. *"Heavens"* and *"earth"* stand for the universe as in Gen. 1:1. The phrase *"there is no searching"* (*"unsearchable"*) ties verse 3 to verse 2, where the king's task is "to search out" (Hebrew root *ḥqr* is used in both verses) the facts in any matter brought before him. The king searches, but his way of thinking and deciding may not always be understood and appreciated by those around him. In this, he is like God with whom "there is no searching of His understanding" (Isa. 40:28; see also Ps. 145:3; Job 5:9; 9:10). That comprehensive outlook is something that leaders, especially heads of organizations, need badly. Our way of dividing administrative responsibilities often results in a team of specialists each of whom is a passionate advocate for his or her area of concern. In my case, for instance, there are student leaders, three deans of schools, a board of trustees, a finance officer, and vice-presidents for academics, development, and administration. They rightly lobby for the importance of their divisions. My task is to grasp the overall picture, balance the specific interests, and make sure we all think long term and not merely short range. This is something like what kings, prime ministers, and presidents do, only they do it on a much larger canvas. Those who do not have either the responsibility or information for massive decisions will always be puzzled by those who do. Our text suggests that they should also be humbly appreciative of the magnitude of the tasks that wise leaders perform.

In the catalog of royal duties nothing outranks righteousness (Ps. 72:1–2; see on Prov. 1:3; 2:9).

> 25:4 Take away the dross from silver,
>   And it will go to the silversmith *for* jewelry.
>   5 Take away the wicked from before the king,
>   And his throne will be established in
>   righteousness.
>   *Prov. 25:4–5*

Whatever else the king must search out (v. 2), he must uncover the presence of *"the wicked"* among his courtiers or among those who plead their causes before him. Only then will *"his throne,"* his whole manner of ruling, his entire regime, be built on the solid foundation (*"established"*) *"in righteousness,"* justice, integrity, and equity. Again the form of the sayings is a comparison, here a comparison of admonitions in which the command *"take away"* (separate, remove) serves as the link between the verses. The illustration is found in verse 4, the application in verse 5. The same refining process that brings *"dross"* (see Isa. 1:21–26; Jer. 6:27–30; Ezek. 22:18–22) to light in metallurgy and enables *"the silversmith"* (Judg. 17:4) to produce a "vessel" or "artifact" (*"jewelry"*) of value and beauty must be applied by the king in court. What dross is to precious metal, a wicked person is to an upright system of justice. In either case, purging is a matter of prudent necessity. Until that is accomplished the full artistry of the smith or the ruler in crafting a beautiful vessel or shaping a righteous state cannot be displayed. Solomon's tactics of purging were extreme to say the least (1 Kings 2:13–46), but it is just possible that without them Judah's throne would have been undermined by corruption at the outset of his reign.

A number of proverbs in chapters 28–29 help to define further the mandate of royal righteousness.

> *Like* a roaring lion and a charging bear
> *Is* a wicked ruler over poor people.
> *Prov. 28:15*

The imagery of *"a roaring lion"* (see Isa. 5:29–30 for a description of Israel's enemies on the march) and *"a charging* ["rushing"; Joel 2:9] *bear"* (see the ferocious picture of God in Hos. 13:8) recalls Amos's parable of the Day of the Lord with its inescapable destruction (Amos 5:19). Blatant, cruel savagery is the point. Woe to the *"poor people"* whose welfare depends on such a ruler! Woe to the *"ruler"* who so viciously defies the divine mandate of just governance. For the Jeroboams (see Amos), Shallums (Jer. 22:11–17), Neros, and Hitlers of this world, divine judgment must be awesome.

Abuse of power seems to come more easily than moderation.

> A ruler who lacks understanding *is* a great
>   oppressor,
> *But* he who hates covetousness will prolong *his*
>   days.
> *Prov. 28:16*

A *"ruler"* (Heb. *nāgîd,* "prominent person" whether "king," "governor or" other "high official," 1 Chron. 5:2; 9:11) does not have to set his mind deliberately to become an *"oppressor"*; he merely has to be devoid of ("*lacks*") the basic "*understanding*" or perception of how to rule wisely and graciously. Justice does not come naturally; oppression does. The person in power, therefore, cannot be neutral but has to hate bribery and graft (as "*covetousness*" seems to mean; see 1:19; 15:27, "gain"), acts that necessarily result in advantage to the guilty at the price of oppression of the innocent.

> When the righteous are in authority, the people
>   rejoice;
> But when a wicked *man* rules, the people groan.
> > *Prov. 29:2*

And with almost infallible intuition, "*the people*" sense the difference and voice it with shouts of joy ("*rejoice*") or "*groans*" (like Israel's sighs in Egypt [Exod. 2:23] or Jerusalem's lament over captivity [Lam. 1:4, 8, 11, 21]) of pain (see 28:12, 28 for similar pictures of contrast). "*Authority*" is literally "in multitudes" (Anchor Bible, "numerous"), a reminder that righteousness is best enforced when the king and the officials are in one accord in support of it.

Any breach of justice undercuts the stability of a kingdom.

> The king establishes the land by justice,
> But he who receives bribes overthrows it.
> > *Prov. 29:4*

"*The king*" may do all that he can to cause "*the land*" to stand tall and firm ("*establishes*") by regarding the rights of every citizen ("*justice*"; see on 1:2; 2:9), but greed or overambitious plans on his part or that of his administrators topple ("*overthrows*") the whole enterprise. "*Bribes*" may be taken literally here, but more likely some form of excessive taxes or "forced contributions" (NEB) is the problem. The word *t⁽ᵉ⁾rûmāh*, "something lifted up" is translated "contribution" in the ritual laws of Exod. 29:27–29 and "offerings" in Mal. 3:8. "The power to tax is the power to destroy" was the way our founding fathers paraphrased the thought of this proverb. Good rulers use that power carefully. Rehoboam learned the lesson the hard way when he refused to lighten "the burdensome service" and "the heavy yoke" which Solomon had placed on the people's shoulders in order to support and construct his temple, palace, and fortified cities (1 Kings 12:4).

A righteous ruler refuses to reward bad behavior.

> If a ruler pays attention to lies,
> All his servants *become* wicked.
>   *Prov. 29:12*

A case in point is paying *"attention* [hearing and believing] *to lies."* There are a lot of filters between a king and the people who report to him. These filters distort reality by shading the truth and making bad news better, exaggerating the good deeds of the staff, spreading false rumors about competitors, bearing inaccurate witness in legal matters, quoting false prophets and not true ones. When the ruler fails to search out the matter (see 25:2–3) and accepts the deceitful statements at face value, he unwittingly is encouraging *"all his servants,"* of whatever rank or station, to trim the truth and thus join the ranks of the *"wicked"* whose influence wars against righteousness and erodes the stability of the kingdom. A recent news clipping cites a statement from a retired chief of police whose officers did not own up to their overaggressiveness until the facts caught them red-handed: "They wouldn't lie all the time, but in a shaky arrest where excessive force was used and they felt it was, I felt that they would lie." The wise teachers understood the problem: it is sometimes difficult to tell the law enforcers from the criminals without a program.

This saying is a bottom line of royal responsibility.

> The king who judges the poor with truth,
> His throne will be established forever.
>   *Prov. 29:14*

It captures the chief duty of the king—he *"judges,"* distributes equity, guards the rights of persons against all who would pervert justice. It highlights the chief constituency of the king—*"the poor"* who have no strong base of political support and are most readily taken advantage of. It summarizes the results of such righteousness—the permanence of the dynasty (*"throne"*) and all it stands for (see 28:5). The variations and elaborations on this simple theme are played loud and clear in the coronation hymn of Psalm 72, especially verses 12–14.

The proverbs on royal responsibility are balanced by a set that touch on the official responses due the king from those who serve him.

> 25:6 Do not exalt yourself in the presence of the king,
>   And do not stand in the place of the great;

> 7 For *it is* better that he say to you,
> "Come up here,"
> Than that you should be put lower in the
> presence of the prince,
> Whom your eyes have seen.
>
> *Prov. 25:6–7*

Humility stands at the heart of wise protocol. The admonition (v. 6) reminds us that our importance as leaders or servants is determined not by our estimate of our importance but by how others view us. Self-accorded honor (*"exalt yourself"*) is never in place and especially *"in the presence of the king"* or his chief officials (*"the great"*). The king alone has the right to decide the pecking order of his court. The message of the motivation (v. 7) is that to overvalue our own importance is to risk the embarrassment of being *"put lower"* in the presence of a nobleman (*"prince"*; 17:7; 19:6). The verbs *"stand," "come up,"* and *"be put lower"* suggest an assembly of some kind that takes place on a tiered platform where the king occupies the highest level and other dignitaries stand on various steps or stages according to rank. The last line (v. 7c) should be linked to verse 8 (Anchor Bible, NEB, NIV, JB; see chap. 26 for the discussion of 25:7c–10). Jesus' parable (Luke 14:7–11) makes the same point as this proverb but transfers the setting to a dinner.

I have some sense of the loss of face which the proverb counsels us to avoid. During my tenure on the California State Board of Education, I had a falling out with the president of the board. In a matter-of-fact way, he removed me from the chairmanship of a key committee and appointed my replacement. The memo in which this change was noted looked so routine that I failed to read it carefully. When, at the next meeting, I boldly sat in my normal chair at the head of the committee table, a discreet staff member had to remind me delicately that I had been replaced. That memory, now over fifteen years old, still prompts me to double check before I presume where I should sit.

Diplomacy along with humility is always the order of the day.

> By long forbearance a ruler is persuaded,
> And a gentle tongue breaks a bone.
>
> *Prov. 25:15*

Patient persuasiveness will accomplish what hot words and ill manners never can. A *"ruler"* or *"judge"* (Heb. *qāṣîn;* see 6:7; Isa. 1:10; Mic. 3:1, 9) likes almost anything better than being put on the spot.

Pushiness is his public enemy. The techniques of courting, one of the root meanings of *"persuaded"* (Heb. *pth* means "prevail upon" in Hos. 2:14 ["allure"] or even "seduce" in Exod. 22:16 ["entices"]) hold up well in court. *"A gentle* [4:3; 15:1] *tongue"* can accomplish more than a sword when it comes to influencing a tough decision or changing the mind of an intransigent official—a task akin to breaking a bone.

Patience is the last of the trio of courtly virtues. It is also the most openly theological.

> Many seek the ruler's favor,
> But justice for man *comes* from the LORD.
> *Prov. 29:26*

It testifies to the ultimate trustworthiness of *"the Lord"* who outranks the ruler and has final say in all matters of *"justice."* *"Favor"* is literally "face" and may suggest that the *"many"* who petition (*"seek"*) *"the ruler"* are asking for special privileges which would result in injustice by making the ruler a "respecter of persons" (faces; see on 24:23; 28:21; Acts 10:34). Such pressure on the ruler should be replaced by patience in waiting on the Lord. What is right in the case He will decide in His own good time. "Rest in the Lord, and wait patiently for Him" is the way another wise person put it (Ps. 37:7). That is equally true in the palace or the cottage.

REGARD FOR PROPER SPEECH

Words are the stock in trade of persons in places of responsibility. This does not mean that all who lead, teach, or supervise others must be skilled rhetoricians—sons and daughters of Demosthenes. It does mean, however, that the ability to instruct, explain, express feelings, convey encouragement or correction with clarity and grace is essential equipment for all who would carry well the privilege of managing others. Work anywhere, and especially in the church, is done best by persons who understand the mission and their part in it. That mission and all that it takes to accomplish it can be explained only with words.

Accurate, honest, sensitive, prudent speaking is a theme threaded through Proverbs as consistently and strongly as any other. We have already seen its imprint in chapters 15 and 18 and are ready to look at a dozen more instances where it appears (25:11–14; 26:4–5, 7, 9). The sayings occur in chains, reinforcing and expanding the theme by the way they are clustered—a further sign of the topical editing of this section of the book. We can group our proverbs under three main headings:

Competence in speech	
in rhetoric	25:11
in reproof	25:12
in reliability	25:13
in rectitude	25:14
Confidence in speech	
in answering a fool	26:4–5
in contrast to a fool	26:7, 9; 27:3
Consideration in speech	
the right setting	27:14
the right timing	29:20
the right reputation	27:21

Comparisons are the dominant literary form in this set of sayings. The wise teachers not only urged effective speech on their pupils, they demonstrated it by a bouquet of effective metaphors and one simile (25:13). Usually the figure of speech is laid back to back with the point it illustrates without any connecting word in the Hebrew text. The form itself pays tribute to the unity of life which God's creative activity had produced. The created order and human experience are so held together by Yahweh's hand that, when appropriately understood, the one can illustrate the other.

The sequence of sayings on speech in chapter 25 are all comparisons. Competence seems to be their unifying theme.

> A word fitly spoken *is like* apples of gold
> In settings of silver.
>
> *Prov. 25:11*

The illustrative line is drawn from the crucible of the smith who works with precious metals to cast fine jewelry. *"Apples"* (see Song of Sol. 2:3, 5; 7:9) made *"of gold"* were the centerpiece of *"settings"* (lit., figures or images; Lev. 26:1; Num. 33:52) cast *"of silver."* "Apples" may suggest a love gift with romantic significance, since the word has an erotic tone to it in the Song of Solomon. Pendant, broach, or mantelpiece may have been the form in which the artifact was shaped. The instructive line comes second in the Hebrew and is not as clear as the first. *"Fitly"* is the problem. A rare word, it has been read to describe timing, "in season" (see 15:23 for a similar thought but a different Hebrew word), or form, "well-turned"

(McKane, based on the suggestion that the word means "wheels") and therefore speaks of balance and proportion in rhetoric. In any case, the value and beauty of a well-chosen, well-shaped *"word"* or *"decision"* (van Leeuwen, p. 83) is celebrated as though it were an exquisite art object.

Again beautiful jewelry, this time a ring and an ornament both of gold, forms the illustration.

> *Like* an earring of gold and an ornament of fine gold
> *Is* a wise rebuker to an obedient ear.
>
> *Prov. 25:12*

The pairing of the two ornaments matches the pairing of the *"rebuker"* (or *"arbiter"* as van Leeuwen reads it, p. 83; see also 3:12; 9:7; 24:25) and the person with the *"obedient* [hearing] *ear."* The two qualities of wise counsel and ready hearing complement each other as do the matching pieces of jewelry, at least one of which is probably an *"earring."* Even the choice of the jewelry is designed to highlight the truth that the rebuke of a wise tongue does little good without a receptive ear.

The comparisons in verses 13–14 switch from ornaments to weather.

> Like the cold of snow in time of harvest
> *Is* a faithful messenger to those who send him,
> For he refreshes the soul of his masters.
>
> *Prov. 25:13*

Only in verse 13 is the comparison made explicit with *"like."* The picture is the refreshment of ice or *"snow"* water in the heat of *"harvest,"* which took place in the hot months from May to October depending on the crops to be worked. Garbled communications and misunderstood messages must have been as much of a problem in antiquity as they are now. To be competent, speech not only has to be winsome and forceful, it has to be reliable. The *"faithful messenger"* (Heb. ṣîr; see 13:17; Obad. 1) not only arrives where he is supposed to, when he is supposed to, but relays precisely the message he is supposed to. *"His masters"* believe they can count on him and when they receive the news that the correct message got through, they are refreshed as surely and thoroughly as if they discovered chilled water in the heat of harvest. Do you suppose that's how God feels when we messengers deliver His Word with reasonable accuracy?

Again the illustration comes first, although NKJV reverses the lines.

> Whoever falsely boasts of giving
> *Is like* clouds and wind without rain.
> *Prov. 25:14*

It speaks of show without performance, of hopes dashed, and expectations crushed. In drought-plagued years, we Californians know the frustration of seeing *"clouds"* blown in with the *"wind"* and yet refusing to drop their *"rain."* Our seasons are like those in Palestine. We need heavy rain from November to January and again in March and April. When that does not come in adequate measure we deplete our supplies and submit to rationing. As I write, Lake Cachuma, Santa Barbara's main reservoir, is at a record low. Weather satellites seem to make the matter worse. We watch storm clouds blow in from Alaska and Hawaii only to be bumped aside by the high pressure area that hovers tenaciously over the Southern California coast. Feigned generosity is one form of incompetent speech. It *"boasts"* (lit., *"praises itself"*) of what it intends not to deliver. The rectitude which must be part of wise speaking is altogether absent, and instead of the refreshment of generosity there is the drought brought by miserliness.

This famous pair of supposed contradictions introduces the subject of confidence in speech. They demonstrate the principle that knowing what to say and when to say it is the essence of prudence.

> 26:4 Do not answer a fool according to his folly,
>   Lest you also be like him.
>   5 Answer a fool according to his folly,
>   Lest he be wise in his own eyes.
>   *Prov. 26:4–5*

Both admonitions picture a *fool* babbling on, pouring out folly after folly. That situation poses a problem to the wise: how should one *"answer"* the fool? The opposite bits of advice—*"do not answer"* and do *"answer"*—show that there is no automatic formula to be applied. Each situation calls for a response that the wise must have confidence to discern on the spot. In one case, to answer would lead to prolonged argument in which the wise might be trapped into babbling like a fool. Where there is a chance of that, silence is the prudent way, *"lest"* the wise come to look *"like"* the fool (*"him"*) before the curious audience. In another case, one prick of the fool's balloon may bring him back to reality and burst the bubble of his conceit ("*wise in his own eyes*"). To answer in that circumstance does a favor to everyone, including the fool. Judging how the fool will respond, what he needs, and how the audience will react is part and parcel of applied wisdom. Both proverbs are valid, each in its own setting.

The encounters with the fools introduce some sayings that describe a fool's ineptness in the use of proverbs. The confident speech of the wise is seen in contrast to the fumbling attempts of fools to ply the wise man's trade. Sad humor hangs over the scene.

> *Like* the legs of the lame that hang limp
> *Is* a proverb in the mouth of fools.
> *Prov. 26:7*

> *Like* a thorn *that* goes into the hand of a drunkard
> *Is* a proverb in the mouth of fools.
> *Prov. 26:9*

Simply put, the first comparison matches the dangling ("*hang limp*") "*legs*" of a "*lame*" person (like Saul's son Mephibosheth; 2 Sam. 9:13) with the "*proverb*" that lies powerless in "*the mouth of fools.*" The second comparison is more bold in its satire. It shows a "*drunkard*" (Joel 1:5) clutching "*a thorn*" branch or thistle in his "*hand*" and waving it as though it were a mighty weapon. This picture captures both the Hebrew wording and the illustrative force better than the thorn "*into*" the hand of NKJV. The proverb is not a burr in the fool's saddle; it is a ridiculous instrument which he alone thinks will accomplish anything. In contrast with such mindless clowning, the most nervous wise person is the soul of confidence.

Any fool is a nuisance to bear with patiently. But one full of wrath is too burdensome for words.

> A stone *is* heavy and sand *is* weighty,
> But a fool's wrath *is* heavier than both of them.
> *Prov. 27:3*

The pictorial line which begins the saying is drawn from the language of construction. In building a wall, a cistern, or a house, "*stone*" and "*sand*" are two key ingredients. If they have to be lugged a long way, they become backbreaking in their weight. The stone has sharp edges that chafe; the bag of sand is cumbersome to hang on to. But if you have your choice, choose "*both of them*" anytime to dealing with a fool whose "*wrath*" has overwhelmed him. He cannot control it so he insists on dumping it on you. He will not listen to sound reason or logical explanation; they make his anger only heavier. It will break the back of anyone who tries to manage it for him. A twofold word this is: it tells us to give angry fools plenty of room; it also tells us to deal wisely and promptly with our own anger.

Honest speech is marked by competence, confidence, and finally consideration.

> He who blesses his friend with a loud voice, rising
>   early in the morning,
> It will be counted a curse to him.
>
> *Prov.* 27:14

The question posed is whether the error is pretense of friendship without substance to back it up or insensitivity to the setting. Perhaps it is some of both, but I lean to the note of setting, largely because of the specific description *"rising early in the morning."* Calling out loud blessings to a *"friend"* is all well and good when the situation is right. But a wrong setting stems from lack of consideration where the greeting of blessing or peace (*shālôm!*) is as welcome as *"a curse"* to the man whose sleep is disturbed. Phoning at 2:00 A.M. to tell a friend you wish her well will be joyfully received only in very rare instances. For other acts of conduct that test the mettle of neighborliness, see 26:18–19.

Consideration calls for minding the timing as well as the setting.

> Do you see a man hasty in his words?
> *There is* more hope for a fool than for him.
>
> *Prov.* 29:20

Whether 29:20 begins with a question or a statement cannot be determined from the Hebrew, but the sense comes out the same either way. It points to a rash person who is *"hasty* [19:2; 21:5; 28:20] *in his words,"* does not weigh or measure them. They blurt out as though they controlled him not he them. He speaks without regard for accuracy, circumstances, audience, or emotions. He makes *"a fool"* of himself and worse, if one can imagine what that might be. So intemperate is he that he leaves a conversation in wrack and ruin and may make a shambles both of the subject and of his hearers. Talk without thought is a hard trait to correct, which accounts for the absence of any *"hope"* of improvement. "Look before you leap" can be interpreted as "think before you speak."

Our final saying in this section brings us back to the bench of the silversmith where we began (25:11–12).

> The refining pot *is* for silver and the furnace for
>   gold,
> And a man *is valued* by what others say of him.
>   *Prov. 27:21*

Here the point is not the beauty of the product but the process of *"refining"* that lies behind the crafted artifacts. *"Refining pot"* (17:3) and *"furnace"* (17:3; Deut. 4:20) are the means of making the metal castable but especially of ridding it of all dross and other imperfections. That illustrative line is followed by a terse application that reads literally "and a man for the mouth of [or "in regard to"] his reputation [or praise]." The parallelism of thought indicates that society has its own testing and refining process as useful and effective as the smith's pot and furnace. Sham speech or feigned integrity will be melted out by the fires of public scrutiny. The fire that sloughs off the dross reveals the gold and silver. Consideration in speech means that we hold each other's reputations in our hands. Hence, we have the high duty to speak as well as possible of each other, to scotch rumors, to pare down exaggerations, and to give the other person the benefit of the doubt. Consideration also suggests that we praise firmly and speak warmly of those whose reputations are tried and true. There are few enough of them among us. We should salute them gladly.

RESPONSIBILITY FOR GENEROSITY

A trio of proverbs (25:21–22; 28:27; 29:7) prompt their hearers to extraordinary generosity. It was incumbent upon Israel's young leaders both to set examples of covenant loyalty by caring for the needy and to promote communal harmony by showing kindness to their personal adversaries. Neither selfishness nor peevishness were qualities to be cultivated, and their education would not be complete without specific instructions along these lines.

As for the enemy ("the one who hates you"), he is to be treated according to his need, not his disposition.

> 25:21 If your enemy is hungry, give him bread to eat;
>   And if he is thirsty, give him water to drink;

22 For *so* you will heap coals of fire on his head,
And the LORD will reward you.

Prov. 25:21–22

Basic necessities are to be supplied: *"bread"* and *"water."* Survival
seems to be at stake, and no one who fears the Lord dare stand by
and let another person suffer if he has the means to meet the need.
The admonitions (v. 21) are more easily explained than the motivations (v. 22). The customary reading of *"heap* [or *"rake together"* in
Isa. 30:14] *coals of fire* ["burning charcoal"; 6:28; 26:21]*"* has to do
with shaming the enemy into contrition and repentance so that his
hatred dissipates. Whether an actual ritual act, like dust and ashes,
is in view, we cannot tell. More recently the suggestion has been
made that this clause describes the salutary effects of giving a
parched person a flask of water. The refreshment eases the fever of
thirst as though one "raked hot charcoal from upon the head" of the
sufferer (see van Leeuwen, p. 60). This removes the note of possible
vindictiveness from the act of generosity and segues naturally to the
promise of divine reward.

He who gives to the poor will not lack,
But he who hides his eyes will have many curses.

Prov. 28:27

As for the poor—who by virtue of their number, their helplessness,
and their prominence in the covenantal instructions on justice in
society merit special attention—the assurance is given that generosity will be rewarded and those who will thus give will still have the
means to care for themselves and their households (*"not lack"*). The
one, on the other hand, *"who hides his eyes"* so as not to see the plight
of the poor will experience *"many curses"* (3:33; see also the curses
on the unfaithful priests in Mal. 2:2; 3:9). The source of the curses is
not only the poor man who may raise his voice in protest against the
blatant indifference of the officials who ought to care, but undoubtedly Yahweh Himself who is the Maker of the poor and everyone
else (14:31; 17:5; 22:2).

Compassion for the poor is one litmus test of righteousness.

The righteous considers the cause of the poor,
But the wicked does not understand *such*
    knowledge.

Prov. 29:7

"Considers" is literally "knows" and means here "pays attention," "cares about." Just as the Lord "knows" the way of the righteous (Ps. 1:6), so the righteous "knows" the "case" (*"cause"* is Heb. *dîn,* a legal word implying rights to be defended or justice to be rendered) *"of the poor"* and makes it his passion to do something about it. Not to perceive (*"understand"* is *bîn,* the standard verb of insight and discernment) is to join the camp of *"the wicked." "Knowledge"* here must be the knowledge of Yahweh's will and way (see on 1:2, 7). The point is that the wicked are wicked precisely because they do not see life from God's angle and do not know that the poor, who have no one else to depend on, are especially precious to God. To care for them is an act of righteousness for many reasons, not the least of which are that their helplessness instructs us of our own helplessness and that our grace to them demonstrates that we have grasped the magnitude of God's grace to us.

CHAPTER TWENTY-SIX

Honest Speech and Careful Conduct

Proverbs 26:1–28

My heart meant well (at least I thought so) but my words turned Ruth's face white and her eyes moist. I was trying to help her make a decision by stating how important it was to me. But what she heard and felt was a put-down, an act of rejection as though she were solely to blame for the problem with which we were dealing. When she regained composure and had freedom to respond, her words were brief and strong: "What you said hurt me as much as if you had slapped my face."

Words can be worse than weapons. The wise teachers labored to put that point across. Their students were to bear large responsibility, to carry weight in their society, to command the respect of the citizenry. They held in their hands the "big stick," as Teddy Roosevelt called it, the big stick of prestige and authority. That meant that they had special need to speak softly because the people viewed their words as larger than life. What liars, deceivers, scoffers, and other fools said, they could not say. Their tongues, as Israel's leaders, were to do other things—pronounce blessing, confront injustice, dispense fair decisions, persuade their colleagues to do right, plead sound causes before their ruler.

The importance of all this we have already seen at chapter 12. The collection restored and released by Hezekiah's scribes (chaps. 25–29) returns to the theme and reinforces it with a battery of illustrations most of which show the brutality and stupidity of foolish, dishonest, and insensitive words. Leaders had to protect their followers from the potential damage of wicked speech, and, even more vitally, they had to guard their own tongues, given their powerful place in Israel's society. Wise leaders keep watch over their tongues as the Swiss Guards protect the pope, and we also defend the rights of others to express themselves as freely as they choose within the bounds of common decency.

Control of speech, as taught in Proverbs, is akin to the general caution in conduct demanded of those whose lives charged them to be examples of prudence (see chap. 22). A handful of sayings in this section of Proverbs spell out this caution and remind us how every area of our comportment needs scrutiny since a serious misstep on a leader's part is rattling to the structure of the whole community. No wonder Paul could not complete his catalog of the Spirit's fruit without the inclusion of self-control (Gal. 5:23).

DANGER IN ILL-CHOSEN WORDS

With a couple of exceptions (26:20; 28:23) all the proverbs dealing with this theme stress the negative impact of words used mindlessly or treacherously. The comparisons are extreme, as though hyperboles are deliberately chosen to show how vicious dishonest speech can be. And wherever the language is more literal it is calculated by the choice of words and phrases to depict abuse of language as a crime akin to murder (see esp. 26:24–26). The range of subjects is wide, as though pointedly to illustrate the almost infinite variety of bizarre ways in which speech can inflict damage on its hearers. Since the context and sequence of the sayings in chapters 25–26 seems to indicate the work of a careful editor, we shall treat the proverbs in their numerical order in the text.

As frequently in the use of comparisons, the words of illustration in the Hebrew text come first in each of these sayings and the words of advice follow. The first line creates suspense and the second line carries the punch of the message.

> 25:18 A man who bears false witness against his
>   neighbor
>   Is *like* a club, a sword, and a sharp arrow.
>
>   19 Confidence in an unfaithful *man* in time of
>   trouble
>   Is *like* a bad tooth and a foot out of joint.
>   *Prov. 25:18–19*

Damage done to others is the point of verse 18. As a battle hammer ("*club*"), "*sword*," and sharpened "*arrow*" can inflict untold damage on an enemy in war or a wild beast in hunting, so the person who fabricates *"false"* testimony in court does savage harm to the one on trial and, indeed, to the whole community that counts on justice to hold it together. (See comments in chap. 12, esp. at 14:5, for the legal background.)

Verse 19 pictures the damage done to the person who naively puts *"confidence"* (or "trust") in the liar. If the court scene in the village gate is the setting here as in verse 18, the *"unfaithful"* person (full of deceit and treachery as Heb. *bôgēd* implies) is the one who bore false witness and the *"time* [lit., "day"] *of trouble* [narrowing, squeezing pressure]" is the trial itself. The defendant had hoped that the witness would vindicate him; instead false evidence was given that guaranteed a verdict of guilty. The whole faithless affair left the innocent man as frustrated as a man who sits down to a bountiful meal only to find that a molar has crumbled (*"bad"* should be translated "broken"; the Hebrew roots are close: r^c and r^{cc}) and as powerless as a runner poised to begin the race only to find that his *"foot"* totters with palsy.

The arena of wild speech is widened from the gate to the marketplace, well, or workshop—all places where gossip was prevalent.

> The north wind brings forth rain,
> And a backbiting tongue an angry countenance.
> *Prov.* 25:23

"A backbiting [lit., "secret" or "hidden" like a shelter or covering; see 9:17; 21:14] *tongue"* produced a predictable response—*"an angry"* ("cursing" or "scolding" 22:14; 24:24) face, just as surely as a *"north wind"* ("northwest" might be more geographically accurate in Palestine, 1 Kings 18:41–44) could *"blow"* rain from the mountains or the sea. Gossip is never a gesture of friendship toward its target and cannot result in the edification of those who bear it or those who hear it.

The curse is viewed as a form of crooked speech.

> Like a flitting sparrow, like a flying swallow,
> So a curse without cause shall not alight.
> *Prov.* 26:2

It has no substance or power to it unless God Himself is behind it. Otherwise it is a piece of harmless magic able to do no more damage to the life it was supposed to *"enter"* (*"alight"* is a paraphrase) than do *"a flitting* [or fleeing] *sparrow"* and *"a flying swallow"* (for the birds see Ps. 84:3). It is blasphemy to utter such a *"curse,"* since the curser usurps the authority of God. It is folly to believe such a curse, since the inflicter has no power to implement it.

The series of sayings from verse 17 through verse 28 should be seen as an intentional collection of proverbs about the perils of rash and evil speech and how they are to be dealt with. The comparisons make the language vivid, while the more literal sayings (vv. 24–26, 28) make it clear by alleviating any doubt or uncertainty as to their meaning. This combination of figurative and literal is a frequent technique in Hebrew poetry amply documented in the Song of Songs and the prophets like Hosea.

> He who passes by *and* meddles in a quarrel not his
> own
> *Is like* one who takes a dog by the ears.
>> *Prov. 26:17*

Where dispute is involved, whether an official law case or personal *"quarrel"*—the Hebrew *rî^b* (see 15:18; 17:1, 14; 18:6, 17; 25:9; 26:21; 30:33) can mean either—no one not a party to the problem should get entangled in the debate. Lack of information means that the outsider can make no contribution and is in danger of becoming angrily embroiled (*"meddles"* is too weak a translation of the Hebrew; see 14:16; 20:2; where *"anger"* lies at the root) and of making the situation worse. *"Passes by"* probably modifies the *"dog"* not the outsider. The illustration thus is strengthened: clutching a passing, therefore, strange dog *"by the ears"* is both disturbing because of the yapping and dangerous because of the nipping. No good can come from either. You may remember that scores of people sent this proverb to President Lyndon B. Johnson when a nationally circulated photograph showed him lifting his pet beagle by the ears. The fact that some of his correspondents saw him as meddling *"in a quarrel not his own"* (Vietnam) added dark humor to the scene.

Practical joking is as dangerous as meddlesome interference.

> 26:18 Like a madman who throws firebrands, arrows,
>> and death,
> 19 *Is* the man *who* deceives his neighbor,
>> And says, 'I was only joking!'
>>> *Prov. 26:18–19*

"Madman" (the Hebrew word occurs only here) may depict a person who "horses around," a clowning joker bent on having mindless fun

at other people's expense. The lame apology *"I was only joking"* ("sporting" or "getting a laugh"; see 8:30–31) does not assuage the hurt done by lying to or misleading (on *"deceives,"* see Gen. 29:25, where Laban has painfully and shamefully tricked Jacob) the *"neighbor."* Friendship depends on trust and even "humorous" deceit is as dangerous to its bonds as *"firebrands* [see the kindred word in Isa. 50:11], *arrows* [25:18], *and death."* The guffaw gained from sending a friend on a wild goose chase on a stormy night eases not at all the pain caused by the news that the friend was seriously injured when his speeding car skidded off the slippery road.

> 26:20 Where *there is* no wood, the fire goes out;
>   And where *there is* no talebearer, strife ceases.
>   21 *As* charcoal *is* to burning coals, and wood to
>   fire,
>   So *is* a contentious man to kindle strife.
>   22 The words of a talebearer *are* like tasty trifles,
>   And they go down into the inmost body.
>   *Prov. 26:20–22*

These sayings all picture the harm done by those who deliberately use their tongues to damage the reputations of others, to spark *"strife,"* and hence to disrupt the peace of the community. The *"talebearer"* ("slanderer" is the stronger translation and brings out the malicious character assassination which can be the result of vile gossip; 16:28; 18:18) is pictured as causing two kinds of damage: (1) he can fuel a quarrel between friends or families and flame it into a feud (for *"strife,"* Heb. *mādôn,* see 6:19; 10:12; 17:14; 28:25; 29:22), with the same incendiary impact that sticks of *"wood"* have on a *"fire"*; his absence, which is relished here, has the opposite calming effect; the *"strife ceases"* (Heb. *shātag*) as Jonah's storm calmed when the seamen tossed him overboard (1:11–12); (2) his *"words"* (v. 22) can insinuate themselves deep in the belly of society including their victim's "inner chamber" and hence do irreparable and permanent damage (see 18:8 for the full explanation of this saying which occurs verbatim there). The *"contentious"* man (v. 21; the Hebrew root is the same as that of "strife" in v. 20) is cousin if not brother to the slanderer (*"talebearer"*) of verses 20, 22. "Quarrel" (Heb. *rîb* is read here "strife"; see on 26:17) is his game; he has the same talent for setting it off that *"charcoal"* (Isa. 44:12) has to keep *"coals"* (6:28; 25:22) blazing or *"wood"* to feed the flames of a "fire."

"Deceit" (vv. 24, 26) is the theme of these three proverbs as "strife" was of the previous trio.

26:23 Fervent lips with a wicked heart
    Are like earthenware covered with silver dross.

24 He who hates, disguises *it* with his lips,
    And lays up deceit within himself;
25 When he speaks kindly, do not believe him,
    For *there are* seven abominations in his heart;
                                  Prov. 26:23–25

The illustration of verse 23 sets the tone of the series: a simple clay pot (*"earthenware"*; Jer. 19:1) is *"covered with"* the leaves of *"silver dross"* (25:4) to give it the appearance of beauty and value. But close examination exposes it as sham. So *"lips"* that appear to burn (*"fervent"*; Obad. 18 where the Hebrew *dlq* is used of fire) with love or concern or truth can only momentarily mask an evil (*"wicked"* is Heb. *rāʿ*) heart.

Hatred (v. 24) seems to be specifically the evil in view. The malicious person may dress up in foreign garb the look of hatred and disguise it, as Joseph disguised himself from his brothers (Gen. 42:7), but the ruse is not to be trusted (*"do not believe"* is a direct command in v. 25). The "gracious" (*"kindly"* translates Heb. *ḥnn*, a root conveying "pity" or "tender compassion") speech is from a heart crammed full (*"seven"* speaks of the utmost completeness) of *"abominations"* (3:32), acts and attitudes of the most hateful horror.

The final three sayings reveal the disastrous results of the multiple evils accomplished by the tongue.

26:26 *Though his* hatred is covered by deceit,
    His wickedness will be revealed before the
    assembly.

27 Whoever digs a pit will fall into it,
    And he who rolls a stone will have it roll back
    on him.
                                    Prov. 26:26–27

Try as he will to cover his hostility (*"hatred"*) by a cloak of *"deceit"* (see Obad. 3, 7 for the Hebrew verb *nāshāʾ* that underlies this noun), the reality of his *"wickedness"* ("evil," Heb. *rāʿāh*) will be exposed (*"revealed"*) because such duplicity cannot permanently be contained. The whole community (*"assembly"* here is probably not an official tribunal but the society that surrounds the culprit and is put in danger by his malice) will call his bluff and deal with him appropriately. Life is like that—geared to trap him in the *"pit"* (Pss. 49:9; 103:4,

where "pit" virtually means death in the grave) the culprit "digs"
(Gen. 26:35) and to crush him under the "stone" he rolls forward to
smash someone else. No court is necessary here; the universe made
by God and operating at His orders exacts its retribution.

An effective summary of the section that begins in verse 17 is
stated in verse 28.

> A lying tongue hates *those who are* crushed by it,
> And a flattering mouth works ruin.
>
> *Prov. 26:28*

The first line encapsulates three main themes that have dominated
these proverbs: (1) the "lying tongue" is the central source of disruption in the community; (2) its crime is motivated by hatred, the utter
disdain of all whom it attacks; (3) its impact is crushingly oppressive
(for Heb. *dakkāyw,* see Pss. 9:9; 10:18). The second line seems, in the
context, to be a condensed version of verse 27: its force is to state
briefly the self-defeating nature of treacherous speech. The "mouth"
that works so hard at the deceitful task of "flattering" (lit., "slickness";
5:8) "works" to the "ruin" (Heb. *dāḥah* means "knock down") not so
much of others, though it can do that, but especially of itself. The
lying mouth is a gun that shoots its owner in the foot.

Honest speech may call for confrontation.

> He who rebukes a man will find more favor
>   afterward
> Than he who flatters with the tongue.
>
> *Prov. 28:23*

The leader of society, the elder in the gate, the administrator of the
government, the teacher of the children—any of these finds himself
in a situation where he points out what is wrong ("rebukes" or reproves; 1:30). The words may sting at the time but if their recipient
is wise he will "afterward" take them as an act of kindness ("favor";
Heb. *ḥēn*), since they encouraged him to change his ways for the
better, something that flattery ("slick talk"), which temporarily may
have been welcomed, would not have done.

Rationalization like flattery is dishonest speech.

> Whoever robs his father or his mother,
> And says, "*It is* no transgression,"
> The same *is* companion to a destroyer.
>
> *Prov. 28:24*

The person who *"robs"* (or defrauds, 22:22) his parents may claim
"'It is no transgression'" (Heb. *pesha‹* means "insubordination," almost "mutiny"; 10:12, 19) by arguing that the money or property
will come to him anyway at the death of the *"mother"* or *"father."*
The wise rightly branded the argument as specious and pinpointed
the viciously cruel conduct of one who broke faith with those who
gave him life and burdened their later years with regrets about their
son's behavior and anxiety about their means of sustenance.
"Companion to a destroyer" is intense language indeed (see 6:32; 11:9;
Gen. 6:13 for the verb *"destroy"*) to be applied to one called to make
a father glad (10:1).

Another grim act of dishonesty is described here.

> Whoever is a partner with a thief hates his own life;
> He swears to tell the truth, but reveals nothing.
> *Prov. 29:24*

Someone who shares the lot (*"is a partner"*) of a *"thief"* stands in
court and *"hears the curse"* pronounced on any who withhold or
pervert the truth (NKJV gives the Hebrew a somewhat different turn
with *"swears to tell the truth"*). He then refuses to reveal what he
knows and thus is guilty of false witness. His fate is the "curse"
pronounced in Lev. 5:1. His silence is ample proof that he *"hates his
own life"* which is sorely threatened by the curse which God Himself
will enforce.

For the final word on the importance of honest speech we reach
back in the book to a statement that features self-interest and the
way our egos distort our words.

> Most men will proclaim each his own goodness,
> But who can find a faithful man?
> *Prov. 20:6*

"Most [or *"many"*] *men"* will raise their voices to *"proclaim"* (or "call
out") *"each his own goodness"* (or "loyalty"; Heb. *ḥesed*) toward his
neighbors, his community, his Lord. But a person who really be-
haves in goodness—a man of *"faithful"* words and deeds is so scarce
as to be virtually undiscoverable (*"who can find?"*). Bragging is easier
than performing. And self-evaluation may be sorely lacking in accuracy. For honesty to overcome our built-in prejudices, many of us
need to lower the volume of self-praise and raise the volume of self-
criticism.

HAZARDS OF HASTY ACTION

The warnings against a lying tongue in chapters 25–26 are matched by sayings that denounce rashness of conduct. Prudence for the sages involved the careful weighing of risk and the delicate measuring of the dangers of hasty conduct in many areas of life:

In litigation with a neighbor	25:7c–10
In imposition on a neighbor	
whether visiting	25:17
or comforting	25:20
In curiosity about mysteries	25:27
In delegation of responsibility	26:6

These verses anticipate the graphic saying about grabbing a stray dog by the ears discussed above (26:17). What is dealt with pictorially there is treated more prosaically and in more detail here.

> 25:7c Whom your eyes have seen.
>
> 8 Do not go hastily to court;
>   For what will you do in the end,
>   When your neighbor has put you to shame?
> 9 Debate your case with your neighbor,
>   And do not disclose the secret to another;
> 10 Lest he who hears *it* expose your shame,
>   And your reputation be ruined.
>
> *Prov. 25:7c–10*

The setting is a dispute with a *"neighbor"* that one party is tempted to settle by litigation in court. The last line of 25:7 needs to be attached to 25:8. When it is, the picture seems to be of casual observation, what (not *"whom"*) *"your eyes have seen"* of some apparent misbehavior which needs correcting. The admonition urges the observer not to bring the matter *"hastily"* out *"to court."* "Bring out" involves a slight change in the vowels of the Hebrew verb but makes clear that it is the issue, not the person, that is under discussion. "Out" also points to the public setting of legal hearings in the city gate. The motivation for caution (*"for,"* v. 8) makes clear that the observation of the neighbor's conduct was superficial and misleading. The neighbor's public explanation will clarify the matter but at the cost of *"shame"* (Heb. *klm*, 28:7) to the impetuous observer/reporter.

The follow-up admonition (v. 9) urges a private discussion (*"debate your case"*; both noun and verb are *rîb*; see on 26:17) to ascertain the facts and merits of the case before any legal action is pursued and before the *"secret"* circumstances supposedly witnessed are disclosed to anybody else. The motivation (v. 10), as in verse 8, is to avoid the *"shame"* or insult (for the negative meaning of *ḥsd*, see 14:34; Lev. 20:17) of being proven wrong. Credibility in the community is such a valued asset that a *"reputation"* (the word is "report," usually an evil one; 10:18) once set aside will "not return" (as *"be ruined"* means literally). "Look before you leap" and "ask before you act" are maxims that have a long and noteworthy history. Nothing in our modern era has made them obsolete.

Imposing on a neighbor carries risks to be avoided.

> Seldom set foot in your neighbor's house,
> Lest he become weary of you and hate you.
> *Prov. 25:17*

The admonition is straightforward, free of metaphor or comparison. *"Seldom"* (lit., "make rare or precious"; Isa. 13:12 uses the verb of "fine gold") warns the hearer against planting his *"foot"* too often on the threshold and taking for granted the hospitality of a *"neighbor's house."* In a culture where hosts felt keen obligation to welcome, make comfortable, and protect their guests, the privilege was not to be abused. The host would be hard put to withhold hospitality but could become so "fed up" (the literal reading of *"weary"*) that he would resent the neighbor's presence and at least *"hate"* to see him coming, if not dislike him personally (as "hate" may mean here).

Imposition is especially inappropriate when a neighbor is ill or depressed ("heavy heart" below is literally "heart of evil," "heart that suffers from something wrong").

> *Like* one who takes away a garment in cold weather,
> *And like* vinegar on soda,
> *Is* one who sings songs to a heavy heart.
> *Prov. 25:20*

Singing *"songs"* pictures intrusive, insensitive behavior toward a person who needs quiet and gentle comfort. Job's friends sat silently with the sufferer "seven days and seven nights, and no one spoke a word to him, for they saw that his grief was very great" (Job 2:13). Their silence was their greatest gift to Job. When they began to speak, their comfort ceased, and they fulfilled the illustration of line one of the proverb: their arguments (though they were not songs!) became as ill-suited to Job's needs as if they had snatched away his outer cloak (*"garment"*) on a *"cold"* day. Their raucous counsel was as perturbing as the bubbling of the acid of *"vinegar"* on the alkali of bicarbonate of *"soda."* Careful conduct is almost always welcome, especially where suffering is prolonged and painful.

Caution calls for some things to be enjoyed in small doses. *"Honey"* is one of them (see 16:24; 24:13; and esp. 25:16).

> *It is* not good to eat much honey;
> So to seek one's own glory *is not* glory.
> *Prov. 25:27*

The second line, which has provoked a number of explanations from commentators and translators, may be best understood by reading *"one's own glory"* as *"weighty"* (the literal meaning of *"glory"*) or *"difficult"* things, and by carrying over from the first line the *"not"* of *"not good"* to negate the second use of *"glory,"* as does the NKJV. The proverb would then comment on the dangers of unchecked curiosity which investigates (*"seek"* or *"search"*) things too weighty for the human mind to grapple with:

> It is not good to eat [too] much honey;
> and to search out difficult things is [no] glory.

So understood, the proverb recapitulates the warnings about the differences between God and the king and between the king and the commoners which introduced the chain of sayings in 25:2–3 (see R. van Leeuwen, p. 60, for these suggestions).

Here caution is counseled in the delegation of responsibility.

> He who sends a message by the hand of a fool
> Cuts off *his own* feet *and* drinks violence.
> *Prov. 26:6*

In Hebrew, as usual, the illustration comes first and deliberately exaggerates the danger to make the warning as stern as possible. We can inflict irreparable permanent harm on ourselves—like amputating one's *"own feet"* or drinking the *"violence"* of poison—if we entrust an essential, perhaps lifesaving *"message,"* to *"the hand of a fool."* A royal letter seeking peace, a commander's missive of battle strategy, a bid on a crucial parcel of property, a notice to a business colleague of a radical change in plans—those all require prompt, accurate, and responsible delivery. The fool may dally on the way, take the wrong turn in the road, give the message to the wrong person, or lose it altogether. And in so doing he may botch the sender's plan beyond recovery. Caution is the watchword because the message must go through. We count on the trustworthiness of the messenger. For us as communicators, the proverb stands as incentive to consistency, obedience, and accuracy. God has entrusted history's most important message to us. Woe to us if we play the fool!

CHAPTER TWENTY-SEVEN

Labor, Love, and Grace

Proverbs 27:1–27

HARD WORK

For biblical men and women, work is the way of life mandated both by our creation in God's image and our fall from God's favor. The Creator's command is clear: no sooner has He announced the plan to make humankind "in Our image, according to Our likeness," than He lays upon us the responsibility of "dominion over the fish of the sea, over the birds of the air, and over the cattle, over all the earth and over every creeping thing that creeps on the earth" (Gen. 1:26). That dominion was to be like God's dominion—full of care, protection, and provision, not a blatant display of power and exploitation but a sensitive duty of management and conservation. "Then the Lord God took the man and put him in the garden of Eden to tend and keep it" (Gen. 2:15). We work because our creation demanded it.

And we work because our fall dictated it. Greed in the garden meant the loss of the garden's goodness. Grasping for more dominion than God offered brought a reduction in the dominion we enjoyed. Keeping and tending (Gen. 2:15) became toiling and sweating (Gen. 3:17–19). The impact of the fall was double-barreled. Work became harder to do, and we lost some of our motivation and competence to do it. What we, as human beings, should have done by natural inclination we now have to do with deliberate intention, and even then we do not perform our work as well as we would like. The memory of Eden lies deep in our human consciousness and goads and shames us by its reminders of what we should be and what we are not.

Where that memory does not shout loudly enough or shine brightly enough, other voices like those of our parents and other lights like those of our teachers come into play. The Hebrew sages understood all this (see chap. 10) and made it their aim to serve their pupils, their society, and their Creator by their insistence that work be given its rightful priority and laziness be branded as a menace to human welfare and divine purpose.

Two aspects of the call to diligence are featured in the proverbs of the Hezekiah section (chaps. 25–29):

The range of vocations for work	
Servant	27:18
Shepherd	27:23–27
Farmer	28:19
The round of excuses for laziness	
Fear	26:13
Fatigue	26:14–15
Fatheadedness	26:16

The servant's vocation can be one of fruitfulness.

> Whoever keeps the fig tree will eat its fruit;
> So he who waits on his master will be honored.
> *Prov. 27:18*

The wide application of this saying can enlarge our understanding of the use of the proverbs. We have stressed the view that the primary audience was the group of potential leaders being groomed for the prominent places in the national administration. But the use of proverbial wisdom was by no means restricted to them. They passed it on to others until it was disseminated far and wide throughout the populace and helped shape the ethos of the entire nation. In a way, these teachings went full circle: many of them began in the clan, were collected in the court, taught in its schools, and then spread again, perhaps in more polished form, to the common people. If the one who *"waits on* [guards or watches the needs of] *his master"* will be esteemed, respected, and seen to carry weight in society (*"be honored"*), any one in any station of life can be encouraged to find meaning and value in life. The illustration of this is drawn from the persistence and patience of the orchard keeper who faithfully plants, cultivates, waters, prunes, and protects from animals and birds the fledgling tree for a period of several years. Then at last he is able to *"eat its fruit."* No denial of the tedium; no ignoring of the toil. Every job has its menial sides. All of us who see ourselves as servants know that. One day I came upon a painter at the seminary; he had been chipping for hours at crinkled paint on a steel pole. We chatted a minute and then I went to my office, leaving him with one remark, "Lem, you may be surprised to know that much of what I do every day is like chipping paint." Let the *"fig tree"* be the sign. Stay with the most repetitive and boring work and it will ultimately bear its fruit: the master's (and Master's) approval.

> 27:23 Be diligent to know the state of your flocks,
>   *And* attend to your herds;
>   24 For riches *are* not forever,
>   Nor does a crown *endure* to all generations.
>   25 *When* the hay is removed, and the tender grass
>   shows itself,
>   And the herbs of the mountains are gathered in,
>   26 The lambs *will provide* your clothing,
>   And the goats the price of a field.
>   27 *You shall have* enough goats' milk for your
>   food,
>   For the food of your household,
>   And the nourishment of your maidservants.
>   *Prov.* 27:23–27

The "shepherd" addressed in the imperatives, *"be diligent to know* [lit., "knowing, know," i.e., "truly know"; the repetition of the verb root gives the command high intensity] *and attend* [lit., "direct your heart/mind"]," is not a lonely peasant roaming the hills with staff in hand. He is the landowner who raises *"your flocks,"* both *"lambs"* and *"goats"* (v. 26), has a considerable investment at stake (v. 24), expands his sheep-raising opportunities by generating profit to buy another *"field"* (v. 26), and maintains a substantial *"household"* including an entourage of *"maidservants"* (v. 27). Given the fact that the young leaders were probably drawn from landed families, we need not find a change of audience in this expanded admonition. It may well be a warning not to let the pressures of urbane activities and the lure of get-rich-quick schemes seduce attention from the enduring and indispensable tasks of feeding and clothing one's household and providing *"nourishment"* (lit., "life" or "livelihood") for one's helpers. Beyond that, of course, are the joy and responsibility of producing surpluses to sell to those without adequate flocks and lands.

"Crown" (v. 24), though normally used in a literal sense, *"royal diadem"* (2 Sam. 1:10), may here be synonymous with *"riches"* and mean a *"royal way of life."* The wise were well aware of the fleeting nature of rash investments (see Eccles. 11:1–2). Well-kept sheep will produce wool and milk for years, in a manufacturing process by which they take cheap *"hay"* and free *"grass"* (*"herbs"* is a synonym

of "grass" describing rain-prompted grassy/shrubby growth) that grow in successive crops and add substantial value to them by the miracle of metabolism (vv. 25–27). The lasting worth of well-kept flocks and fields is signaled in their contrast with "riches" and "crown" which do not necessarily last for ages ("forever") and are not always passed along from generation to generation ("all generations"). The parallels between the good shepherding policies described here and duties of leaders who ought to govern righteously may be found in Ezekiel 34.

The word to the farmer is expressed in the typical antithesis that plays wisdom against folly.

> He who tills his land will have plenty of bread,
> But he who follows frivolity will have poverty
>   enough!
>
> *Prov. 28:19*

For the partner to this saying (12:11), see chapter 10. There the emphasis was on the empty-headedness of the person who makes "frivolity" (empty, mindless, idiotic pursuits), perhaps senseless, high-risk investments; *rēqîm* is the same root as the word for "fool" or "idiot" (*Raca*) that Jesus bans in the Sermon on the Mount (Matt. 5:22). Here the point is the dire result of failing to work ("till") the "land" with diligence: "poverty [see on 6:11] enough," literally, "he will be sated with poverty." Again it is the importance of agriculture, as the backbone of the economy, that the teachers are striving to safeguard.

The one thing at which the lazy were not sluggish was the art of coining alibis for their laziness. A round of excuses is listed in 26:13–15, followed by the conclusion of the wise that fatheadedness is the true reason for the sluggard's behavior.

> The lazy *man* says, "*There is* a lion in the road!
> A fierce lion *is* in the streets!"
>
> *Prov. 26:13*

Fear is the first excuse. "*The lazy man*" (or "sluggard"; 6:6, 9) stays locked comfortably in the house, claiming that to venture out would be life-threatening because of the "*lion*" (Hos. 5:14; 13:7) that purportedly roams the district, bold enough to leave cover and stalk the "*road*" and "*streets.*" The two words for "*lion*" or "*fierce lion*" are virtually identical. The Semitic languages enjoy coining words for "lion," especially Arabic, which has hundreds of them. That lions in

Palestine could be harmful is demonstrated in the Old Testament (Judg. 14:5; Amos 5:19); they were ferocious carnivores, close kin to the lions of Africa. The crusades apparently wiped them out in Palestine, but they continued to appear in Syria, Iraq, and Iran into the nineteenth and twentieth centuries. The saying in 26:13 has a fraternal, not identical, twin in 22:13, which mentions specifically the threat of death (see chap. 10).

Fatigue is the second excuse.

> As a door turns on its hinges,
> So *does* the lazy *man* on his bed.
> Prov. 26:14

The saying is a comparison in which whatever movement the *"lazy"* person (see 26:13) makes leads nowhere and produces nothing; it is like the swinging of *"a door."* Turning over in *"bed"* requires all the energy he can muster.

The fatigue is further illustrated in a scene at the table (see 19:24 in chap. 10).

> The lazy *man* buries his hand in the bowl;
> It wearies him to bring it back to his mouth.
> Prov. 26:15

The sluggard (*"lazy man"*) can stir from bed periodically when hunger pangs prod him. But even then his ennui wins out: the combined weight of the bread he dipped and the sauce *"in the bowl"* (2 Kings 21:13) *"wearies him"* so that *"his hand"* cannot manage the return trip *"to his mouth."*

The sluggard has his real problem exposed in the concluding verse. Not fear nor fatigue but fatheadedness is the trouble.

> The lazy *man is* wiser in his own eyes
> Than seven men who can answer sensibly.
> Prov. 26:16

He is not only lazy but unteachable because he deems himself wise. A vast cadre (*"seven"* describes completeness, not a literal number) of discerning, sensible (the root word *ṭ'm* describes good taste, reliable judgment; 11:22) persons can explain his problems to him and make no dent in his faulty thinking. As usual, the teachers did not have in view persons of physical limitations—the lame, maimed, or mentally infirm. The persons they described had competence enough to care for their own and contribute to society and with dogged stubbornness refused to do so.

WARM AFFECTIONS

Achievement gained by hard work and relationships nurtured by firm love should go hand in hand. I try to measure my effectiveness as a leader with a two-column scorecard. The left-hand column gauges my effectiveness in accomplishing the goals I set out to reach in a given time frame, for me an academic year—September through June. There I evaluate how I have done in long-range planning, recruiting and orientation of new trustees, implementing new academic programs, raising funds to meet the operating budget and the capital needs of the seminary, and making progress in writing books like this one. The right-hand column rates relationships; the morale and well-being of my family members so far as they are dependent on how I have treated them, the personal growth of those with whom I work closely, the levels of joy or anxiety in the seminary community, the contribution I have made or not made to my circle of intimate friends. The left-hand column is an index of my work; the right-hand column is a window on my love. My aim, which I have never reached, is to keep both columns high and equally so. I am so geared for achievement that I do not find it difficult to shortchange relationships.

I have a hunch that Israel's young leaders who were the first students of Proverbs were a lot like me. That may be why sayings about love stand side by side with sayings about work (see chap. 17). A cluster of them in chapter 27 touch on the following aspects of love:

> Love's limits   27:4
> Love's labor   27:5–6
> Love's loyalty   27:10

Love's limits are set by three boundaries: what is good for the one being loved, for the one doing the loving, and for the community to which both belong.

> Wrath *is* cruel and anger a torrent,
> But who *is* able to stand before jealousy?
> *Prov. 27:4*

Those limits are exceeded when *"jealousy"* (or *"envy"*; see 6:34; 14:30; Song of Sol. 8:6) kidnaps love and uses it for selfish purposes. Jealousy is out of bounds. It strikes the parties involved and those who care for them with far greater force than the red-hot *"wrath"* (or *"rage"*; 6:34; 15:1, 18; 22:24) that is *"cruel"* (5:9; 11:17; 12:10; 17:11) at the time but often short lived. It is like the snorting *"anger"* (22:24) that bowls over its victim with the rush of a rain-filled gully (*"torrent"*; Ps. 32:6) but also may spend itself quickly, like a temper tantrum (in Hebrew to be *"short of wrath"* is to be quick tempered, 14:17; to be *"slow to wrath,"* lit., *"long of wrath,"* is to be patient, 14:29).

Jealousy, in short, is impossible. It purports to love while it distorts love. It addles the thinking of the jealous person to misinterpret every word and act of the *"loved"* one. It threatens the beloved person by fencing in his or her freedom so that all actions have to be judged by one criterion: how will the jealous person react? It jeopardizes the peace of family and friends by thrusting the sword of irrational thinking into their midst and making normal relationships impossible. Jealousy topples life to its knees and makes everyday walking and standing an achievement beyond reach. What the New Testament calls *philadelphia* (Rom. 12:10; 1 Thess. 4:9; Heb. 13:1), the kind of love that stable families enjoy, the willingness to suffer and sacrifice for each other, is shattered.

Love's labor is expressed in the willingness to make the effort to confront a friend when such action (*"open rebuke"* below; see 1:23; 3:11) is necessary.

> Open rebuke *is* better
> Than love carefully concealed.
> *Prov. 27:5*

Reproof that confronts is much preferred (*"better"* signals the contrast) to *"love"* that is too timid, too fragile (*"concealed"*) to say the needed thing. Indeed, confrontation done in the right way and for the right reasons is a high act of love (see Eph. 4:25–27), a worthy labor of love (see 1 Thess. 1:3); silence, in such circumstances, is no love at all. For those of us who minister as public communicators of the faith, it is often easier to preach on love to an audience—protected by pulpit, robe, and rank—than to confront face to face in love those who need our rebuke. Jesus' version of this proverb, set in the form of an admonition, gives us a definition of how such laboring love ought to work: "If your brother sins against you, rebuke him; and if he repents, forgive him" (Luke 17:3). I fear that our love is not usually good enough either to rebuke or to forgive.

Love's labor is depicted even more graphically in the antithesis between the wounds inflicted by a friend and the kisses feigned by an enemy.

> Faithful *are* the wounds of a friend,
> But the kisses of an enemy *are* deceitful.
>   *Prov.* 27:6

The *"faithful"* nature of the wounds expands on the theme of verse 5: the *"friend"* can be trusted since his intentions are loving ("well-meant," Scott, p. 161) even when he states the truths that hit home and hurt. The *"enemy"* is no less an enemy when he pretends affection with a lavish display ("effusive"; McKane, p. 610) of *"kisses"*; the public show, the overplayed scene of attachment, marks him more, not less, the enemy. Volume and ostentation are necessary only when treachery is the aim. The excess gestures of endearment are themselves badges of treason (*"deceitful"*). The chidings Jesus often gave His disciples are *"the wounds of a friend."* The kisses Judas gave Jesus are the deceit of an enemy (Mark 14:43–45).

Love's loyalty is described in the admonitions of verse 10.

> Do not forsake your own friend or your father's
>   friend,
> Nor go to your brother's house in the day of your
>   calamity;
> Better *is* a neighbor nearby than a brother far away.
>   *Prov.* 27:10

One may wish that the picture were clearer: (1) the three-line form is unusual; (2) the command not to enter *"your brother's house"* seems strange in light of 17:17, where the opposite is stated; (3) no mention of the reasons for the apparent contradiction between 17:17 and 27:10 is noted. The best way to catch the flow of the text seems to be to reconstruct circumstances from the brief saying, perhaps originally a self-contained proverb, in the last line. The basic question is this: how do you behave *"in the day of your calamity"*? Where do you seek help? Close to home from *"your own friend"* or an older family (*"your father's"*) *"friend."* But why not from your brother? Probably because your brother's house is *"too far away."* Why seek help from a relative who is removed from you by geographical circumstances, when a loving friend or neighbor is available nearby?

Other backgrounds may be posited. Perhaps the sufferer, wracked by financial or physical calamity has outworn his brother's welcome. Or possibly he has taken literally the warning of 25:17 against frequenting a neighbor's house too often. In any case the basic command, as interpreted by the final line, seems clear: where love's loyalty is available from friends, do not run away from it; use it as you need it. After all, those faithful friends will probably welcome an opportunity to reciprocate the deeds of kindness that evoked their friendship in the first place. Hence it can be an act of loyal love to ask for help just as it is to render help. In the covenant of neighborliness, love flows in both directions.

FEMININE DIGNITY

The proverbs say almost nothing about women in general; their subject is women in relationship to men—women as mothers (1:6; 4:3; 6:20; 10:1; 15:20; 19:26; 20:20; 23:22, 25; 28:24; 29:15; 30:11, 17; 31:1), women as daughters (31:29), and women as wives (virtually all the sayings in this section, except 22:14, where the theme of seductive immorality is resumed from the earlier parts of the book; see 2:16–20; 5:1–23; 6:20–35; 7:1–27; 23:26–28; see also 30:20). Even more important to notice is that no proverb is spoken directly to a woman. The audience was entirely male—the generations of potential leaders of Israel's commonwealth.

Men are told to listen to their mothers, to honor their mothers, and to behave in ways that bring them neither pain nor shame. And men are told to take care in the choosing of a wife, lest they be embarrassed in their community, and uncomfortable at home. Almost nothing is said specifically about how a man should treat the woman to whom he is married. We must assume that the general maxims about patience, self-control, kindness, and gentle speech and wise deeds were meant to apply in the home as well as in social relations or public service. In addition, the instructions against fornication and adultery point to an emphasis on love and loyalty to a covenant partner (see 5:15–23). No mention is made of divorce, and no license is given to abuse a wife under any circumstances.

What are celebrated both directly and obliquely in these sayings are the grace and graciousness of womanhood and the marvelous contribution that an inwardly lovely woman makes to the building of a stable family. Since the proverbs deal largely with relationships and relatively few persons of either gender remained single in Israelite society, the focus is on marital and family life. And since public careers, as we know them, were rarely open to women, the center of activity is the household, though the range of duties and opportunities in the households of the wealthy, influential families whose sons were instructed by the teachers was huge (see 31:10–31).

The sayings that touch on female behavior as a guide to the establishing of sound marriages may be organized along these lines:

Introduction	
role	11:16
responsibility	14:1
Discretion	11:22; 12:4
Harmony	21:9, 19; 25:24; 27:15–16
Integrity	22:14
Conclusion	
providence	18:22; 19:14

> A gracious woman retains honor,
> But ruthless *men* retain riches.
> *Prov. 11:16*

The point of this saying seems to be a contrast between the role of women and that of men in Israel's upper classes. For a *"woman,"* the chief aim in life should be the *"honor"* and respect that cause her and her household to carry weight and win regard in the community. For a man, financial security (*"riches"*; see chaps. 19 and 28 for sayings on the advantages and use of wealth) should be the prime concern, enabling him to care for his family, share his goods with his neighbors (see chaps. 11 and 25 for the theme of generosity), and praise God from whom all blessings flow.

The outstanding quality necessary for persons of each gender to play these roles is plainly stated. (1) For the woman, grace is the key—not merely outward beauty, but poise under pressure. This includes the steady intuition of what to say and do under all circumstances, no matter how surprising or trying. (2) For the man, "vigor" or "energy" is the key—not merely physical strength or stature, but the ability to keep motivation high and concentration firm so that nothing diverts him from the goal of providing for his household. This interpretation (and the text may lend itself to several other possibilities including a much expanded form in the Greek Septuagint) rests on the probability that the word read *"ruthless"* in NKJV (ʿārîṣ) can also, as is evident in its Arabic form, have the positive meaning of "vigorous" or "energetic" (see McKane, p. 431). As with all proverbs, we must read this one as a generalization applicable to many but not all situations. Personal aptitudes and circumstances may encourage or necessitate other qualities and even reversals of roles.

> The wise woman builds her house,
> But the foolish pulls it down with her hands.
> *Prov. 14:1*

The lesson of this antithetical saying has to do with the responsibility of the woman: to exercise her wisdom (Kidner correctly translates *"wise woman"* as "womanly wisdom," p. 105) in building, that is, establishing and maintaining her household on a solid foundation. *"House"* is much more than a material structure; it describes the persons who live and work together and their whole way of life. The term *"foolish"* should be interpreted to mean "womanly folly," the negative counterpart of line one. Whether such folly expresses itself in contentiousness, lack of discretion, laziness, or immorality we are not told. What we do know is that the stability of the family and its entourage of servants and helpers hinges on the conduct of the woman who leads and guides the household. Her behavior can make the ultimate difference between its welfare and its destruction. The more general contrast between wisdom's ability to construct and folly's skill to destroy (chap. 9) is given a personal setting in this saying.

Discretion (lit., "taste"; Exod. 16:31; its figurative meaning comes to be "discernment" or "accurate perception"; for the noun, see 26:16; for the verb, 31:18) is a highly desired quality in either a man or woman.

> As a ring of gold in a swine's snout,
> So *is* a lovely woman who lacks discretion.
> *Prov. 11:22*

Without it, no amount of physical beauty will provide adequate compensation. In fact the disjunction between loveliness in face and form and churlishness in speech and behavior is as jarring as the waste of *"a ring of gold"* mounted in the pierced *"snout"* of a pig. I think it was John Gardner, one of our generation's articulate spokespersons on leadership and its character, who said, "When I choose persons to work with me, I look for two things: taste and judgment. Everything else is for sale by the pound."

The presence or absence of discretion must lie at the heart of the contrast in this proverb.

> An excellent wife *is* the crown of her husband,
> But she who causes shame *is* like rottenness in his
>   bones.
>
> *Prov. 12:4*

"Excellent" (see 31:10) translates a many-splendored word that begins by meaning "strength" and then branches out to include "ability," "merit," and "reputation." Its antithesis, *"she who causes shame,"* suggests the utter lack of discretion, whether in speech, manners, ability, attitude, or morality. The community and perhaps some of her own household have branded her as unworthy, and her husband's morale is affected right to *"his bones"* (which in Hebrew can stand for his whole inner self, not just his skeletal frame), which turn weak as though hollowed by *"rottenness"* (see 14:30 for the noun; 10:7, for the verb). The impact of emotional suffering on the bones is well documented in Ps. 32:3. A pastor friend of mine, pressured for years by a combination of overwork and conflict with a congregation, expressed to me his need for relief from distress like this, "I want six months just to soak my weary bones." The contrast between *"crown"* (or "wreath"; see 4:9) and *"rottenness"* is apt: stellar conduct of a spouse brings a tone of royalty to anyone's life; public embarrassment caused by a partner gnaws at the vitals of anyone's inner being.

Harmony is the quality valued in a wife in five of the proverbs that deal with feminine behavior.

> Better to dwell in a corner of a housetop,
> Than in a house shared with a contentious woman.
>
> *Prov. 21:9*

> Better to dwell in the wilderness,
> Than with a contentious and angry woman.
>
> *Prov. 21:19*

> *It is* better to dwell in a corner of a housetop,
> Than in a house shared with a contentious woman.
>
> *Prov. 25:24*

All of these reach for strong comparisons to describe a woman who picks fights as a way of life, a trait from which men are in no way exempted (see 26:21). *"Contentious"* in each of these proverbs is a word that suggests constant quarreling about decisions—who, how, what, and why. The gist of 21:9, 19, and 25:24 is that isolation and solitude, no matter how uncomfortable, are preferable to continual conflict. In 21:9 and 25:24, which are identical sayings, the isolation is to stay (*"dwell"*) *"in a corner of a housetop,"* perhaps a tiny attic room, used for storage and an occasional guest, with few of the basic amenities that the Shunammite offered Elisha (2 Kings 4:10). In 21:19, the preferred solitude is starkly and simply the desert (*"wilderness"*), with no farms, no houses, and only the marauding animals and passing bedouin as occasional companions. *"Angry"* (12:16; 17:25; 27:3) is added to lend bite to the meaning of contentious.

The contentious woman is one who never backs away from her nagging commitment to quarrelsomeness.

> 27:15 A continual dripping on a very rainy day
>   And a contentious woman are alike;
>   16 Whoever restrains her restrains the wind,
>   And grasps oil with his right hand.
>   *Prov. 27:15–16*

The perpetual repetition of her arguing has the maddening effect of rain's *"continual dripping,"* perhaps like a leak which is so unrelenting that we become wild to escape it (see 19:13). Tradition has it that an outraged homeowner phoned Frank Lloyd Wright with the complaint that the roof of the new house which the distinguished architect had designed was leaking badly—and directly over the owner's favorite chair. Wright's response was classic: "Move your chair." No way to check the dripping, so to get out of the house was the harassed husband's only recourse. Two other comparisons (v. 16) describe the impossibility of stopping the pugilistic prattler. To restrain her (lit., "put her in a hiding place where she won't disturb anyone") is about as easy as grabbing *"the wind"* to hold it back (see Eccles. 2:11, etc., for the futility of clutching at the wind) or picking up olive *"oil"* with the *"right hand."* The latter comparison is rendered more literally by Scott (p. 162)—"One cries out that 'his hand is slippery'"—who compares the image to our "butterfingers." Compulsiveness of any kind and of either gender is hard to live with. You can't stand it, and you can't stop it.

The integrity of a fine wife (see 12:4 above) is exalted by the contrast between her and the immoral woman whose dangers are highlighted in 22:14.

> The mouth of an immoral woman *is* a deep pit;
> He who is abhorred by the LORD will fall there.
>
> *Prov. 22:14*

Immoral could be translated "strange" or "foreign" (2:16; 5:3, 17, 20; 6:1; 7:5). In the Israel of the monarchy, most women, especially those from noble or landed families, would have been sheltered from the ploys of sexual opportunists by their servants, family, and daily routines. Foreigners living in Palestine, whether for business or political assignments, seemed less bound by local custom. At times they must have flaunted their moral indifference so that "foreign woman" came to connote "immoral woman." If Israelite women aped their ways, they too could be branded "foreign." Israelite men on the prowl seemed to feel that they could dally with such loose types with less reproach and greater anonymity. Hence the reminder that her *"mouth"*—both her seductive words (see 7:14–21) and her profligate kisses (5:3)—was *"a deep pit,"* a fatal trap for the wild or unwary.

"Abhorred" is literally "scolded" or even "cursed" (see 24:24). *"The Lord"* who demands integrity of all His people, male and female, does not let sexual promiscuity go unpunished. Acts of immorality, in ways that we cannot always comprehend, carry their own judgment. We are plagued by guilt, our reputations are tarred in the community, our children are put to shame by our conduct and confused by our double standard, our partners may feel the need to remove themselves from a situation where betrayal has become the rule, and venereal disease may rob us of health. In all this, God's hand is on us bringing harm to us as we have to others and pressing us by the pain of judgment to seek His face and turn from our wicked ways.

God is not always Lord of punishment; He is Lord of providence as well.

> Houses and riches *are* an inheritance from fathers,
> But a prudent wife *is* from the LORD.
>
> *Prov. 19:14*

His providence shines with special brilliance in His gift of *"a prudent wife."* *"From the Lord"* stands at the head of its Hebrew clause and is thrust thereby into prominence. If a contentious mate makes one yearn for isolation, a wise, clever, effective (on the root *śkl*, *"prudent,"* see 1:3; 10:5) partner ought to prompt gratitude to God in lavish measure. Such a gift outranks any kind of *"inheritance"* no matter how bountiful the *"house"* and the *"riches."* They may be the best that our fathers ("ancestors") can bequeath us. But God can do better. He can give as He did to the first man a "bone of my bones" and "flesh of my flesh" companion, lover, and coworker (Gen. 2:23).

> *He who* finds a wife finds a good *thing,*
> And obtains favor from the LORD.
> *Prov. 18:22*

This saying connects marriage to divine *"favor"* (see 8:35, for the identical clause; also 12:2). The institution itself is ordained by God, affirmed by Jesus in His first miracle at the wedding in Cana (John 2), and acclaimed by Paul to be a demonstration of Christ's relationship to the church (Ephesians 5).

The proverb may not have had all this in mind, though biblical revelation as a whole teaches this understanding of marriage and therefore calls divorce sin (Mal. 2:13–16; Mark 10:12). Within the framework of God's gracious provision of marriage as the setting for love, child bearing, family nurture, and lifelong care, and as the chief way of reflecting God's covenantal loyalty to His people, the teachers are encouraging their students to be thankful for the *"wife"* God has given. Though no adjective is attached to wife—remember "excellent" in 12:4 and "prudent" in 19:14—some description like that must be implied. Nothing in any proverb suggests that a quarrelsome wife is a gift of God. But then neither do the proverbs seem to make explicit the truth that the husband may be partly responsible for her pugnacious disposition. What the proverb seems to say is that wherever the relationship between husband and wife is satisfactory, the husband should thank God for the *"good"* (*"thing"* is supplied in translation and should probably be omitted since it borders on depersonalizing the woman) that has came into his experience, see her as a gift of God's favor, pursue a righteous life with her, and shower her with the love that God's grace has poured out on him.

CHAPTER TWENTY-EIGHT

Poor and Rich;
Righteous and Foolish

Proverbs 28:1–28

This chapter plays variations on familiar themes. The subject of wealth which rises to prominence in almost every chapter of Proverbs is treated here in a minor key. Its risks and dangers are the dominant message, not its blessings and advantages (see, in contrast, chap. 19). No incentive is given to acquire it, only warnings about its pitfalls. These sayings are clear illustrations of the checks and balances in which the teachers specialized. On the one hand, they affirmed the joy of wealth in the opportunities it afforded and the philanthropy it enabled. On the other hand, they cautioned against the greed and dishonesty which many paid as the price of wealth. Wealth ill-gotten was a much worse fate than poverty. So taught the six sayings discussed in the first part of this chapter.

The second major theme reprises the notes sounded so clearly and consistently in chapters 10 and 21 about the rewards of righteousness and the calamities that follow folly. The advice centers more in the general outcomes and their striking contrasts. The two ways they are generally labeled: the way of blessing that is the lot of the righteous and wise (remember those terms are virtually synonymous) and the way of doom that is the destiny of the wicked and foolish. Since the conceptual background of these emphases has been treated in the earlier chapters, it remains for us only to sketch briefly the force and contribution of each saying.

RISKS OF WEALTH

The negative lessons about wealth were as necessary as the positive ones. The brashness of youth can encourage us to overvalue wealth, to seek it for the wrong reasons, or to look down on those who have less than we. The six sayings in chapter 28 can be organized like this:

> Priorities of wisdom
>> The importance of integrity   28:6
>> The superiority of understanding   28:11
>> The centrality of justice   28:21
> Dangers of greed
>> The loss of wealth to the poor   28:8
>> The punishment by poverty   28:20, 22

> Better *is* the poor who walks in his itegrity
> Than one perverse *in his* ways, though he *be* rich.
>> *Prov. 28:6*

The *"better"* proverbs compare extremes in such a way that what is generally valued—here, being *"rich"*—is far outweighed by what is generally denigrated—here, being *"poor."* But the contrast of economic status is not the central point of the saying. It is the radical difference between *"integrity,"* an upright and admirable life that centers in the finer values of the community as a perpetual habit (*"walks"*), and *"perverse"* (28:18) patterns of conduct (*"ways"*) that violate both the laws of God and the mores of society. No amount of wealth can assure blessing, success, or honor when integrity is absent. *"Better"* in such contexts not only means a better example; it also denotes a better result. We could virtually translate it with the phrase *"better off"* is the upright poor person than the crooked rich one. God will bless the one and judge the other.

> The rich man *is* wise in his own eyes,
> But the poor who has understanding searches him
>   out.
>> *Prov. 28:11*

"Understanding" (Heb. *mēbîn*; 1:2, 6; 8:9) as well as integrity is a value to be treasured beyond material wealth. In the antithetic form of the saying it plays against *"wise in his own eyes"* and wins. Wealth without objective power to evaluate oneself is a loser. The *"poor"* person who is perceptive can see right through (*"searches him out"*) the pretense, vanity, and emptiness of the wealthy person who lacks judgment. Good judgment may help one acquire riches, but to be *"rich"* without that judgment is infinitely inferior to poverty in the priority system of the wise.

Justice also outweighs material goods.

> To show partiality *is* not good,
> Because for a piece of bread a man will transgress.
>
> *Prov. 28:21*

The young administrators charged with the high duty of deciding lawsuits and other kinds of litigation had to know this. They themselves had to live above reproach, resisting all temptation *"to show partiality"* (see on 24:23). They had also to beware of false witnesses who would violate the law (*"transgress"*) and sell the truth for a price as low as *"a piece of bread."* To condone such bribery caters to greed and may drive both the giver and the recipient to raise the ante. Illgotten gain is contagious and habit forming. A trial is taking place in Chicago as I write this. The prosecution claims that a public official was first corrupted by a $20 bill passed to his hand surreptitiously in a handshake. That handshake led to a pattern of accepting bribes that allegedly totaled $70,000. What began as a piece of bread created an appetite that ultimately craved the entire bakery. No society can stay decent and pander justice at any price.

God's way of working is often tinged with irony.

> One who increases his possessions by usury and
>   extortion
> Gathers it for him who will pity the poor.
>
> *Prov. 28:8*

Greed is fraught with surprising dangers as the synthetic parallelism, where the final line is a surprising climax, shows. *"Usury"* and *"extortion"* were banned by law (Lev. 25:36). The latter (Heb. *tarbît*) is excessive interest that takes advantage of the borrower's misfortune. The former (Heb. *neshek*) is a fixed loan fee that withholds part of the loan at the beginning of the transaction. The borrower gets nipped both ways: he borrows less than he needs (usury) and pays back more than he should (extortion). The irony is that none of this will ultimately profit the lender but will, presumably in a stroke of divine justice, fall into the hands of someone who will take *"pity"* on *"the poor"* and give it to them. On the seriousness with which the prophets judge unscrupulous lending practices, see Ezek. 18:8, 13.

> A faithful man will abound with blessings,
> But he who hastens to be rich will not go
>   unpunished.
>
> *Prov. 28:20*

"Faithful" and greedy (*"he who hastens to be rich"*) are opposites. The former term speaks of reliability toward fellow members of the community, of trustworthiness in word, deed, and motive. The latter clause describes persons who cut corners of honesty, ride roughshod over commitments, and place profit above relationships. Such topsy-turvy values will lead either to crimes that merit punishment or to the judgment of the Almighty One before whose eyes all of our deeds are bare and naked.

> A man with an evil eye hastens after riches,
> And does not consider that poverty will come upon
>   him.
>
> *Prov. 28:22*

The *"evil eye"* (see 23:6) is a graphic figure for an attitude of ill-will toward others, motivated by jealousy, hatred, or some kindred disposition. Greed is surely its chief expression in this passage, as *"hastens after riches"* (see v. 20) attests. As often with evil pursuits, what results is the opposite of what is sought. *"Poverty"* is greed's reward not wealth. The God of justice will see to it, though He may use natural means like gambling losses or bad investments to enforce His judgment.

RIGHTEOUSNESS AND FOLLY: PERPETUAL ENEMIES

In a cluster of comparisons and contrasts, the dangers of foolishness and the wonders of righteousness are pounded home. No literary device is spared, no illustration is left unused. This section, credited to Hezekiah's scribes (25:1), feels as though it needs to treat the issue from every possible angle before the space runs out and the book is completed. Chapter 28 is especially ardent in teaching the last word on the subject with a zeal that borders on compulsiveness. Three major headings may be used to embrace the proverbs treated here:

The calamity of righteousness that fails	
Corruption of others	25:26
Catastrophe to the wicked	28:10
The absurdity of honoring a fool	
The cause: self-deception	28:26
The comparisons	26:1, 8, 10
The consequences	
The harm of flattery	29:5
The indelibleness of folly	26:3; 27:22

The failure of righteousness is nothing less than a calamity.

> A righteous *man* who falters before the wicked
> *Is like* a murky spring and a polluted well.
> > *Prov. 25:26*

NKJV inverts the order of the lines. The Hebrew begins with the comparison for the sake of drama and to highlight the magnitude of the crime: to foul the water supply, say with animal excrement or poisonous plants, was an atrocity of high order, threatening the livelihood and even life of a whole community. Our massive modern problem of the contaminating effects of hazardous wastes gives us empathy with the ancient setting of this saying. What is not so clear is the precise nature of the calamity described by *"falters"* (or *"totters"*). It could picture the moral collapse of a *"righteous"* person who succumbs to the lures of the *"wicked"* man and imitates his godless way. That certainly would have a negative impact on the community. Yet it is hard to account for the dramatic double image of the *"murky," "polluted"* water source. Better, I think, is the interpretation that reads *"falter"* as a failure to confront, oppose, or resist the wicked person, who then bulldozes the righteous one out of his way and is thus free to work his godless will in the community with the death-dealing corruption that the befouled water envisages. A reminder this, that while the ultimate fate of the wicked is in God's hands, and He will triumph, our interim role is to battle wickedness for the sake of the spiritual health of family, church, and society.

This saying looks at the situation from the opposite side.

> Whoever causes the upright to go astray in an evil
>   way,
> He himself will fall into his own pit;
> But the blameless will inherit good.
> > *Prov. 28:10*

In 25:26 the emphasis was on the failure of the righteous to withstand the juggernaut of the wicked. Now attention is focused on the seductive wiles of an evil person who lures *"upright"* people (the Hebrew noun is plural) to leave the straight and narrow way and fall into sin and its harmful effects. *"Evil"* can mean both the bad act and its consequences. A literal instance of such vicious misleading is cursed in Deut. 28:18.

The promise of judgment in line 2 with its yawning *"pit"* waiting to trap the culprit is a catastrophe of his own making suggests that his evil intent was not only to divert persons of integrity ('upright') from the path but to bury them in a cavity of rebellion from which they could not extricate themselves. The *"blameless"* are those who neither mislead nor are misled. Their lot is to inherit *"good"* things, blessings both material and spiritual.

> He who trusts in his own heart is a fool,
> But whoever walks wisely will be delivered.
> *Prov. 28:26*

A dominant theme in this section is the absurdity of honoring a fool. One major cause of folly is to place ultimate confidence (*"trusts"*) in one's own thinking (*"heart"*). Such self-destruction has several forms: one may pay no heed to the lessons of experience and plow ahead on one's own mindless path; one may not seek the safety found in listening to other wise counselors (11:14; 15:22; 24:6); worst of all one may squeeze the fear of the Lord out of all decision-making and pay the costly price of living as though God did not matter (see chap. 14). The one who *"walks wisely"* does all that the *"fool"* neglects and escapes (*"will be delivered"*) the disastrous consequences.

Three comparisons use humor to mock the absurdity of granting honor (weight, repute) to a fool.

> As snow in summer and rain in harvest,
> So honor is not fitting for a fool.
> *Prov. 26:1*

> Like one who binds a stone in a sling
> *Is* he who gives honor to a fool.
> *Prov. 26:8*

First, to do so is as out of place as *"snow in summer"* and *"rain in harvest"* (26:1)—particularly apt sarcasm for a land that has almost no rain between April to October and where snow is usually limited to the areas of higher elevation in Galilee and the highlands of Gilead. Second, to render tribute to a *"fool"* is as inappropriate as trying to bind *"a stone in a sling"* (28:8); it is almost impossible to tie a smooth, round stone (see David's sling stones in 1 Sam. 17:40, 49–50) in the sling's pouch and, more absurd yet, to do so would render the sling unusable and defeat the entire purpose of having one.

> The great *God* who formed everything
> Gives the fool *his* hire and the transgressor *his*
>   wages.
>
> *Prov. 26:10*

The Hebrew text of 26:10 is one of the more difficult in Proverbs. Most modern translations take a very different tack from that of NKJV. *"God"* does not occur in the Hebrew, and *"great"* is frequently translated "archer" (see Gen. 49:23, where the verb *rbb*, which resembles words for "great" means to "shoot arrows"). The precise comparison is not easy to ascertain but van Leeuwen's reading (p. 87) is as accurate as any:

> An archer who wounds all
> One who hires a fool or passing drunkard.

To hire ("hire" and drunkard look much alike in Hebrew) is in a sense to honor by showing confidence and trust. To do that to those unworthy of such responsibility is downright dangerous, as dangerous as a wild-eyed archer taking potshots at random in a crowded marketplace. Honor to the fool is a double error: it rewards stupid behavior, further encouraging folly; it also undercuts the effort of the righteous by giving honor where it is not due.

The consequences of such misplaced honor are stated in two sayings.

> A man who flatters his neighbor
> Spreads a net for his feet.
> *Prov. 29:5*

Any flattery (lit., "smooth talk") is dangerous because it makes the one who is flattered—here the *"neighbor"*—susceptible to any ploy or plot the flatterer has in mind. Flattery swells the ego and dulls the judgment both at once. It makes a manipulator if not a liar out of the one who practices it; it gulls the one who receives flattery into false self-confidence and makes him vulnerable to the wiles (the hunting *"net"*) of the flatterer. When the victim is a fool, the consequences are extreme: he has incentive to behave even more foolishly and is set up to hurt others by exaggerated folly and be hurt in return, like a bird or small animal whose *"feet"* are snared in a trapper's net.

A further fate of a fool is to be stamped indelibly with foolishness.

> Though you grind a fool in a mortar with a pestle
>   along with crushed grain,
> *Yet* his foolishness will not depart from him.
> > *Prov. 27:22*

No amount of pounding, pressure, or grinding—*"mortar,"* a hollowed stone, and *"pestle,"* a rodlike stone, are the standard tools for grinding grain or vegetable to make flour or sauce—can beat it from the *"fool."* It permeates every part of his person and becomes inextricable. One of Proverbs' more memorable sayings carries us from the kitchen to the fields and makes the same point.

> A whip for the horse,
> A bridle for the donkey,
> And a rod for the fool's back.
> > *Prov. 26:3*

The structure resembles the numerical sayings of chapter 30. Without using numbers it lists two things in order to emphasize the third. *"Fool"* not *"horse"* or *"donkey"* is the subject, not only of the verse but of the whole series of sayings in the twelve verses that begin chapter 26. The question is how to get the proper response from a slow-witted or rebellious-spirited fool. The answer is treat him like an animal: use external force. The point is not abuse. The *"whip"* (1 Kings 12:11, 14) is not used to punish a horse, but to prompt it to move quickly and maneuver skillfully in battle (21:31). The *"bridle"* is not to break the donkey's neck but to guide it over the rocky twists and turns as it carries its precious cargo. The *"rod"* then is an instrument of instruction to encourage the fool to wiser, more productive behavior, because the folly is so deeply stamped in him that words alone do not prove adequate. Foolishness here is not an occasional lapse of judgment but a pattern of behavior, thought, and choice that utterly saturates the fool's personality. It is a tragic case of how practice can make perfect.

We may introduce the series of contrasts between the righteous and the wicked by noting that each is an abomination to the other.

> An unjust man *is* an abomination to the righteous,
> And *he who is* upright in the way *is* an abomination
>   to the wicked,
>   *Prov. 29:27*

The polarity between the two ways of life is pushed to its extremes by that horrible word which suggests unrelieved antipathy, total revulsion of each by the other. Few passages in Scripture deal more starkly with the unspannable gulf between people who love God and God's ways (called here *"righteous"* and *"upright"*) and people who live to spurn God's care and flout God's will.

We have outlined the contrast by spotlighting the behavior of the righteous as that behavior is made all the more attractive by the obnoxiousness of its opposite.

> A prudent *man* foresees evil *and* hides himself;
> The simple pass on *and* are punished.
>   *Prov. 27:12*

Foreseeing danger is a skill of a *"prudent"* (shrewd, clever; 12:16, 23) person, who is not only perceptive but sensibly practical enough to hide himself for protection. The *"simple"* (naive, unseasoned) persons, on the other hand, keep going (*"pass on"*) and pay the price or fine (*"are punished"*; 22:3) for their callow stupidity. In such cases an ounce of prevention is worth much more than a pound of cure.

The lionlike (for "lion," see 19:12; 20:2; 26:13; 28:15; 30:30) courage exhibited by the righteous is due to their firm confidence (*"bold"* is literally *"trusting"*) in the Lord's commitment to vindicate their God-fearing behavior.

> The wicked flee when no one pursues,
> But the righteous are bold as a lion.
>   *Prov. 28:1*

Conversely, the *"wicked"* person lives charily and moves skittishly (*"flees"*) even when no one is out to get him, not only because of a tainted conscience but because of a deep-seated fear that his sins will find him out and the divine gavel of judgment will rap out his punishment.

> Because of the transgression of a land, many *are* its
>   princes;
> But by a man of understanding *and* knowledge
> Right will be prolonged.
>
> *Prov. 28:2*

The scene seems to shift here from the personal to the political arena (though the variety of translations witness to the difficulty of the Hebrew text of 28:2) and contrasts the instability of a realm where an ingrained pattern of *"transgression"* (lit., "mutiny" or "rebellion"; see on 10:12, 19) leads to a high rate of turnover in royal leadership (*"many are its princes"*). Hosea documents such a period in the life of the Northern Kingdom from 753 to 723 B.C., when three of the six kings had reigns of two years or less each of which ended violently. "[They] have devoured their judges, / All their kings have fallen. / None among them calls upon Me" describes the chaos (Hos. 7:7), which is further documented in Hos. 8:4; 10:3; 13:10–11; 2 Kings 15:8–26. Exceptions may be cited to the rule that transgression leads to short reigns and *"right"* (a word not in the Hebrew text but supplied for clarity in NKJV) to *"prolonged"* ones. Manasseh, a paragon of wickedness, held sway in Judah some fifty-five years (2 Kings 21) while Josiah, an exemplar of virtue, died young after about three decades of reign (2 Kings 22:1). Yet the exceptions do not nullify the basic principle of God's protection of and provision for the rulers that walk in His ways.

Righteousness may be defined as loyalty to keep the law.

> Those who forsake the law praise the wicked,
> But such as keep the law contend with them.
>
> *Prov. 28:4*

The general tone of Proverbs suggests that *"law"* (Heb. *tôrāh*) means the wise, reliable instruction of parents and teachers (1:8; 3:1) rather than the commandments of Moses, though we cannot tell for sure. Abandoning the law and its call to personal and social integrity and obedience puts us in a position to admire and cheer for (*"praise"*) the *"wicked"* who lead the way in lawlessness and rebellion. We contribute to their sin by lauding their deeds and hence become accessories to the crime. We are like the persons who gape at and gloat over a neighborhood rape even though they may never initiate such an act. To care about right behavior means not only to practice it ourselves but to *"contend"* or *"engage in war"* (see Deut. 2:5, 9, 19 for the literal use of the same form of the verb *gārāh*) with those who behave lawlessly. Complacency is itself a form of crime, as the gang warfare and drug dealing on our city streets ought to remind us.

Understanding justice is something that true believers (those who seek the Lord in worship and obedience) are good at.

> Evil men do not understand justice,
> But those who seek the LORD understand all.
> *Prov. 28:5*

They *"understand all,"* that is, all about *"justice"*—how it works, what it means, why it is important (see on 1:3)—because they know the God from whom all justice flows. *"Evil men,"* who ignore God's call, reject God's will, and follow their own savage impulses can not grasp the ABC's of the rights of others within the community. Selfishness has dulled their perception with a stupor akin to drunkenness. To know God, whose attributes alone are worth imitating, is the only sure way to know how to behave decently as human beings.

The social impact of good and bad behavior is highlighted in these sayings.

> When the righteous rejoice, *there is* great glory;
> But when the wicked arise, men hide themselves.
> *Prov. 28:12*

> When the wicked arise, men hide themselves;
> But when they perish, the righteous increase.
> *Prov. 28:28*

Verse 12 describes the *"great glory"* (or *"elation"*; NIV) that prevails when persons loyal and faithful to God and therefore concerned about the community (*"the righteous"*; see 2:20; 3:33; 4:18 and the discussion in chap. 10) win out over the forces of evil: *"rejoice"* should be understood as joy gained from victory—"triumph" (NIV). When *"the wicked"* gain the upper hand (*"arise"*), people *"hide themselves"* in fear, fear both of catastrophe and persecution. Think of the thousands, if not millions, of Christians who have "gone underground" in totalitarian states during our lifetime. Verse 28 reverses the thought of the two lines and puts the emphasis on the triumph of the wicked which drives good people into hiding until such time as divine justice rescues them by causing the wicked to *"perish"* and allowing *"the righteous"* to *"increase"* in numbers and hence in prominence and influence.

> He who covers his sins will not prosper,
> But whoever confesses and forsakes *them* will have
>   mercy.
>
> *Prov. 28:13*

Here is a happy reminder that the wise teachers understood the meaning of confession and forgiveness which the psalmists and prophets made so plain. Covering *"sins"* ("transgressions"; see 28:2) is itself an expression of sin and consequently cuts down on the possibility of prosperity with which God blesses the righteous. The opposite activity to *"covers"* is *"confesses"* (see Ps. 32:5) and *"forsakes"* ("abandons"; 2:13, 17) one's transgressions; the noun (*"sins"*) carries over to serve as the object of the second line as well as the first. *"Will have mercy"* recalls the name of Hosea's daughter "Not Pitied" or "Not shown mercy" (1:6, 8) and especially the reversal of the name as the sign of divine forgiveness (Hos. 2:1, 23). Here alone in Proverbs does this verb of compassion (Heb. *rḥm*) occur. The entire saying demonstrates the wise teachers' understanding of covenant relationship with God which underlies their moral and spiritual lessons. "Confess" and "forsake" are an apt summary of what the Bible means by repentance, and the whole verse is a foreshadowing of John's pivotal teaching about the sin of self-righteousness and the release of forgiveness (1 John 1:8–9).

> Whoever walks blamelessly will be saved,
> But *he who is* perverse *in his* ways will suddenly
>   fall.
>
> *Prov. 28:18*

To walk *"blamelessly"* includes following the pattern of confession and abandonment of sin described in 28:13. "Blamelessly" means "maturely," depending on God and seeking His help and strength to be what He wants us to be. It includes trust and faithfulness and, hence, carries with it the blessings of salvation. God's arm is there to rescue us from the narrow places and to snatch us from falling off life's tight ledges (see 20:22). The one who *"is perverse in his ways"* has the opposite experience. He *"will suddenly fall"* and keep falling at every turn. He neither acknowledges his sin, seeks God's mercy, nor obeys God's will. Therefore he has cut himself off from God's resources and is open to all that life throws at him. The divine order has become his enemy because he does not acknowledge any accountability to the Lord of creation and covenant.

> By transgression an evil man is snared,
> But the righteous sings and rejoices.
> *Prov. 29:6*

This saying charts the doom of the *"evil man"* in the first line: his rebellion against God (on *"transgression"* see 28:2, 13) has become his snare or more literally the "springer bar" on which bait was placed to set off the trap or drop the net (for Heb. *môqēš* see 12:13; 13:14; 14:27; 18:7; 20:25; 22:25; 29:25). To set foot on a sinful act is to trigger your own captivity. One dose of "crack" in some cases assures permanent addiction; sin can be like that. The blessing of freedom, in contrast, belongs to *"the righteous"* one who *"sings"* songs of rejoicing, while the ensnared transgressor can only curse his fate and lamely call for help.

The concluding verse rings with hope even for days that look ominous.

> When the wicked are multiplied, transgression
>   increases;
> But the righteous will see their fall.
> *Prov. 29:16*

When *"wicked"* people *"are multiplied"* as the covenant seems to break down and what was once a rebellious, troublesome remnant in the community has gathered both numbers and influence, the consequences seem dire: *"transgression increases"* and the mutinous forces, openly defying the ways of wisdom, both corrupt the community and threaten to control it. The mood of *"the righteous,"* loyal and obedient, people can turn glum, even desperate. This saying speaks to that outlook by announcing what the righteous should already know: the justice of God will right the imbalance, and His faithful people will live to see and take heart in the fall, the utter collapse in influence and strength of those whose hearts are set against the will of Him who created them.

Few verses capture the essence of the doctrine of the two ways more clearly and more concisely than this one. As leaders, managers, organizers, and communicators, the art of compromise plays a large part in how we work. We look for the "Solomonic middle" and cut the issue in half, dividing it equally between aggrieved and contending parties. And so we often should do. But not where righteousness and wickedness are at stake, not where wisdom and folly are the adversaries. There the doctrine of the two ways is our guideline and we learn from the wise teachers and the great Teacher who is our Master to vote and act for righteousness and wisdom whatever be the price.

CHAPTER TWENTY-NINE

Discipline: Ourselves and Our Families

Proverbs 29:1–27

Like parent, like child. This more modern proverb is a clue that our two themes—Self-Control (see chap. 14) and Discipline of Children (see chap. 20)—belong together and are as crucial today as in those remote centuries when sages were readying their pupils for government service. It is hard for youngsters to rise above the levels of behavior practiced by the elders who have most influence upon them. Where do kids learn violence, selfishness, profanity, deception, greed, explosive anger? The answer is not simple but it is important. The aptitude for all these perverse skills seems to be there by virtue of their participation in the human rebellion which Adam and Eve perpetrated. Original sin we call this. It does not mean that every child is equally bad or that every child is as bad as he or she could be. With some effort we all could be worse! Original sin means that each of us is born with a bent to sin within us that makes it impossible for any human being not to sin—that is, to hurt others and displease God.

At the same time, that original sin can have more frequent and more flagrant expressions as we grow up depending on the outside influences in our lives. That is why one of the first and best pieces of counsel in Proverbs is, "If sinners entice you, do not consent" (1:10). Bad companionship fosters bad behavior.

Well and good to know that. But what if parents turn out to be the bad companions that nurture their young in bad behavior? To some extent that happens to all of us. Our sinful habits, dispositions, attitudes, and actions rub off on our children, and often theirs bring out the worst in us. These family dynamics were not the chief concern of Israel's teachers. They focused on the shame and dishonor that rebellious youngsters brought to their families and hence, centered their counsel in the need for sound discipline and firm training of children.

At the same time they put great stress on self-control—control of passions, appetites, temperament, and especially anger. The consequences of not exercising self-discipline were monumental, both to the person and to the community. In this exposition I choose to couple self-control with discipline of children in a way the sages only hinted at, because in our society, as I suspect in theirs, they go hand in hand. We cannot expect more righteousness of our children than we demonstrate to them in our daily lives.

DISCIPLINE OF SELF

The outcomes of a life that lacks discipline are a primary subject of the eleven sayings in chapters 25–29. Positive advice is always there, sometimes explicitly, often implicitly. But damage control is a prime motive. How can we keep our appetites and tempers in check so that we don't blow ourselves up and explode into shrapnel that maims our whole community? By looking to the consequences is the chief answer found here:

Personal consequences	
Fed-upness	25:16; 27:7
Vulnerability	25:28
Loneliness	27:8–9
Frustration	27:20
Social consequences	
Strife	28:25; 29:9, 22
Loss of influence	29:11
Destruction	29:8

Too much of a good thing presents its own problems.

> Have you found honey?
> Eat only as much as you need,
> Lest you be filled with it and vomit.
> *Prov. 25:16*

A binge of wild *"honey," "found"* unexpectedly in a remote place where bees have parked their hive (1 Sam. 14:26–27), carries risks, namely, a surfeit, a fed-upness that forces one to *"vomit"* (see 23:8). The rule of discipline is to *"eat only as much as you need."* Physical need, not emotional need, is the point. The richness of the flavor, the thickness of the viscosity, and the sudden injection of sugar into the system combine to force the stomach to reject the overdose. And the whole serendipitous discovery is wasted in the rash quest for pleasure, when it might have been meted out to add delight to a whole week or two.

Honey is a good thing, a symbol of wisdom in 24:13. Here the context (25:17) suggests that fellowship in a neighbor's house is one good thing that can be overdone. Self-discipline is needed not only to ward off temptation to evil acts but also to stem the abuse of good ones. Luxury in excess can turn to ugliness as honey to vomit.

> A satisfied soul loathes the honeycomb,
> But to a hungry soul every bitter thing *is* sweet.
> *Prov. 27:7*

Having too much dulls the "appetite," as *"soul"* may also be translated. The *"hungry"* "appetite," on the other hand, will find even the *"bitter"* to taste *"sweet."* As is often the case in Chapter 27, no clue is given as to the specific application of this saying. We can assume that the collectors deliberately left it open to cover a wide range of meanings. The general sense seems to be that control of the appetite whether for food, luxury, or power, leaves space for further delight, together with the joy and gratitude such delight provides. Nothing seems exciting to one who has everything. "I'm so thirsty I could drink a dozen Cokes," I panted to my two high-school buddies. Tired of my callous bragging, they took me up on my grandiose claim, bought the dozen Cokes, and gave me an hour in which to quaff them. Sixty minutes and seventy-two ounces later, I was up to my eyeballs in caffeine, carbonation, and the secret formula. Like a seasick sailor I headed for the heaving room. My color varied from green to yellow to gray as I rid myself of the sickening syrup. It was weeks before I could look at a soft drink bottle, and to this day, some forty-five years later, I still try to be more modest in my assertions as to what I can do.

> Whoever *has* no rule over his own spirit
> *Is like* a city broken down, without walls.
> *Prov. 25:28*

The illustration (or comparison) comes first in the Hebrew text. *"A city broken down,"* its *"walls"* so severely breached that they fail to act as walls, is totally vulnerable to wicked men and wild beasts. Any vagrant can roam its streets, any invader loot its goods, any animal pillage its supplies. It is so damaged that it cannot fulfill any of its basic purposes: affording shelter, protecting community, encouraging commerce. Helplessness and uselessness are its dominant features. So it is with one who cannot keep in check (*"rule"* translates a noun used only here and whose verbal root means "hold back," "retain"; see Gen. 16:2; 20:18 for uses that describe God's restraining of women from pregnancy) his *"spirit,"* that is, his attitudes, disposition, and emotion. The virtues of self-restraint are lauded in 16:32 as being acts of heroism that outstrip military conquest. To be out of control is to be susceptible to a wide range of dangers and to be incapacitated for any productive activity.

Loneliness may be another by-product of the failure to employ self-control.

> 27:8 Like a bird that wanders from its nest
>   *Is* a man who wanders from his place.
>
> 9 Ointment and perfume delight the heart,
>   And the sweetness of a man's friend gives
>   delight by hearty counsel.
>   *Prov. 27:8–9*

Wanderlust seems to be the specific problem in verse 8. It stems from lack of contentment or refusal to bear responsibility at home. *"Place"* must mean home territory, the place where one is born and raised. In a society where millions wander frequently from *"nest"* to nest, the force of this passage may be blunted. More than 20 percent of Americans change their addresses each year, yet even they carry goods with them to make the new nest feel like the old one. And they add, most of them at least, to their sense of stability and continuity by frequent use of phone and mail that keeps them in touch with their past. A minority of them—runaways of all ages—deliberately cover their tracks and block out their past. They lack the self-discipline to make life work at home or the people at home lack the skill to make home a home. Flitting birds are one thing; roaming adolescents or adults are another. Rejecting friendship at home, they often find it in bizarre circumstances on the road, a tacit acknowledgment of the truth of verse 9.

When self-control prevails, friendship can take the very fragrance of royalty as *"ointment"* (lit., "olive oil") and *"perfume"* (lit., "incense"; Exod. 30:1, 8, 27, 35) suggest. The precise meaning of the second line (v. 9b) is hard to recover. A recent study suggests, "a friend's sweetness [gladdens, the verb *"delight"* carries over from v. 9a] more than one's own counsel" (van Leeuwen, p. 124). The point is that fellowship when kept within the bounds of propriety and free from inordinate demands (see 25:17) offers a security and wisdom that enrich life as do the luxuries ordinarily available only to the wealthy. No one need wander from the home nest when such friendship is possible. And to cultivate such friendship ought to be a chief preoccupation of us all.

Frustration prompted by greed is another personal consequence of lack of discipline.

> Hell and Destruction are never full;
> So the eyes of man are never satisfied.
> *Prov.* 27:20

The devilish nature of human avarice is made clear in the comparison of our appetites with those of *"Hell and Destruction."* The capital letters catch the fact that Hell (or *sheʾôl*; see 1:12; Song of Sol. 8:6, the grave or realm of the dead) and *Abaddon*, which is translated "Destruction" (see 15:11 for the combination of terms), are treated personally, as powerful forces or realms of death. They are virtually deified, not to place them in competition with Yahweh but to feature their domination over the human family. At all ages, in all circumstances, in all places, they snatch people from life to death with yawning maws that have endless capacity to devour (for sheol's greed, see 30:15–16). Human envy, greed, and covetousness are like them. What a grim mirror to hold before us when we want what we do not need and will not well use! And what a telling portrait of one of our key characteristics: the more we have the more we want! Appetites like a bottomless pit! (See Eccles. 1:8 for a similar picture of how difficult it is to satisfy human desires.)

The social consequences of losing self-control are as obvious and dangerous as the personal.

> He who is of a proud heart stirs up strife,
> But he who trusts in the LORD will be prospered.
> *Prov.* 28:25

"Strife" is among the worst consequences (for Heb. *mādôn*, a quarrel that may have legal overtones, see 6:19; 10:12; 15:18; 16:28; 17:14; 22:10; 26:20; 29:22). It is often the product of the *"proud* [lit., "wide," "expansive"; see 21:4] *heart,"* the person of selfish pushiness, who wants more than a fair share and will use all his muscle and weight to get it, usually at someone else's expense. Hence the

harsh disruption of the community whose peace is always jeopardized by such behavior. Proud hearts put their neighbors in a lose-lose situation. If their greed prevails, the community is rightly miffed and the greedy person wrongly encouraged to be even more greedy. If the greed fails, then the arrogant grasper may become more aggressive than ever.

How much better says line two is a person *"who trusts in the Lord"* both to defend his cause and to provide for his needs. He *"will be prospered"* (for Heb. *dāshēn,* see 11:25; 13:4; 15:30) like a well-fed calf, or more personally he will be anointed with the oil of God's blessing as the psalmist attested (Ps. 23:5). Prosperity gained through the grace of trusting God rejoices in a community with whom it is shared and who learns lessons of self-control from the one who waits in patient trust.

> If a wise man contends with a foolish man,
> Whether *the fool* rages or laughs, *there is* no peace.
> *Prov. 29:9*

The strife here seems clearly to be a court case as *"contends"* (lit., "goes to judgment" or "court") implies. The outcome is grim, given the *"foolish"* character of the one litigant. He makes his argument not by logic, reason, or clear evidence but in a range of wild responses in which he *"rages* [a verb for "earthquake" in 30:21; Amos 8:8] *or laughs,"* probably in a mocking, sneering fashion to try to sway the verdict. The *"peace"* that ought to come from reconciliation, or at least a sound decision, is impossible. The matter bubbles on interminably to the pain of the wise and the distress of the community. (On "peace" or rest, see Eccles. 4:6; 6:5; 9:17.) Surely one point of this saying is to avoid litigation with a mindless person whenever possible. Self-control may at times include the control of the use of one's full right. Christian love knows this and "does not seek its own" but "bears all things" and "endures all things" (1 Cor. 13:5, 7).

> An angry man stirs up strife,
> And a furious man abounds in transgression.
> *Prov. 29:22*

The disruptive power of the *"angry"* (lit., "snorting") or *"furious"* (lit., "hot") man is pictured in the synonymous lines of this saying. Like the proud heart (28:25) he incites *"strife,"* and more than that, he *"abounds in* [or "multiplies"] *transgression* [Heb. *peshaʿ*]," which here is directed not primarily against God but against the community. He overrides its proprieties, defies its norms, and scoffs at its moral standards. A rebel without cause, a mutineer motivated by sheer gall, he seeks to turn his town on its ear and ruin its stable, peaceful way of life.

> A fool vents all his feelings,
> But the wise *man* holds them back.
> *Prov. 29:11*

The loss of control here is habitual; the man is branded *"a fool,"* which is a permanent not a temporary title in Proverbs. He has no power to restrain the expression of what he feels: literally, "all his spirit he sends forth." Whatever feeling, emotion, attitude, gripe, insult wells within him he lets erupt. Neither influence nor respect can be his lot. His responses in any conversation or social setting are predictable: they will inevitably be unacceptable whatever form they take. The *"wise"* person may feel all sorts of emotions and sense their expression bubbling to the tip of the tongue, but he or she has the sense, poise, and discipline to stifle those expressions, bite the tongue, count to ten, change the subject or whatever else it takes. Saying too little has rarely led me into trouble; saying too much has done so time after time—and always with some loss of credibility, influence, and self-respect.

Scoffers are at the bottom of Israel's list of scoundrels (1:22; Isa. 28:14).

> Scoffers set a city aflame,
> But wise *men* turn away wrath.
> *Prov. 29:8*

They not only violate God's way, they joke about their wickedness and mock all who try to live uprightly. Their crude, rude lack of judgment attacks the integrity of their community and sets loose all the tensions and strains that are present. As an earthquake cracks the pavement, loosens the foundations, and shakes down the unsecured plaster so the scoffers' behavior threatens the security of their community. Setting *"a city aflame"* is based on the picture of blowing on embers or coals to spark them into fire. In contrast to the *"scoffers"* and their practice of social arson, the *"wise men"* of the town are the volunteer firefighters who *"turn away* [lit., "cause to turn back"] *wrath* [lit., "snorting"]" by their calm analysis of the situation and their refusal to panic at the brushfires being set by the wicked scoffers. They prevent the destruction which is the ultimate consequence of loss of self-control by remaining cool enough to say and do the right things under pressure.

DISCIPLINE OF FAMILIES

Household order is an important theme in chapter 29. The security, stability, and productivity of the family depended on it. So did the parents' level of joy and satisfaction. Three sayings and one admonition deal with the discipline of children and slaves. The latter were usually acquired in one of two ways: (1) Prisoners of war were retained by their captors and put to work in agriculture and construction; prisoners may also have been purchased from those who captured them; note Gaza's and Tyre's transactions with Edom (Amos 1:6, 9). (2) Debtors were forced to serve their creditors as slaves; note Amos's outrage, "Because they sell the righteous [innocent] for silver, / And the poor for a pair of sandals" (2:6).

The laws of Israel, geared to forestall the development of a slave class, ordered a debtor-slave to be offered freedom after six years of service (Exod. 21:2–6; see Deut. 15:12–18 where the slave is called "your brother"). Runaway slaves were to be received humanely, given a choice of where to live, and guarded from oppression (Deut. 23:15–16). The motivation for this call to consideration of a slave's well-being is the Exodus in which Israel's enslaved state was overcome by Yahweh's redemptive intervention (Deut. 5:14–15).

This background on the treatment of slaves sheds light on the ways in which they came to be included as virtual members of the owner's household. This was the case for the women especially, who seemed to have formed strong bonds to the householders, who were restrained by law from selling them to foreigners (Exod. 21:7–11). Treated as persons more than property and protected by law from inhumane treatment, servants were nevertheless distinguished from blood relatives in the teachings of the wise. The basic difference was the way in which the teachers stressed the impact of the children's behavior on their parents' well-being. Blood was thicker than water, and the children's power to bring joy or shame to their parents was greater than any influence wielded by the servants.

This influence is featured in two proverbs that deal with child raising.

> The rod and rebuke give wisdom,
> But a child left *to himself* brings shame to his
> mother.
>
> *Prov. 29:15*

> Correct your son, and he will give you rest;
> Yes, he will give delight to your soul.
>
> *Prov. 29:17*

The alternatives set out in verse 15 are discipline (for *"rebuke,"* see 1:23, 25, 30; for *"rod,"* see 23:13–14) or *"shame,"* a dreadful outcome to any of us but especially to an Oriental. Wisdom is gained in many ways according to the sages: by listening to wise parents and teachers, by answering wisdom's call, by fearing God as the beginning of wisdom, by observing how good and bad conduct work and are rewarded. An even more practical source of the wisdom is to be scolded and corrected with the reinforcement of some punishment or deprivation for which "rod" serves as the symbol. Without those loving reprimands etched into the memory by a measure of firm but bearable pain, the whole structure of family love breaks down. *"A child left to himself"* (lit., "sent away") without sound teaching and strong connection will not develop the self-control featured so strongly in Proverbs (see first half of this chapter) and will almost inevitably behave badly. The most tender, vulnerable person, *"his mother,"* will be hurt the worst. She will "lose face" ("shame") and be branded in her failure as an authority figure, teacher, example, and counselor (remember that Deborah, as a wise leader, was called a *"mother* in Israel"; Judg. 5:7).

Verse 17 is addressed to the father. The imperative verb *"correct"* (Heb. *yāsar;* see 9:7; 19:18) is masculine as are the pronouns *"you"* and *"your."* Here the positive results of discipline are stated: (1) *"rest"*—from worry, anxiety, disappointment, and especially shame; (2) *"delight"*—a culinary figure of speech, drawn from the "delicacies" or "dainties" that tickle the palate of the royal (Gen. 49:20) and the wealthy (Lam. 4:5); exquisite, inexpressible, luxurious delight is the force. It is a superlative way of saying that the pain, patience, and persistence of raising children will bring the highest possible payoff.

Attention turns now to the servant.

> A servant will not be corrected by mere words;
> For though he understands, he will not respond.
>
> *Prov. 29:19*

He who pampers his servant from childhood
Will have him as a son in the end.

Prov. 29:21

For him *"words"* alone are not enough. That is no surprise because it almost always takes more than words to get the full attention of any of us. Yet *"a servant,"* feeling that he has less to gain than a child and heir, may be slower to *"respond"* ("answer and act") even to instructions that he *"understands."* Implied in this saying is the need for a heavy hand, even a rod (v. 15). But the lack of specific instruction in dealing with a balky servant leaves the way open for us to consider other forms of motivation, including encouragement when work is well done and promise of further praise and reward when doing well begins to become habitual.

The important thing, warns verse 21, is to hold a servant accountable *"from childhood,"* as early as he is able to assume any responsibility. *"He who pampers"* (a Heb. root occurring only here, its meaning is deduced from the context and confirmed by an Arabic verb meaning "indulge") does precisely the wrong thing, perhaps by giving the young servant less work than others do, letting him off the hook when he fails to perform, believing his excuses, and rewarding him beyond any warrant. I wish we knew exactly the negative outcome of such coddling, but the second line is not clear, notably the meaning of the rare word translated *"son."* Among the alternative suggestions are "ungrateful" (NEB), "weakling," "bring grief" (NIV following the LXX), "refractory" (Anchor Bible, in keeping with the Vulgate text). The point is that failure to discipline a servant raised from childhood in the household brings the heartache of an unsatisfactory relationship as surely as lack of reproof of one's own child will eventually bathe his mother in shame (v. 15).

Part of self-discipline is to force ourselves to exercise responsibility faithfully, regularly, kindly, and fairly over all those whose nurture is in our care. This is one of my least favorite things to do. I have continually to remind myself of the havoc to be wrought if I shun this distasteful duty. As pastors and teachers as well as parents and employers, the sayings of this chapter ought to speak volumes to us.

Words of Agur

Proverbs 30:1–33

CHAPTER THIRTY

Words of Agur

Proverbs 30:1–33

The feast of wisdom to be enjoyed in chapter 30 seems to come from a table other than Solomon's. The change of chef in no way diminishes the quality, whether of content or artistry. Indeed, this chapter is unmatched in the book in its variety of forms—from dispute, to prayer, to instruction, to description of social chaos, to playful numerical games whose wry humor catches our consciences.

TITLE

> 30:1 The words of Agur the son of Jakeh, *his* utterance. This man declared to Ithiel—to Ithiel and Ucal:
>
> *Prov. 30:1*

The sayings, whether through verse 9 or perhaps verse 14, are credited to one *"Agur,"* a name otherwise unknown in the Old Testament. And *"Jakeh"* his father is mentioned only here. If we transliterate rather than translate *maśśāʾ* (*"his utterance,"* a common prophetic word for "oracle," Isa. 13:1; 15:1; Nah. 1:1; Hab. 1:1; Mal. 1:1, but used in Proverbs just twice—here and 31:1), we may gain further information about "Agur, the son of Jakeh," the man of Massa or the Massaite (see Ishmael's son in Gen. 25). This reading would identify Agur as a tribal sage or chief of Massa's tribe in North Arabia, an area whose wisdom was legendary (1 Kings 4:29–34). As confusing as it may seem, if *"utterance"* should be read as the proper name Massa, Ithiel and Ucal, who defy identification, should be translated as phrases. What the phrases mean is more difficult to say. Despair seems to be the mood: "I am weary, O God, I am weary and worn out" (NEB). Or even more desperately: "There is no God, there is no God and I am exhausted" (McKane, p. 258; see Anchor Bible). Thus is set the melancholy tone for the dialogue that follows (vv. 2–9).

In what sounds like skepticism and doubt, Agur's words are closer to those of Job or Ecclesiastes than to the bulk of Proverbs. They demonstrate that dealing with the uncertainties of faith was part of the ministry of the teachers along with the instruction in wise conduct (see Psalm 73 for another example).

CONFESSION/DISPUTE OF IGNORANCE

30:2 Surely I *am* more stupid than *any* man,
     And do not have the understanding of a man.
  3 I neither learned wisdom
     Nor have knowledge of the Holy One.

  4 Who has ascended into heaven, or descended?
     Who has gathered the wind in His fists?
     Who has bound the waters in a garment?
     Who has established all the ends of the earth?
     What *is* His name, and what *is* His Son's name,
     If you know?

                                        Prov. 30:2–4

For *"surely,"* read "for": it introduces the reason for the despair that borders on agnosticism. Human limitation is the theme. "I am more beast than man" would accurately paraphrase the first line (see Ps. 73:22 for Heb. *ba'ar* as "beast"; Prov. 12:1 contains similar wording). The thought is expanded and clarified in verse 3. The *"understanding"* (Heb. *bînâh*; 1:2) that he lacks is *"wisdom"* that stems from the fear of God and *"knowledge"* (see 1:7) of the will and ways *"of the Holy One"* (see 9:10). The Hebrew plural form of "holy" expresses the excellence and majesty of God, as the Being utterly different in power, glory, and purity from anything in the whole creation.

The three synonyms, "understanding," "wisdom," "knowledge," echo the opening verses of Proverbs, but with all the joy and confidence drained away. What the wise teachers held out as the purpose of their training, Agur confesses to have missed.

All the questions in verse 4 call for God as the answer. Their nearest biblical parallel is Job 38, when the Lord's voice blasts from the whirlwind with questions that force Job to acknowledge his ignorance and yield to God's wisdom. It is likely, in light of these similarities to Job, that God is speaking, whether directly or indirectly through the lips of a sage. Agur can hardly be the speaker. The knowledge of God's activities implied in the questions does not fit the stupidity which he confessed.

The point God seems to make in the questions is that no unaided human knowledge can probe these mysteries—a theme sounded in Job 28. Agur should not despair of his ignorance. It is a problem he has in common with all who have not learned to fear and trust God in His revealed word. *"Name"* stands for character. To know the name, especially the covenant name "Yahweh" is to know the person of God as Creator and Redeemer (Exod. 3:13–14). *"Son"* here may have initially stood for a wise teacher, since "son" is regularly used of an apt pupil in Proverbs. But the wording *"what is His Son's name"* opens the passage for a New Testament interpretation: "No one knows the Son except the Father. Nor does anyone know the Father except the Son, and the one to whom the Son wills to reveal Him" (Matt. 11:27).

The mystery of God's ways has more than one meaning. God threw that mystery at Job to shake his complacency and self-confidence. God pressed that same mystery on Agur to relieve him of his depression and assure him that he was not alone in his doubt and ignorance.

My seat mate looked at his watch as we neared Chicago on a flight from Louisville. He had just found out the nature of my occupation. His statement came quickly and bluntly: "You have twenty-two minutes to convince me that I should not be an agnostic." I continued our conversation on a nonreligious topic. He interrupted to repeat his challenge: "Twenty-two minutes." I looked him in the eye and said, "I'm not even going to try."

He took charge immediately. "Well, I'll tell you one thing: no one can convince me that the universe is here by chance. There's too much pattern and design in it. It could not have happened by itself." I answered slowly and quietly. "You have just drummed yourself out of the agnostics' corps. They have ripped the epaulets from your shoulder and stripped the sword from your side. No one can say what you said about creation and remain an agnostic."

Then I paused a minute and smiled. "I'm sure glad you acknowledge God's power in the universe. I was afraid that he might have to let the plane crash before we landed in Chicago so that I could hear you pray."

ADMONITION ON GOD'S WORD

30:5 Every word of God *is* pure;
He *is* a shield to those who put their trust in
Him.

        6 Do not add to His words,
           Lest He rebuke you, and you be found a liar.
                                              Prov. 30:5–6

These verses contain the teacher's comments on the divine word
to Agur. They underscore the reliability of what God has said: It is
"pure," unmixed with any dross of error, bright and shiny like refined silver (see Ps. 12:6); it is strong like a military *"shield"* (see
2:7; Song of Sol. 4:4), probably a reference to the small round or
rectangular protective devices made of leather, wood, or metal and
carried by hand or slung over the shoulder. Paul's *"shield of faith"*
(Eph. 6:16) connects *"shield"* and *"trust"* as does this proverb.

Such reliability cannot be improved on. Therefore, in what is
called *"an integrity formula"* expressing the completeness of God's
word (see Rev. 28:18) and based on Ps. 18:30 and Deut. 4:2, the
hearer, probably Agur, is warned against adding thoughts of his
own, which if contrary to divine teaching would brand him as *"a
liar."*

PRAYER FOR MODERATE BLESSINGS

30:7 Two *things* I request of You
        (Deprive me not before I die):
     8 Remove falsehood and lies far from me;
        Give me neither poverty nor riches—
        Feed me with the food alloted to me;
     9 Lest I be full and deny *You,*
        And say, "Who *is* the LORD?"
        Or lest I be poor and steal,
        And profane the name of my God.
                                              Prov. 30:7–9

The conversation between Agur, God, and a teacher closes with
the teacher's model prayer which picks up the theme of lying from
verse 6 and in the *"of You"* makes clear that the Lord has been party
to the whole discussion. The prayer is an example of persistence:
"before I die" means *"as long as I live."* This is not a cry for rescue
from immediate crisis but for continual help with never-ending
problems. The first petition, which uses the imperative mood like an
admonition—*"remove falsehood and lies"*—requires no expansion or
motivation clause. The damaging results to the person who deals in
dishonesty and to his victims are obvious. "Falsehood" (Heb. *shāw*;

here only in Proverbs; frequent in Psalms, see 12:2, and prophets; see Jer. 2:30; 4:30) is literally "emptiness," worthless behavior or speech. Lies are regularly condemned in Proverbs for their disruptive impact on the social and especially judicial welfare of the community (6:19; 19:5, 9, 22).

The second petition (again an imperative)—"*Give me neither poverty nor riches*"—is more subtle and is accompanied by the substantial explanation of verse 9. Both petitions place the nouns—falsehood, lies, poverty, riches—at the head of the Hebrew sentence to thrust them, not the verbs, into prominence. The petitioner knows what help he needs in terms both of protection and supply, and he asks for it in the straightforward manner of the children of God (Matt. 7:7–11). He counts on the Lord to determine his basic needs and to meet them. "*Feed me*" in its Hebrew form portrays the divine hand extending a loaf of bread ("*food*") and telling him exactly what his portion is to be. The idea of allotted food brings to mind memories of my Depression boyhood, namely, the picture of my watchful mother dispensing equity among five children at the dinner table. "Give us this day our daily bread" (Matt. 6:11) is the New Testament form of this request.

The most fascinating thing about the prayer is the balanced and worldly wise wisdom present in the motivation clauses beginning with "*lest*" (v. 9). Overabundance ("*full*") may lead to an arrogant self-sufficiency that loses all sense of dependence on God. "*Who is the Lord?*" is a question in form but a statement in intent—"I have no need of the Lord." Poverty, on the other hand, may drive a person to the desperate act of stealing. Theft has profound theological consequences. It profanes—the word means to "seize" or "snatch" in a violent way, as Potiphar's wife clutched at Joseph's garment (Gen. 39:12)—"*the name of my God.*" It does so by breaking God's law against stealing (Exod. 20:15; Deut. 5:19) and by declaring that God will not provide for His own as God has promised.

The world-view expressed here is remarkable. The supplicant knows both the frailty of his own human nature and also the sanctity of God's name. Earthly sins have heavenly significance. And the ultimate result of human crime is to insult the name of the Lord who made us, and who made us for better things than lying and stealing.

The brief yet dramatic discussion introduced by Agur's name seems to end here. In verse 10 the subject changes sharply. A word on the flow of the structure may be the best way to sum up the gist of the passage.

vv 1–3   Agur confesses an inability to know God.

vv 4   God raises questions that show both the mystery and
            majesty of God.

vv 5–6   A teacher affirms the trustworthiness of God's words
            and warns against adding to them.

vv 7–9   A teacher offers a model prayer illustrating dependence
            on God for life's basic spiritual and physical provisions.

The prayer, then, may be seen as the practical conclusion to a
discussion that began with doubt and disbelief. We come to know
God not by speculation or meditation but by calling on Him daily
for His practical help at our neediest points.

Admonition on Slandering a Servant

Do not malign a servant to his master,
Lest he curse you, and you be found guilty.
                                                Prov. 30:10

The close, almost familial, bond between servant and master (see
chap. 29) is the background of this warning. *"Malign"* suggests a
harsh use of the tongue in words of *"slander"* or *"false condemna-
tion"* (see the same verb root *lāshan* in Ps. 101:5 where *"neighbor"* is
the target). Meddling seems to be the crime involved, since the servant is given the right to defend himself by dressing down (*"curse"* is
not used here in a technical sense) his accuser. The *"guilty"* verdict
(the verb *ʾāshēm* is frequent in the law, see Lev. 4:13, 22, 27, and
prophets, see Jer. 2:3; Ezek. 22:4; Hos. 4:15, but used only here in
Proverbs) does not place the scene in a courtroom but suggests guilt
in the eyes of the servant, the master, any one in the community
who overheard the meddling and the meddler himself. It is the master's role to handle a servant's or a child's misbehavior. To interfere
with that responsibility is to ask for guilt and shame. Busybodies
win no popularity contests.

Description of Spiteful Behavior

30:11   *There is* a generation *that* curses its father,
        And does not bless its mother.
   12   *There is* a generation *that is* pure in its own
          eyes,

> Yet is not washed from its filthiness.
> 13 There is a generation—oh, how lofty are their
>   eyes!
> And their eyelids are lifted up.
> 14 There is a generation whose teeth *are like* swords,
> And whose fangs *are like* knives,
> To devour the poor from off the earth,
> And the needy from *among* men.
>
> *Prov. 30:11–14*

A significant sector of Israel's society seems to have run amok. Life is out of hand in ways that the prophets denounced. *"Generation"* at the head of each verse calls repeated attention to a substantial group within the land that bears wretched characteristics. The passage anticipates Jesus' use of "generation" as reference to a group or circle of His countrymen (Matt. 3:7; 12:34; 23:33). Whereas most of the proverbs focus on the foolish or wicked as individuals, here the suggestion must be that a substantial minority or even a majority of the citizenry are bound together in the four kinds of rebellious conduct described. *Dishonor of parents* heads the list (v. 11), in defiance of the first admonition of the book (1:8) and the commandment given with a promise in the law (Exod. 20:12; Deut. 5:16; see chap. 17 for this theme in Proverbs). Next (v. 12) is *flagrant self-righteousness*, described in the contrast between claiming to be *"pure,"* newly washed, unsoiled, while being caked with *"filthiness,"* a mild translation of the Hebrew ṣoᵓāh which is *"excrement"* as 2 Kings 18:27 shows. Third (v. 13), there is *lofty pride* symbolized in the snooty looks that pour barrels of haughtiness on the heads of those thought to be beneath them (see 6:17). Finally (v. 14) comes *oppressive greed* that (note the *"swords"* and *"knives"*; see Abraham's knife in Gen. 22:6, 10 for the same word) consumes (*"devour"*) the *"poor"* and *"needy"* with a savage ferocity, feeding on their meager goods, shrunken land, and well-bent backs with a cannibalism that Micah so graphically described (3:1–3). *"Men"* (v. 14) perhaps should be read as "land" (by adding an *h* in Hebrew) to complete the parallelism with *"earth"* and to acknowledge the rapacity with which the rich robbed the poor of their lands.

NUMERICAL SAYINGS ON GREED

> 30:15 The leech has two daughters,
> "Give *and* Give!"

> There are three *things that* are never satisfied,
> Four never say, "Enough!":
> 16 The grave,
> The barren womb,
> The earth *that* is not satisfied with water—
> And the fire never says, "Enough!"
>
> *Prov. 30:15–16*

The first saying, though not strictly a numerical proverb since it contains one number not two (on the x, $x + 1$ structure of numerical sayings see 6:16), is attached to verse 15 both because it contains the number *"two"* and because its implicit subject is greed. The *"two daughters"* of *"the leech"* are probably the two suckers found at the head and tail. Their endless appetite is voiced in *"Give and Give!"* Whether this is what they cry as many versions suggest or what they are named, the point is the same: they crave inordinate amounts of blood and serve as an object lesson from the creation of the greed that motivates much human behavior. Though very different in form from verses 11–14, these numerical sayings pick up some of the themes and sound them another way. Hence, verses 15–16 play off the note of greed in verse 14.

Four items of insatiable appetite are listed, items that never say *"Enough!"* (Heb. *hôn* means wealth and power and describes what is plentiful or bountiful): The *"grave"* with its bottomless capacity to absorb the dead (on Sheol see 1:12); the *"barren* [lit., "shut up" or "oppressed"] *womb"* which craves conception and birth to sustain the family line and name, as well as to fulfill its basic purpose; the *"earth"* ever and always open to receive the moisture of dew, rain, and melted snow, especially in the dry Middle Eastern climes where these sayings were spawned; *"fire"* which, whether in a friendly setting like an oven or firepit or in a hostile one like the burning of houses or crops, feeds endlessly on fuel. Often, the last item in the numerical series is both the climax and the main point. That does not look to be the case here.

These sayings like most of the numerical family are not mere observations on how the created world works, though they are insightful at that level. At heart they are illustrations drawn from creation to shed light on the behavior of creation's most puzzling creature: the human being, whether individually or in community. No wonder, given the endemic nature of our greed, God capped the Decalogue with commands against coveting (Exod. 20:17; Deut. 5:21)! No wonder Paul concluded an epistle on joy with one of the chief keys to it: "I have learned in whatever state I am, to be content" (Phil. 4:11)!

SAYING ON RESPECT FOR PARENTS

30:17 The eye *that* mocks *his* father,
And scorns obedience to *his* mother,
The ravens of the valley will pick it out,
And the young eagles will eat it.

Prov. 30:17

This proverb harks back to the theme of verse 11, while featuring the haughty *"eye"* of verse 13. Note that mockery and lack of *"obedience"* (for the other Old Testament use of this word see Gen. 49:10; another reading supported by LXX is "seniority") do not have to be voiced or acted out. The set of the eye can convey volumes of disrespect. God so hates such dishonor that He has geared the creation to inflict punishment for it: *"ravens,"* the strong, loud black birds that scouted for Noah (Gen. 8:7) and fed Elijah (1 Kings 17:4), will join with the *"young eagles"* ("vultures" may be a better translation here) to inflict fearsome judgment on the arrogant eye. The parental disrespect may have to do with refusing them proper burial. The fitting judgment then would be the exposure of the ungrateful son's body so that birds of carrion would scavenge from it.

NUMERICAL SAYING ON LOVE

30:18 There are three *things which* are too wonderful
for me,
Yes, four *which* I do not understand:
19 The way of an eagle in the air,
The way of a serpent on a rock,
The way of a ship in the midst of the sea,
And the way of a man with a virgin.

Prov. 30:18–19

Here the point is made in the final line: the venturesome and mysterious ways of the soaring *"eagle"* (often a symbol of vigor and vitality; Ps. 103:5; Isa 40:31), the slithering *"serpent"* (not usually poisonous in Palestine, but see Amos 5:19; 9:3), the sailing *"ship"* (a source of wonder to Israelites who, unlike the Phoenicians, were not at home in the sea and on ships)—these all build to a climax in the mystery and adventure of affection and attraction between a young man and an eligible young woman. The Bible provides accurate and detailed documentation of *"the way of a man with a virgin"* and of her way with him in the Song of Solomon. The repetitions of "way" form a sort of pun on a key word of Proverbs which usually stands for a total pattern of life and behavior but here focuses on one important component of it. The positive picture of romance here contrasts with the warnings against illicit relations (2:16–19; 5:1–14; 6:20–29; 7:1–27) and connects with the admonitions to marital fidelity (5:15–23), while preparing for the picture of a competent and virtuous woman in 31:10–31.

Description of a Callous Adulteress

This *is* the way of an adulterous woman:
She eats and wipes her mouth,
And says, "I have done no wickedness."
Prov. 30:20

The contrast between the last line of verse 19 and this saying is patent. *"Way"* connects the two. The virgin entered the wonders of love with wide-eyed expectation and eager openness to its surprises. The *"adulterous woman"* (for the adulterous man, see 6:32) treats the act of intercourse as though it were a casual meal, a snack grabbed on the run. No mystery, no wonder, no commitment, no real pleasure! And to top it off, no admission of guilt or shame! Her covenant with her husband seems meaningless, and her sense of responsibility to God appears to have evaporated. However, her denial of *"wickedness"* (on Heb. ʾāwen, see 6:12, 18) may be a left-handed confession of guilt. "Beware of what you deny" was the way a therapist friend of mine put it.

Numerical Saying on Social Chaos

30:21 For three *things* the earth is perturbed,
Yes, for four it cannot bear up:
22 For a servant when he reigns,
A fool when he is filled with food,
23 A hateful *woman* when she is married,
And a maidservant who succeeds her mistress.
Prov. 30:21–23

The stability of a community is the theme. Four instances are listed that upset it. Their impact is described by humorous exaggeration:

"perturbed" can also describe an earthquake (Amos 8:8), and *"for"* is literally "under," with the implication that the earth itself rattles and loses its poise under the influence of these acts of social upheaval. *"A servant"* is not trained to serve as king (*"reigns"*) and may mishandle the authority either by complacency or by abuse of power. *"A fool"* stuffed with *"food"* (lit., "bread") may become crude, rude, loud, and boorish, thinking he has merited such lavish fare and is welcome in such high-class company. *"A hateful,"* or better "unattractive" and therefore previously rejected as a suitable marriage partner, *"woman"* may react high-handedly in overcompensation for her years of being looked down on. *"A maidservant"* may become puffed up with haughtiness and treat with disdain the rest of the household, including her fellow servants if she *"succeeds"* or usurps the position of *"her mistress."* In the ordered structures of Israelite society changes of station were not the norm and the education and preparation for such changes were usually lacking. Rash promotions can lead to illustrations of the "Peter principle," the assigning of persons to tasks beyond their competence, with substantial hurt to them and to others. On the other hand, the Old Testament celebrates the success of Joseph, Esther, and Daniel, who were gifted with the talents and attitudes to rise from servitude to high places and rendered distinguished service.

NUMERICAL SAYING ON WISE BEHAVIOR

30:24 There are four *things which* are little on the earth,
　　　But they *are* exceedingly wise:
　25 The ants *are* a people not strong,
　　　Yet they prepare their food in the summer;
　26 The rock badgers are a feeble folk,
　　　Yet they make their homes in the crags;
　27 The locusts have no king,
　　　Yet they all advance in ranks;
　28 The spider skillfully grasps with its hands,
　　　And it is in kings' palaces.

Prov. 30:24–28

This lesson seems especially fitting for younger or less gifted students. Its point is that persistent, thoughtful effort will pay off even for those who seem less promising. The form departs from the usual numerical saying in listing only one number—*"four"* (see the leeches' two daughters in v. 15). Furthermore, the verses seem not to build to a climax; each illustration from nature contains an importance lesson, to amplify the theme that size does not count nearly as much as wisdom (v. 24).

"Plan ahead" is what we learn from the *"ants"* (v. 25) who overcome their lack of physical strength by starting their *"food"* preparation *"in the summer"* and setting aside enough to carry them through the winter. The *"rock badgers"* (v. 26), animals about the size of rabbits but with smaller ears and shorter legs like guinea pigs, illustrate the maxim, "Make wise choices," by living in rocky crags where they can hole up to escape animals of prey or human hunters (Ps. 104:18). "Hang together or you'll hang separately" is the motto of the *"locusts"* (v. 27) who without an apparent leader (*"king"*) move across the land in ordered *"ranks"* like a well-drilled army (see Joel 2:7). "If at first you don't succeed, try and try again," is the slogan of the "lizard" (a better translation than *"spider"* of the Hebrew word found here only in the Old Testament); probably a type of gecko, harmless and awake at night to feed on insects, who can slip through tiny cracks, lie quietly and blend into stone or wood surroundings to make itself comfortable in royal *"palaces."* I have never slept in a royal palace. But I did enjoy the company of a pet lizard in a room that I occupied in a state guest house in India. Its surefooted tenacity and sneaky persistence testify to the veracity of this proverb. In an age where brilliant thinking and high technology are admired, it is good to hear again the importance of basic virtues like careful planning, wise choosing, community loyalty, and dogged (or "lizarded") persistence. The little engine that said "I think I can, I think I can, I think I can" is no fairy tale but a true symbol of how progress is made and service rendered by those whose determination may be greater than their stature or talent.

NUMERICAL SAYING ON STATELINESS

> 30:29 There are three *things which* are majestic in pace,
> Yes, four *which* are stately in walk:
> 30 A lion, *which is* mighty among beasts
> And does not turn away from any;
> 31 A greyhound,
> A male goat also,
> And a king *whose* troops *are* with him.
>
> *Prov. 30:29–31*

The subject changes from the small (v. 24) to the stately. *"Majestic"* and *"stately"* translate the same Hebrew word, which literally means "those who do things well." The point is the importance and impact of behaving like leaders. The first two verses are clear in Hebrew and show where the saying is headed, even though it is very difficult to translate with precision. The proud courage of the *"lion"* sets the pace; it will not shy away from any foe (v. 30; see Isa. 30:6; Job 4:11). *"Greyhound"* (v. 31) is also translated "cock" or "horse"; the Hebrew word occurs only here and cannot be rendered with certainty. Any of these animals could be cited for its preeminence among others of its kind. The same is true of the *"male goat"* that marks off its territory and fights all other claimants to its ewes. The last line seems to be the climax that makes the point about how a *"king"* should behave and be viewed. Unfortunately the line is not clear: *"troops"* represents a guess at the Hebrew word, though not a wild guess (see "lead his army," NEB; similarly NIV); "at the head of his people" is McKane's reconstruction.

Appropriate words these are for would-be leaders. They frame a how-much-more argument: if animals perform with dignity their roles as prominent members of the pride, flock, or herd how much more should human beings called to be heads of the government or its various branches! "King" (v. 31) may link these verses to the preceding ones, especially verse 27: if the locusts who have no king perform together in such an orderly fashion, how much more should Israel's daughters and sons who have leadership ordained by God!

ADMONITION ON ANGER

> 30:32 If you have been foolish in exalting yourself,
> Or if you have devised evil, *put your* hand on
> *your* mouth.
> 33 For *as* the churning of milk produces butter,
> And wringing the nose produces blood,
> So the forcing of wrath produces strife.
> *Prov. 30:32–33*

This concluding proverb reaches back to the words on pride in verse 12, highlights *"wrath"* (v. 33) as one of its inevitable by-products, and features *"strife"* (Heb. *rîb* which covers a range of arguments from personal quarrels to formal lawsuits; 15:18; 17:1, 14) as the bottom line. Only one hope is offered for checking this inevitable process: *"put your hand on your mouth."* Don't say what you feel about your inflated sense of self-importance (*"exalting yourself"*) or about the scheming way (*"devised evil"*) you are going to get and retain the upper hand on your neighbor.

If you miss that one checkpoint and fail to cool down and think soberly about the impact of your words, the chain reaction sets in and moves step by step from pride to scheme to anger to quarrel. The relentless nature of the process is twice illustrated and once stated. The language is deliberately repetitive. The same Hebrew word (*mîṣ*) which means "pressing" or "pressure" is used three times with appropriate translations: with *"milk,"* *"churning"*; with *"nose,"* *"wringing"*; with *"wrath,"* *"forcing."* And as the English indicates, the same verb is used to point to the results in all three cases: *"produces."* The argument says that unchecked pride will lead to anger and strife with the same predictable effect that tells a farmer that churning milk will always result in butter and that tells a wrestler that twisting and pushing an opponent's nose will regularly draw blood.

So the collection of numerical sayings, admonitions, and descriptions ends at verse 33 where it began in verse 15—with examples of lessons learned from the way God's created order works. The lessons are to be studiously and faithfully applied in everyday life to honor the covenant Lord, to work peace and harmony in society, and to fulfill our potentials as human beings.

Words of Lemuel

Proverbs 31:1–31

CHAPTER THIRTY-ONE

Words of Lemuel

Proverbs 31:1–31

In the first admonitions of Proverbs, we find the command, "And do not forsake the law of your mother" (1:8). A specific sampling of that maternal instruction begins the closing chapter of the book. And sound advice it is. Whether the words of Lemuel's mother extend beyond 31:9 we are not told. The subject of 31:10–31, however, is surely appropriate to the concern and experience of a queen-mother. Who would know more or care more about the qualities of excellence in family life, business acumen, and compassion for her community, and fear of the Lord than a woman thoroughly accustomed to that wide range of responsibilities?

Whatever its specific origin, the magnificent poem with which the book closes provides both an exquisite conclusion and a practical balance to Proverbs. With all the attention to masculine achievement that dominates the teachings, it is fitting that the last words belong to and deal with women, from whom every man is born and without whom neither a present of significance nor a future of continuity is possible. Whatever value achievements have—and they are many—without covenantal relationships they will mean little. And at the heart of these relationships stand mother and wife, the figures with whom the conclusion is occupied.

These figures describe roles for men—for the Lemuels of this world from kings to peasants—that can draw out the very best in us. Not roles as hunters, tillers, smiths, captains of industry, dealers in commerce, purveyors of learning, but roles that plumb the depths of our masculinity and teach us who we really are and want to be— roles as listeners, as admirers, as persons loved and loving. If *mastery* is the curriculum of most of Proverbs, *dependence* is the lesson here. *Achievement* is how we selfishly label gifts made possible by others. The final words that the sages collected are designed to provide a constant reminder of who those important others are.

TITLE

31:1 The words of King Lemuel, the utterance which
his mother taught him:

Prov. 31:1

Like Agur (30:1) Lemuel seems to be an Arab king or chieftain of
the tribe of Massa (see 30:1, for this reading of the Hebrew word
translated *"utterance"*). The *"words"* are his only in the sense that he
relays what *"his mother taught him."* "Taught" is Hebrew *yāsar* a pivotal word in Proverbs (for the verb see 9:7; 19:18; 29:17, 19; for the
noun *mûsār,* see 1:2, 3, 7). Disciplined instruction or instruction in
discipline is its main thrust, with overtones of correction or even
punishment of bad behavior.

ADMONITIONS ON ROYAL DISCIPLINE: WHAT TO AVOID

31:2 What, my son?
And what, son of my womb?
And what, son of my vows?
3 Do not give your strength to women,
Nor your ways to that which destroys kings.

4 *It is* not for kings, O Lemuel,
It is not for kings to drink wine,
Nor for princes intoxicating drink;
5 Lest they drink and forget the law,
And pervert the justice of all the afflicted.
6 Give strong drink to him who is perishing,
And wine to those who are bitter of heart.
7 Let him drink and forget his poverty,
And remember his misery no more.

Prov. 31:2–7

The commands flow from an intense intimacy and concern that
only a mother can know. *"My son,"* *"son of my womb,"* and *"son of my
vows,"* with their repetitions and building to a climax, express both
her right and her motives in telling her son how to behave. There is
an Aramaic flavor to the passage, especially in the word for "son,"
that may retain a taste of the mother's original dialect. "Womb" calls
attention to the blood ties and the months of prenatal nurture.
"Vows" suggests how desperately she desired to conceive and bear
him. Hannah's vows that preceded the birth of Samuel illustrate the

background and power of the phrase (1 Sam. 1:11, 17). Part of what Lemuel's mother promised in the vows must have been to raise her son well and wisely. Her admonitions show her doing just that.

"What" is the enigma in verse 2. It has been read to mean "Now then!" (Anchor Bible, p. 184), "what shall I say to you" (NEB based on LXX), or "listen" (from an Arabic *ma*, whose spelling resembles the Heb. *māh*, "what?" or "how?"). In any case it is obviously an attention-getting device that plays the role of "hear" or "give attention" like the calls in 4:1; 22:17; 23:22, etc.

"Women" (v. 3) and *"wine"* (v. 4) are her first concerns. If "power is the ultimate aphrodisiac," as one of our modern statesmen put it, then kings and leaders face special sexual temptations. Solomon's harem and the pain it brought on his kingdom (not to speak of its occupants) were the Bible's Exhibit A (1 Kings 11:1–13). Who the women were is not specified. His own concubines and wives or those of his countrymen and courtiers are all possibilities. The warnings seem based more on practical than moral considerations: to *"give"* away *"strength"* is to dissipate physical energies and personal wealth—the word can mean both; *"ways"* with a slight change in Hebrew spelling becomes "loins," which is a closer parallel to *"strength"* and keeps the focus on sexual excess with its destructive powers.

The three lines of verse 4 are designed as steps to climb to a high point of intensity by building suspense and delaying the double punch line, with its warnings about *"wine"* (see 20:1; 23:31) and *"intoxicating drink"* (or "beer"; see on 20:1). A diet of alcohol is unthinkable for those who need constantly to be in possession of sound wit and solid judgment. On *"princes"* see 8:15. The motivation sentence (v. 5) anchors the case for sobriety in the bedrock of *"justice,"* a prime responsibility of leaders in any organization, but especially in government (Ps. 72:1–2). *"Forget the law"* means to become so addled in thinking that the statutes that define right and wrong are ignored and the regulations or customs that define the limits of royal power are overridden. It is especially easy and dangerous to do this in the case of the poor and *"afflicted"* who have few advocates in high places and are at the mercy of the royal sense of righteousness. Besides, God insists that they get extra attention (14:31; 17:5; 22:2).

Alcoholic beverages were to be viewed as remedies more than refreshments. They had a role in emergencies (vv. 6–7): to revive or comfort someone on the point of collapse (*"perishing"*) as did the brandy cask offered by St. Bernards to people trapped in Alpine avalanches or the shot of whiskey to aid the frontier cowboy who faced the pain of amputation; a flask of *"wine"* might ease the agony of those who had suffered intolerable financial reverses and were ruthlessly held in the grips of *"poverty"* with its grinding *"misery"* that came from toil that was grueling but fruitless (Heb. *'āmāl;* see 24:2; the word is common in Ecclesiastes, used six times in chap. 2 alone).

Even in our chemically dependent culture, the wisdom of Lemuel's mother is catching on. The percentage of adults that drink has dropped a few points in the last five years. I have been increasingly impressed with the numbers of leaders in politics, and business, and the professions that avoid alcohol completely. The recent refusal of the U.S. Senate to confirm the appointment of a cabinet nominee, partly on the grounds of alcohol abuse, may be a sign that our society is catching up with the wisdom of ancient Israel.

What to Advocate

> 31:8 Open your mouth for the speechless,
>   In the cause of all *who are* appointed to die.
>   9 Open your mouth, judge righteously,
>   And plead the cause of the poor and needy.
>   *Prov. 31:8–9*

If Lemuel's *"mouth"* is to be closed to carousing, it is to be *"open"* to correcting. Again (see v. 5) the concern is for those who cannot help themselves: *"speechless"* does not here mean literally *"dumb"* (Isa. 35:5) but so overwhelmed with fear, anxiety, and isolation as to be rendered speechless before the accusers; *"appointed to die"* translates an obscure Hebrew word which more likely, in parallel to *"speechless,"* means *"stupefied"* and *"devoid of understanding"* (D. Winton Thomas cited by McKane). Judicial procedures of which the defendant had no previous knowledge may be the setting as verse 9 suggests. The perspective on the role of the monarch is remarkable. Not a word about amassing military might, negotiating shrewdly with foreign emissaries, or garnering economic advantage through trade agreements. The whole passage focuses royal responsibility on the need to *"judge righteously"* and *"plead"* ardently for *"the cause of the poor and needy."* Equity, not aggrandizement is the first duty of leadership, according to Lemuel's mother. What wisdom! What a woman! Would that we could hear more about her in Mother's Day sermons!

Acrostic Sayings on an Excellent Woman

This alphabetic poem, in which each verse begins with the succeeding letter of the Hebrew alphabet from *aleph* to *tau*, is a wonderful blend of form and content. This *acrostic* pattern, as the alphabetical sequence is called, occurs a number of times in the Old Testament. The best known examples are Psalm 119 and Lamentations 1–4. The poets apparently used the acrostic to accomplish a number of purposes. First, they were an *artistic labor* to demonstrate the importance and beauty or pathos of the topic; the very task of selecting words that fit the alphabetic structure was a labor of love, a self-imposed burden which the poet carried as a badge of his desire to offer a pleasing sacrifice to the wonder and winsomeness of womanhood.

Second, the acrostic could serve as an *aid to the memory* of the pupil whose recall of each successive verse would be triggered by which letter it had to begin with. Third, and perhaps uppermost in the mind of the artist, the acrostic was an *expression of comprehensiveness.* The topic was fully covered from A to Z (or *aleph* to *tau*), and the very act of canvassing the alphabet demonstrated the completeness of the virtues, skills, and accomplishments of the ideal wife.

The acrostic form has one drawback. Picking a word with the right letter to begin each verse means that the poem may skip from subject to subject without the inner coherence of carefully crafted stanzas. Actually, the poet has done a remarkable job given this limitation. The poem begins with introductory verses that describe the woman's worth, reliability, and virtue (vv. 10–12) and concludes with a lengthier encomium paying tribute to her character, wisdom, industry, love, and piety (vv. 25–31). Between the introduction and conclusion are a cluster of descriptions of her specific tasks, habits, and accomplishments (vv. 13–24) that demonstrate why she is so eminently trustworthy and praiseworthy. Seventeen of the verses are synthetic parallelism, a form suited to packing the most information into the two-line structuring.

The most puzzling matter raised by the poem is the question of for whom it is intended. One suggestion has seen it as a list composed for young women of privilege to help them prepare for marriage. On the other hand, it could as well be a guide sheet for young noblemen to use in the selection of a wife of character and quality. In any case it is a wondrous contribution to a book packed with sage advice, since it sets a standard of excellence in charity, diligence, diversity, and responsibility that any woman would do well to live up to.

31:10 Who can find a virtuous wife?
      For her worth *is* far above rubies.
   11 The heart of her husband safely trusts her;
      So he will have no lack of gain.
   12 She does him good and not evil
      All the days of her life.
   13 She seeks wool and flax,
      And willingly works with her hands.
   14 She is like the merchant ships,
      She brings her food from afar.
   15 She also rises while it is yet night,
      And provides food for her household,
      And a portion for her maidservants.
   16 She considers a field and buys it;
      From her profits she plants a vineyard.
   17 She girds herself with strength,
      And strengthens her arms.
   18 She perceives that her merchandise *is* good,
      And her lamp does not go out by night.
   19 She stretches out her hands to the distaff,
      And her hand holds the spindle.
   20 She extends her hand to the poor,
      Yes, she reaches out her hands to the needy.
   21 She is not afraid of snow for her household,
      For all her household *is* clothed with scarlet.
   22 She makes tapestry for herself;
      Her clothing *is* fine linen and purple.
   23 Her husband is known in the gates,
      When he sits among the elders of the land.
   24 She makes linen garments and sells *them,*
      And supplies sashes for the merchants.
   25 Strength and honor *are* her clothing;
      She shall rejoice in time to come.
   26 She opens her mouth with wisdom,
      And on her tongue *is* the law of kindness.
   27 She watches over the ways of her household,
      And does not eat the bread of idleness.
   28 Her children rise up and call her blessed;
      Her husband *also,* and he praises her:
   29 "Many daughters have done well,
      But you excel them all."
   30 Charm *is* deceitful and beauty *is* passing,
      But a woman *who* fears the LORD, she shall be
        praised.

> 31 Give her of the fruit of her hands,
> And let her own works praise her in the gates.
> *Prov. 31:10–31*

Scarcity and rarity are the emphases of verse 10.

> Who can find a virtuous wife?
> For her worth *is* far above rubies.
> *Prov. 31:10*

The rhetorical *"Who can find"* calls for the response, "Almost no one." The comparison with *"rubies"* (or "beads of coral") links this woman to the personified wisdom in 8:11. The introductory verse is appropriately superlative and general, setting the tone for all the specific accolades that follow. *"Wife"* (or "woman") is the first word in Hebrew, beginning with *aleph*. *"Virtuous,"* which modifies it, is a wondrously inclusive term, embracing strength, resourcefulness, character, and wealth. "Capable" (Anchor Bible; NEB) is on the right track, but "noble character" (NIV) and "perfect" (JB) convey more of the ideal of total strength.

> The heart of her husband safely trusts her;
> So he will have no lack of gain.
> *Prov. 31:11*

"Trust" (*bāṭaḥ*) begins the verse in the Hebrew word order and sets the theme. The completing line identifies the reason for the husband's deliberate and willful (*"heart"*) trust: not marital fidelity, which is assumed in the poem, but economic security. *"Gain"* translates a term usually read as "booty," "plunder" (1:13; 16:19) but which must mean "profit" or "substance" here. An alternate suggestion connects the Hebrew *shālal* with an Arabic word for "wool," citing a proverb: "A clever woman is never without *wool"* (D. Winton Thomas, cited by McKane).

> She does him good and not evil
> All the days of her life.
> *Prov. 31:12*

The introductory summary concludes with the general description of the "blessings" that she brings (*"good"*) instead of the "harm" (*"evil"*) that some women inflict on their husbands. It is the persistence and continuity of her beneficence that helps to set her apart. What she *"does"* (Heb. *gāmal* is to *"render"* an act toward someone) is not a sporadic, temporary deed of kindness but a consistent way of life.

> She seeks wool and flax,
> And willingly works with her hands.
> *Prov. 31:13*

"Seeks" (Heb. *dārash*) continues the acrostic and describes the woman's eagerness to accomplish her carding and weaving with *"flax and wool."* *"Willingly"* (lit., with *"delight"*) underscores the eagerness. The two materials cover the summer and winter needs of her family. Her provision of family clothing is featured in verses 19, 21, 22, while verse 24 depicts the commercial side of her textile activities.

> She is like the merchant ships,
> She brings her food from afar.
> *Prov. 31:14*

The word *"she is"* (Heb. *hāyᵉthāh*) provides the alphabetic sequence. The text features her enterprising quest for *"food"* beyond what is produced locally. It may indicate that her sales of goods to places afar off (note *"merchant ships"*) generate profit (lit., *"bread"*) to support her family.

Food preparation is the logical sequence to food acquisition (v. 14).

> She also rises while it is yet night,
> And provides food for her household,
> And a portion for her maidservants.
> *Prov. 31:15*

"And she rises" (Heb. *wattāqām*) continues the emphasis on diligence, the *"and"* (*w*) furnishing the appropriate beginning letter. The word for *"food"* usually means *"prey,"* portions torn up by wild beasts, but see Job 24:5; Mal. 3:10, Ps. 111:5 for uses that illustrate our proverb. *"Portion"* may describe work assignments rather than meals, thus picturing the woman as organizing the tasks of her staff as part of her daily routine.

Agri-business was another of her skills.

> She considers a field and buys it;
> From her profits she plants a vineyard.
>
> *Prov. 31:16*

"Considers" (Heb. *zām͏ᵉmāh*) contains a touch of shrewdness or scheming (30:32), as she weighs the potential value of the *"field"* against the asking price and probably, in good Middle Eastern fashion, bargains hard before she *"buys* [lit., "takes" or "gets"] *it."* *"Profits"* is "fruit of her palms" and describes the funds generated by her handiwork, perhaps the weaving pictured in verses 19 and 24. The value added to the field by planting the *"vineyard"* will open new possibilities of economic expansion. She understands the workings of the free market and will make the most of them.

Strength of body and will are required for such a schedule of vigorous activities.

> She girds herself with strength,
> And strengthens her arms.
>
> *Prov. 31:17*

The metaphor of *"girding"* (*ḥāg͏ᵉrāh*) furnishes the next letter and describes the intensity of the labor. To "gird the loins," as the text reads in Hebrew, means to get ready to fight or work hard by wrapping the tunic (v. 24) tightly around the torso so it won't interfere with bodily movement.

> She perceives that her merchandise *is* good,
> And her lamp does not go out by night.
>
> *Prov. 31:18*

"Perceives" is a paraphrase of "tastes" (Heb. *ṭāʿᵃmāh*) which begins the verse. *"Merchandise"* may be either what she makes and grows or the profit from it. The long-burning *"lamp"* may suggest diligence, of which she has plenty, but more likely it describes the affluence that results from her diligence: she does not have to skimp on olive oil, the lamp's fuel, since she either produces it in large quantities or has ample cash to buy it.

> She stretches out her hands to the distaff,
> And her hand holds the spindle.
>
> *Prov. 31:19*

"Hands" starts the sentence with the letter *yodh*. The picture is of industry in spinning thread from flax or wool (v. 13) *"Distaff,"* the

rod on which the rough fibers are wound before they are stretched into thread on the *"spindle,"* may not be in view here. The Hebrew word *kîshôr* is probably the *"whorl,"* the weighted disk with a hole in the center through which runs the spindle stick. The pulling, stretching process to make the thread or yarn begins with a hand (lit., *"palm"*) holding the spindle while the other *"she stretches out"* to give the whorl a spin and thus furnish the momentum to turn the spindle and wind the taut thread on it. The two parallel lines are virtually synonymous.

> She extends her hand to the poor,
> Yes, she reaches out her hands to the needy.
> *Prov. 31:20*

"Her hand" (lit., *"palm"*; Heb. *kaph* continues the alphabetic sequence) does more than wield whorl and spindle. It *"extends"* in gifts of charity to the *"poor"* and *"needy"* (note the same two Hebrew words in 31:9), a royal act indeed. Again the poetry is synonymous.

> She is not afraid of snow for her household,
> For all her household is clothed with scarlet.
> *Prov. 31:21*

"Not afraid" opens the sentence, since Hebrew *lō›* *"not"* begins with the needed letter. The spinning and weaving described or implied in verses 13 and 19 are insurance against the coldest winter (*"snow"*). Jerusalem experiences flurries of snow almost every year but only occasionally does it stay on the ground. Perhaps once in twenty years it may block roads and require clearing. Even for those once-a-generation storms the strong wife is ready. *"Scarlet"* should probably be translated *"double"*—the two Hebrew words are formed from the same consonants. The bright color would not guarantee warmth; the double thickness would.

> She makes tapestry for herself;
> Her clothing *is* fine linen and purple.
> *Prov. 31:22*

Quality and beauty are her concerns as well as warmth. *"Tapestry"* leads off the saying and probably indicates couch coverings (*marbaddîm* is from *rbd*, *"to prepare a couch"* in 7:16). *"Fine linen"* is well carded, tightly woven, and perhaps bleached to purge it of impurities. *"Purple"* is the premier cloth of the Eastern Mediterranean coast, dyed with the bright, indelible coloring that comes from the secretions of certain mollusks, especially near Tyre and Sidon. One authority estimates that it took the fluid from eight thousand mollusks to produce one gram of dye. No wonder the Roman soldiers valued the purple cloth from Jesus' robe which they rent in pieces at the foot of the cross (John 19:2, 5).

Her excellence contributed to her husband's reputation.

> Her husband is known in the gates,
> When he sits among the elders of the land.
> *Prov. 31:23*

"Known" (Heb. *nôdā'*), which continues the acrostic, suggests prominent recognition, ready acknowledgment. The *"gate"* was the center of political and judicial life in the Israelite cities. There *"the elders"* (or *"authorities"*) gathered to decide policy for the community, settle grievances, and adjudicate legal claims. The wife's accomplishments not only increased her husband's stature but enhanced his freedom to participate in public life. Those of us whose wives have carried far more than their share of burdens at home and in the church have some idea of how blessed this husband was.

> She makes linen garments and sells *them*,
> And supplies sashes for the merchants.
> *Prov. 31:24*

"Linen" tunics (Heb. *sādîn*) or undergarments, over which one wore a robe for warmth or more formal dress, are part of her household's productivity. Their surplus was put up for sale along with the *"sashes"* or cloth belts that cinched (see *"girds,"* v. 17) the tunics around the waist. The whole transaction with its producers and *"merchants"* (the Hebrew word is *"Canaanite"*) is a reminder of what a mercantile hotbed Canaan was, with its access to Egypt, Phoenicia, Syria, Mesopotamia, and the cities of the Hittites in Asia Minor.

She peddles clothes to others (v. 24) and displays elegant material herself (v. 22).

> Strength and honor *are* her clothing;
> She shall rejoice in time to come.
> *Prov. 31:25*

But what really outfits her in a way that turns all heads are *"strength"* (Heb. *'ōz*, the acrostic word), which expresses financial stability

among other qualities, and *"honor"* that drives away all fear of shame
that comes from want or deprivation. "Strength" and "honor" garb her
against the hazards of an unknown future. *"Time to come"* is literally
the "day afterward."

> She opens her mouth with wisdom,
> And on her tongue *is* the law of kindness.
> > *Prov. 31:26*

Like the pupil's mother in 1:8 and Lemuel's mother in 31:1, she
teaches *"wisdom"* anytime she *"opens her mouth"* (*pîhāh* the alphabetic key). The synonymous second line contains one of Proverb's
most beautiful phrases—*"the law of kindness"* (Heb. *ḥesed;* 3:3). It
suggests that all her instruction to her staff, family, and friends are
motivated by covenant love that treats others with the loyal consideration that graced God's dealings with His people. Her conduct
anticipates James's "perfect law of liberty" and "royal law" (1:25; 2:8)
and Paul's "law of Christ" (Gal. 6:3). What a contrast between her
and the contentious woman of 25:23!

The summary of the excellent woman's activities continues with a
note on her vigilance.

> She watches over the ways of her household,
> And does not eat the bread of idleness.
> > *Prov. 31:27*

"Watches" (Heb. *ṣôphîyyah*) continues the acrostic and combines the
idea of constancy with accuracy. Its other use in Proverbs describes
the eyes of the Lord "keeping watch on the evil and the good" (15:3).
The detailed supervision needed to keep her household running
smoothly and justly permits no *"idleness,"* a word built on the familiar term for "sluggard" (6:6, 9). *"Bread of idleness"* implies that whatever she eats she has earned. By changing the form of the verb
slightly, Scott (Anchor Bible, p. 186) applies the clause to her insistence that her whole household imitate her diligence: "she permits no
one to eat food in idleness," a thought that Paul echoes in 2 Thess.
3:10: "If anyone will not work, neither shall he eat."

> Her children rise up and call her blessed;
> Her husband *also,* and he praises her:
> > *Prov. 31:28*

"Rise up" (Heb. *qāmû;* the acrostic calls for *q*) is both a sign
of respect (Job 29:8) and preparation for public speech. The verb

carries over to the second line and defines the posture of *"her hus-band"* as well as *"her children." "Call her blessed"* or *"happy"* (Gen. 30:13; Song of Sol. 6:9) and *"praises her"* (the root is the same as that found in the title of Psalms) are synonymous and convey unqualified regard of her worth and accomplishments.

The husband's praiseful words are quoted.

> "Many daughters have done well,
> But you excel them all."
>
> *Prov. 31:29*

"Many" (Heb. *rabbôt*) fits the acrostic and provides the setting for the dramatic comparison. *"Well"* translates the word read as "virtuous" or "excellent" in verse 10; and thus forms a subtle bracket tying together the opening and closing of the poem. *"Excel"* means literally to "rise above," "stand on top." However high other women—*"daughters"* here speaks of gender not relationship—have climbed in the pursuit of excellence, the subject of this poem is deemed "Queen of the mountain" by those who know her best.

Here alone the poetic form turns antithetic.

> Charm *is* deceitful and beauty *is* passing,
> But a woman *who* fears the LORD, she shall be
>   praised.
>
> *Prov. 31:30*

The comparison of verse 29, which held high praise for many women, becomes here a strong contrast between external *"charm"* (or *"grace"*) and *"beauty"* (or "attractiveness"; 6:25) and inward devotion (or fear of the Lord, see 1:7 and chap. 14). The contrast is based on the difference between the deceptive and the genuine. Charm is *"deceitful"*; Hebrew *sheqer*, the acrostic word, is used frequently in Proverbs to denote lies and falsehoods (6:17, 19); beauty is *"vain"*; Hebrew *hebel* is the theme word of Ecclesiastes; see 1:2. Together they warn that physical beauty may be faked with cosmetics, jewelry, and clothing, and even when it is not faked it may not carry with it the strength of faith in and obedience to the Lord which are the true marks of human beauty.

The poetry returns to synonymous parallelism to underscore by repetition the praiseworthy character of her life and deeds.

> Give her of the fruit of her hands,
> And let her own works praise her in the gates.
>
> *Prov. 31:31*

"Give" (Heb. *tᵉnû;* the acrostic has reached its ending in *t*) is the first imperative verb in the poem. Its plural form, combined with the mention of the *"gates"* where public deliberations took place, indicates that the open recognition begun in verse 28 with the family blessings continues here. What she has meant to her household is worthy of acclamation in the whole community. She deserves at least the "Woman of the Year" award. In light of the verb *"praise"* in line two, we may wish to consider the suggestion that *tᵉnû,* "give," be spelled *tannû* which means "laud" or "extol" (G. R. Driver, cited by McKane, p. 670; see NEB: "Extol her"). This change preserves the parallelism precisely: *"fruit of her hands,"* then, refers not to her rewards but to her achievements as do *"her own works,"* that is, everything she has accomplished in every area of life. This verse, with its public recognition and its all-embracing mention of *"fruit"* and *"works,"* is an ideal climax to the description of a woman who has a lot of ability and uses every bit of it in ways that serve others and surely satisfy her.

Wisdom, the other dominant woman in Proverbs, officially addressed her invitations and advice to the young men of Israel (1:22–23; 8:4). And the book has been crammed with her words to the budding leaders of the land. But listening and watching all the while must have been a whole set of remarkable women. They sensed that neither giftedness nor righteousness were matters of gender. They grasped the truth that society's well-being rested on their shoulders as surely as on the backs of the men who held office.

Quietly but steadily they too ate at wisdom's table and found life and favor from the Lord (8:35). As they did, they took on wisdom's attributes and demonstrated both her beauty and her bounty. In turn, they became teachers, proclaiming and demonstrating wisdom's sense of piety, prudence, and fairness. Because of their lives, wisdom's call to the people took on clarity and credibility. No wonder the sages, wise men that they were, found no better way to conclude their canon of wisdom than with profound counsel from Lemuel's mother and the striking portrait of an excellent woman.

Bibliography

Alden, Robert L. *Proverbs: A Commentary on an Ancient Book of Timeless Advice.* Grand Rapids, Mich.: Baker Book House, 1983.

Crenshaw, James L. *Old Testament Wisdom: An Introduction.* Atlanta: John Knox Press, 1981.

Delitzsch, F. *Biblical Commentary on the Proverbs of Solomon.* 2 vols. Biblical Commentary on the Old Testament. Edited by C. F. Keil and F. Delitzsch. 1890. Reprint. Grand Rapids, Mich.: William B. Eerdmans Publishing Co., 1950.

Kidner, Derek. *Proverbs: An Introduction and Commentary.* Tyndale Old Testament Commentaries. Chicago: InterVarsity Press, 1964.

————. *An Introduction to Wisdom Literature: The Wisdom of Proverbs, Job, and Ecclesiastes.* Downers Grove, Ill.: InterVarsity Press, 1985.

van Leeuwen, Raymond C. *Context and Meaning in Proverbs 25-27.* SBL Dissertation Series 96. Atlanta: Scholars Press, 1988.

McKane, William. *Proverbs: A New Approach.* Old Testament Library. Philadelphia: Westminster Press, 1970.

Murphy, Roland. *Wisdom Literature: Job, Proverbs, Ruth, Canticles, Ecclesiastes, Esther.* The Forms of the Old Testament Literature 13. Grand Rapids, Mich.: William B. Eerdmans Publishing Co., 1981.

von Rad, Gerhard. *Wisdom in Israel.* Nashville, New York: Abingdon Press, 1972.

Scott, R. B. Y. *Proverbs, Ecclesiastes.* Anchor Bible 18. Garden City, N.Y.: Doubleday and Co., 1965.

Toy, Crawford H. *A Critical and Exegetical Commentary on the Book of Proverbs.* International Critical Commentary. Edinburgh: T. & T. Clark, 1899.

Whybray, R. N. *The Book of Proverbs.* Cambridge Bible Commentary. Cambridge: Cambridge University Press, 1972.